ADVANCES IN AUTOETHNOGRAPHY AND NARRATIVE INQUIRY

Advances in Autoethnography and Narrative Inquiry pays homage to two prominent scholars, Arthur Bochner and Carolyn Ellis, for their formative and formidable contributions to auto-ethnography, personal narrative, and alternative forms of scholarship.

Their autoethnographic—and life—project gives us tools for understanding shared humanity and precious diversity; for striving to become ever-more empathic, loving, and ethical; and for living our best creative, relational, and public lives. The collection is organized into two sections: "Foundations" and "Futures." Contributors to "Foundations" explore Carolyn and Art's scholarship and legacy and/or their singular presence in the author's life. Contributors to "Futures" offer novel and innovative applications of autoethnographic and narrative inquiry. Throughout, contributors demonstrate how Bochner's and Ellis' work has created and shifted the terrain of autoethnographic and narrative research.

This collection will be of interest to researchers familiar with Bochner's and Ellis' research. It also serves as a resource for graduate students, scholars, and professionals who have an interest in autoethnographic and narrative research. This collection can be used in upper-division undergraduate courses and graduate courses solely about autoethnography and narrative, and as a secondary text for courses about ethnography and qualitative research.

Tony E. Adams is a Professor and Chair of the Department of Communication at Bradley University. He is the co-author and co-editor of nine books. He is a co-editor of the *Writing Lives: Ethnographic Narratives* book series (Routledge) and founding co-editor of the *Journal of Autoethnography* (University of California Press).

Robin M. Boylorn is an Associate Professor of Interpersonal and Intercultural Communication at the University of Alabama. She is the author, co-author or co-editor of three books. She is also an Associate Editor of the *Journal of Autoethnography* (University of California Press).

Lisa M. Tillmann is an activist researcher, documentary filmmaker, and professor at Rollins College. The author of two books and producer or co-producer of four documentary films, she holds the William R. Kenan Chair of Critical Media and Cultural Studies.

INTERNATIONAL CONGRESS OF QUALITATIVE INQUIRY (ICQI) FOUNDATIONS AND FUTURES IN QUALITATIVE INQUIRY

Series Editors: Michael Giardina and Norman K. Denzin.

From autoethnography, observation, and arts-based research to poststructural, new materialist, and post-qualitative inquiry, interdisciplinary conversations about the practices, politics, and philosophies of qualitative inquiry have never been stronger or more dynamic. Edited by Michael D. Giardina and Norman K. Denzin and sponsored by the International Congress of Qualitative Inquiry (www.ICQI.org), the Foundations and Futures in Qualitative Inquiry series showcases works from the most experienced and field-defining qualitative researchers in the world. Engaging critical questions of epistemology, ontology, and axiology, the series is designed to provide cornerstone texts for different modes and methods in qualitative inquiry. Books in this series will serve the growing number of students, academics, and researchers who utilize qualitative approaches to inquiry in university courses, research, and applied settings.

Volumes in this series:

Advances in Autoethnography and Narrative Inquiry
Reflections on the Legacy of Carolyn Ellis and Arthur Bochner
Edited by Tony E. Adams, Robin M. Boylorn, and Lisa M. Tillmann

Wayfinding and Critical Autoethnography
Fetaui Iosefo, Stacy Holman Jones, and Anne Harris

For a full list of titles in this series, please visit:
https://www.routledge.com/International-Congress-of-Qualitative-Inquiry-ICQI-Foundations-and-Futures/book-series/ICQIFF

ADVANCES IN AUTOETHNOGRAPHY AND NARRATIVE INQUIRY

Reflections on the Legacy of Carolyn Ellis and Arthur Bochner

Edited by Tony E. Adams, Robin M. Boylorn, and Lisa M. Tillmann

Routledge
Taylor & Francis Group

LONDON AND NEW YORK

First published 2021
by Routledge
2 Park Square, Milton Park, Abingdon, Oxon OX14 4RN

and by Routledge
52 Vanderbilt Avenue, New York, NY 10017

Routledge is an imprint of the Taylor & Francis Group, an informa business

© 2021 selection and editorial matter, Tony E. Adams, Robin M. Boylorn, and
Lisa M. Tillmann; individual chapters, the contributors

The right of Tony E. Adams, Robin M. Boylorn, and Lisa M. Tillmann to be
identified as the authors of the editorial material, and of the authors for their
individual chapters, has been asserted in accordance with sections 77 and 78 of
the Copyright, Designs and Patents Act 1988.

British Library Cataloguing-in-Publication Data
A catalogue record for this book is available from the British Library

Library of Congress Cataloging-in-Publication Data
Names: Adams, Tony E., editor. | Boylorn, Robin M., 1978- editor. |
Tillmann, Lisa M., 1971- editor.
Title: Advances in autoethnography and narrative inquiry : reflections on the
legacy of Carolyn Ellis and Arthur Bochner / Edited by Tony E Adams, Robin
M Boylorn and Lisa M Tillmann.
Identifiers: LCCN 2020047698 (print) | LCCN 2020047699 (ebook) |
ISBN 9780367476670 (hardback) | ISBN 9780367476694 (paperback) |
ISBN 9781003035763 (ebook)
Subjects: LCSH: Ethnology--Authorship. | Narrative inquiry (Research method) |
Bochner, Arthur P. | Ellis, Carolyn, 1950-.
Classification: LCC GN307.7 .A38 2021 (print) | LCC GN307.7 (ebook) |
DDC 305.80072--dc23
LC record available at https://lccn.loc.gov/2020047698
LC ebook record available at https://lccn.loc.gov/2020047699

ISBN: 978-0-367-47667-0 (hbk)
ISBN: 978-0-367-47669-4 (pbk)
ISBN: 978-1-003-03576-3 (ebk)

Typeset in Bembo
by Taylor & Francis Books

CONTENTS

FIGURES

ACKNOWLEDGEMENTS

We are grateful to Michael Giardina and Norman Denzin for the opportunity and privilege to publish in the *Foundations and Futures in Qualitative Inquiry* series, as well as the Routledge staff for their endless support, especially Matt Bickerton and Hannah Shakespeare. We are also grateful to the contributors of this collection; without them, this book would not exist. Their enthusiasm, responsiveness, and patience have been treasured. Finally, we are forever indebted to Carolyn Ellis and Art Bochner, the inspiration for this book. Your passion, love, and support of us, and many of the contributors, continue to shape who we are, what we care about, and what it means to live a moral and just life, within and away from the academy.

Tony: I am grateful for Robin and Lisa, my esteemed co-authors and academic siblings, for collaborating on this collection; it has been a privilege to work with you both. I am grateful for Art and Carolyn as well; indeed, they are my adoring mentors, role models, and life guides. I would also like to thank the many others who have made my writing life possible, including Mitch Allen, Keith Berry, Bernard Brommel, Derek Bolen, Marcy Chvasta, Norman Denzin, Andrew Herrmann, Stacy Holman Jones, Lenore Langsdorf, Patricia Leavy, Nicole Neuman, Ron Pelias, Sandy Pensoneau-Conway, Jillian Tullis, and Jonathan Wyatt; Sharon Rome, my mother; and my funny, patient, and loving husband, Jerry Moreno.

Robin: This project has been a labor of love to anchor and make concrete my deep admiration, appreciation, and love for Carolyn Ellis and Art Bochner. I am indebted to your decades-long research centering autoethnography and personal narrative, and for (y)our decades-long love. Your work made it possible and legible to be a storytelling researcher. Thank you for your bravery and vision! I also thank H. L. "Bud" Goodall, Jr., my mentor and friend, whose memory and legacy I will always honor, and whose words and encouragement still ring in my head when words won't come. Tony and Lisa, I love you both so much. Our work together is not only a homage to our academic parents and family, but to each other. Your love and support, during what has been one of the most challenging and emotionally exhausting times in my memory, made it more bearable. We collectively imagined how to forge forward when the world is falling apart. Thank you for your brilliance, generosity, kindness and friendship. I am honored to be in chosen family relationship with you.

Lisa: The chaos of 2020 has been unparalleled in my lived experience. Viruses rage: COVID-19, racist violence, authoritarianism. Through it all, Art Bochner and Carolyn Ellis love, stand with, and buoy me—as they have since 1993. Through them, I met Tony and Robin, my tireless and uber-talented coeditor-siblings. I have been fortunate to devote my academic career to Rollins College, which has given me the freedom to create courses and programs explicitly grounded in social justice values. At Rollins, I have been privileged to learn about, with, and from so many gifted student storytellers. I also have been blessed with colleagues who feel more like brothers and sisters, including Steve Schoen and Denise Cummings. Outside Rollins, an extended family of narrative inquirers—including Jay Baglia, Keith Berry, Elissa Foster, the late Bud Goodall, Stacy Holman Jones, Christine Kiesinger, Lesa Lockford, Csaba Osvath, Ron Pelias, Lori Peterson, Chris Poulos, Carol Rambo, and Bill Rawlins—has inspired and nourished me. I am grateful for the unwavering generosity and devotion of my parents, Beth and John Tillmann. Family of choice includes my calm and steady yet hilarious partner Shane; his beautiful children Xander and Halle; and my sisters/co-mentors/co-conspirators Kathryn Norsworthy and Deena Flamm. May our collective love—and rage—carry us toward systemic change and lasting peace.

CONTRIBUTORS

Author X may or may not exist as a contributing author or postmodern place-holder. Their research interests include strange accounting and topics that may carry stigma, taboo, the fear of retaliation, or that need a protective layer of *strangeness*.

Brandi Barnes holds an MA in Sociology from the University of Memphis. Her research interests include the medicalization of experiences within chronic illness, stigma, liminality, racial inequalities and social injustice, and autoethnography as a method of research.

Silvia M. Bénard Calva (PhD, University of Texas at Austin) is a Professor in the Department of Sociology and Anthropology at Universidad Autónoma de Aguas-calientes in Mexico. Her research focuses on identity and subjectivity as they intersect with the sense of belonging in different urban and national settings. Most recently, she edited a book, *Voces desde la diversidad*, presently in press.

Keith Berry is a faculty member in Communication at the University of South Florida. His research adopts a cultural approach to studying relational commu-nication and identity. Much of his recent research has focused on bullying, reflex-ivity in autoethnography, and LGBTQ cultures and identities. He is the author of *Bullied: Tales of Torment, Identity, and Youth* (Routledge) and most recently (with Catherine M. Gillotti and Tony E. Adams) *Living Sexuality: Stories of LGBTQ Relationships, Identities, & Desires* (Brill/Sense).

Arthur P. Bochner is Distinguished University Professor Emeritus of commu-nication at the University of South Florida and an NCA Distinguished Scholar. He is the author of *Coming to Narrative: A Personal History of Paradigm Change in the* xii List of contributors

Human Sciences (Left Coast Press, 2014) and co-author (with Carolyn Ellis) of *Evocative Autoethnography: Writing Lives and Telling Stories* (Routledge, 2016). He has contributed chapters to more than a dozen handbooks and published more than 100 articles and book chapters. He is currently working on a new book project, *Living an Autoethnographic Life.*

Deborah C. Breede is a Professor of Communication, Coordinator of Graduate Programs, and Affiliate Professor with Women's and Gender Studies at Coastal Carolina University. Her research, teaching, and service interests focus on the formation, development, and maintenance of community within and around a variety of contexts: interpersonal, pedagogical, social, and cultural; sites and experiences of trauma; and end of life experiences.

Darren Cummings is pursuing a PhD in Education: Language, Culture and Teaching at York University, Canada. His research interests include queer theory, critical theory, feminist research, and autoethnography. His research seeks to challenge deficit discourses often associated with queerness, and particularly within rural contexts. He currently resides in Toronto, Ontario and misses his rural home.

Carolyn Ellis is Distinguished University Professor Emerita at the University of South Florida. She has contributed to the narrative and autoethnographic study of human life through integrating ethnographic, literary, and evocative writing to portray and make sense of lived experience in cultural context. Her recent publications include *Revision: Autoethnographic Reflections on Life and Work* (revised), *Final Negotiations: A Story of Love, Loss, and Chronic Illness* (expanded/revised), and *Evocative Autoethnography: Writing Lives and Telling Stories* (with Arthur Bochner). She co-edits the Routledge book series, *Writing Lives: Ethnographic Narratives* (with Arthur Bochner and Tony Adams).

Mark Freeman is Distinguished Professor of Ethics and Society in the Department of Psychology at the College of the Holy Cross. His many writings include *Rewriting the Self: History, Memory, Narrative* (Routledge, 1993); *Finding the Muse: A Sociopsychological Inquiry into the Conditions of Artistic Creativity* (Cambridge, 1994); *Hindsight: The Promise and Peril of Looking Backward* (Oxford, 2010); and *The Priority of the Other: Thinking and Living Beyond the Self* (Oxford, 2014).

Nathan Hodges is writing this bio in third-person. He teaches in the Communication Studies Department at Coe College in Cedar Rapids, *Iowa*, legally obligating him to say, "I-ow(e)-a guy five dollars" every time he says "Iowa." He's published autoethnographies on topics ranging from "The American Dental Dream" to "The Chemical Life." He also performs standup comedy at open mics and local comedy clubs, though audience members might disagree with the "comedy" part of that statement.

Stacy Holman Jones is Professor and Director of the Centre for Theatre and Performance at Monash University in Melbourne, Australia. Her research focuses broadly on performance as socially, culturally, and politically resistive and transformative activity. She specializes in critical qualitative methods, particularly critical autoethnography and critical and feminist theory. She is the author of more than 90 articles, book chapters, reviews, and editorials and the author/editor of 14 books.

Barbara J. Jago, PhD, is Chair and Associate Professor of Communication Arts and Sciences at the University of New Hampshire, where she teaches courses in relational communication. Her autoethnographic research explores mental health and family relationships, and has been published in the *Journal of Contemporary Ethnography, Qualitative Inquiry*, and *the Journal of Loss and Trauma* as well as edited collections. Barbara is the vice-chair of the New Hampshire State Advisory Committee to the U.S. Commission on Civil Rights.

Elaine Bass Jenks is Professor of Communication and Media at West Chester University. She studies interpersonal communication among individuals who are blind, sighted, or visually impaired from an ethnographic perspective. Her ongoing research addresses parenting a visually impaired child and the interpersonal communicative experiences of elite blind athletes who play the Paralympic sport of goalball.

Marcin Kafar is an interdisciplinary scholar working at the intersection of human and social sciences; to express his own voice he combines fields of e.g. anthropology of culture, education, literary studies, sociology, and philosophy. He is an assistant professor at the Department of Educational Studies of the University of Lodz. He is the editor-in-chief of the book series "Biographical Perspectives" conducted by the Lodz University Press. He authored, co-authored and edited several monographs, e.g. *Scientific Biographies: Between the "Professional" and "Non-Professional" Dimensions of Humanistic Experiences* (Lodz–Krakow, 2014), and *Autoethnographic "Proximities" and "Distances." On Autoethnography in Poland* (originally *Autoetnograficzne zbliżenia I oddalenia. O autoetnografii w Polsce*, Lodz 2020). He is the recipient of internships (2010, 2016) and a visiting professorship (2018) at the Department of Communication, University of South Florida, as well as a promoter of autoethnography in Poland.

Lesa Lockford is Professor and Chair of the Department of Theatre and Film at Bowling Green State University in Ohio. She teaches courses in acting, voice for the stage, performance studies and qualitative methods. Her publications have appeared in *Text and Performance Quarterly, Liminalities, the International Review of Qualitative Research, Qualitative Inquiry, Cultural Studies ←→ Critical Methodologies* among others. She is also a performer whose work has appeared in a variety of academic and non-academic venues as well as a frequent narrator of audiobooks.

Csaba Osvath is a doctoral candidate at the University of South Florida, pursuing literacy studies with a special focus on qualitative methods and arts-based inquiry. Csaba's work explores the epistemological, pedagogical, and existential roles/functions of artmaking within the context of higher education and academic research. His current project centers on the integration of evocative autoethnographic writing and contemplative artmaking (mixed media collage), establishing a maker-centered method within the field of autoethnography and narrative inquiry.

Chris J. Patti is an Associate Professor in the Department of Communication at Appalachian State University, where he is also an Affiliate Faculty member of the campus Center for Judaic, Holocaust, and Peace Studies. His research examines compassionate communication and navigating suffering through listening to and writing with survivors of trauma.

Christopher N. Poulos, PhD is Professor of Communication Studies at the UNC Greensboro. He teaches relational and family communication, autoethnography, ethics, dialogue, and film. He is the author of *Accidental Ethnography: An Inquiry into Family Secrecy* (2008) and *The Essentials of Autoethnography* (2021). His work has appeared in *Qualitative Inquiry, Cultural Studies<=>Critical Methodologies, Communication Theory, Southern Communication Journal, International Review of Qualitative Research, Qualitative Communication Research*, and in many edited books.

Ronald J. Pelias is a Professor Emeritus from Southern Illinois University, Carbondale, IL. His most recent books exploring qualitative methods are *Writing Performance, Identity, and Everyday Life* (2018), *The Creative Qualitative Researcher* (2019), and *Lessons on Aging and Dying: A Poetic Autoethnography* (2021).

Brittany Presson is a doctoral candidate at the University of Missouri in Columbia, MO. Her research focuses on everyday life, qualitative methodology, and identity. Research topics include the lived experiences of former self-injurers and meaning making practices among gold star families.

Carol Rambo is Professor of Sociology at the University of Memphis in Memphis TN. She was the editor of the journal *Symbolic Interaction* from 2007–2011. Her past research has delved into topics such as Striptease Dancing, Mentally Disabled Parenting, Childhood Sexual Abuse, Trauma, and theorizing the craft of writing Autoethnography. She has published her work in a variety of outlets including *Deviant Behavior, Journal of Contemporary Ethnography*, and *Qualitative Inquiry*.

William K. Rawlins is Stocker Professor Emeritus of Interpersonal Communication at Ohio University. His publications examine the unique challenges and dialectical tensions of communicating in friendships across life, how they accomplish well-being for individuals and communities, and the role of dialogue and narrative in co-authoring identities with other persons. Bill also embodies musical performances to address the aesthetics of interpersonal and relational communication, music as communication, and the musicality of social life and interpretive inquiry.

Lisa P. Z. Spinazola earned her PhD in Communication at the University of South Florida where she currently serves as Visiting Instructor. Research interests are autoethnography, narrative reframing, trauma/loss, empathy/compassion, and pedagogy. Recent publications include an article examining lifelong struggles with body image; a narrative on aftereffects of a traumatic car accident; and a co-authored evocative autoethnography in a textbook on research methods for librarians. She is under contract with Routledge for a co-edited autoethnographic book project exploring the stigma and shame surrounding familial estrangement.

Gresilda A. Tilley-Lubbs is Associate Professor of Social Foundations at Virginia Tech. She combines autoethnography and critical pedagogy to examine power and privilege in her work in vulnerable Spanish-speaking communities. Currently she is conducting research in Spain for a critical autoethnography of her perspectives as a student studying in Spain during Franco's dictatorship following the Spanish Civil War.

1

RIGHTING AND WRITING (FOR) OUR LIVES

Turning inward when the world falls apart

Tony E. Adams, Robin M. Boylorn, and Lisa M. Tillmann

In the final song of the Broadway musical, *Hamilton* (Miranda & McCarter, 2016), Eliza ponders what her husband, Alexander, could have done had he lived longer: "He acted and wrote as if *running out of time*." She invites us to think about who will tell *our* stories after we are gone and whose stories remain untold or shrouded in secrecy.

As editors, we approached this collection of stories and essays in a spirit resonant of Eliza's meditation on time and absence, which we see as akin to the calling of autoethnography. We pay tribute to Carolyn Ellis and Arthur Bochner (Art and Carolyn)—our friends, mentors, and writers with whom we have bonded as family over many years. They too have written as if running out of time, while providing us the guidance, tools, and inspiration to write our own stories about the people, things, ideas, and issues we care about before time runs out.

We write—and invite you to write—as if running out of time as well, because on many fronts our world feels wounded and haunted by rampant individualism and authoritarianism; predatory capitalism and widening economic inequality; and systemic and intractable racism, sexism, xenophobia, transphobia, ableism, ageism, and religious-centrism. COVID-19 has brought into focus the many ways in which the most vulnerable populations among us are punished and endangered by economic, social, and healthcare inequality.

As (auto)ethnographers, we feel called to turn outward, looking to others in society, then inward to reflect, understand, and figure out what to say, write, and do. In no year has this felt more urgent than 2020. Under quarantine, stay-at-home orders, social distancing guidelines, and travel restrictions, our project of documenting life and crafting narratives has helped us to process uncertainty, anxiety, fear, and grief; to preserve old connections and forge new ones; and to organize politically and spiritually. Storying this moment has helped demonstrate that hashtags, petitions, and posts can move beyond "slacktivism" and promote consciousness-raising, community-building, and power-holder accountability, driving even vulnerable and at-risk physical bodies into the streets.

We write to navigate, record, and challenge these turbulent times.

We write through terror and towards a shared and just security.

We write knowing we won't always be here—but perhaps our stories will.

***

"Writing Lives." Carolyn and Art both taught a class by this title at the University of South Florida, where each of us received our PhD. They later adopted this title for their Routledge book series. As autoethnographers, we mobilize their phrase to ask: what does it mean to write (for our) lives, to live writing lives, and to make lives live on the page?

Autoethnographers mindfully mine the past, attend to the present, and chart paths toward more humane and just futures. As composers of autoethnography, we sometimes follow closely the footsteps of our autoethnographic ancestors, including Art and Carolyn; at other times, we blaze new trails of critical and creative engagement. We use texts to promote empathy, to live more meaningful and fulfilling lives, to become better versions of ourselves, and to transform unjust structures. As readers of autoethnography, we listen and bear witness to others' stories, seeking advice and comfort in times of distress.

In this introduction, we describe how we write for our lives, how we maneuver in/ through the intersections of personal experience, relationships, and social problems. We demonstrate such maneuvering by understanding autoethnography from the perspectives of the "micro" (personal), "meso" (relational), and "macro" (structural). A micro analysis asks: how does the practice and composition of autoethnography affect us individually—bodily, emotionally, psychologically, existentially? At the meso level, we ponder: how might autoethnography affect our immediate spheres of influence—our relations with family, friends, coworkers, and community members? A macro view considers: how can analysis of systems of power and inequality affect our autoethnographic practices, and how might autoethnographic practices sharpen our and others' ability to engage in such analysis and mobilize for change? We use these perspectives to provide an overview of Carolyn and Art's work and offer a preview to this collection.

The micro of autoethnography

At the micro (personal) level, autoethnography invites identity work: who am I; how did I become *this* variant of myself; how might I become more compassionate, understanding, and engaged; what social locations do I occupy, and how do those foster, shape, and constrain my opportunities and challenges? By centering the intrapersonal, autoethnography cultivates the introspection, sensitivity, and reflexivity needed to write our way through difficult experiences, moving from frustration, pain, and grief toward meaning, fulfillment, and hope. Autoethnographers reframe and re-story experiences in ways that leverage positionality and can build agency and empowerment.

Autoethnography can help us make sense and meaning of both mundane and extraordinary lived experiences, including trauma. For example, we have written about mental illness (Boylorn, 2014), same-sex attraction (Berry, Gillotti, & Adams, 2020), and eating disorders (Tillmann-Healy, 1996; Tillmann, 2009) to make visible, normalize, and destigmatize experiences often shrouded in shame. We find the therapeutic effect of autoethnography to be one of the method's greatest strengths, especially during uncertain, fearful, and devastating times.

When effective, autoethnography unlocks and expands emotional and empathic capacity. We look deeply within and feel deeply for ourselves so that we also might feel for and with others. Autoethnographers share micro-experiences—secrets, epiphanies, traumas—to encourage others to consider, listen, and respond. We say,

> This happened to me. This is how I—in this place, at this time—make sense of what took place. This is how power, privilege, marginalization, inequality, and oppression operate on/in/alongside me in these particular contexts. As a result of this exploration, this is how I might live differently.

Autoethnographers tend not to instruct, "This is how you should generalize from the events portrayed." Instead, we invite readers to ask, "How does the author's experience resonate—or not—with my own? What might I learn about myself, others, and the social world from such resonances and disjunctures?"

Autoethnography recognizes singularity and particularity *as situated in cultural, social, and political contexts.* It centralizes *auto* (self) and involves creative composition (*graph*). Systematic engagement with culture (*ethnos*) distinguishes autoethnography from autobiography.

Personal narratives that fail to stretch beyond one's inner life and cultural analyses unmoored from lived experience are not autoethnographies. We resist the neoliberal urge to individualize and privatize social problems, while remaining mindful that social problems impact actual bodies and beings.

The meso of autoethnography

Though an autoethnographer often introspects and composes alone, there is no truly "lone" autoethnographer. One may examine and write through a personal epiphany (Denzin, 2014), but all lived experience is situated within relationships and systems. When we attend the meso of autoethnography, we focus on relational *patterns* of personal experience—encounters, reactions, and interactions that happen repeatedly—and our close connections with friends, families, workplaces, and face-to-face and virtual communities.

For example, a meso approach to understanding and navigating this historical moment, one shaped profoundly by COVID-19, could explore our fear that beloved ones will contract the virus, suffer, and die alone. Each of us struggles to manage the anxiety and loneliness of being unable to share space with family, close friends, and students. The pandemic infuses the global community (macro) but is lived and felt most acutely as it impacts particular bodies (micro) and relationships (meso).

This moment also draws attention to individual and systemic racism in the United States, exemplified by the murders of Breonna Taylor, George Floyd, and countless other Black people. Our analysis of systemic racism might begin with the micro, focusing on one person, one body, one life cruelly extinguished; we say the person's name (#SayTheirNames) and demand the killer and accomplices be held accountable. We move to the meso when considering how that person's death affects families, organizations, and local communities. Although the three of us did not know Breonna Taylor or George Floyd personally, their deaths reverberate through our relationships. One of us watched his White mother and her White best friend acquire "conceal and carry" licenses granting them the ability to possess a loaded gun in public; the two women fear not police brutality *but those protesting it*. For us, their guns symbolize not freedom and safety but racism and danger. In a conversation with Trump-voting Republican family members, another of us was asked *sincerely*, "What do they mean when they say, 'Racism is a systemic problem'?" This prompted what felt like a productive discussion. As a Black woman, still another of us fears for her own life and those of her family members. She listened in rage and sadness as her cousin recounted being targeted by emboldened White supremacists. They followed her on the highway, attempted to run her off the road, and threw bricks and debris at her car, causing costly damage. In terror, she waited on the side of the road for the authorities, not knowing whom to fear most: the White supremacists or the police.

The macro of autoethnography

As indicated, the identity (*auto*, micro) and relational (meso) aspects and implications of autoethnography bear recursive relationships to the macro (*ethnos*). The macro level draws our attention to canonical narratives and institutional forces. We argue that autoethnography—as a method, mode of representation, and way of life—already advances a collective consciousness and can, if mobilized effectively, make broader and deeper contributions to social change and justice.

As we write (August 2020), COVID-19 and police violence dominate the news cycle. The pandemic has laid bare long-standing structural and intersecting inequities (e.g., racism and poverty) related to the environment, water, food, housing, health care, jobs, education, criminal "justice," and the political system.

Analyzing U.S. Centers for Disease Control and Prevention (CDC) data, Ford, Reber, and Reeves (2020) conclude that COVID-19 death rates among Black and Latinx people aged 45–54 in the U.S. "are at least six times higher than for whites." The virus also exacerbates health inequities among Native Americans, who suffer disproportionate rates of diabetes and asthma—conditions that render one more likely to die from the disease. How telling that many states in the U.S. classify Native Americans as racially "other" (Nagle, 2020), undermining our ability to make reliable comparisons between the dominant racial group and survivors of what may have been the largest-scale genocide in human history, rivaled only by the trans-Atlantic slave trade. We receive daily reminders that the U.S. lacks the infrastructures we need—*and could well afford*—if power-holders did not direct trillions of dollars to policing and incarcerating at home and dominating and colonizing elsewhere.

We recoiled at testimony provided by nurse anesthetist Derrick Smith (Elassar, 2020), who described a gasping COVID patient. About to be placed on a ventilator, the man asked Smith, "Who's going to pay for it?" These may have been the man's last words. The U.S. stands alone: the most expensive healthcare in the world yet with mediocre health outcomes and no universal coverage. When 24.7 million people lost jobs in the pandemic's wake (Kochhar, 2020), millions also lost access to employer-based health insurance. We don't know how many of the hundreds of thousands of U.S. casualties to date asked themselves the same question posed to Smith and then delayed or avoided care.

White supremacy and a pandemic are macro problems. At long last, the U.S.—an individualistic, "every-man-for-himself" (gendered language intended) country—has a critical mass of people calling for systemic solutions. We hear more demands for Medicare for All, if not the abolition of for-profit healthcare, as well as for defunding, demilitarizing, and even dismantling the police. Powerful cultural institutions already have shifted: the NFL announcing players may kneel during the national anthem,[1] NASCAR banning confederate flags, the Washington Redskins yielding to decades of pressure to change their racist name.

Alongside, and in addition to the micro and meso, interrogating the macro advances our roles not only as autoethnographers but also as critical and *public* intellectuals. Autoethnographers are well positioned to help channel the moral outrage of this moment by giving media interviews, writing op-eds, contacting elected officials, and documenting our activism—all *story-centered* pursuits that connect the *personal*, the *relational*, and the *structural*.

***

There is no single or linear path from the micro to the meso to the macro—and back. As Ellis and Bochner (2000) write, "back and forth autoethnographers gaze" by focusing "outward on social and cultural aspects of their personal experience" and then "inward, exploring a vulnerable self that is moved by and may move through, reflect, and resist cultural interpretations" (p. 739). Doing autoethnography requires toggling between our experiences and larger relational and social contexts and then creating micro (personal), meso (relational), and macro (structural) analyses and critiques.

Throughout their life's work, Art and Carolyn have demonstrated how to do such toggling, and it would be surprising to meet an autoethnographer of the past three decades who has never encountered their writings. Individually and collectively, they have been architects and fierce advocates of autoethnography and personal narrative. They have published more than a dozen books as well as hundreds of articles, chapters, and essays, some of which have thousands of citations; given more than 50 national and international workshops and keynotes; and edited more than 40 books about autoethnography and narrative inquiry for their *Ethnographic Alternatives* and *Writing Lives* series. Art and Carolyn have received numerous article, book, and lifetime achievement awards, and their individual and collaborative contributions have been celebrated in many conference sessions, articles, and journal issues (e.g., Denzin, 2005; Holman Jones, 2004; Kafar, 2019; Santoro & Boylorn, 2008). Their legacy extends beyond their home disciplines of communication and sociology and beyond the geographic boundaries of the United States. Art and Carolyn have traveled extensively to bring the ethics and practices of autoethnography and narrative inquiry to scholars in various regions. They have been referenced in disciplines as diverse as music, education, nursing, accounting, architecture, drama, and medicine, and their writing has been translated from English to Polish, Finnish, German, Spanish, Chinese, and Thai.

Art and Carolyn's autoethnography has engaged the micro, meso, and macro in several ways. Their micro explorations have documented internal feelings and struggles as they cared for aging, ill, and frail parents (Bochner, 2002a; Ellis, 1996, 2001) and partners (Bochner, 2014; Ellis, 2018); coped with bodily stigmas, failures, and ailments (Bochner, 2020; Ellis, 1998, 2014); processed and carried loss and grief (Bochner, 1997, 2012; Ellis, 1993, 2014); managed trials and tribulations of academic life (Bochner, 1997, 2001, 2014; Ellis, 2019); and worked toward and through difficult relational decisions such as abortion (Bochner & Ellis, 1992; Ellis & Bochner, 1992; Ellis, 2020). At the meso level, they've engaged extant research, theories, interviews, and fieldwork to explore and explain close relationships (Bochner, 2014) and community life (Ellis, 1986, 1995, 2007). From a macro perspective, they have used personal experience to challenge canonical narratives and explore systemic problems such as racism (Ellis, 1995a, 2009a), xenophobia, sexism, and authoritarianism (Bochner, 2018; Ellis & Rawicki, 2018), and COVID-19 (Ellis & Rawicki, 2020).

Further, Carolyn and Art have changed the landscape of communication, sociology, and qualitative inquiry (see, e.g., Bochner, 1994; Bochner & Ellis, 2002, 2016; Ellis 2004, 2009b; Ellis & Bochner, 1992, 1996, 2000). They have organized conferences, taught undergraduate and graduate courses in autoethnography and narrative inquiry, supervised theses and dissertations, and edited several journal issues and books—at every turn offering generous feedback and support. Within and across their oeuvre, they never privileged their own experience and stories over others'. Indeed, they have used their experiences to create an extended *family* and scholarly community. Each of this book's editors (and some of the contributors) refer to them as "parents" and to each other as "siblings." Art and Carolyn have demonstrated the importance of narrative and story in/as research (Bochner, 1994, 2001, 2002b, 2014) and guided us through ethical issues we encounter when writing about ourselves and others (Bochner, 2007, 2012; Ellis, 1995b, 2007). They have contributed greatly to creating and sustaining the infrastructure for recognizing the significance of personal experience, establishing meaningful and sustained relationships, and challenging injustices.

Granted, autoethnography is not without detractors. Autoethnography has been criticized by some traditional qualitative researchers for being self-indulgent and lacking in ethics; or as lacking reliability and validity; or for over-privileging the humanist self. But these criticisms, all of which cut across epistemological and ontological lines and reinforce positivist and post-positivist rejections of the inter-pretive paradigm itself, have lessened in the past decade. And although we have always firmly rejected such criticisms (as have Art [2001] and Carolyn [2009c]), it is important to acknowledge that autoethnography in general, and the works of this volume in particular, exist in a "contested methodological present" (see Denzin & Giardina, 2015); doing autoethnography can indeed entail *personal* and *professional* risks (see Poulos, 2019). Yet, Carolyn and Art have shown us one way forward in terms of the practice of autoethnography, and many of the contributors to this volume have taken their lead, extending it into new and innovative formations. This volume, then, con-nects the past to the future—showing where autoethnography has been, and where it might—and can—go.

About this collection

In August 2018, Art and Carolyn retired from the University of South Florida. For more than three decades, they mentored hundreds of students and championed the development and application of autoethnography and narrative inquiry. In cele-bration of their retirement, more than a hundred friends and colleagues assembled for a symposium, "Autoethnography and Narrative Inquiry: Reflecting on the Legacy of Carolyn Ellis and Art Bochner." The symposium was held January 3–5, 2019 at the Dolphin Beach Resort in St. Pete Beach, Florida.[2] Some attended in deference to the ways Carolyn and Art's work promotes a nuanced, compassionate approach to understanding oneself, relating with others, and unpacking the sig-nificance of cultural, social, and political life. Others attended because Art and Carolyn model not only how one might produce work of significance but also how one might *live* meaningfully, responsibly, and ethically. Friends and colleagues also organized two tribute panels at the 2018 International Congress of Qualitative Inquiry. This collection originates from those panels and the symposium.

We organize the collection into two sections: "Foundations" and "Futures." Contributors to "Foundations" explore Carolyn and Art's scholarship and legacy and/or their singular presence in the author's life. Informed by their work, con-tributors to "Futures" offer novel and innovative applications of autoethnographic and narrative inquiry.

Throughout the collection, we see autoethnography operate at micro, meso, and macro levels. Several authors spotlight their particular relationships with Carolyn and Art (micro-meso) and show how their influence reverberates through connections the author has with significant others. Some authors describe how a concept drawn from Art and/or Carolyn (e.g., institutional depression, relational ethics) informs not only their individual research but also how they teach, discuss, evaluate, and use research. Authors show how interact-ing with and learning from two people, Art and Carolyn, shape their practices of teaching and mentoring; researching, composing, and editing; and serving others, institutions, and communities. Each year, these practices continue to connect Carolyn and Art to thousands of students, readers, and fellow travelers.

After thinking and feeling with/for these chapters, we reexperience our immense gratitude for Art and Carolyn and for ways they humanize social scientific research and writing and challenge the notion that such work can—or should—be objective, neutral, and apolitical. That they exemplify working and living as if running out of time makes possible our writing and living to/with/for each other. Carolyn and Art ground and guide us. We see, hear, and feel this directly in how they care for us, converse with us, and facilitate our work, and indirectly through their insight, influence, and inspiration. They show us how to live with adversity and how to learn from formative, epiphanic, and scarring experiences. They help us fuse the personal and the academic; the arts, humanities, and social sciences; the head (intellect) and the heart (emotion). They give us permission to get stuck and tools to break loose. They help us face pain and despair with hope. They encourage us to challenge unethical and abusive attitudes, values, beliefs, and practices. They exemplify how to use stories to craft meaningful lives; to undertake creative, analytical, and critical interventions in the academy and beyond; and to seek equality and social justice.

This collection pays homage to two prominent scholars who have left an indelible imprint on our lives and scholarship. No one has shaped us more as autoethnographic methodologists and composers than Art and Carolyn. But as the collection demonstrates, this influence expands beyond two people—beyond the micro and meso. Their autoethnographic and life project gives us tools for understanding both shared humanity and precious diversity; for striving to become ever-more empathic, loving, and ethical; and for living our best creative, relational, and public lives—as if running out of time.

Notes

1 An even more systemic solution would be to abolish "The Star-Spangled Banner," written by a slave owner and slavery advocate.
2 The Dolphin Beach Resort is notable for an additional reason: It hosted two earlier conferences focused on autoethnography and lived experience. The conference, "Ethnography for the 21st Century: Alternatives and Opportunities" (2000), served as the impetus for *Ethnographically Speaking: Autoethnography, Literature, and Aesthetics* (Bochner & Ellis, 2002); and the conference, "Sociology of Subjectivity" (1990), served as the impetus for *Investigating Subjectivity: Research on Lived Experience* (Ellis & Flaherty, 1992).

References

Berry, K., Gillotti, C., & Adams, T. E. (2020). *Living sexuality: Storying LGBTQ relationships, identities, and desires*. Brill | Sense.

Bochner, A. P. (1994). Perspectives on inquiry II: Theories and stories. In M. Knapp & G. R. Miller (Eds.), *Handbook of interpersonal communication* (2nd ed., pp. 21–41). Sage.

Bochner, A. P. (1997). It's about time: Narrative and the divided self. *Qualitative Inquiry, 3*(4), 418–438. https://doi.org/10.1177/107780049700300404.

Bochner, A. (2001). Narratives virtues. *Qualitative Inquiry, 7*(2), 131–157. https://doi.org/10.1177/107780040100700201.

Bochner, A. (2002a). Love survives. *Qualitative Inquiry*, *8*(2), 161–170. https://doi.org/10. 1177/1077800408002009.

Bochner, A. (2002b). Perspectives on inquiry III: The moral of stories. In M. Knapp & J. Daley (Eds.), *The handbook of interpersonal communication* (3rd ed., pp. 73–101). Sage.

Bochner, A. (2007). Notes toward an ethics of memory in autoethnography. In Norman K. Denzin & M. Giardina (Eds.), *Ethical futures in qualitative research: Decolonizing the politics of knowledge* (pp. 197–208). Left Coast Press.

Bochner, A. P. (2012). Bird on the wire: Freeing the father within me. *Qualitative Inquiry*, *18*(2), 168–173. https://doi.org/10.1177/1077800411429094.

Bochner, A. P. (2014). *Coming to narrative: A personal history of paradigm change in the human sciences*. Left Coast Press.

Bochner, A. P. (2018). The night of and the mourning after: Truth and transference in the election of Donald Trump. *Qualitative Inquiry*, *24*(5), 309–317. https://doi.org/10.1177/ 1077800417745428.

Bochner, A. P. (2020). Autoethnography as a way of life: Listening to tinnitus teach. *Journal of Autoethnography*, *1*(1): 81–92. https://doi.org/10.1525/joae.2020.1.1.81.

Bochner, A. P., & Ellis, C. (1992). Personal narrative as a social approach to interpersonal communication. *Communication Theory*, *2*(2), 165–172. https://doi.org/10.1111/j.1468-2885.1992. tb00036.x.

Bochner, A. P., & Ellis, C. (2002). *Ethnographically speaking: Autoethnography, literature, and aesthetics*. AltaMira Press.

Bochner, A. P., & Ellis, C. (2016). *Evocative autoethnography: Writing lives, telling stories*. Routledge.

Boylorn, R. M. (2014). A story and a stereotype: An angry and strong auto/ethnography of black womanhood. In R. M. Boylorn & M. P. Orbe (Eds.), *Critical autoethnography: Intersecting cultural identities in everyday life* (pp. 129–143). Left Coast Press.

Denzin, N. K. (Ed.) (2005). Carolyn Ellis's contributions to Symbolic Interaction and Communication. *Studies in Symbolic Interaction*, *28*, Elsevier. https://doi.org/10.1016/ S01632396(04)28030-28039.

Denzin, N. K. (2014). *Interpretive autoethnography* (2nd ed.). Sage.

Denzin, N. K., & Giardina, M. D. (Eds.), (2015). *Qualitative inquiry—past, present, & future: A critical reader*. Left Coast Press.

Elassar, A. (2020, April 11). A nurse revealed the tragic last words of his coronavirus patient: "Who's going to pay for it?" *CNN Health*. Retrieved from www.cnn.com/2020/04/11/ health/nurse-last-words-coronavirus-patient-trnd/index.html.

Ellis, C. (1986). *Fisher folk: Two communities on Chesapeake Bay*. University Press of Kentucky.

Ellis, C. (1993). "There are survivors": Telling a story of sudden death. *The Sociological Quarterly*, *34*(4), 711–730. https://doi.org/10.1111/j.1533-8525.1993.tb00114.x.

Ellis, C. (1995a). The other side of the fence: Seeing Black and White in a small, southern town. *Qualitative Inquiry*, *1*(2), 147–167. https://doi.org/10.1177/107780049500100201.

Ellis, C. (1995b). Emotional and ethical quagmires in returning to the field. *Journal of Contemporary Ethnography*, *24*(1), 68–98. https://doi.org/10.1177/089124195024001003.

Ellis, C. (1996). Maternal connections. In C. Ellis & A. Bochner (Eds.), *Composing ethnography: Alternative forms of qualitative writing* (pp. 240–243). AltaMira Press.

Ellis, C. (1998). I hate my voice: Coming to terms with bodily stigmas. *The Sociological Quarterly*, *39*(4), 517–537. www.jstor.org/stable/4120826.

Ellis, C. (2001). With mother/with child: A true story. *Qualitative Inquiry*, *7*(5), 598–616. https://doi.org/10.1177/107780040100700505.

Ellis, C. (2004). *The ethnographic I: A methodological novel about autoethnography*. AltaMira Press.

Ellis, C. (2007). Telling secrets, revealing lives: Relational ethics in research with intimate others. *Qualitative Inquiry*, *13*(1), 3–29. https://doi.org/10.1177/1077800406294947.

Ellis, C. (2009a). At home with 'real Americans': Communicating across the urban/rural and Black/White divides in the 2008 presidential election. *Cultural Studies<=>Critical Methodologies*, *9*(6), 721–733. https://doi.org/10.1177/1532708609348566.

Ellis, C. (2009b). *Revision: Autoethnographic reflections on life and work*. Left Coast Press.

Ellis, C. (2009c). Fighting back or moving on: An autoethnographic response to critics. *International Review of Qualitative Research*, *2*(3), 371–378. https://doi.org/10.1525/irqr.2009.2.3.371.

Ellis, C. (2014). No longer hip: Losing my balance and adapting to what ails me. *Qualitative Research in Sport, Exercise and Health*, *6*(1), 1–19. https://doi.org/10.1080/2159676X.2014.880505.

Ellis, C. (2018). *Final negotiations: A story of love, loss, and chronic illness* (rev. ed.). Temple University Press.

Ellis, C. (2019). Failing to communicate in a communication department: A former chair calls her spirit back. In J. Brower & W. Benjamin Myers (Eds.), *Critical administration in higher education: Negotiating political commitment and managerial practice* (pp. 49–76). Lexington.

Ellis, C. (2020). *Revision: Autoethnographic reflections on life and work* (rev. ed.). Routledge.

Ellis, C., & Bochner, A. P. (1992). Telling and performing personal stories: The constraints of choice in abortion. In C. Ellis & M. Flaherty (Eds.), *Investigating subjectivity: Research on lived experience* (pp. 79–101). Sage.

Ellis, C., & Bochner, A. P. (Eds.). (1996). *Composing ethnography: Alternative forms of qualitative writing*. AltaMira Press.

Ellis, C., & Bochner, A. (2000). Autoethnography, personal narrative, reflexivity: Researcher as subject. In N. K. Denzin & Y. S. Lincoln (Eds.), *The handbook of qualitative research* (2nd ed., pp. 733–768). Sage.

Ellis, C., & Flaherty, M. (1992). *Investigating subjectivity: Research on lived experience*. Sage.

Ellis, C., & Rawicki, J. (2018). Remembering the past/Anticipating the future: A professor from the white working class talks with a survivor of the Holocaust about our troubled world. *Qualitative Inquiry*, *24*(5), 323–337. doi:10.1177/1077800417741387

Ellis, C., & Rawicki, J. (2020). A researcher and survivor of the Holocaust connect and make meaning during the COVID-19 pandemic. *Journal of Loss and Trauma*. doi:10.1080/15325024.2020.1765099.

Ford, T., Reber, S., & Reeves, R.V. (2020, June 16). Race gaps in COVID-19 deaths are even bigger than they appear. *Brookings*. Retrieved from www.brookings.edu/blog/up-front/2020/06/16/race-gaps-in-covid-19-deaths-are-even-bigger-than-they-appear/.

Holman Jones, S. (2004). Building connections in qualitative research: Carolyn Ellis and Art Bochner in conversation with Stacy Holman Jones. *Qualitative Social Research*, *5*(3). Retrieved from http://nbn-resolving.de/urn:nbn:de:0114-fqs0403284.

Kafar, M. (Ed.) (2019). Legacy of masters: Honoring the retirement of Professors Carolyn Ellis and Arthur P. Bochner. *Master and mastery in culture, society, art, and education*, *1*(8), 241–280.

Kochhar, R. (2020, June 9). Hispanic women, immigrants, young adults, those with less education hit hardest by COVID-19 job losses. Pew Research Center. Retrieved from www.pewresearch.org/fact-tank/2020/06/09/hispanic-women-immigrants-young-adults-those-with-less-education-hit-hardest-by-covid-19-job-losses/.

Miranda, L., & McCarter, J. (2016). *Hamilton: An American musical*. Grand Central Publishing.

Nagle, R. (2020, April 24). Native Americans being left out of US coronavirus data and labelled as "other." *The Guardian*. Retrieved from www.theguardian.com/us-news/2020/apr/24/us-native-americans-left-out-coronavirus-data.

Poulos, C. N. (2019). Trouble in paradise. *International Review of Qualitative Research*, *12*(3), 268–277. https://doi.org/10.1525/irqr.2019.12.3.268.

Santoro, P., & Boylorn, R. M. (2008). Re-imagining possibilities: Honoring the work of Carolyn Ellis and Art Bochner. *Qualitative Inquiry*, *14*(2), 192–211. https://doi.org/10.1177/1077800407304422.

Tillmann, L. M. (2009). Body and bulimia revisited: Reflections on "A Secret Life." *Journal of Applied Communication Research*, *37*(1), 98–112. https://doi.org/10.1080/00909880802592615.

Tillmann-Healy, L. M. (1996). A secret life in a culture of thinness: Reflections on body, food, and bulimia. In C. Ellis & A. P. Bochner (Eds.), *Composing ethnography: Alternative forms of qualitative writing* (pp. 76–108). AltaMira Press.

PART I
Foundations

2

RISK AND REWARD IN AUTOETHNOGRAPHY

Revisiting "Chronicling an Academic Depression"

Barbara J. Jago

November 2000. From beneath my bed covers, I spy the clock. 9am. 10am. 11am. Insistent cat screams drift into half-waking stress dreams.

I have to feed them.

I slip into my nightshirt, fill cat bowls, move to the couch. Cocooned in my PJs and a pink blanket. Flooded by tears. Speechless.

Time is punctuated by Lifetime TV. *The Golden Girls. Designing Women. Moment of Truth* movies. I push the remote buttons from tactile memory, smoke cigarettes, drift.

I consider all the ways I might end my pathetic life: razor blades, car crash, bullet to the brain. Every day I weigh my options. Who would care? But I am too tired to act. They say suicides tend to happen when you are coming out of major depression, still caught up in the darkness, but energized enough to take action, the ultimate irony of recovery (Solomon, 2001).

Guilt fogs my thoughts. Cancelled classes. Angry students. Frustrated colleagues. The tenure clock stopped. Reputation ruined. My mother's worried voice on the phone, reaching across the 1400 miles from Tampa, hoping for an affirmative response, "Are you okay?"

***

What you have just read is a story I tell in "Chronicling an Academic Depression" (Jago, 2002), my autoethnography published 18 years ago in the *Journal of Contemporary Ethnography* (*JCE*). In my major depression[1] story, I highlight the mental health challenges I faced as an assistant professor. That story connects to what Art Bochner (1997) has referred to as "institutional depression," which he defines as "a pattern of anxiety, hopelessness, demoralization, isolation, and disharmony that circulates through university life" (p. 289).

In this meta-autoethnography (Ellis, 2009), I examine the life my autoethnography has lived since publication and consider the risks and rewards inherent in autoethnographic writing. As I write, I hear the voices of Art Bochner and Carolyn Ellis, voices that have guided me in my career—and in my life. In this layered account (Ronai, 1995), I include their voices as well as a chorus of others that have contributed to this autoethnography's meaning as it has evolved over time. In this way, this meta-autoethnography is also a tribute to Art, Carolyn, and other guides and companions.

Every autoethnographer knows that writing about life's challenges requires honesty and vulnerability (Bochner & Ellis, 2016; Ellis, 2007). *It isn't easy.* The ethics of auto-ethnography can be difficult to navigate, especially when our self-presentations open us to criticism, judgement, and worse. Moreover, as Carolyn (Ellis, 2007) has told us about relational ethics, we need to exercise great care when we write about others. "The bad news," she explains, "is that there are no definite rules or universal principles that can tell you precisely what to do in every situation or relationship you may encounter, other than the vague and generic 'do no harm'" (p. 5). Of course, the more experience we have, she explains, the better we are at navigating these some-times-tumultuous waters (Ellis, 2007).

When we publish our stories, we hope they are used and used well (Coles, 1989)—but we have no control over the meanings others bring to our accounts. Once our stories appear in print, they lie out of our interpretive control. Ultimately, publishing autoethnography can be risky, to our careers and to our close relationships. But as Art and Carolyn write in *Evocative Autoethnography* (2017),

> Sometimes we just have to put our story out there and accept the consequences. We have to figure out how important it is to tell it, think about the potential rewards and risks, and determine if the work has something important to offer others by putting meanings into motion. Nobody can make these judgements for you.
>
> *(pp. 152–153)*

So, I ask, what have been the consequences of publishing my major depression autoethnography? What meanings did others attribute to my words? How did they use my story in their own lives? What are the risks and rewards of living an autoethnographic life?

***

This meta-autoethnography starts long before the publication of my major depression story. It begins in August of 1993, when I enroll in the doctoral program in Communication at the University of South Florida (USF). After a difficult period in my twenties, including substance abuse and my first bout of major depression, I am intimidated to begin the program, having never taken a communication course before. Thankfully, my background in cultural anthropology, cinema studies, and education positions me well.

In my first semester, I enroll in Art's course, "Interpretive Perspectives in Communication," and my life changes. In this course, Art teaches us to think about academic research and scholarly writing in a new way, to employ an interpretive perspective, to consider the value of including the personal and spiritual in our academic work, to embrace stories. In the following semesters, I take "Narrative" and "Writing Workshop" with Art as well as "Communicating Emotion" with Carolyn. In these courses, we read Jerome Bruner, Robert Coles, Laurel Richardson, George Herbert Mead, Gregory Bateson, Barbara Myerhoff, Clifford Geertz, Richard Rorty, Erving Goffman, Norman Denzin, Carol Rambo, and so many others; we read Art and Carolyn's work; we discuss epistemology and ontology; and we write stories.

At the time, I am fascinated by the ideas we are discussing, but I don't yet know how privileged I am to participate in the paradigm shift Art and Carolyn are helping to propel in the social sciences. Years later, when I devour Art's *Coming to Narrative* (2014), I am back in his class, listening to his argument for an interpretive perspective and the incorporation of personal narratives in academic research.

> We need to face up to the ways we use orthodox academic practices to discipline, control, and perpetuate ourselves and our traditions, thus stifling innovation, discouraging creativity, inhibiting criticism of our own institutional conventions, making it difficult to take risks, and severing academic life from emotional and spiritual life. No matter how much they may threaten us, we need to consider alternatives—different goals, different styles of research and writing; different ways of bringing the academic and the personal into conversation with one another.
>
> *(p. 291)*

As I take classes with Art and Carolyn, I find a new way of thinking about academic research and knowledge, a new way of writing, a new way of being in academia, and a supportive community of people who truly honor the "human" side of human communication research. I embrace autoethnography. As I write autoethnography, I make sense of my experience and find my voice. At the risk of sounding schmaltzy, I also find an intellectual and emotional home. Work and life become one, with all the risks and rewards that integration brings. As a graduate student, I am already living an autoethnographic life.

The vulnerability inherent in autoethnographic research is apparent to me from the beginning. Putting my stories in print and sharing them with others proves challenging and even frightening at times—but also invigorating and satisfying. I am amazed at the conversations this work prompts, the understandings that develop, the resulting potential for positive change. When Norm Denzin publishes my first autoethnography (written under Art's guidance) about my family (Jago, 1996) in *Qualitative Inquiry*, I finally feel like a "real" academic. When I decide to write an autoethnographic dissertation later that year, Eric Eisenberg, my advisor, warns me I might be taking a risk with my burgeoning career. "Not everyone appreciates this methodology," he says. "And you will be on the job market." I appreciate Eric's sincere concern for my future but, in my heart, I know autoethnography is not *an* option; it is the *only* option for me. So, I write about growing up without a father and interview six other "father-absent" women (Jago, 1998). The process is grueling but also richly satisfying. Together, my co-researchers build a community of understanding about fatherlessness. Eventually, I publish an autoethnography about one of my co-researchers (Jago, 2006).

In 1998, I graduate from USF and accept a position as an assistant professor at the University of New Hampshire (UNH) in Manchester. In my first year at UNH's commuter campus, I participate in delivering the communication program housed in Durham ("the mother ship"). Soon after I arrive, my colleague, Associate Professor Jeff Klenotic, and I begin to create a new program in "communication arts," an applied program that will live on the Manchester campus and be under our control. I am overjoyed to create the relational communication area of the curriculum. As I build courses, I apply everything Art and Carolyn taught me. My favorite class is a seminar entitled "Narrative" where my students learn about narrative theory and write auto-ethnography. I teach the course almost every spring for years to come. When *Evocative Autoethnography* (Bochner & Ellis, 2016) is published, I am overjoyed to have such a rich text for teaching. Even though I live far away from USF, Art and Carolyn are with me in the classroom. I cherish their presence—and so do my students.

***

In the fall of 2000, in my second year as an assistant professor, I fall apart; another bout of major depression renders me unable to do my job. With the support of my colleagues and dean, I go on medical leave for a year. With the help of good therapists and psychiatrists, I recover, and start writing my depression autoethnography. The process is overwhelming. I revisit the depths of depression with every keystroke, always fearful of falling back into the black hole. But the process of writing is therapeutic and cathartic. I render myself vulnerable, and hope the rewards, for me and others, will outweigh the risks. The idea that autoethnography can inspire dialogue about difficult and often marginalized experiences motivates me (Bochner & Ellis, 2016).

In early 2002, I take a deep breath and submit my story to JCE.

***

JCE Reviewer:
   I have read, studied and critiqued a number of narratives that aim to give voice to the depth, darkness, and despair of the depressive experience. Few come close to this manuscript[,] which offers readers a compelling, brutally honest glimpse of what depression is, how it "feels," and how one struggles to cope and manage through it. I'd like to see this piece in print as soon as possible. I deal with a large number of students who are experiencing depression for the first time. They need to know they are not alone.

(Anonymous, personal communication, May 21, 2002)

***

JCE Reviewer:

I do worry somewhat about Barbara's career given the story in this paper. She says [on page 9] that she wants to enhance others' understanding, but I wonder if this work might not also enhance others' fears. Might it not be best for her left unpublished? That doesn't mean I don't see benefit from her writing it for herself and others in her situation. Only Barbara can answer this and I guess for the most part it should not be our job to protect writers. Or should it?

(Anonymous, personal communication, May 21, 2002)

***

When I receive the reviews from *JCE*, I am overwhelmed. The comments from the three reviewers and the editor are generally positive, but one reviewer (whom I later find out was Carolyn) encourages me to address the risks of publishing. I am surprised by the reviewer's concern; I am so committed to sharing a story I worked hard to write (and live), a story I need to publish for tenure, that I haven't fully considered the potential risk to my career. Am I being naïve about publishing? Self-destructive? I wonder, do the benefits outweigh the potential harm?

But I am an autoethnographer. This is what I do. Risks be damned, I decide to publish.

In the reviews, there are also many suggestions for revisions, good suggestions from smart people. But I can't go back into the story; I can't relive the trauma. Not right now. I make only minor changes, and *JCE* publishes it. I regret not addressing the reviewers' comments more fully.

To this day, the story remains true for me. I still struggle with depression every day. Some days are better than others, but the feeling never goes away.

***

In *Revision* (2009), Carolyn writes:

There are many "secrets" we walk around with that perhaps don't need to be hidden. We think sharing them will make us feel vulnerable. Perhaps sharing them will make us feel less vulnerable, or maybe we will find that vulnerability is not necessarily a bad thing. Besides, sharing events in our lives opens the possibility that we will get feedback that might help us change our lives for the better. Perhaps we might learn from others in similar circumstances and offer them insights from our experiences.

(p. 188)

***

Excerpted from an email I receive from an associate professor of sociology:

I just read your article in [*JCE*]. It was recommended to me by someone who loved it. I love it. And I have in turn forwarded it to others. Bipolar lives with me. Wish it didn't, but there it is. Thus, your work really resonated with me at a personal level.... Have you heard from others like me?... Your article rang "so true" for me. In so many ways. Thanks for writing it. As a qualitative researcher, I think it is a contribution to the qualitative literature. From the perspective of someone who is ill, it also informed my personal life.

(Anonymous, personal communication, February 3, 2003)

***

Excerpted from an email I receive from an assistant professor of sociology:

Just wanted to let you know how moved I was by your article.... From reading your article, it sounds like you and I have a lot in common—professionally, being new faculty members, making the transition from grad student to [assistant] professor, and personal things like being fatherless and being plunged into depression because of the end of a relationship. It was actually a bit spooky in places ... because I could have written so many parts of it. Anyway, I'd love to talk if you'd like.

(Anonymous, personal communication, January 9, 2004)

***

Excerpted from an email I receive from a first-year doctoral student:

I really related to your experiences and enjoyed the article very much.... I have gone through many similar episodes. And unfortunately, just as I begin my doctoral program, when I really need to focus on some difficult classes, it all happens again (due to a completely unforeseen development). I've spent 2–5 AM the last several nights just crying and crying. Also, I am a bit scared to give out my name for now, but I am wondering whether you'd be willing to give me advice?

(Anonymous, personal communication, September 12, 2004)

***

In a handwritten note, the writer says:

[In your major depression autoethnography], you talked about your "former self disappearing." I disappeared once too, for different reasons, but I have reappeared and my dark time is well back on my timeline. Life imperfect is still life. I am alive now. I have important thoughts and accomplishments yet unfinished, thank God. ... My charming mother told me that life is good and bad, unless you are a cat, whereas life is only good. For us, the contentment is not so easily lived.

(Anonymous, personal communication, 2004)

***

When I answer the phone in my NH apartment, Mom offers her usual greeting. "It's your mother calling from Tampa!" She sounds cheerful. "How are you?"

"Hi, Mom! I'm ok." I imagine my 73-year-old mother relaxing in her living room Barcalounger with her TV tuned to a tennis match or an equestrian event. "How are you?"

"I just read your depression story," she tells me. "You are such a good writer!" She pauses. Then her tone lowers, her voice cracks, her words come hesitantly. I can hear the sadness in her voice. "I didn't know how bad it was. I knew it was bad, but I didn't think it was *this* bad. I'm sorry I wasn't there for you."

Tears roll down my cheeks. "No, Ma! It's not your fault. You helped me *every day*. I don't know if I could have gotten through without you." I pause for emphasis. "I LOVE YOU!"

"I love you, too."

***

In 2003, I receive an email from Professor Kimberly Myers at the Penn State College of Medicine asking to include a version of my depression story in *Illness in the Academy: A Collection of Pathographies by Academics*. I agree (Jago, 2007).

***

In 2012, I receive an email from Professor Pat Sikes from the University of Sheffield in the UK. She wants to reprint my depression story in her two-volume collection *Autoethnography*. I agree (Jago, 2013).

***

In 2016, I receive an email from Sarah Brown, a journalist for *The Chronicle of Higher Education*. *The Chronicle* is doing a story on professors coping with mental illness.

"I read your depression story," Sarah says. "And I want to interview you. Of course, I'll let you give me feedback on what I write before publication."

I am thrilled at the prospect of my story reaching more people and potentially helping them, so I eagerly accept. I have a phone interview with Sarah, and two weeks later, a photographer comes to my office to shoot photos for the article.

He asks me not to smile.

On September 23, 2016, "How 4 Professors Built Careers Despite Mental-health Struggles" (Brown, 2016) is published, without my editorial feedback. Not only does my photo make me look depressed (which I was not at that time), but the article suggests I hid my condition from the university, which is absolutely NOT true. But it's too late; the story is published.

I imagine it showing up in the inboxes of academics across the country. I am simultaneously gratified and horrified.

Despite the misrepresentation, I still want UNH to add the story to the UNH Newsroom, the curated site of popular press articles featuring UNH faculty. I want to do anything I can to push back against the stigma of mental illness in the academy. They don't respond to my inquiry, leaving me with the sense that having a mentally ill faculty member is something UNH would like to hide, that I embarrass them.

Fuck them, I think. The academy still has such a long way to go in addressing the mental health challenges faculty face.

***

In the 20 years I have been teaching Narrative at UNH, I have guided approximately 300 students through the challenging journey that is autoethnographic scholarship. As a gesture of camaraderie and to help them understand the ethics of autoethnography, I require students to read my depression story.

Risky?

Yes.

Do the details of my story undermine my credibility? Our professional relationship?

Perhaps.

Is sharing my story rewarding?

Absolutely.

Whenever my students read my story, I am gifted with stories about their own mental health challenges—and there are many, many more with each passing year, especially recently. In fact, a 2019 analysis of evidence from two national surveys of the mental health of undergraduates, including a total of 788,235 students in U.S. colleges and universities, reported significant increases in rates of depression from 2012 to 2018. In one survey, rates for students with moderate to severe depression increased 74% in women and 49% in men over that time period (Duffy, Twenge, & Joiner, 2019). I see these statistics mirrored in my students and together, we create a safe space for conversation about our experiences.

In 2014, 20-year-old Amanda (who has granted me permission to identify her) sits across from me at my office conference table to discuss her autoethnography project.

"I read your article," she says, sounding hesitant, her blue eyes fixed on mine. "Thank you for writing it. I saw so much of myself in your story. I suffer from major depression too."

I put my hand to my heart and lean toward her. "Oh Amanda. I am sorry to hear this. I know how hard it can be."

"Thank you. I am taking two different medications. They help, but …" Her voice trails off. She licks her lips, a sign of the dry mouth that can accompany some antidepressants. "I want to write about my own depression."

I smile, so proud of her honesty and bravery. "Ok. But before you begin, I need to ask a question. Are you sure you want to do this? It won't be easy—and you'll be sharing your story with me and the rest of the class. I want to make sure you're up to the task. It's my responsibility as your professor to protect you." As I say these words, I think about Carolyn's *JCE* review of my depression autoethnography.

Amanda sits up straight in her chair and looks right at me. "Yes. I am sure."

During the next three months, Amanda writes "Depressed—Proceed with Caution: An Autoethnography of Depression" (Cote, 2016). Her beautifully written story is a gift to her classmates, to her family, and to me. "The writing process … was liberating," she says in her autoethnography.

Once past the tsunami of emotion found in my memory of the time, I felt the urge to write. It felt as if a higher being was pulling me to the table, my fingers to the keys, my words to the screen. I couldn't get away from it. A sign, perhaps, telling me I had to do this. In the end, writing this story left me with peace.

(p. 33)

Six months later, Amanda (Cote, 2017) bravely publishes "The Healing Power of Storytelling: An Exploration into the Autoethnographic Process," a commentary on her autoethnographic adventure, in UNH's *Inquiry Journal*, a publication that highlights undergraduate research.

***

In May of 2018, I receive an email from Tony Adams.

"Stacy Holman Jones, Carolyn Ellis, and I are starting work on a second edition of the *Handbook of Autoethnography*.... We write to ask if you would be interested in including your article as an exemplar" (Adams, personal communication, May 23, 2019).

I respond immediately, "I'm in! Thanks for thinking of me."

***

In January 2019, I present a version of this paper at the Symposium on Auto-ethnography and Narrative Inquiry: Reflecting on the Legacy of Carolyn Ellis and Art Bochner. I am the first speaker on a panel Art has organized, and I am honored to be chosen. But due to back problems that have hampered my ability to travel, I haven't presented at a conference in four years. So, as I sit next to Art at the long table in front of a room full of autoethnographers, friends, acquaintances, and strangers alike, my stomach tightens. I sip water and clutch my nine-page 18-point font script. I never present without a script; in fact, I hate presenting, laying myself bare to others, sharing intimate details of my life in a face-to-face setting. It's nerve-wracking—but going personal is inherent in autoethnography. Nonetheless, I worry. How will others see me? My work? Am I sharing too much? What is the self I am presenting (Goffman,1959)?

As I read my presentation, I take care to speak clearly. I try to bring my story to life through thick description (Geertz, 1973), dialogue, tone of voice, inflection, pacing. Interjections of humor help to lighten the mood, and audience laughter calms me.

At the end of my presentation, I look over at Art and notice tears in his eyes.

I gently put my hand on his shoulder. "It's ok," I say.

He turns to me. "It's not what you think."

"I know." And I do. Or at least I think I do. I believe Art feels compassion for me, for the pain I have suffered, not in a pitying way, but with sincere concern and love. I hold back tears.

I appreciate his concern, but I also wonder if my presentation of self over the years in my work has portrayed me as a troubled and sad person. In my auto-ethnographic work, I have written about many aspects of my life, including my family (Jago, 1996, 1998, 2011a), my mental health (Jago, 2002, 2007, 2014), cohabitation (Jago, 2011b), loss (Jago, 2004, 2015) and most recently, the challenges of being alone at mid-life and the importance of friendship (Jago, 2019). Currently, I am working on a project about the pain I have experienced over a lifetime of back problems and four recent spine surgeries (Jago, 2019). All of these experiences have been difficult, but I have also had many joyous and uplifting moments in my life. Why don't I write about them more often? Does autoethnography lend itself much more easily to stories of difficulty, pain, and loss? And if so, what are the identity consequences? I see myself as a survivor, a strong woman who perseveres. But do others?

***

My depression story continues to be lived and written, including one new episode of major depression after an emergency appendectomy in 2011 and a horrifying experience with antidepressant medications in 2014 (Jago, 2014). I continue to see both a therapist and a psychiatrist, two relationships that help me keep the darkness at bay. I am not living a restitution story, one where my life has been restored to what it was before (Frank, 1995), but I cope with mental illness on a daily basis.

When I wrote "Chronicling an Academic Depression," I never imagined the life my autoethnography would live. As a result of publishing my autoethnography, people around the world continue to reach out to thank me and to share their own stories of mental illness. Together, we have supported one another. But more importantly, we are building a community of understanding that I believe has created spaces for challenging the stigma around mental illness that persists in the academy and beyond. Nonetheless, we have a long way to go.

When I began the USF graduate program in 1993 and took courses with Art and Carolyn, I never imagined the career I would have. Writing autoethnography has been so rewarding. Making sense of my experience and sharing those stories with others, including friends, family, and colleagues; engaging in dialogue about life's challenges; making a contribution to academic research; and building communities of understanding continues to be gratifying. But there are always risks—personal and professional. In the end, for me the rewards of writing autoethnography have definitely outweighed the risks. I continue to embrace the vulnerability that comes with living an autoethnographic life.

I wouldn't have it any other way.

***

Postscript
At the end of every spring semester Narrative students tell me that writing an autoethnography and listening to the stories of their classmates has been the

highlight of their undergraduate careers. I always think of Art and Carolyn and how I felt at the end of their courses. I think about the classes they have taught; the articles and books they have produced; the workshops they have conducted around the world; and I think about the value of storytelling and autoethnography in academic research. Art and Carolyn have impacted the lives of so many people, especially their graduate students. They taught us, gently critiqued us, inspired us, and loved us. They have changed our lives, the lives of all the students we continue to teach, and the students our students will teach for years to come. As Robert Coles (1989) says, "the beauty of a good story is its openness—the way you or I or anyone reading it can take it in, and use it for ourselves" (p. 47). In their work—and in their lives—Art and Carolyn have shared so many good stories with us—and I know we will continue to use them well. From the bottom of my heart, I thank them for all they have given me. May this narrative inheritance (Goodall, 2008) continue to be passed on to many future generations.

Note

1 I am referring to major depressive disorder (MDD). Please see the *Diagnostic and Statistical Manual of Mental Disorders, 5th edition* for a complete definition of MDD. MDD is not synonymous with the everyday sadness that people often refer to as depression. MDD is a clinical diagnosis.

References

American Psychiatric Association (2013). *Diagnostic and statistical manual of mental disorders, 5th edition*. American Psychiatric Publishing.

Bochner, A. P. (1997). It's about time: Narrative and the divided self. *Qualitative Inquiry, 3*(4), 418–438. https://doi.org/10.1177/107780049700300404.

Bochner, A. P. (2014). *Coming to narrative: A personal history of paradigm change in the human sciences*. Left Coast Press.

Bochner, A. P., & Ellis, C. (2016). *Evocative autoethnography: Writing lives and telling stories*. Routledge.

Brown, S. (2016). How 4 professors built careers despite mental-health struggles. *The Chronicle of Higher Education, 63*(4).

Coles, R. (1989). *The call of stories: Teaching and the moral imagination*. Houghton Mifflin.

Cote, A. (2016). *Depressed—proceed with caution: An autoethnography of depression*. Unpublished manuscript.

Cote, A. (2017). The healing power of storytelling: An exploration into the autoethnographic process. *Inquiry Journal, 8*. https://scholars.unh.edu/inquiry_2017/8.

Duffy, M. E., Twenge, J. M., & Joiner, T. E. (2019). Trends in mood and anxiety symptoms and suicide-related outcomes among U.S. undergraduates, 2007–2018: Evidence from two national surveys. *Journal of Adolescent Health 65*(5), 590–598. https://doi.org/10.1016/j.jadohealth.2019.04.033.

Ellis, C. (2004). *The ethnographic eye: A methodological novel about autoethnography*. Alta Mira Press.

Ellis, C. (2007). Telling secrets, revealing lives: Relational ethics in research with intimate others. *Qualitative Inquiry, 13*(1), 3–29. https://doi.org/10.1177/1077800406294947.

Ellis, C. (2009). *Revision: Autoethnographic reflections on life and work*. Left Coast Press.

Frank, A. W. (1995). *The wounded storyteller: Body, illness and ethics.* University of Chicago Press.

Geertz, C. (1973). *The interpretation of cultures.* Basic Books.

Goffman, E. (1959). *The presentation of self in everyday life.* Doubleday.

Goodall, H. L. (2008). Narrative inheritance: A nuclear family with toxic secrets. *Qualitative Inquiry, 11*(4), 492–513. https://doi.org/10.1177/1077800405276769.

Jago, B. (1996). Postcards, ghosts, and fathers: Revising family stories. *Qualitative Inquiry, 2*(4), 495–516. https://doi.org/10.1177/107780049600200406.

Jago, B. (1998). *Ambivalence and agency: Women's narratives of father-absence.* (Unpublished doctoral dissertation). University of South Florida: Tampa.

Jago, B. (2002). Chronicling an academic depression. *Journal of Contemporary Ethnography, 31*(6), 729–757. https://doi.org/10.1177/089124102237823.

Jago, B. (2004). The car radio: A autoethnographic short story. *Journal of Loss and Trauma, 10*(1), 1–6. https://doi.org/10.1080/15325020490890598.

Jago, B. (2006). A primary act of imagination: An autoethnography of father-absence. *Qualitative Inquiry, 12*(2), 398–426. https://doi.org/10.1177/1077800405284599.

Jago, B. (2007). Coming out with my academic depression. In K. R. Myers (Ed.), *Illness in the academy: A collection of pathographies by academics* (pp. 110–122). Purdue University Press.

Jago, B. (2011a). Chasing Laurie: An autoethnographic short story. *Qualitative Inquiry, 17*(9), 780–786. https://doi.org/10.1177/1077800411423193.

Jago, B. (2011b). Shacking up: An autoethnographic tale of cohabitation. *Qualitative Inquiry, 17*(2), 204–219. https://doi.org/10.1177/1077800410393889.

Jago, B. (2013). Chronicling an academic depression. In P. Sikes (Ed.), *Autoethnography, 4,* (pp. 59–82). Sage.

Jago, B. (2014). My sleep fest: An autoethnographic short story. *Health Communication, 30*(1), 1–4. https://doi.org/10.1080/10410236.2014.891453.

Jago, B. (2015). Tracing Mom: An autoethnographic short story. *Qualitative Inquiry, 21*(8), 675–677. https://doi.org/10.1177/1077800414563807.

Jago, B. (2019). *Narrating pain: Autoethnographic stories of chronic back pain and its treatment.* Unpublished manuscript.

Jago, B. (2019). Solid as cracked granite: An autoethnography about living alone at midlife. In L. W. Peterson & C. E. Kiesinger (Eds.), *Narrating midlife: Crisis, transition, and transformation* (pp. 25–42). Lexington Books.

Ronai, C. (1995). Multiple reflections of child sex abuse: An argument for a layered account. *Journal of Contemporary Ethnography, 23*(4), 395–426. https://doi.org/10.1177/089124195023004001.

Solomon, A. (2001). *The noonday demon: An atlas of depression.* Scribner.

3

COMING HOME TO NARRATIVE AUTOETHNOGRAPHY

Encounters with Bochner and Ellis

Christopher N. Poulos

I offer this essay as a tribute to the pioneers of autoethnography. I first met Carolyn Ellis and Art Bochner the way most of us who aren't their (direct) students do: On the page. In graduate school, as I did background research for a course in qualitative research methods, I stumbled across their co-authored piece on abortion (Ellis & Bochner, 1991). They begin with this: "The act of telling a personal story is a way of giving voice to experiences that are shrouded in secrecy" (p. 79). A simple, elegant statement—but to me, an epiphany. Or maybe just a confirmation of my own experience—you see, I grew up in a family shrouded in secrecy, with so many stories waiting to be told!

More importantly, it was the first time I'd read any communication scholar claiming that storytelling was a legitimate form of scholarship.

I was suddenly hopeful.

I have always been drawn to a good story.

It's true that I "met" (stumbled upon) them because I was desperate. I had entered a doctoral program in the discipline of Communication Studies sideways—from a background in religious studies, philosophy, film studies, and corporate organizational development. I was quickly terrified that I had made a huge mistake, as there seemed to be a lot of emphasis in my new field on quantitative research. As a lifelong storyteller from a long line of storytellers, most with no penchant for numbers, I was quite sure this new field was not going to work for me. I was on the brink of quitting.

What I needed was a new story.

While I was familiar with the tradition of using personal stories to open up and explore deep religious, spiritual, and philosophical insights—mostly from my deep studies of existentialist literature—Ellis and Bochner's essay was among the first gut-wrenching personal narrative texts I'd read in my foray into this new (for me) "social science" literature. The other lifeline for me was the work of Bud Goodall.

And once I'd read their work, I was off and running. Narrative ethnography would be my bridge into my new discipline. Their work would profoundly shape my work.

This way of reading their piece—as intensely emotional, powerful, moving—was radical. You see, so-called social science had not trafficked much in the wrenching of the human gut, or the breaking of the human heart, as Ruth Behar (1996) would have it. It had, up until this point, largely stuck with crass generalizations. Speaking directly to me, this person, this flesh and blood person right here, and reaching into my heart instead of just my head—well, that was radical. Of course, I admit I was taken both by the quality of the writing, and because the piece directly implicated and reflected my own experience.

You see, I, too, had gotten a young woman pregnant, not far into our relationship. And like "Ted" in their story, I had struggled with my personal internal battle between my rights and my obligations, between a queasy feeling that the decision was both quick and final and someone else's (though I was implicated) and knowing it was the right decision, even if a bit tortured. And I had mourned the loss of our (potential) child. As it turned out, my partner and I later married, and have stayed together for 38 years now. So Bochner and Ellis' story came to me many years after my experience with abortion, as I was embarking on my doctoral studies in the autumn of the year our second (actual) child was born. The direct personal resonance of their (controversial) story of decision-making and "the constraints of choice in abortion" impacted me in a way I cannot begin to calculate, much like reading H. L. Goodall, Jr.'s *Casing a Promised Land: The Autobiography of an Organizational Detective* (1989) had (a book I read while I was a practicing organizational detective working in organizational development and training).

These people had my number.

But, of course, as I read on through the emerging body of work in personal narrative and autoethnography, both from these pioneers and from others, it quickly became obvious that most autoethnographic writing would *not* be so directly relevant to my own experience. I have never cared for and struggled with a dying life-partner (Ellis, 1995). I have never had a mentally retarded mother (Ronai, 1996). I have no direct experience with child sexual abuse (Fox, 1996). I have no experience in the closet, or coming out of it (Adams, 2011). I have not gone on the road with a rock band (Goodall, 1991). I have no direct experience of cancer and death (Vande Berg & Trujillo, 2008). And I have not been a young black girl growing up in rural North Carolina (Boylorn, 2012). But thanks mostly to great writing, I have visited all these spaces, empathized with all these experiences.

Autoethnography, it seems to me, brings emotion and empathy to the surface, draws it out of the reader, puts me in the position to draw upon my experience and teach me something about my fellow humans. When I read evocative auto-ethnography, I am *moved*. I am moved by these stories of emotion, emotionally rendered, evocatively written. Autoethnography expresses, invokes, provokes, and evokes deep feeling, rich connection, vibrant *identification*.

And I quickly realized that what this kind of writing actually does is open up *possibility* by opening up (and sometimes breaking) the heart of the reader (Behar, 1996). Autoethnography offers an opening—to evocation and understanding, to close examination of the deeper contours of human social-emotional experience.

Ellis and Bochner, in their attempts to map and evoke the rocky terrain of a diffi-cult/ tortuous/tumultuous/tormented personal decision-making process, opened up the possibility of crafting a scholarship largely consisting of evocative narratives that speak into the central—but so often overlooked, avoided, and suppressed (especially in research)—human experience: *emotion*. Scholars, up until this point, had often attempted to avoid (and even deny) the obvious fact that much of human life is colored by (or at least infused with) our deeply emotional responses to situations in our lives. And yet, human authors and their human readers, overtaken by the intensity of human emotion, may find ourselves

> battling madly, if you will, for possibility, because possibility is the only salvation. When someone faints, we call for water, eau de Cologne, smelling salts; but when someone wants to despair, then the word is: Get possibility, get possibility, pos-sibility is the only salvation. A possibility—then the person in despair breathes again, he revives again, for without possibility a person seems unable to breathe.
>
> *(Kierkegaard, 1980, pp. 38–39).*

Of course, hints of this move toward evocative/emotional personal narrative had been coming in ethnography since the early days of journal/diary writing in the field, and surely at least since Geertz (1973) wrote his "thick description" of his experience studying Balinese cockfighting. Ethnographers had long been searching for new methods that could evoke what it is actually *like* to be a living, breathing, feeling, embodied human studying human social-communicative *praxis*. What Bochner and Ellis offered, in fact, was both a revolution and a kind of homecoming. In pioneering a new way to navigate the complex intersections of emotion, lived experience, introspection, and scholarship—through *writing as a method of inquiry* (Richardson, 2005), this new method dubbed *autoethnography*—they took us into new, raw, open territory, and at the same time they took us back to the original "dwelling place" (Greek: *ethos*) of writing about human social life.

In the beginning—even deep in the caves of southern France, or in the hills of ancient Greece, or in the pyramids of Egypt, or out in the deserts of Palestine, or in the dense forests of southeast Asia, or in the jungles and deserts of Africa, or in the Outback of Australia, or in the Arctic Circle, or in the high mountains of South America, or the steppes and hills of Asia—there was *story*, and drama, and human struggle. Indeed, at the heart of our communicative *praxis* lies the deep understanding that *logos* (the word) is deployed, first and foremost, in the service of *mythos* (story) and speaks to us through *pathos* (feeling) in the ancient and eternal return to the *ethos* (dwelling place, home) of our shared humanity (Campbell, 1948). As Walter Fisher declares, *of course* humans ought to be understood as *homo narrans*, the story-telling and story-consuming creature. It's what we do.

The power and the *call* of story is at the very heart of our being (Coles, 1989). Narrative is the heartbeat and the hearthstone of our humanity's home.

And autoethnography carries on that ancient core human tradition in a new and powerful way.

In stumbling upon narrative auto/ethnography, I had found my way home.

A few years later, in 2002, at the invitation of Bud Goodall, I found myself on a panel at the National Communication Association (NCA) Conference in New Orleans. There I joined giants in the field of narrative ethnography and auto-ethnography. I, a second-year Assistant Professor, was on a panel with Art Bochner, Carolyn Ellis, Bud Goodall, Nick Trujillo, and Ron Pelias. Not for the last time, I was sandwiched between giants (Poulos, 2016). As I listened to their words, I knew I was forever to be caught up in the stream of autoethnography. And then, at the Ethnography Division's Business meeting, Art Bochner referred to Bud Goodall's *Writing the New Ethnography* (2000) as "the little red Bible."

Damn, I found myself thinking, *I just got religion. Won't Dad be proud?*

Side note: My Dad was a preacher.

Just a few years after autoethnography was widely mocked (Bochner, 2001), our words had taken on a new aura.

We were deep in the mystery and the magic.

We had ourselves a *BIBLE*.

We were, as they say, on a roll.

And a few years after that, as my paper titled *The Ties that Bind Us, the Shadows that Separate Us: Life and Death, Shadow and (Dream)Story* (Poulos, 2006) won the Ellis-Bochner Autoethnography and Personal Narrative Research Award, Art approached me at NCA to talk about contributing to the *Writing Lives* book series at Left Coast Press. I was, frankly, both star-struck and dumb-struck. Not only had I been invited to the party, but I was about to be certified as one of a growing wave of "new ethnographers" (Goodall, 2000), with my very own book.

I had gained entry to the club. I had arrived. It has been my honor to follow these pioneers in the wave of autoethnographic work that progressed, over about twenty years or so, from a highly controversial and contested research method to a powerful mode of qualitative inquiry with the solidity and weight and seriousness of a 736-page *Handbook*, currently undergoing its second edition revisions (Jones, Adams & Ellis, 2013).

I had met the autoethnography pioneers, and I had hitched a ride on their narrative wagon.

I've always had an affinity for pioneers.

When I was a kid, growing up in the 1960s, there was a popular television show about Daniel Boone. There was also an LP record album that I wore out on our Hi-Fi set (look it up if you don't know what that is; I don't have time to explain) about Davy Crockett. Oddly, both the TV Daniel Boone and the movie Davy Crockett were played by the same actor, Fess Parker, but I didn't care. I was really into a good story, and I willingly suspended disbelief. Besides, I had my own coonskin cap, and a genuine bullwhip and axe, though I had no bulls to whip, and nary an axe to grind at the time. After all, I was only about six or seven. I was deep in what I like to call my "pioneer phase," which came just after my cowboy phase, and my superhero phase, but just before my astronaut phase. Let's just say I was into pioneers. Of course, I had no idea at the time that my heroes had actually committed genocide. I didn't know such a thing existed, and anyway, the stories I was consuming were sanitized for my consumption. (Pioneers and Indians could be friends in this TV-world; Daniel Boone's best friend on the show was his Cherokee sidekick, Mingo, played by Ed Ames.)

In my defense, I was just a kid, and I wasn't into complexity then.

Anyway, there is something I've always loved in that pioneer spirit. I think it's the idea of breaking new ground—a pure admiration of the kind of courage that would allow you, as they say on *Star Trek: The Next Generation*, to "boldly go where no one has gone before." Watching Neil Armstrong walk on the moon in July of 1969 rocketed me right out of my Western frontier pioneer phase and into my space pioneer phase (astronaut). That giant leap was just what I needed to take me to the next level of pioneer worship. Bold adventurers were, quite simply, inspiring.

Truthfully, *all* my heroes were pioneers.

So, naturally, I was quite taken when I first "met" the pioneers of autoethnography.

Of course, there is more to the story than my personal (though hardly revolutionary or original) epiphany that striking (or startling, or evocative, or gut-wrenching, or heart-breaking, or vivid, or ground-breaking) stories are, for lack of a better phrase, "my jam" (though they are). There is more to this story than my personal revolution revelation. This work, this "new ethnography" was a revolution and a revelation for scholarship across many disciplines, and now around the globe. I now turn to a brief discussion of how the work of Bochner and Ellis (and their pioneer friends Norman Denzin and Bud Goodall and Ron Pelias and Laurel Richardson, among others) has shaped the foundations and movements of qualitative inquiry.

By breaking new ground in qualitative inquiry, these pioneers showed us what was possible; they stuck their necks out, staking their careers on the power of the "new ethnography" to overcome the resistance put up by the gatekeepers of what counts as inquiry in the academy. In fact, they powered right through that wall, like the Kool-Aid man. Boom! *Oh Yeah!* The barrier was broken! A whole new world of inquiry had opened up before (and for) us all!

Art Bochner's ground-breaking work in laying out the philosophical foundations for autoethnography is, at least from my perspective, his most powerful and lasting contribution. In his foundational essay, *Narrative's Virtues* (2000), Art crafts a stunning repudiation of the critics of the "narrative turn" in ethnography by weaving together a powerful personal narrative response to the critics with a strong philosophical argument in favor of the profound and enduring power of narrative—a power that reaches well beyond the analytical/objective essay into the *heart* of what it means to be human. This essay is nothing short of brilliant! Art deftly lays the groundwork for the narrative turn, giving the new ethnographers a way forward. It also set the stage for his own continuing work in narrative autoethnography, which is most thoroughly represented in his latest book, *Coming to Narrative: A Personal History of Paradigm Change in the Human Sciences* (2014). In my view, this book puts the nail in the coffin of the armchair critics of narrative (auto)ethnography.

Meanwhile, Carolyn Ellis has shown, throughout her career, how to build an evocative emotional narrative grounded in and driven by systematic introspection. She has actively and repeatedly torn down the veil between scholarship and emotion, seeking always to build a case for—and a literature in—evocative inquiry into the deeper emotional terrain we all experience but often fear to enter. Ellis opened the "ethnographic I" (2004) so each of us could open our own ethnographic I/eye, and thus find our way to evocative autoethnography. From her early book *Final Negotiations* (1995) to her most recent book-length collaboration with Art, *Evocative Autoethnography* (2016) to her work on collaborative witnessing with Holocaust survivors (Ellis & Rawicki, 2013), Carolyn has brought gut-wrenching stories to the page, offering the rawest and most painful moments of human lives for our edification.

Opening that door has given permission to a large contingent of scholars to explore, through evocative writing as the method of inquiry, what it means—*really means*—to be a feeling human being co-inhabiting social spaces with other feeling human beings. In the *oeuvre* of Ellis, thinking is, of course, important, but it's overrated. Or at least it's not more important than feeling deeply. In fact, I see a kind of sweet balance in her work between the evocative and the interpretive-analytical. Above all, in her most recent work, she has shown us how to practice a relational ethic of care while invoking the "ethnographic I" in the face of the ethnographic other.

The quest for both powerful evocation of the emotional landscape of human life and deeper understanding/interpretation of human social experience is the hallmark of the many individual works by these pioneers, and of the many fruitful collaborations between Art and Carolyn over the years. Together and separately, they've broken new ground that has led to three remarkable turns in qualitative inquiry:

First, this work takes us directly into the *praxis* of re-centering the "I" in social inquiry after many years of absence. This achievement might be easy to underestimate. It is nothing less than monumental. The I, as Kenneth Gergen (2009) so deftly points out, is only available because of the we who socially co-construct our shared realities. In other words, we are *relational beings;* all possibility of human Being is grounded in our fundamentally *intersubjective* nature. The narrative turn in ethnography took a fundamentally intersubjective turn with the work of Bochner and Ellis.

To achieve this movement toward fuller, richer narrative intersubjectivity, the pioneers of autoethnography had to overcome powerful social and political forces that had pushed the "I" to the sidelines in the name of the pipe dream that is objectivity, leaving social science research sterile, detached, clinical, and far removed from the lived, embodied experiential realities of human social actors. This inter-subjective turn set the stage for the current critical turn in autoethnography, as well as other movements across the larger world of qualitative inquiry. The re-centering of intersubjectivity (the "ethnographic I") was a necessary condition for the opening up of powerful critique of cultural systems of power and oppression (the Critical

Ethnographic eye), and was clearly a sufficient condition for authors to re-claim authorship and agency and presence in their writings.

Second, their work has generated a powerful momentum for the narrative turn in qualitative inquiry writ large. Through their impressive record of narrative scholarship, along with their vibrant advocacy for narrative qualitative inquiry, years of teaching courses and workshops, public presentations, keynotes, and their ongoing active presence at the International Congress of Qualitative Inquiry, they paved the path for students, collaborators, colleagues, and others around the world to pick up the torch of narrative auto/ethnography and follow, and even boldly open up the possibility of new paths. They have actively recommended and supported the centering of the narrative voice that now infuses the many path-branches and forks now in play across many qualitative methodologies (not just autoethnography) after so many years of dynamic, engaged action by these two pioneers.

Third, as they forged the path, they invited us all to join them. They have actively helped to construct—and unflinchingly supported—the careers of many of the second and third waves of new ethnographers who followed them on this journey. In my own case, they, along with Denzin, Goodall, and Pelias literally saved my career (Poulos, 2010). We all owe them a deep debt of gratitude. Their spirit of generosity has been a force of nature, and their tireless advocacy and support of narrative autoethnography has been a true gift to the world of qualitative inquiry. Taking this "road less traveled" with Art and Carolyn has been intellectually, emotionally, and spiritually invigorating to most of us who have followed along.

As my moment to pay tribute to my pioneer heroes for their foundational work draws to a close, I find myself reflecting on the arc of the narrative turn in qualitative inquiry, the emergence and growth and sustenance of autoethnography in particular, and on my own good fortune in accidentally stumbling upon autoethnography as a way of life. Mostly, I find myself reflecting on the many gifts that this movement, now a tradition, and its pioneers have bestowed upon us all.

I have found my way home.

Thank God, and thank you, Art Bochner and Carolyn Ellis.

References

Adams, T. E. (2011). *Narrating the closet*. New York, NY: Routledge.

Behar, R. (1996). *The vulnerable observer: Anthropology that breaks your heart*. Boston: Beacon Press.

Bochner, A. (1997). It's about time: Narrative and the divided self. *Qualitative Inquiry, 3*, 418–438.

Bochner, A. (2001). Narrative's virtues. *Qualitative Inquiry, 7*, 131–157.

Bochner, A. (2014). *Coming to narrative: A personal history of paradigm change in the human sciences*. New York: Routledge.

Bochner, A., & Ellis, C. (2016). *Evocative autoethnography: Writing lives and telling stories*. New York: Routledge.

Boylorn, R. (2012). *Sweetwater: Black women and narratives of resilience*. New York: Peter Lang.

Campbell, J. (1948). *The hero with a thousand faces*. Princeton, NJ: Princeton University Press.

Coles, R. (1989). *The call of stories: Teaching and the moral imagination*. Boston: Houghton Mifflin.

Ellis, C. (1995). *Final negotiations: A story of love, loss, and chronic illness*. Philadelphia: Temple University Press.

Ellis, C. (2004). *The ethnographic I: A methodological novel about autoethnography*. Walnut Creek, CA: AltaMira Press.

Ellis, C., & Bochner, A. (1991). "Telling and performing personal stories: The constraints of choice in abortion." In C. Ellis & M. Flaherty (Eds.), *Investigating subjectivity: Research on lived experience*, 79–101. Thousand Oaks, CA: Sage.

Ellis, C., & Bochner, A. (Eds.) (1996). *Composing ethnography: Alternative forms of qualitative writing*. Walnut Creek, CA: AltaMira Press.

Ellis, C., & Rawicki, J. (2013). Collaborative witnessing of survival during the Holocaust: An exemplar of relational autoethnography. *Qualitative Inquiry, 19* (5), 366–380.

Fox, K. (1996). Silent voices: A subversive reading of child sexual abuse. In *Composing ethnography: Alternative forms of qualitative writing*. In C. Ellis & A. Bochner (Eds.), Walnut Creek, CA: AltaMira Press.

Geertz, C. (1973). *The interpretation of cultures*. New York: Basic Books.

Gergen, K. (2009). *Relational being: Beyond self and community*. Oxford: Oxford University Press.

Goodall, H. L. (1989). *Casing a promised land: The autobiography of an organizational detective as cultural ethnographer*. Carbondale: Southern Illinois University Press.

Goodall, H. L. (1991). *Living in the rock n roll mystery*. Carbondale: Southern Illinois University Press.

Goodall, H. L. (2000). *Writing the new ethnography*. Walnut Creek, CA: Alta Mira Press.

Jones, S. H., Adams, T. E., & Ellis, C. (Eds.) (2013), *Handbook of autoethnography*. Walnut Creek, CA: Left Coast Press.

Kierkegaard, S. (1980). *The sickness unto death* (H. V. Hong & E. H. Hong, Trans.). Princeton, NJ: Princeton University Press.

Poulos, C. N. (2006). The ties that bind us, the shadows that separate us: Life and death, shadow and (dream)story. *Qualitative Inquiry, 12*(1): 96–117.

Poulos, C. N. (2009/2019). *Accidental ethnography: An inquiry into family secrecy* (Classic ed.). New York: Routledge.

Poulos, C. N. (2010). Transgressions. *International Review of Qualitative Research, 3*, 67–88.

Poulos, C. N. (2016). A giant sandwich: Reflections on Laurel Richardson and qualitative inquiry. In J. White (Ed.). *Permission: The international interdisciplinary impact of Laurel Richardson's work*. Boston: Sense Publishers.

Richardson, L. (2005). "Writing: A method of inquiry." In N. K. Denzin & Y. S. Lincoln (Eds.), *Handbook of qualitative research* (2nd ed.). Thousand Oaks, CA: Sage.

Ronai, C. R. (1996). *My mother is mentally retarded*. In C. Ellis & A. Bochner (Eds.), *Composing ethnography: Alternative forms of qualitative writing*. Walnut Creek, CA: AltaMira Press.

Vande Berg, L., & Trujillo, N. (2008). *Cancer and death: A love story in two voices*. New York: Hampton Press.

4

BECOMING WILD

Autoethnography as feral pedagogy

Stacy Holman Jones

Scene: Living room in a large, comfortable house in Tampa, Florida.

The lights are low, the air is cool, and there is a peace about the house. The living room is cozy, even though occupants aren't home. They're away in the mountains for the summer, escaped to their cabin in North Carolina, a long-realized dream.

In the still and quiet of the house in Tampa, I stand in the kitchen, serving dinner to my toddler in the waning hours of a June day. After I tuck her into bed, I sit on the edge of the sprawling round couch in the living room and cry.

I cry with fear and wonder. I cry with relief for this cozy house, for the home it makes for my toddler and me at the precise moment we needed it. I cry with gratitude for the two people who made this moment—and so many other moments in my life—possible.

***

That moment, so many years ago, is one of the many happenings that I've reflected on as I contemplated how I might describe the legacy of Carolyn Ellis and Art Bochner. I recognize how that moment, on the face of it, isn't about the *work* of Carolyn and Art. But that's the thing: those kinds of moments are not outside of or adjacent to the work of this amazing duo, it *is* the work.

In that moment, I was an assistant professor at the University of South Florida, a new mother, just separated from my husband, barely out as a queer woman. I was desperately trying to pull a new life together out of—seemingly—nowhere. And just like that—without me asking—Carolyn and Art proposed that I housesit while they were away for the summer. They didn't need a house sitter, of course, but they offered their home to my toddler and me under the guise that I would look after the house and look out for hurricanes. And in that gentle and humble act—like so many acts that preceded and followed it—Carolyn and Art made new life possible.

It's not surprising that Carolyn and Art's work is intertwined with how they've touched and marked our lives with their words and their presence and for most of us, their very material actions: the time they give us, the spaces they make for us in conferences and workshops, on the pages of their books and essays, in university programs and departments, and through the homes they offer to us as scholars and as people. Though perhaps what is surprising is that such unwavering generosity still exists in the very material world that is the contemporary academy.

But how to describe the trailblazing and making possible that Carolyn and Art have brought to their work inside the academy and out? In their book *Evocative Autoethnography* (2016) they describe that trailblazing as "breaking bad"—though they're both a lot more lovable than Walter White. In Art's words, "When Carolyn and I started calling what we were doing evocative autoethnography, we considered our work both transgressive and critical. We were breaking bad, misbehaving, and defying the rules" (p. 60).

When I read this, I thought about another description of their work and the work of "breaking bad" in the academy. I borrow this from my friend and colleague Alyson Campbell (2019), a queer-identifying artist and researcher working in theatre institutions and in the academy. The latter position she regards with deep ambivalence because, as she asks, what does it mean to make your homeplace within a normative system when your principles as an academic and a human being are to resist and even rage against the normative? How do we stay true to our commitment to resist and rage against the "machine"—our commitment to "breaking bad"—while living with and within the normative constraints of the academy?

Alyson's answer has been to develop a set of strategies for "exploiting" her privileged position within the academy, strategies she terms "feral pedagogies" (Campbell, 2018). Those strategies—and that term—come close to how Carolyn and Art have been breaking bad in the academy and in our lives for so long. Merriam-Webster defines "feral" as "having escaped from domestication and become wild" (qtd. in Campbell, 2019, p. 177). Campbell (2019) suggests that the "condition of de-domestication" includes being excluded from normative modes of family life—because you are queer, because you are non-assimilating, because you do not behave or belong in expected and predictable ways. José Esteban Muñoz (1999) deems this "productive disidentification," which, as Campbell (2018) argues, "builds companionship on new terms" (p. 61).

Carolyn and Art's work and "badness" in the academy are built on a productive disidentification with the unemotional and impersonal in sociological and communication scholarship—scholarship claiming to generate new knowledge and insight about interpersonal relationships and emotions within those contexts. Their "turn" to emotion, narrative, and the role of the person and the personal in research (see, for example, Bochner, 2012, 2014; Bochner & Ellis, 2016; Ellis, 1993, 1995; Ellis & Bochner, 1996) provides a blueprint for "feral pedagogies: community engagement with teaching and learning in a spirit of generosity that is removed from the elitism of academic institutions and the professionalization of arts [and other] training" (Campbell, 2018, p. 62). What possibilities do feral pedagogies hold for those of us who make comfortable homes *within* the stability, status and salaries of the academy? Campbell posits that using "feral strategies" within the academy urges us to "take the money and knowledge from the institution and run wild" (2019, p. 177). Reflecting on strategies for "going feral" in the academy helps us see more clearly how Carolyn and Art create not only interesting and vibrant living and research spaces for themselves but also a research community marked by a spirit of generosity and a commitment to "running wild."

One strategy for "going feral" that Campbell (2019) outlines is consciously rejecting the normative trajectory of academic "success": established, "traditional" social-scientific research programs' status, audiences, funding possibilities, and "street cred." But what to pursue instead? One possibility (admittedly one that undermines professional and economic stability) is to pursue hybrid, multidisciplinary, and "new" questions, methods, and modes of representation. For example, Carolyn's and Art's work in narrative inquiry (Bochner, 2014), autoethnography (Bochner & Ellis, 2016; Ellis, Adams, & Bochner, 2011) and collaborative witnessing (Ellis & Rawicki, 2013)—all (at some point) new forms of research—required that they stop moving ever-forward on established academic pathways and, instead, "go the other way" (Campbell, 2019, p. 178). Their willingness and commitment to going the other way meant that they turned their attention away from individual academic success and toward building audiences, legitimating alternative approaches to research and writing, and the continuous nurturing and mentorship required to sustain and grow these (and other) new research communities. Those who joined them along the way have also charted their own paths, following new and nascent forms of inquiry, including layered accounts (Rambo, 1995) friendship as method (Tillmann-Healy, 2003), critical autoethnography (Boylorn & Orbe, 2017; Holman Jones, 2016), queer autoethnography (Adams 2011; Adams & Holman Jones, 2008; Holman Jones & Adams, 2010; Holman Jones & Harris, 2018), posthuman autoethnography (Gale & Wyatt 2019; Harris & Holman Jones, 2019; Simmons 2016) among many others.

Another strategy of "going feral" has to do "with how we train future leaders in the academy" (Campbell, 2019, p. 178). Campbell writes that theatre training in the academy

> is still to a large extent governed by sets of ideas about truth, reality/realism, and "transformation" that cling on to liberal humanist ideas of "the human experience" as an homogenous entity unbridled by inequality or dis/advantage. This has got to change.
>
> *(p. 178)*

The same can be said about sociological, communication, and other "human-centered" (and centric) research. That too must change. How does the feral student of narrative inquiry or autoethnography fit into an essentially conservative institution governed by liberal humanist and homogenizing ideas about truth, reality, and knowledge- building? For more than 25 years, Carolyn and Art have shown us multiple ways of asking and answering that question. And they continue asking that important question of themselves and those whom they train and mentor, including Tony Adams, Robin Boylorn, Tasha Dunn, Andrew Herrmann, Nathan Hodges, Csaba Osvath, Blake Paxton, Chris Patti, David Purnell, and Lisa Till-mann. Training future leaders who challenge received and destructive ideas about human experience (and indeed, human exceptionalism and the humanist ideals it props up) is one kind of feral pedagogy; it recognizes that changing the hearts and minds of students in the academy is political work (Campbell, 2019).

Third, Art and Carolyn help us recognize how the academy is a place of deeply-felt exclusions, a place in which many of us have never felt quite comfortable or "domesticated." They create instead a home for the "feral outsider"—a personal and political strategy that allows us to operate powerfully from that from which we are excluded. By "going feral," Carolyn and Art have exploited their "domesticated" insider knowledge and privilege to channel resources to others who might otherwise have been excluded or "left to fend for themselves in the academy" (Campbell, 2019, p. 178). This includes making research, teaching, writing, and publishing opportunities for others. The disciplines to which many autoethnographers and narrative inquiry scholars belong have been slowly—and in many cases unwillingly—attending to the harms exclusionary practices have wrought on so-called "outsiders" (see Chakravartty, Kuo, Grubbs, & McIlwain, 2018); thus such "power from without" strategies are not only needed but indeed essential.

As Carolyn and Art have shown us, moment after moment, the feral is a very powerful position. And while "de-domesticating is hard, and actually may require relinquishing the spoils of capital instead of merely writing about the perils of it" (Campbell, 2019, p. 179), the work of autoethnographic and narrative scholarship is "inextricably bound up with life in an unavoidable, but also *galvanizing"* way (p. 179). Borrowing again from Alyson, what are we for, as autoethnogaphers and narrative scholars, if we "cannot use our training to think through our own positions and lives" (p. 179)? To resist the neoliberal and stultifying humanist academy by "skewing it from within" and "harnessing the potential and possibilities of the domestic turned feral" (p. 179)?

That's the thing about Carolyn and Art: going feral and doing the intellectual and emotional labor of feral pedagogy is not outside of or adjacent to the work we claim to do in an increasingly hostile landscape.

It *is* the work.

It is the work of going in the opposite direction and training those who come after us to do the same.

Of being "Robin Hood academics" and begging, borrowing, and stealing the resources of the rich academy to feed the minds and hearts of people the institution has kept out or left to fend for themselves.

Of escaping domestication.

Of making possible.

***

Scene: Living room in a cozy house in Melbourne, Australia.

It's mid-afternoon on a sunny Thursday, what would be Thanksgiving Day if we celebrated the U.S. holiday here in the southern hemisphere. I miss those few days in November reserved for gathering together, resting, and giving thanks for community. In the absence of those who have been "actively excluded"—exterminated, really, and thus left out—from the comfortable domestic sphere that Thanksgiving holidays cover over, it is important to remember how feral kinship is often "built around being forced outside traditional and family networks" (Campbell, 2018, p. 61). If it weren't for the friendship, sense of family, scholarly community, and quite literally a place for my daughter and me to live and lay our heads while I got a new life together—if it weren't for the feral kinship of Carolyn and Art—I wouldn't be sitting in my cozy living room in Melbourne enjoying the sun and writing this essay. Autoethnography as feral pedagogy is something for which to give thanks. It is also something to remember and to actively work at—turning and going the other way, abandoning the domestic, embracing the feral. It is something to strive for: breaking bad and becoming wild.

References

Adams, T. E. (2011). *Narrating the closet: An autoethnography of same-sex attraction*. Left Coast Press.

Adams, T. E., & Holman Jones, S. (2008). Autoethnography is queer. In N. K. Denzin, Y. S. Lincoln, & L. T. Smith (Eds.), *Handbook of critical and indigenous methodologies* (pp. 373–390). Sage.

Bochner, A. P. (2012). Bird on the wire: Freeing the father within me. *Qualitative Inquiry, 8*(2), 168–173. https://doi.org/10.1177/1077800411429094.

Bochner, A. P. (2014). *Coming to narrative: A personal history of paradigm change in the human sciences*. Routledge.

Bochner, A. P., & Ellis, C. (2016). *Evocative autoethnography: Writing lives and telling stories*. Routledge.

Boylorn, R., & Orbe, M. (2017). *Critical autoethnography: Intersecting cultural identities in everyday life*. Routledge.

Campbell, A. (2019). Going feral: Queerly de-domesticating the institution (and running wild). In P. Eckersall & H. Greehan (Eds.), *The Routledge companion to theatre and politics* (pp. 177–180). Routledge.

Campbell, A. (2018). GL RY: A (w)hole lot of woman trouble. HIV dramaturgies and feral pedagogies. In A. Campbell & D. Gindt (Eds.), *Viral dramaturgies: HIV and AIDS in performance in the twenty-first century* (pp. 49–68). Palgrave Macmillan.

Chakravartty, P., Kuo, R., Grubbs, V., & McIlwain, C. (2018). #CommunicationSoWhite. *Journal of Communication, 68*(2), 254–266. https://doi.org/10.1093/joc/jqy003.

Ellis, C. (1993). There are survivors: Telling a story of sudden death. *The Sociological Quarterly, 34*(4), 711–730. https://doi.org/10.1111/j.1533-8525.1993.tb00114.x.

Ellis, C. (1995). *Final negotiations: A story of love, loss and chronic illness*. Temple University Press.

Ellis, C., Adams, T. E., & Bochner, A. P. (2011). Autoethnography: An overview. *FQS, 12*(1). Retrieved from www.qualitative-research.net/index.php/fqs/article/view/1589/3095.

Ellis, C., & Bochner, A. P. (eds.) (1996). *Composing ethnography: Alternative forms of qualitative writing*. AltaMira Press.

Ellis, C., & Bochner, A. P. (2000). Autoethnography, personal narrative, reflexivity: Researcher as subject, in N. K. Denzin & Y. S. Lincoln (Eds.), *Handbook of qualitative research* (2nd ed., pp. 733–768). Sage Publications.

Ellis, C., & Rawicki, J. (2013). Collaborative witnessing of survival during the Holocaust: An exemplar of relational autoethnography. *Qualitative Inquiry, 19*(5), 366–380. https://doi.org/10.1177/1077800413479562.

Gale, K., & Wyatt, J. (2019). Autoethnography and activism: Movement, intensity and potential. *Qualitative Inquiry, 25*(6), 566–568. https://doi.org/10.1177/1077800418800754.

Holman Jones, S. (2016). Living bodies of thought: The 'critical' in critical autoethnography. *Qualitative Inquiry, 22*(4), 228–237. https://doi.org/10.1177/1077800415622509.

Holman Jones, S., & Adams, T. E. (2010). Autoethnography and queer theory: Making possibilities. In M. Giardina & N. K. Denzin (Eds.), *Qualitative inquiry and human rights* (pp. 136–157). Left Coast Press.

Holman Jones, S., & Harris, A. (2018). *Queering autoethnography*. Routledge.

Muñoz, J. E. (1999). *Disidentifications: Queers of color and the performance of politics*. University of Minnesota Press.

Rambo, C. (1995). Multiple reflections of child sex abuse: An argument for a layered account. *Journal of Contemporary Ethnography, 23*(4), 395–426. https://doi.org/10.1177/089124195023004001.

Simmons, J. (2016). Memories of Venice. *Departures in Critical Qualitative Research, 5*(1), 83–89. https://doi.org/10.1525/dcqr.2016.5.1.83.

Tillmann-Healy, L. (2003). Friendship as method. *Qualitative Inquiry, 9*(5), 729–749. https://doi.org/10.1177/1077800403254894.

5

A COLLABORATIVE DIALOGUE ON THE DIALOGIC INFLUENCE OF ART BOCHNER AND CAROLYN ELLIS

Lesa Lockford and Ronald J. Pelias

When we learned that there would be a symposium honoring the legacy of Carolyn Ellis and Art Bochner, we knew we wanted to be present and to underscore their many contributions to autoethnography and narrative inquiry and to us personally. As we began to consider what we might say, we realized very quickly that we could only reside in a small area in the vast territory of their offerings. We elected to focus on their use of dialogue, a defining narrative feature found in much of their work and one of the earliest strategies they employed to challenge prevailing modes of scholarly writing. We gave ourselves the task of doing a dialogue between the two of us that would mirror what we see their dialogue accomplishing. We considered putting the dialogue within a narrative form as is common to their work, but elected to put our dialogue in the form of a play script to call more attention to the dialogue itself. What follows is our dialogue about their early influence on our careers and about their use of dialogue. It is our hope through this mimetic practice to accentuate the potency of relational discourse, a feature so central to their work and to the ethics of qualitative inquiry. What Ellis and Bochner embody through their dialogues is relational care, a privileging of the co-constitution of meaning-making, an acknowledgment of the partiality of perspectives, and the epistemological centrality of communication that funds autoethnography and narrative inquiry.

LESA: What do you think we should do for our Art and Carolyn paper? I know you just got here and you're probably not ready to jump in, but we should get to work.

RON: Remember the last time we were here. We were so busy we didn't even walk on the beach. That's what we should do: let's go for a walk on the beach.

LESA: We have to get our paper done. We're running out of time.

RON: What if we talk about it as we walk?

LESA: Okay, but you have to promise to stay on topic.

RON: I promise.

LESA: Alright. Remind me of what we said in our abstract.

RON: If I remember correctly, we said we wanted to discuss the continuing influence of Carolyn and Art on the field, our work, and our careers. Our intent was to model the collaborative dialogue we've seen them frequently use in their work with one another.

LESA: Yes. That is what we said, but that's not easy. One thing they have in each other is a great dialogical partner.

RON: Are you saying that you don't think I'm a good dialogical partner just because we're going to the beach?

LESA: No, not at all. Let me finish. What I mean is, they get to live and work together and essentially eat and breathe autoethnography every day. As The Ethnogs said, ethnography really is a way of life. Can you imagine what it must be like for them? All that reflexivity in their everyday life? For Art and Carolyn, I would imagine that, well, almost everything they do is a possible subject for an autoethnography.

RON: That's fun to consider, thinking of them of turning back on themselves in endless cycle of "What do you make of this? What do you make of what we just made of this? Now what about this? About this? About this?"

LESA: They probably don't live in a constant state of reflexivity. Instead, I see them living with a keen sense of the possibilities in the pause … [She stops and looks out to the sea] Oh, wait! Look at that view! There is something so wonderfully calming about the shoreline. It just makes my whole body breathe. It invites breathing in, doesn't it?

RON: Yes, it does pull you in. By the way, I can't tell you how times I've turned to your construction of "pausing" from your book, *Performing Femininity* (Lockford, 2004).

LESA: Lovely for you to say that. But I should say it is in the chapter in the book that Art and Carolyn edited, *Ethnographically Speaking* (Bochner & Ellis, 2002), where I talk about the move from stillness to action. We pause, reflect, and then move. In *Performing Femininity* I speak of thinking and thinking again. A similar motif, arguably. But different.

RON: I think over the years I've collapsed them. Sorry. *Ethnographically Speaking* came out in 2002 and your book was published in 2004, right?

LESA: Right.

RON: I know Art worked with you on your book. Did he also work with you on your essay in *Ethnographically Speaking*?

LESA: Art edited my book for AltaMira's *Ethnographic Alternatives* Series, the same series in which they published your *Methodology of the Heart* (Pelias, 2004). Art and Carolyn supported my early work and really helped launch my career. That essay in *Ethnographically Speaking* first appeared as a response I gave to a panel of essays at the 2000 Couch Stone Symposium right here at the Dolphin Beach Resort.

RON: That was the last time we were here. That was the conference when we didn't walk on the beach.

LESA: That's right. Art and Carolyn have always been so good about encouraging young scholars. I remember really fretting about that essay because there I was, relatively fresh out of my doctoral program, and I was the respondent to some senior scholars! They have a way of both nurturing and pushing people to new heights. The same combination of nurturing and pushing happened with my book.

RON: I think I too was nurtured and pushed along by Carolyn and Art, although when I first met them I was further into my career than you were. I've told the story of how Bud Goodall's (1989) *Casing the Promised Land* brought me to the door of autoethnography. But it was Carolyn's (Ellis, 1995, 2018) *Final Negotiations* and Art's (Bochner, 1997) classic piece about his father that I read shortly after Bud's book that solidified my desire to walk through that door. And they were both so generous with me by including my work in one of their early anthologies and in their book series. By the way, did you know Carolyn has just published a second edition of *Final Negotiations*?

LESA: I saw that, but I haven't had a chance to get to it.

RON: I found revisiting it a true joy. It made me pause. It made me think twice.

LESA: The pause, the space given to reflexivity, is one of the gifts that Art and Carolyn display in their work. Through their modeling, they have instilled the practice of reflexivity in those of us who do autoethnography. That's what their dialogues do. They model reflexivity constituted between discursive partners. I mean, we all know that each word of those dialogues is written with care, even though they most likely came from actual conversations. It is the ease of their dialogue on the page that reminds us of the reflexivity we need as we practice autoethnography. Indeed, we need it as we move through life! The world moves so fast these days. And now, even more than ever, people are so quick to point, to jump, to indict. Reflexivity is a peaceful habit of thought, which should be the mode of academic life; it is too often forsaken in the maelstrom of the academy and, more generally, in everyday life.

RON: There is something considered and peaceful about Art and Carolyn's dialogues and in their work more generally. You feel the pause, the alertness in their work.

LESA: Yeah. Even when, for example, they have their dogs run into a story, trying to pull their attention away from their talk, you get the sense that it's a happy intrusion.

RON: It's not an intrusion, really. It's a celebration of the little moments that make life meaningful.

LESA: Yes, they take readers there. Communication happens in context. Their dialogues foreground how meaning making is context dependent.

RON: [Ron notices a shell and stoops to pick it up]. Look at that shell. Look at that color. I think I'll keep it as a remembrance of walking on the beach instead of working.

LESA: It's lovely. But we *are* working. It's those small day-to-day interactions Carolyn and Art include in their writing that, taken together, make up our world, make us human, and guide us to be better humans. That seems to be a fundamental aspect of their project for autoethnography: to help us move more consciously and intentionally in all our daily doings.

RON: And they model it in their dialogues.

LESA: That's right. They put their voices and others' voices right on the page. They take us into a situation; they capture a simple moment in time, with all its sensory detail so we can feel our way into the moment.

RON: They write situationally, scenically, with an always present contextual and cultural backdrop.

LESA: Like how we might include in our paper the privilege of being able to attend a conference and take the pause to revisit the work of two influential people.

RON: I do enjoy how they manage to capture the intimacy and everydayness of their conversations together, the warm interactional flavor of their one-on-one chats with students, and the welcoming and informative talk in classroom and workshop settings.

LESA: And, they weave the voices of theorists who've influenced them and do so without it jarring you away from the situation.

RON: That's no easy task, particularly when they establish a framework where they have so much information that needs to be presented, and they want to create the feel of a real conversation.

LESA: I also enjoy when they bring in their interior voices. Like when Art learns of his father's death in the piece you referenced earlier (Bochner, 1997). The guiding voice in that moment is his inner voice. He takes us into the heart of the situation. He brings us there, inside his mind and body, makes us feel the chill of the realization, the many things in his life calling for his attention. He shows himself being summoned by his conference roommate from the shower to answer the phone call about his father's death, the water dripping from his towel-clad body, mixing with the tears that begin to fall. He is both literally and psychically naked in that moment.

RON: I think you are exactly right. Another time Art works with interior dialogue is in his Epilogue in *Coming to Narrative* (Bochner 2014). Remember how he establishes the scene as if talking with his therapist, Milton. Readers later learn that Milton has been dead for fifteen years, and Art was having a dream. We hear two vulnerable voices inside Art in dialogue, exposed, available.

LESA: Yes, Art and Carolyn's writing carries an intimate proximity, a nearness between self and other and between writer and reader.

RON: I do feel that closeness in their dialogues with others. They manage to capture a keen attentiveness, a caring presence, in their represented conversations, but that shouldn't surprise me since that's how I experience them whenever we talk.

LESA: That sense of closeness I think would be present even if you only met them on the page.

RON: Yeah, I think so too.

LESA: That intimate proximity also comes forward as they merge observation and emotion. Whatever they are examining, they pull it close; they look carefully and feel it so vitally.

RON: Do you think their willingness to speak from the most personal aspects of their lives connects to their vulnerability?

LESA: Absolutely. Certainly, they mine themselves and look to those moments of vulnerability to speak about that which matters most. But it's a self that's in relation to others: to the reader, to the community, to the world. Through telling and showing, they invite us to feel that vulnerability with them and in so doing, they narrow the relational distance.

RON: And that demands that we account for our position in the world, from the most mundane and trivial to the most extraordinary and profound.

LESA: Right. Just as they do.

RON: This urging, this mandate really, can be found in all their work.

LESA: That constant reflexive move that deploys the self on behalf of us all gives their work such meaning.

RON: Look at what Carolyn does in her book, *Revision* (2009).

LESA: Yes, she calls it a meta-autoethnography. The entire book is an exemplary production of reflexivity. The overriding questions are: who was she then, and who is she now in relation to that self who wrote those essays in the past? *Revision* recursively tracks a trajectory of self across time and in relation to her various projects and to her readers.

RON: It really is quite amazing what Art and Carolyn accomplish in their dialogues.

LESA: Yes, their co-constructed narratives address specific others on the page as well as readers who are willing to listen in, who are willing to meet Art and Carolyn's vulnerability with their own.

RON: Carolyn and Art make it difficult to resist being the person they ask us to be. They entice through intimacy.

LESA: At the same time, they make it difficult to be the person they ask us to be. Didn't we say that we were going to model their dialogues in our paper? How can we possibly do that?

RON: I doubt we can. I take as our objective not to make fools of ourselves.

LESA: Well, if that's our objective, I think we should head back and try to get something down on paper.

RON: Maybe we could write about what we just said, maybe put our dialogue into narrative form, make it into a story.

LESA: I don't know. Maybe we should pause a bit before we go in that direction. Turning what we've said into narrative form is easier said than done. I'm not sure if we've said anything worth saying. I think everyone—symposium attendees and one day readers–will know what we just said.

RON: Yes, perhaps. But I agree; it's easy to take their dialogues for granted. The ease with which they speak lets you overlook the work they do. They model a way in the world that should, with continued attunement, become easy, a way of being. It doesn't, however, come without effort. They make us think and think again as we strive to find an ethical relational foothold for our work. Speaking of footholds, let's go back. My old legs are beginning to wear out, and we should get to work.

LESA: Do you still have your shell?

RON: Yes.

LESA: Good. I like knowing you have it.

Leaving our dialogue about dialogue within Carolyn and Art's narratives, we shift to four lyric summary claims to offer a poetic feel for the possibilities of Art and Carolyn's work. They lead us to see how dialogue carries the desire to hold us together, to understand dialogue as:

care, a relational intimacy that takes in, holds you as if this moment is yours, as if eyes have learned how to see and ears how to listen, as if words could work their way to your skin, enter through your pores, making you feel a presence, a calming vibration surrounding you like warm water.

making, a gathering of what you want to see, what you need to see, together, shaping it, forming it into something you might hold in the pleasure of agreement, in the obligation of respect, or in the struggle of divergence until you settle into the satisfaction that's gained by collaborative labor, into the harmonious rhythm made by mutual effort.

taking, pieces collected into perspectives that comfort, reassuring you that what you hold has resonance, a mallet to a bell, and into perspectives that disturb, become a troubling rub against your grain, and you search for ways to allow its scrape against your sensibilities to reside in you, even when you continue to resist.

communicating, not just by continuous talk, but by connecting, sharing for shared understanding, discovering what empathy might allow, until you make a bed of words that holds, that supports like a steel bridge, that lets you get a step closer, that turns you into the person you want to be.

References

Bochner, A. (1997). It's about time: Narrative and the divided self. *Qualitative Inquiry, 3*, 418–438. https://doi.org/10.1177/107780049700300404.

Bochner, A. P. (2014). *Coming to narrative: A personal history of paradigm change in the human sciences*. Left Coast Press/Routledge.

Bochner, A. P., & Ellis, C. (Eds.). (2002). *Ethnographically speaking: Autoethnography, literature, and aesthetics*. AltaMira Press.

Bochner, A. P., & Ellis, C. (2016). *Evocative autoethnography: Writing lives and telling stories*. Routledge.

Ellis, C. (2004). *The ethnographic I: A methodological novel about autoethnography*. AltaMira Press.

Ellis, C. (2009). *Revision: Autoethnographic reflections on life and work*. Left Coast Press/Routledge.

Ellis, C. (2018). *Final negotiations: A story of love, loss, and chronic illness*, rev. ed. Temple University Press.

Ellis, C., & Bochner, A. (Eds.). (1996). *Composing ethnography: Alternative forms of qualitative writing*. AltaMira.

Ellis, C., & Bochner, A. P. (2000). Autoethnography, personal narrative, reflexivity. In N. K. Denzin and Y. S. Lincoln (Eds.). *Handbook of Qualitative Research* (2nd ed., pp. 33–68). Sage.

Goodall, H. L. (1989). *Casing a promised land: The autobiography of an organizational detective as cultural ethnographer*. Southern Illinois University Press.

Lockford, L. (2002). Breaking habits and cultivating home. In A. P. Bochner & C. Ellis (Eds.). *Ethnographically speaking: Autoethnography, literature, and aesthetics* (pp. 76–86). AltaMira Press.

Lockford, L. (2004). *Performing femininity: Rewriting gender identity*. AltaMira.

Pelias, R. J. (2004). *A methodology of the heart: Evoking academic & daily life*. AltaMira.

6

TRAVELING WITH CAROLYN ELLIS AND ART BOCHNER, OR HOW I BECAME HARMONIZED WITH THE AUTOETHNOGRAPHIC LIFE

An autoformative story[1]

Marcin Kafar

Introduction

The aim of this chapter is to reconstruct and show through a set of short personal stories (small autoethnographies) the process of getting conscious of what living the autoethnographic life means. Working in a mode of reflexive thinking, I am trying to discover how my way to the academic *ethos* endemic to the world of autoethnography (and autoethnographers) has been developed.

My scientific (scholarly) biography is marked by a few turning points, among which the most profound was a passage—to use the vocabulary of Alexander Romanovich Luria (1987)—from the "Classical Science" to the "Romantic Science." As a young researcher I was brought up in a school of thought based on, to put it concisely, critical thinking in the field of anthropology. Yet, I always desired to be closer to "real life" and people living their lives. Even though the "utmost importance to romantics" is to "preserve the wealth of living reality" (p. 6), I never had a chance to fully do so it until I encountered both autoethnographic discourse and those who established it—root autoethnographers. When I say "root autoethnographers," I relate to a certain thought-collective, acting within its "esoteric circle" (Fleck, 1979), and I include the inventors of autoethnography, namely Carolyn Ellis and Art Bochner. I was most interested in how I started doing autoethnography, learned about its various stages, and negotiated the possible consequences for doing autoethnography, particularly in contexts of science and neoliberalism.

These interests opened up an experiential space in which I began to write my stories. My primary proposal is to call them "autoformative stories," but the Reader might see them as "trans-formative" stories (Bochner, 2019, p. 255), ones that reveal *a gradual, changing* sense of my move from being a total stranger to being a neophyte of autoethnography. Four significant events led to *the trans-formative* experiences I describe below. The first is coming across the book *Final Negotiations*

(Ellis, 1995) and feeling a special connection to its author who I had not yet met, Carolyn Ellis. The second is my initial travel (2010) to Tampa, Florida, where I had an opportunity to complete an internship at the Department of Communication at the University of South Florida—the place broadly recognized as a cradle of autoethnography. During this month-long visit, I sat in on two of Carolyn Ellis's and Art Bochner's classes and felt a sense of an academic community unlike anything I had previously imagined. Parallelly, I had to recognize the socio-cultural alienation that inhibited my ability to live the autoethnographic life. The third event was Carolyn's trip to Warsaw (2013), the capital of my home country, Poland. There, I felt acknowledged as something more than a bystander, a person—a collaborator—who helped make that visit memorable for Carolyn and her co-researcher, Jerry Rawicki, a Warsaw ghetto survivor. The fourth event happened at the Tampa International Airport (2018), where I met anew with Art just before leaving Florida and where I felt a familial connection with him; he became a father-teacher for me. These four events were accompanied by rich conversations among Carolyn, Art, and myself; in a period of several years (2013–2019) we held regular talks about "work" and "life" as mingled and meaningful. They resulted in hours of taped, partially transcribed interactions, some of which are included in this chapter. Taken together, these events constitute what I call "the distinctive feature(s) of my personal experience" that generated a revised understanding of autoethnography, and they illustrate *autoethnographicity*—a way of (academic) life referring to particular "*ideas, values and beliefs.*"

Crossing the borders of oblivion

In the novel *Wymazane* [*Erased*] (2017), Michal Witkowski describes a utopian provincial town. The title captures its chronotopic specificity through vignettes of local peculiarities of events, people, and places. Among the palette of images is Witkowski's description of the unusual library:

> The library was a multi-story building, with stairs, quite crooked due to the location on an extremely swampy area, which made the books fall off the shelves. Whenever some book fell down, I picked it up and I took it blindly, because the swamp always chose the most interesting publications for me. Even when it was seemingly nothing interesting, I took it home, read it from cover to cover and I always found the passage that caused the swamp to choose this book for me.
>
> *(p. 59)*

Remembering this part of Witkowski's novel blurs the "borders of oblivion" in me, and I begin a journey to Edinburgh. I recover Edinburgh in my memories after a dozen or so years since my last stay there—*the* Edinburgh where I lived from 2002 to 2006. In Poland, I had been writing my doctoral thesis in the so-called free-form mode, i.e. not requiring any formal duties at the university; in

Edinburgh, I had the time and freedom to work and write. I spent the autumn, winter, and early spring months in Poland, running, among other things, anthropological research in the hospice and the Social Welfare Home for Chronically Ill People, while the rest of the year I resided in Edinburgh. Given its regularity, my life there did not deviate much from the life of a monk. The work (mainly in restaurants and hotels) usually lasted 12–13 hours a day, and I spent the occasional day off on trips to the library of the University of Edinburgh, or to other city libraries. My interests were broad, but their core motif was the lived experience of illness. In my search I tried to not restrict myself to a certain discipline or paradigm. I yearned to learn about worlds of thought about illness across the human sciences. I would define this strategy as "waiting"—I was not hurrying anywhere, but let myself succumb to the hypertextual "flow" (Csíks-zentmihályi, 1990). I immersed myself in book contemplation, and while con-templating I waited. For what? I could not say, until one day I found *Final Negotiations: A Story of Love, Loss, and Chronic Illness* (Ellis, 1995), a book that turned me upside down. The book showed me how I wanted to think, research, and *write* about illness. I did not anticipate that five years later, Carolyn Ellis, the author, would fill the dust-jacket of my copy with a beautiful dedication: "For Marcin, who shares my interest in love, loss, and life."

Dreaming about traveling and conversation

By 2009, I had already defended my doctoral thesis (*I, The Anthropologist—I, The Human Being: On One Variant of Engaged Anthropology*), and I began to settle institutionally at the Faculty of Educational Sciences of the University of Lodz. Colleagues and administrators were open to interdisciplinary activities and interna-tional cooperation, including offering the employees, selected by means of a contest, the opportunity to complete a scientific internship at any chosen institution in the world. Hearing about the planned contest, I decided to submit an application for an internship at the Department of Communication at the University of South Florida (USF).

In February 2010, I got up my courage and sent an email to Carolyn and Art. In the email, I introduced myself as a person who finds the message and community of autoethnography familiar and desirable. Looking back, the word "autoethnography," was not the most important word; instead, I gravitated towards *the social world of autoethnographers*, and thus also to how *specific manifestations of autoethnographic life* could infuse the social sciences with *a humanistic coefficient*.

In *Final Negotiations* I recognized many words, thoughts, and feelings, and I could repeat here what Art recalls in every version of his founding tale of the first meeting with Carolyn, a meeting that took place in 1990 during a talk that Car-olyn gave on *Final Negotiations*: "She's giving my talk. Who is this woman anyway?"[2] (Ellis, 2009, p. 112). My first encounter with Carolyn's work was characterized by similar emotions.

A few minutes after clicking "Send" I received a return email, in which Carolyn and Art expressed their enthusiasm concerning my request for them to host me in Tampa. I read with my face flushed,

> Dear Marcin,
>
> Art and I are delighted to get your letter and find out about your work. Indeed, it appears we are "kindred spirits." We would be happy to talk further about assisting you with a scholarship to come here for a month and would be happy to have you attend our classes and participate in our program....
>
> We also have some interest in visiting Poland, perhaps giving lectures, and meeting some scholars there. I am interviewing Holocaust survivors and taking some of what we have done in narrative, interactive interviewing, and auto-ethnographic writing to this work. We feel that a trip to Poland is a necessary part of this endeavor....
>
> Let us know what the next step might be in terms of your application.
>
> We look forward to more exchange.
>
> Warm regards, Carolyn and Art
>
> *(February 10, 2010)*

Finding myself as the other: my first trip to Tampa, Florida

ART: When were you here the last time—three or four years ago?

MARCIN: Actually, six years ago.

ART: Six years? Oh my! Last time, if I remember accurately, you visited Carolyn's classes and the class I was co-teaching with Charles Guignon. You stayed in our house one night and we had conversations but not as many as this time. You interacted with students and explored Tampa. You were learning what we were doing here. But this visit, I feel like we have had more informal conversation as well as academic conversation.

MARCIN: And both are equally important to us.

ART: Yes, I feel like the last time you were a guest, but this time you're a friend and a colleague.

> *(transcript of a conversation between Art and Marcin, September 30, 2016)*

"I feel like the last time you were a guest," I repeat again and again as I start to think how euphemistic this phrase might sound compared to what I really experienced in Tampa during the first visit.

My first visit to Tampa began at the end of August 2010 and ended at the beginning of October 2010. I open a note file (part of the folder titled *Florida Journal*), dated September 5 and read:

> I am sitting in a hotel room. I got up quite early, I set the alarm clock at 7:30, but I could not get up, I just could not get up...

Before leaving for breakfast, I spoke with M. [my girlfriend]. She told me that she had bought headphones; when I came back from breakfast, we tried to connect, but were unsuccessful.

That day, I remember feeling better than the previous few days; the exception was yesterday afternoon. A trip to Ybor City allowed me some relief, but I felt a hunger for thoughts, working with books. I was at the USF library, the evening before, to answer an email from Carolyn. I wrote that I felt "thought-fever"; I was reinvigorated by the early-morning conversation with M., her assurances of sincerity and depth of devotion, a hint of "organic longing," which acts as *a punctum* in photography.

Ybor City reminded me of Polish open-air museums—it's a kind of cultural park. Before entering it, I stepped into a bar-shop, where there was a counter with food and where you could help yourself to eggs, coffee, and other "Cuban" food. At Palm Street, I was followed by a man who was dressed in a festive way, though I had never had the opportunity to meet him. After a few hours, the same man got on bus number 5, which I was also riding, and shouted from the entrance: "Good mornin' everybody." I was sitting in a seat behind an empty seat meant for a wheelchair, so I was clearly visible. Approaching me, the man raised his right hand and repeated "Good mornin'." Did he really direct this greeting to me? I felt that he did. However, I did not respond. When I am in a new place, I treat any person who signals the slightest indication of understanding like a salvation, so I'm not sure why I didn't respond.

I skip to the file with the date September 18.
"I miss everything I left in Poland," I wrote, and further,

after waking up, I was thinking about the alienation I am experiencing here. I was wondering, among other things, whether my waking up in the early morning is not associated with nostalgia, and, at least partly, with the overwhelming need to be back in Poland. I have only 12 days before I leave. Yesterday I stopped understanding what Jason (the receptionist at the hotel) was saying to me. In this way, did I subconsciously cut myself off from the place where I am?

I read the next portion of notes and memories flush back. I close my eyes and see "A Man with a Bicycle," with whom I regularly chatted at a bus stop located on the border of the university campus. He becomes so vivid, as does Robi *vel* Gipsy, encountered by me in Clearwater. Robi *vel* Gipsy—that's how he introduced himself—accosted me at the bus stop at a mall, as I was trying to return to Tampa. He was a contemporary *hobo*, a short man appearing as a handful of bones encased by sunburned skin. The story of his life, told to me over three beers and seven cigarettes for each of us, resembled images from the classic novel by Eddy Joe Cotton, *Hobo: A Young Man's Thoughts on Trains and Tramping in America* (2002). Our conversation revolved around the motif of traveling around the United States. I listened to him with bated breath for hours, missing four buses going to Tampa. I returned on the last possible bus, succumbing to the remnants of common sense, which won over my desire to commune with the pulse of living life personified by … a U.S. American tramp. How meaningful is the following memorandum in this context:

> I returned to the hotel. It's late evening. My head is spinning with the stories I've heard and the beer I have drunk, which Robi *vel* Gipsy eagerly treated me with…. Tomorrow I'm going to Carolyn's classes in Autoethnography, which I do not feel like going to after what happened today. I have the impression that real life is taking place elsewhere, not at the university.
>
> *(a fragment of the* Florida Journal, *September 21, 2010)*

"Being with" and becoming part of a legacy of love

Event 1: Being with Carolyn and Jerry in Warsaw, or how I became harmonized with collaborative witnessing

March 2013. I receive an email from Carolyn, in which she reports that she is planning to come to Poland. "Hi, guess what?" she writes,

> I am coming to Warsaw on May 19 for a few days. I will visit with one of the survivors [Jerry Rawicki] I have been working with. I could not pass up the experience of being there with him. He is 85 and this is the first time he has returned to Poland. He was in the Warsaw Ghetto Uprising. If you could come to Warsaw during that week (May 20–25), I would love to see you for a few hours. But I know it is a long drive so I do not expect you to come.
>
> *(March 28, 2013)*

Contrary to Carolyn's travel concern (it takes about 1.15h to travel from Lodz to Warsaw by train or 1.5h by car, which, in comparison with 24h that it took to travel to Florida, does not seem to be "a long drive"), I reply enthusiastically to her desire to see me. We determine the details of the meeting. We plan, among other things, a conversation about autoethnography and—prior to that—my assistance in filming Carolyn and Jerry at work.

My memory archive opens by launching a kaleidoscope of scenes that took place seven years ago: my welcoming Carolyn in the lobby of the Novotel hotel; our journey by subway to the neighborhood where Jerry's family rents a house; meeting him (a warm handshake and a conversation in Polish—I gave Jerry a small bouquet of lilies of the valley, and he, charmingly combining Polish with English, called them *lilijki* [lilacs]); an interesting transcultural, trans-ethnical and trans-religious breakfast with Jerry's family; collaborative interviewing (after breakfast we all went to the living room, Carolyn and Jerry settled themselves on a bench, serving as foreground actors, the other participants were the audience. Jerry, encouraged by Carolyn, played the role of the father-in-law, grandfather, witness to the distant past, and autoethnographic co-researcher); a trip to the city visiting significant places, focal points that, in a series of spontaneously evoked memories of Jerry, transferred us into the depths of war experiences, providing the opportunity to understand them by compiling a doubled consciousness, and at times even a tripled "I" (Jerry-a young boy, Jerry-an older man meeting his younger "I," and Jerry-the "naïve autoethnographer"[3]); Viennese cheesecake tasting outside a Warsaw cafe and ordinary-extraordinary being with one other; an evening talk, not only about autoethnography, but also about what happened during the day, as seen with a doubled pair of "ethnographic I's/eyes"[4]:

CAROLYN: I am glad we had this collaborative experience of being in Warsaw with Jerry. I love how we all worked together. You came into this situation not knowing Jerry, and you couldn't have been more compassionate and caring. You figured out what needed to be done, and you helped me there, and you helped him. Sometimes you and I were working together; sometimes you and he were working together—because I don't know Polish so the two of you were taking care of things; and sometimes he and I were working together because we have this intimate connection and really trust each other. But at the end of the day the three of us were working together. He adores you already, you adore him, and I adore both of you. I couldn't have done today without you, and I felt so much gratitude. Jerry needed someone to be watching him every second, but he needed someone watching him in a way that he didn't get upset that we were taking over too much. I didn't realize how much he needed since I haven't spent this kind of extended time with him. So I needed you and you took over doing some of the video recording, finding things, reading the map, getting the taxi. Without you, we couldn't have done much else today, other than make it to the Wall.[5]

MARCIN: Carolyn, you're talking about more technical things, but during the first part of the conversation we had at Jerry's home, when he was describing his feelings, we were, to some extent, in different dimensions. We spoke English to English, Polish to Polish, and English to Polish. In doing so, the meaning of the stories Jerry told as well as the meaning of the whole situation gradually changed. There was a clear process of finding out something and discovering ourselves.

CAROLYN: And Jerry was our main concern, and I appreciated that. He had to be my main concern, but he didn't have to be your main concern. But you made him your main concern, and I thought that was incredible. Very few people can come into a situation and do that. For example, if Art had been with me I know I could have depended on him to do that. It was immediately clear that I could depend on you, and that allowed me flexibility to make things happen. We didn't know what would happen another day—it may pour down rain, he may not feel like going out; so we had today for sure. I wanted to do what I thought were the main things that he would really enjoy, and be meaningful for him. We managed to do that …

MARCIN: We did, yes …

CAROLYN: At some point I thought "we should get a cab, we should get a cab" because that would make things easier for him. But I could see he enjoyed being able to walk and *do* this. He *loved* it.

MARCIN: Yes, I noticed his enjoyment too.

CAROLYN: I understand that because I have my hip issue. To be able to manage all of this—to think of myself as having a problem, and yet I was taking care of him—it was really wonderful. I will never forget today; I will never forget it in my whole life; and I will never forget the part you played in it.

MARCIN: Thank you. I do not feel like I was the most important part of it, but definitely I was/I am a part of what happened today.

CAROLYN: You are a part and I felt strongly connected to you as we were doing this very intimate thing together, which was taking care of Jerry. There were so many layers of Jerry's re-identification with Poland after all these years. You're Polish, his strong connection to you was part of his healing process today. It makes me cry when I think about that because it was so meaningful to reconnect with this part of the ghetto district. Can you imagine how important it is, not just for him, but for healing in general from his unbearable experience?

MARCIN: Do you remember those people standing near the Wall? When they found out Jerry was a survivor, they suddenly left their guide and pushed in to be near him and hear what he said.

CAROLYN: Oh yes! That was amazing.

MARCIN: They wanted to hear his story. He started to become the center of the process and conscious of what was happening. It was unbelievable—the whole situation.

CAROLYN: Yes, and you were recording it. I'm so happy they thought he was my father and I couldn't tell them he wasn't because they would have been disappointed … they had created this story in their minds about his daughter bringing him to the Wall. They surrounded him as soon as he said he was a survivor.

MARCIN: Do you remember how he wanted to be as quickly as possible near the Wall? He was walking faster and faster when he saw people gathered in that space.

CAROLYN: Yes, and I was standing there and I thought "Please—the guy who was leading it—please be who I hope you are going to be because if Jerry hadn't said he was a survivor I was going to say it." And the guide turned out to be just who I wanted him to be, as he turned his attention to Jerry as well.

MARCIN: Incredible.

CAROLYN: Yes, that was a moment, and at that moment I thought "Nothing else has to happen. This is enough."

(transcript of a conversation between Carolyn and Marcin, March 21, 2013)

Event 2: Being with Art, M. and Carolyn, on the move into the realm of love

The day after talking with Art, when he reflected on the changes that took place between us ("I feel like the last time you were a guest, but this time you're a friend and a colleague"), M. and I were ready to embark on the return journey from Tampa to Poland (in 2016 we visited Tampa together). In the early afternoon, we carried our luggage to the hotel's main entrance and, waiting for the arrival of Art to drive us to the airport, we savored the damp, suspension-like air that drew across the city. Incidentally, and trying to avoid the ideological divisions, we chatted with a group of tipsy "rednecks" from Kentucky. Art arrived punctually, as always. Unfortunately, he looked unmercifully tired. He admitted that he had not slept much after reading a chauvinistic entry on Donald Trump's Twitter account (the U.S. presidential elections were in two weeks). Unexpectedly, but luckily for us, after passing a few blocks to East Fowler Avenue, we saw Art at his best—fatigue evaporated, and in return a fantastic sense of humor. "How do you do this?" I asked.

"Do I do what?" he replied.

"You looked so tired just a minute ago," I said.

"Oh, I simply enjoy being with you two. I thrive on it."

Soon we got to the airport and entered the "drop off" zone. After putting our luggage on the sidewalk, we began to say goodbye so profusely that the accompanying intense emotions surprised us. About an hour later I received an e-mail from Art:

> You two are family. I was deeply touched by our departing hugs. We are friends for life. Safe travels.
>
> Love, Art and Carolyn.

On October 19, we replied in a similar tone:

> Dear Carolyn and Art,
>
> A week has already passed since we returned to Poland, but our thoughts and our hearts are still there in Florida. I would like to thank you for all you did for us during our visit in Tampa. The time we spent together was amazing and unforgettable. M. and I talk about our U.S. experiences every day and we agree that this journey was the best we have ever had as a couple. You two became VERY important to us. To experience moments like those is what makes life worthwhile. These are moments when other people start to be your friends and family. When you feel it, it means you are a happy person. Art, M. asked me after I burst into tears at the airport if I would be willing to interpret that situation as having its source in me with my father relationships. It's a long story, but she is probably right trying to find a connection between these two things. I was surprised at how I behaved, usually I am much more reserved about showing emotions, and suddenly something happened.... I am trying to understand it but it is not so easy.... Will write more soon.
>
> With love, Marcin.

Art replied,

> You two are so sweet. I love having you as part of our family. I am sorry you
> feel that your tears call for an apology. I was touched and felt even closer to
> you. This is only the beginning.
>   Love, Art.

(October 19, 2016)

Making transitions in time and understanding what should be known

I have just put aside *The Border of Oblivion* by Sergei Lebedev, since I came across
fragments that allow me to "think further" about *autoethnography* and *autoethnographicity*. Lebedev, presenting one of the heroes of his novels, highlights the
theme of human transition from "non-stranger" to "one of us"—a family member.
The narrator explains that "family is created by a community of relationships built up
in time between different people" (Lebedev, 2018, p. 35). I let those words resonate,
I think *with* them (Frank 1995).
    What does it mean to belong to the autoethnographic family? I wonder, looking for
a similarity between Lebedev's insights and what constitutes the distinctive feature(s) of
my experience. What conditions must be met for someone to be able to give a verdict
of conviction, "He belongs to our family"? And what about myself? What is the significance of being suspended between being "a stranger" and "one of us," of becoming a "household member" in the house of autoethnography? Lebedev mentions the
"power of gradual integration" (p. 36) in this process. Undoubtedly, gradual integration requires symmetry, its strength lies in *both-sides opening to* and *using the potential*,
which emerges from a given relational context. I treat situations of crossing the
"autoethnographic Rubicon" (*Events 1* and *2*) as peculiar "milestones" in approaching
the core of the autoethnographic world, but no less important are the "small steps."
While the former allows one to go through the previously closed gates, the latter
allows one to wander the paths located in front of and behind those gates. I perceive
big and small steps as symbiotic and synergistic. They reflect the movement of
achieving the position of a non-stranger that has been going on for almost a decade,
and then replacing it with the position of being one of us, as well as the position of
being an autoethnographic household member. Art, in the conversation that we held
in February 2019, aptly notices that I came to Tampa in 2010 to try to find myself
"within autoethnography and narrative inquiry," and that, from his point of view, I
"had an anxious edge"; I was in an evolving state of a "gradual commitment to an
autoethnographic way of being."[6] I would now see that experience as being situated
on *the changing scale of my belief in autoethnography* in its available, multiple manifestations. When the reality of autoethnographic words (i.e. autoethnography known to
me only in a textual form) collided with the reality of life (and thus my association
with an effective autoethnographic practice—including also the experience of autoethnographic life) it resulted in emotional and somatic *alienation*, which is evidenced

by the paragraphs I extracted from my *Florida Journal*. However, this alienation was not permanent, and when subjected to a reflexive revision, the intermediary nature distinguishing it, paradoxically, influenced the release and operation of the "force of gradual integration" (equivalent to moving in small steps). For, without the memory of alienation, would I be able to add *the trans-forming* weight to the Warsaw meeting with Carolyn and Jerry, or a meeting with Art at the airport in Tampa? Indeed, would these "meetings-events"[7] have occurred at all?

Sometimes ambivalence is the driving force of *change*. For example, being in a permanent liminal state—living in Poland and Edinburgh; making library searches and finding *Final Negotiations* and other autoethnographic works as evoking the impression of existence somewhere of a community of scholars based on humanistic beliefs that are close to me; an invitation and a trip to the United States—a cultural shock for me; further, triggered or brought by a fluke, situations of *transformative* intercultural encounters. These elements make up a series of cases (small and big steps) that, taken together, led to the place from where I noticed that I am no longer a "non-stranger," nor even "one of us" only visiting the autoethnographic house. I am a full-fledged household member. I am an integral part of the "extended autoethnographic family."[8]

In search of meta-autoethnographic conclusion: towards autoethnographicity

In Laurel Richardson's classic monograph *Fields of Play: Constructing an Academic Life* (1997), I find a passage that proves instrumental in helping me find a proper meta-autoethnographic (Ellis, 2009) conclusion to the story/ies recounted in the preceding sections. Reminding us of what Carolyn Heilbrun suggests, Richardson claims,

> we don't imitate lives, we live "story lines." The process of rereading one's work and situating it in historical and biographical contexts reveals old story lines, many of which may not have been articulated. Voicing them offers the opportunity to rewrite them, to renarrativize one's life. Writing stories about our "texts" is thus the way of making sense of and changing our lives.
>
> *(p. 5)*

A year or so has passed since I wrote a draft version of my autoformative story. The story was later reread and edited several times (including by Carolyn and Art); formal reviewers of this collection also commented on it. The process of reaching a wider audience began pushing me towards re-contextualizing what seemed to be already complete. Surely, I discovered another dimension of reflexive acting through which very "naturally" a new realm of significant experiences started to become vivid. The following paragraphs will shed light on some of these experiences, showing yet another side of living the autoethnographic life.

My story, at least partly, might be understood as a sentimental utterance that raises serious questions: "So what?" "Who cares?" Or to be more precise, what is "the importance of what we care about"? (Bochner, 2008; see also Bochner & Ellis, 2016, p. 118).

Does a story about becoming an "integral part of the 'extended autoethnographic family'" have any universal element in itself, or is its meaningful capacity limited to a set of "beliefs" shared by a certain group of people? Autoethnographers gathered around the "architects of autoethnography," as Tony Adams had called Carolyn and Art elsewhere (cf. leaflet of *The Symposium on Autoethnography and Narrative Inquiry: Honoring the Legacy of Carolyn Ellis & Art Bochner*, January 3–5, 2019).

There is no simple answer to this question. Occupying the position of someone who had a chance to travel to the cradle of autoethnography, I strongly believe that living the autoethnographic life in Tampa has its own rhythm, and that rhythm is unique. Obviously, entering into what I had labeled the "autoethnographic family," as depicted earlier in this chapter, is no easy task. "[O]ur extended family ... includes quite a few folks you don't know some of whom are not academics and some who are but do not relate to us principally through our work," explains Art in an e-mail in which he offers a summary of his experience of reading this chapter (May 5, 2019). From the very beginning, these words were unsettling and inspiring at the same time, they gave a lot to think about as they coincided with other words I had previously heard from Carolyn when I asked her to tell me the story of why I was invited to visit the Department of Communication at USF. First, she said, "I had appreciated what you wrote to me when asking to come. It had intrigued me and I saw we are kindred spirits." She continued,

> A lot of people want to come and work with us, but most of the time we reject those proposals because having visitors is time consuming and draws our attention away from our work. Your letter was different. It was not about completing another scientific project; instead, it was about life in the first place.
>
> *(Kafar & Ellis, 2014, p. 125)*

Carolyn's last sentence shows a hierarchy of values generated and promoted by the root autoethnographers. The well-known dichotomy of "life" and "work," which plays a crucial role in constituting and sustaining autoethnographic discourse, helps me identify the power of *autoethnographicity*—an indispensable component of doing "genuine" autoethnography. For me, "autoethnographicity" is not the same as "autoethnography." We are prone to see autoethnography as exclusively tied up with research practices (in various types of reflexive acts), whereas autoethnographicity refers to *common ideas, values and beliefs of humanistic origin* and with *the concurrent gift of sensitivity*, available only to a few of us, *skillfully used to tell us about the inner and outer life of people*. Thus, in my opinion, an authentically autoethnographic life *must be* permeated by autoethnographicity. At the same time, autoethnography that is devoid of autoethnographicity—which happens rather often, regarding the multiple understandings of "autoethnography" coexisting today—should be understood as one of the many "dehumanized" cognitive tools of social sciences that function on the academic "market." Instead, an autoethnography that is imbued with autoethnographicity becomes *a peculiar challenge that is able to transform reality by making life better, by participating in the process of negotiating meaning and making sense of lived experience* (Bochner & Ellis, 2016, pp. 35–36).

Although autoethnographicity is never expressed explicitly in the stories written by Ellis and Bochner, it should be nonetheless regarded as *a fundamental factor of the evocative autoethnography paradigm.* A profound *exemplum* confirming my intuitions is the very recent work prepared collectively by Carolyn, Art and their "family members," published in the form of a special collection titled *Legacy of Masters: Honoring the Retirement of Professors Carolyn Ellis and Arthur P. Bochner* (2019). The five texts included in the volume connect us to autoethnographicity; they reveal what makes Ellis and Bochner's professional, as well as personal, life meaningful. For instance, Art writes,

> Now Carolyn and I enter a new chapter of our lives, retirement, a coming toward the end and looking back on the beginning together, the two of us, living as we do, as all people do, in the middle. "What are your plans?" friends ask. Their question reminds me that moments before he died Tolstoy was said to have remarked "I don't know what I'm supposed to do." What I want to do, what I find meaningful, is making people feel stuff, continuing my quest to put into circulation self-clarifying, evocative, and transforming stories; and keep alive the conversation in the human sciences about what can make life good.… I don't know if that's what I'm supposed to do, but it does feel like the right thing to do.
>
> *(Bochner, 2019, p. 255)*

Carolyn also contemplates crucial changes taking place in her life similarly:

> [t]he last twenty-plus years were a wonderful and meaningful time, when Art and I often didn't know when we were working and when we were just living and enjoying life together.… But I already miss the kind of energy that can be generated in a graduate classroom: the lively exchange of ideas, the passion and excitement that builds through the semester, the stimulating conversations that have us on the edge of our seats; the happy exhaustion on the ride home and talking to Art over a late dinner about what happened in class that day.… And the talk around the dinner table continues just as before where Art and I are not sure when work ends and the rest of our lives begins. Together, we create a new chapter where talk is still the kiss of life.
>
> *(Ellis, 2019, pp. 247–248)*

Is it utopian to think that talk/conversation, seen as "the kiss of life," can be understood as a remedy for the neoliberal university in which bureaucratic rules organizing everyday academic existence prevail over collective ("family") values? I don't know, but I feel I was lucky to have met Carolyn Ellis and Art Bochner, as well as other people living their lives autoethnographically (some of whom are not even conscious of it). In this way, "experiencing an experience" (cf. e.g. Ellis & Bochner, 1992; Ellis, 2004) turned into lived experience (cf. Ellis & Bochner, 2016) that builds up (intergenerational) bonds among those who are willing to conceive Academia as *ethos*—a homestead for understanding our interdependence and from which to create a better world.

These are old and new directions of autoethnography that is pervaded with *autoethnographicity*, and this is the legacy worth living by.

Acknowledgments

Thanks to Carolyn Ellis and Arthur Bochner for traveling with me through different dimensions of reality, starting from lived experience and ending with reflection; and also for their superb editing skills that made this chapter more readable for an English-speaking audience. Thanks to Marta Kozlowska for sharing my passion for discovering imponderabilia of U.S. American culture, engaging conversations about them, and helping me to clear up the main ideas in this article. Thanks to Robin Boylorn and Tony Adams for their profound remarks that let me revise my story and make it more consistent.

Notes

1   This work was partially supported by The National Science Centre, Poland, decision no. DEC-2017/01/X/HS6/00941, and by the project entitled *Auto/Formative Dimensions of Scientific Biographies—Prolegomena*, an international research grant funded by the Dean of Faculty of Educational Sciences, University of Lodz, Poland (contract no. B1511800000218.01).
2   This talk entitled *Systematic Sociological Introspection and Research on Emotions* was given in the business school, University of South Florida.
3   The notion of a "naïve autoethnographer" does not carry a pejorative meaning. In this case it refers to a person who did not take a professional course on autoethnography, but nonetheless exhibits a natural autoethnographic sense. Jerry Rawicki is someone who I see as possessing a trait of *autoethnographicity* and employs it successfully in his work with Carolyn.
4   I am referring to some of the associations which Carolyn Ellis used in *The Ethnographic I: A Methodological Novel about Autoethnography* (2004).
5   The Wall is a reference to a fragment of the wall that surrounded the Warsaw ghetto in the Muranow district, located on the courtyard between the streets Sienna 55 and Zlota 62. It is a popular location among Jewish people visiting Warsaw. In the conversation with Carolyn, we are referring to a specific situation that became an inspiration for the title of a collaborative documentary film which uses the autoethnographic convention, namely *Behind the Wall* directed by Carolyn Ellis, Michal Golebiowski, and Jerry Rawicki, Total Film Productions 2013.
6   Art locates these remarks in a wider context of different "roads that have led people to autoethnography." This topic appears in one of our conversations in which he explains, "Some arrive [to autoethnography] through methodology or epistemology; others through a life crisis or through a desire to live a more integrated life, one that merges the personal and the academic. Yours, I classify as a gradual commitment to an autoethnographic way of being, an ontology I sometimes call 'living the autoethnographic life.' You strike me as a good example of this ontological path. When I think of our shared time together since you've been here this month and compare it to the way I experienced you the first time, in 2010, your evolution is a quantum leap.

Marcin: It's more revolution than evolution [*laughter*].

Art: I think it's both probably [*laughter*]. When you came the first time, you seemed to be trying to find yourself, or place yourself, within autoethnography and narrative inquiry. Your dedication as a scholar was unmistakable, but you had an anxious edge to you, as if you weren't quite sure. Perhaps you felt intimidated given the circumstances, forging a new relationship in a new city, in a different country. You were finding your footing in it. And that was a lot to take on given the solid footing for autoethnography you found here at the time. But, you know, when I think of where you were starting, you've come so far, and of course, we've evolved since then too. In 2011 I was just in the middle of doing my book [*Coming to Narrative*] and we hadn't done *Evocative Auto-ethnography*—hadn't even thought about it … and the requests to do workshops were mounting, so for all of us it's been a constant evolution. But the big picture for me is how people get hooked on autoethnography. They get permission from us, from you, and from others, to start to think about their own lives in autoethnographic ways, and then they begin to discover, 'Hey maybe I can make a life out of this that is both an academic life and a good personal life as well,' … and then some people fortunately have the opportunity that you had with Jerry and Carolyn, to be involved in the process of living the autoethnographic life" (transcript of a conversation among Art, Carolyn, and Marcin, Tampa, February 1, 2018).

7 When using the term of "meeting-event," I am referring to the concept of the philosophy of drama as it was characterized by the Polish scholar Jozef Tischner. Referencing the opinions of Emmauel Lévinas, Tischner (2006) emphasizes *the reciprocal properties* of similar situations, explaining their deeply dialogical nature in the following way: "To meet some-one is something much more than being aware that someone other is present next to me or close to me. When mixed in a street crowd, I am aware of the presence of other people, however, it does not mean that I have met them. A meeting is an event. A meeting results with a significant change in the space of relations" (p. 19; see also Tischner, 2017).

8 When talking about close friends, Art and Carolyn use the word "extended family" more often that the word "family." Often these people are Tony Adams, Keith Berry, Robin Boylorn, Andrew Herrmann, Christine E. Kiesinger, Csaba Osvath, Lisa P. Spinazola, Jerry Rawicki and Lisa Tillmann.

References

Bochner, A. P. (2008, November 23). *Communication's calling: The importance of what we care about.* Presidential address, National Communication Association.

Bochner, A. P. (2019). A meaningful academic life: Improvised, amusing, unsettling. *Nauki o Wychowaniu. Studia Interdyscyplinarne/Educational Sciences: Interdisciplinary Studies, 1*(8), 250–256.

Bochner, A. P., & Ellis, C. (2016). *Evocative autoethnography: Writing lives and telling stories.* Routledge.

Bochner, A. P., Ellis. C., Kafar, M., Osvath, C., Scheffels, E., Spinazola, L. P., & Tillmann, L. M. (2019). Legacy of masters: Honoring the retirement of Professors Carolyn Ellis and Arthur P. Bochner. *Nauki o Wychowaniu. Studia Interdyscyplinarne/Educational Sciences: Interdisciplinary Studies, 1*(8), 241–280.

Cotton, E. J. (2002) *Hobo: A young man's thoughts on trains and tramping in America.* Harmony Books.

Ellis, C. (1995). *Final negotiations: A story of love, loss, and chronic illness.* Temple University Press.

Ellis, C. (2004). *The ethnographic I: A methodological novel about autoethnography.* Left Coast Press.

Ellis, C. (2009). *Revision: Autoethnographic reflections on life and work.* Left Coast Press.

Ellis, C. (2019). A meaningful academic life: Loving, fulfilling, challenging, flabbergasting. *Nauki o Wychowaniu. Studia Interdyscyplinarne/Educational Sciences: Interdisciplinary Studies, 1*(8), 243–249.

Ellis, C., & Bochner A. P. (1992). Telling and performing personal stories: Constrains of choice in abortion. In C. Ellis & M. G. Flaherty (Eds.), *Investigating subjectivity: Research on lived experience* (pp. 79–101). Sage Publications.

Fleck, L. (1979). *Genesis and development of scientific fact*. (F. Bradley & T. J. Trenn, Trans.). The University of Chicago Press.

Frank, A. (1995). *The wounded storyteller. Body, illness, and ethics*. The University of Chicago Press.

Kafar, M., & Ellis, C. (2014). Autoethnography, storytelling, and life as lived: A conversation between Marcin Kafar and Carolyn Ellis. *Qualitative Sociology Review, 3*(10), 124–143.

Lebedev [Lebiediew], S. (2018). *Granica zapomnienia*. (G. Szymczak, Trans.). Claroscuro sp. z o.o.

Luria, A. R. (1987). *The mind of a mnemonist*. Harvard University Press.

Richardson, L. (1997). *Fields of play: Constructing an academic life*. Rutgers University Press.

Tischner, J. (2006). *Filozofia dramatu*. Wydawnictwo Znak.

Tischner, J. (2017). *Inny: Eseje o spotkaniu*. Wydawnictwo Znak.

Witkowski, M. (2017). *Wymazane*. Znak literanova.

7

DEAR ART AND CAROLYN

A love story[1]

Keith Berry

Dear Art and Carolyn ("names listed alphabetically"),

Calvin O. Schrag (2003) writes, "We never stand at a beginning but are always somehow already begun, held within a web of delivered discourse, social practice, professional requirements, and the daily decisions of everyday life" (p. 4). Schrag's phenomenological position speaks to the processual nature of everyday living, and, more particularly, the ways in which people co-constitute (i.e., make and remake) and use human understanding. Lived experience, or to use the wording you, Art, often use, "lived-through experience," is dynamic and complex. It is also often tensional, contingent, and uncertain. So are human beings and our ways of relating to others and ourselves. So is writing and research that uses autoethnography, including personal letters about scholarly legacies.

How do I begin to write this letter, a love story about academic lives that have been so full and meaningful? How do I sort through the wide array of characters, plotlines, settings, twists and turns, low and high points, loss, pain and suffering, survival, joy and growth that comprise your story? How do I continue to give meaning to your awe-inspiring tale of narrative inquiry—the personal, emotive, and complicated meaning synonymous with evocative autoethnography (Bochner & Ellis, 2016)? How do I do justice to lives you've touched around the world? Your Being-in-the-world (Heidegger, 1996/1953) certainly makes this task formidable. Yet, I am up for the challenge. I am also thrilled to participate in this book.

I could begin by speaking to the ways theory and everyday theorizing provide an instructive pathway on which people learn, love, and grow. As Kurt Lewin (1943) writes, "There is nothing as practical as a good theory" (p. 118). If I did begin this way, I would stress and underscore that there has never been a more crucial time for emphasizing care in the theories and theorizing on culture and cultural identities people espouse and utilize. I know you both agree, even though I also know that you, Carolyn, love to immerse yourself within stories, including memoirs (Bochner & Ellis, 2016; Ellis, 2004). While you, Art, and I love to dwell and tarry in or "with" theory, I suspect if you were writing this letter, you would remind readers that theories are stories, and stories are theories (Bochner, 2002; 1994). Then again, I have witnessed Carolyn also brilliantly engage with theory to deepen the ways readers understand stories. Okay, my description is getting blurry. It is sometimes hard to tell you two apart. I am grateful for that blur, for the ways in which you come together. The merging of similar and distinct ideas, bodies, and beings, the relational "in between" of Carolyn and Art. We all blur in many respects. I digress. Theory and theorizing are imperfect. Sometimes they lead people to orient to each other and the world, in Schrag's (1994) terms, by engaging with "bloodless abstractions" (p. 146), or social constructs too far removed from the things, or persons, about which they purport to describe or explain. This tendency can be dangerous. The more "bloodless" we are, the less human and alive we risk being.

I could begin by writing about how the reflexive life writing endemic to the community of autoethnographers you've led in creating over all of these years has allowed us to perform in ways that *infuse* blood into cultural inquiry. Your guidance continues to invite scholars to convey and explore stories that invite intimate understandings of issues that hinder and help relational lives. As you, Art, write:

> The truths of autoethnography exist *between* storyteller and story listener; they dwell in the listeners' and readers' engagement with the writers' engagement with adversity; the heartbreaking feelings of stigma and marginalization; the resistance to the authority of canonical discourses; the therapeutic desire to live up to the challenges of life and to emerge with greater self-knowledge, the opposition to the repression of the body, the difficulty of finding words to make bodily dysfunction meaningful, the desire for self-expression, and the urge to speak to and assist a community of fellow sufferers. The call of these stories is for engagement from within and between, and not from without.
> *(Bochner, 2012, p. 161, emphasis in original; see also Bochner, 2001)*

Autoethnography creates the conditions for scholars to connect with others in dialogue about ongoing and mundane moments of lived experience by tuning in to the actual ways we live our lives. This makes autoethnography inherently phenomenological. As founder of phenomenology Edmund Husserl (1970) [1954] advocates, we must turn our attention, again and again, to lived experience, to "the things themselves." Lived experience is the space of coherence and resonance. In this sense, autoethnographers immerse ourselves within experiences in bold and risky ways. Working to locate, reflect on, and reckon with circumstances of our cultural lives and beings in ways that bring a one-of-a-kind heart and vitality to inquiry.

Your labor has most certainly benefitted my work on the ways in which people's phenomenological lifeworld (everyday reality) creates the conditions for the possibility, and sometimes the necessity, to use autoethnography rather than other research methodologies and writing practices that are less inclusive of diverse selves

(Berry, 2011); the challenges and opportunities inherent in responding to others' autoethnographies (Berry, 2006); and the ways enacting autoethnographic research and writing often enables novel performances or transformations of auto-ethnographers' subjectivities (Berry, 2013, 2016, 2021a, 2021b). I continue to learn more about the ways in which autoethnography is always and already a concrete instantiation of "communicative praxis" (the thoughtful and emotional doing of communication) (Schrag, 2003) that "implicates" autoethnographers. We are not unaffected bystanders to the meaning-making process of autoethnography, but rather are interpretively "in" this work. In turn, autoethnography implicates readers and audience members, which, given the ways autoethnographers commonly study hardship, pain, and suffering, is sometimes difficult for some people to understand and accept. As you write:

> Maybe [something] that scares people about autoethnography is the kinds of experiences we ask people to reflect on. Often we focus attention on experiences that normally are shrouded in secrecy.… [T]he good stories, the really good ones, grab us by the collar and demand that we listen and that we feel.… Readers can't just sit back and be spectators. They are thrust into scenes that invite them to feel, care, and desire.
>
> *(Bochner & Ellis, 2006, pp. 119–120)*

In these ways, the autoethnography you developed and continue to advocate—interactive, evocative, vulnerable—feels, to me, like the antithesis of a bloodless abstraction. Indeed, evocative autoethnography is alive. The theme of its beats tells the story of hearts that are pulsating, engorged, and scintillating!

I could also begin by also acknowledging the numerous dissertations you have supervised and PhDs you mentored. Dr. Mary Anne Fitzpatrick at Temple University was your, Art's, first advisee in 1976; your last, Dr. Dionel Cotanda in 2019, who completed his dissertation at age 80. Carolyn's first was Dr. Leigh Berger in 2000, her last, Dr. Lisa Spinazola in 2018. So many students, graduate and under-graduate, learned from your instruction, and as I know you will want me to say, you have learned from theirs.

I could also consider the significant ways you have touched and made better students' work and lives. Take, for example, the ways you, Carolyn, guided Dr. Chris Patti as he made his way through the painstaking process in his dissertation study of doing mindful justice to the horrors of Holocaust victims. Or take the ways you, Art, helped create a paradigm shift for Dr. Nathan Hodges during the proposal defense for his dissertation study on working-class scholars. As a member of his committee, I can still envision you drawing that four-paned window on the dry-erase board and challenging him to reflect on his experiences in more layered and expansive ways. I have since used that pedagogical approach multiple times. Lived experience is certainly far more complex than we often imagine. Stories and storytellers are rarely, if ever, one-dimensional. Or take for example, Art and Carolyn, your past PhD student, academic son, co-editor for the *Writing Lives:*

Ethnographic and Autoethnographic book series (Routledge), and international leader of all things evocative autoethnography, Dr. Tony Adams (co-editor of this book). Your mentoring and bond with Tony, whom I'm grateful to call my best friend and collaborator, exemplifies the possibilities of/for love inherent to "chosen family": unstoppable care and support, endless laughs, and real tears.

Of course, I would not begin without sharing that Art and Carolyn, your both being named Distinguished University Professors (DUP) at the University of South Florida (USF) still renders me in awe. DUP is the highest honorific at USF. Extremely difficult to earn, the rank is reserved for the most exemplary scholars, often scientists with notable patents and formulas on their curriculum vitae. What an honor it was to be asked to serve as a faculty reviewer on the "Discipline Committee" in response to the materials you, Carolyn, submitted. Art and Carolyn, no matter how departments, universities, and lives change over time, in good and uncertain ways, having DUP attached to scholarly records comprised largely of autoethnographic inquiry will serve as an indelible verification of the quality and quantity of innovative work you've produced and the lives you've touched.

Not too shabby for a couple of hippie "navel gazers."

Each of the above main ideas offers only a partial starting point from which to honor the community of autoethnographers you've led us in creating and the overall body of work you've produced. Do not get me wrong: My letter already seeps with love. Yet, there is more to the story. There are other personal experiences I have been lucky enough to share with you, which, although not about autoethnography per se, signal additional ways in which you live as good autoethnographic Beings. I orient to these experiences as relational "moments" that speak to your legacy, a legacy of love, engagement, and care. I end my letter by sharing them in the spirit of appreciation for the ways in which you consistently come together with your relational partners, and so often fellow autoethnographers, hand-in-hand and heart-to-heart, openly contributing light and love to a world that feels of late dark and uncaring.

The first moment occurred when you, Carolyn, and I had dinner in 2018. Art was visiting Tony in Chicago, participating on a tribute panel at Northeastern Illinois University for the late family communication scholar Dr. Bernard J. Brommel. You and I took advantage of your temporary bachelorette status and made the evening one of our "date nights" that I cherish so much. It was a rare late April evening when the weather was mild enough to allow us to sit and eat outside comfortably. We ate a yummy diner in Seminole Heights just outside of downtown Tampa. As you often say, you "dressed for me" that evening. I do love the gender- and sexuality-bending aesthetic of your favorite "butch" jeans and boots. After several hours of visiting, sharing, and helping each other with ways of thinking about our current writing projects, it was time to head home. We left the restaurant, said good night with words and hugs, and began to walk to the separate ends of the lot where we had parked our cars.

As I approached my car, thinking and feeling through the talk I had with you about a romantic relationship brewing in my life, your voice called out to me:

"I adore you."

I instantly smiled and responded:

"Love you."

We walked a couple more steps closer to our respective cars, and I heard you, again, say:

"Adore you … I adore you."

Now quite a ways from each other, I shouted back, trying to let my loving tone match yours:

"I adore you, too."

I opened the door and got into my car feeling like I was glowing. Granted, I have felt adored in my life; but this moment was the only time I can remember when someone said goodbye to me in this particular way, and made sure I heard, knew, and felt it.

As I write this letter, I can hear your loving words and feel my glowing. I adore you, too, my dear friend. I adore your heart of gold, which is readily apparent and available in our bond, and in the bonds you share with the countless others I'm sure you have made glow. I adore so much about you; those ways of performing that may seem trivial or momentary to others, but to me they matter and are lasting.

For instance, I adore that, when two of our colleagues at department meetings would occasionally argue, debating about the rightness of their individual positions to little resolve, you would sometimes intervene and say, gently and definitively, "You know, I think *both* of these positions can be right at the same time." Eyes gazing in their direction. Head nodding to complement the utterance. They often went silent, and appeared to contemplate your (wise) position.

I adore the ways in which you are excited by knowing that I and others are working on new writing projects, and your (seemingly endless) ways of encouraging us. I love that you still ask for feedback on your writing (and genuinely want it) this many years into your career. This is to say, I love the love you have for inquiry, openness, engagement, and honesty—the ways you embody your call for revision (Ellis, 2009) and relational ethics (Ellis, 2007) in autoethnographic research and writing.

I adore your strength and perseverance through adversity, across difference, in the face of betrayal, across life's … "stuff." You've frequently expressed to me and others that the forces of institutional life often lead scholars to abandon loyalty and memory (Ellis, 2019). Those forces are real and unhelpful. Nevertheless, you persisted—and persist.

The second moment occurred several years ago when you, Art, and I were having breakfast at Pach's Place, my family's favorite greasy spoon diner in Tampa. That morning you asked me, as usual, about my father's declining health. I responded by letting you know of the increasing complications related to his condition, including the massive number of blood transfusions he had to endure, and the physical and emotional toll his poor health, and the circumstances that led it, had on him and my family (see Berry, 2012, 2021b). You and I had talked about his condition, and life related to it, many times before in the past. In this moment, it felt to me that there was not much new to say. I got the sense that you felt similarly, having lived through the taxing nature of your parents' poor health prior to their deaths. But you did say something to me that touched me in ways that allowed my weary heart to open: "Sometimes the best thing you can do is to relate with him in ways that create the conditions that will facilitate future memories, and allow your memory of him to live on." Your feedback was so gentle and loving and meant the world to me. That moment motivated me to spend more quality time, and to be more present and engaged, with him. It led us to share more moments that mattered.

My dad died in 2015. He was a good man and a loving father. Yet, his struggles with addiction affected his relationships with me and others in my family (see Berry, 2012, 2021b). I love the more intimate bonds he and I created during the five years of his recovery prior to his death. I'm grateful to miss him. I did not always think I would. I now have far more warm and loving memories of my times with him. Memories which you had a hand, and heart, in helping me build. Thank you for that precious gift.

This moment leads me to also reflect on your love for, and the impact you have made on, inquiry and the academic life, more generally. I cherish the ways in which history—of an academic department, for instance, ours at USF—matters, and should matter. History should matter most in times of conflict. Humans are temporal Beings; time matters (Heidegger, 1996/1953). In these times of drastic change in higher education, who will tell the stories made from the memories created during all of your years of passion, vision, and investment? I know I will.

Art, I cherish what you've written about good autoethnographic stories, namely the ways in which they render experiences meaningful and tell the tales of different selves evolving over time, and the ways autoethnography entails an investigation of researchers' subjectivities (see, for example, Bochner, 2000). I admire, relate to, and learn from how you've aimed to live as a teacher and writer, in ways that have sought to bring this orientation to life, and story.

I cherish the ways in which your lived-through experience with others emphasizes the import of living authentically (i.e., sincerely); of practicing good communication, not in ways that assume communicating to be a panacea or quick fix to issues, but in ways that understand how relating is the fertile ground on which this work must begin; of pursuing wisdom over intelligence and the diverse ways in which one can be wise when attempting to live a good life; of matters of the heart and living in open and heartfelt ways, even when living with closed-off hearts might feel easier and safer; and of your ongoing romance with the life-transforming potential of vulnerable story writing and narrative analysis.

You, my friend, are a mensch.

***

Carolyn and Art, the essence of your legacy dwells in the gift of engagement, openness, determination, wisdom, patience, care, and love you have given us, which has made, and continues to make, a positive impact that lasts and that reaches many people and in many ways.

For me and so many others, you have served as an exquisite model of the promise and peril inherent to living "the ethnographic life." The love story I have described—one that embodies reflexive, vulnerable, compassionate, and dedicated teaching, researching, and writing—is a much needed and enduring story. Your current and future work expand on the legacy. Our work that must come as a result of yours continues the story.

This labor calls scholars to use autoethnography in ways that emphasize personal and candid inquiry, as your work has readily demonstrated. "Doing" autoethnography and being autoethnographers often entails uncovering some of the innermost thoughts and feelings pertinent to relational and cultural lives, and exposing experiences and identities, and their meaningfulness, to others in the most sincere ways possible. It means taking risks as we reveal to others the struggles and joys that comprise people's lives. In these ways, *continuing the story means working with soul.*

We also work to continue your story, our story, by taking seriously reflection, writing, and dialogue with others. To orient to work in this way entails embodying a dedication to skillful research and writing, discipline and focus amid the inevitable distractions, and compassion for others and ourselves. It means finding the best ways to join words, sentences, and paragraphs in our writing, and skillfully engaging with the stories of our lives so that others may do the same. In turn, it entails challenging our comfort zones by putting ourselves "on the spot" with difficult memories and realities, all the while making sure that the ways we engage in research allow us to feel safe. In essence, *continuing this story calls us to be warriors of the craft of autoethnography.*

We also continue the story by committing ourselves to strengthening and growing the community of autoethnographers that exists and thrives today. We are an extraordinarily soulful community of warriors who are far better when we work together and support each other. We must work to connect with each other based on the shared and unique struggles we have endured, and our shared interest in bringing this lived experience to our research and writing. As your work has made abundantly clear, this path is not easy—in fact, at times it can be confounding, intimidating, and scary. Yet, staying on it, as best as possible, creates the conditions for a more engaged, aware, and heart-ful way of living as scholars and persons.

This autoethnographic community, much like the Department of Communication at USF, would not exist as it is today without your contributions—contributions of seismic love.

It has been a great honor for me to be your close colleague in the Department, in the Ethnography Division of the National Communication Association, a fellow member of the International Congress of Qualitative Inquiry, a collaborator, an author whose first book you edited (Berry, 2016), and a friend for all of these years.

I am excited for you as you live the next chapter of your academic story. I miss having you down the hallway in the Department of Communication. Yet, the missing I feel is nuanced. After all, you emerge from your many years on the faculty, both the exciting and trying, having made an unmistakable mark on the Department, College, and USF. Your contributions make it unlikely you'll ever be truly and fully "gone." I don't think legacies like yours work that way. All starting points in the community, at least in part, whether explicit or tactic, trace back to your contributions. You are here "with" me, and I suppose that will need to be, and is, enough.

Legacies are created and sustained through the enactment of work and the sharing of memories and stories over time. May the readers of this love letter, and all autoethnographers, give back to you as you have given so generously. Your love story goes on. I can hardly wait to see how you tell it.

Peace and love,

Keith

Note

1 Portions of this chapter were presented at the Symposium on Narrative and Auto-ethnography, January 2019, on St. Pete Beach in Florida, and at the 14th Annual International Congress of Qualitative Inquiry, May 2018, in Urbana/Champaign, IL.

References

Berry, K. (2006). Implicated audience member seeks understanding in autoethnography: Reexamining the "gift." *International Journal of Qualitative Methods*, *15*, 1–12. https://doi.org/10.1177%2F160940690600500309.

Berry, K. (2012). Reconciling the relational echoes of addiction: Holding on. *Qualitative Inquiry*, *18*, 134–143. https://doi.org/10.1177%2F1077800411429088.

Berry, K. (2013). Spinning autoethnographic reflexivity, cultural critique, and negotiating selves. In T. E. Adams, S. Holman Jones, & C. Ellis (Eds.), *The handbook of autoethnography* (pp. 209–227). Routledge.

Berry, K. (2016). *Bullied: Tales of torment, identity, & youth*. Routledge.

Berry, K. (2021a, forthcoming). Autoethnography. In M. Bamberg, C. Demuth, M. Watzlawik (Eds.), *Cambridge handbook of identity*. Cambridge University Press.

Berry, K. (2021b, forthcoming). Meditations on the story I cannot write: Autoethnography, reflexivity, and the possibilities of maybe. In T. E. Adams, S. Holman Jones, & C. Ellis, Eds.), *The handbook of autoethnography*. Routledge.

Bochner, A. P. (1994). Perspectives on inquiry II: Theories and stories. In M. L. Knapp & J. A. Daly (Eds.), *The handbook of interpersonal communication* (2nd ed., pp. 21–41). Sage.

Bochner, A. P. (2000). Criteria against ourselves. *Qualitative Inquiry*, *6*, 266–272. https://doi.org/10.1177%2F107780040000600209.

Bochner, A. P. (2001). Narrative's virtues. *Qualitative Inquiry, 7*, 131–157. https://doi.org/10.1177/107780040100700201.

Bochner, A. P. (2002). Perspectives on inquiry III: The moral of stories. In M. L. Knapp & J. A. Daly (Eds.), *The handbook of interpersonal communication* (3rd ed., pp. 73–101). Sage.

Bochner, A. P. (2012). On first-person narrative scholarship: Autoethnography as acts of meaning. *Narrative Inquiry, 22*, 156–164. https://doi.org/10.1075/ni.22.1.10boc.

Bochner, A. P., & Ellis, C. (2006). Communication as autoethnography. In G. J. Shepherd, J. St. John, & T. Striphas (Eds.), *Communication as … Perspectives on theory* (pp. 110–122). Sage.

Bochner, A. P., & Ellis, C. (2016). *Evocative autoethnography: Writing lives and telling stories.* Routledge.

Ellis, C. (2004). *The ethnographic I: A methodological novel about autoethnography.* AltaMira Press.

Ellis, C. (2007). Telling secrets, revealing lives: Relational ethics in research with intimate others. *Qualitative inquiry, 13*, 3–29. https://doi.org/10.1177%2F1077800406294947.

Ellis, C. (2009). *Revision: Autoethnographic reflections on life and work.* Left Coast Press.

Ellis, C. (2019) A Meaningful academic life: Loving, fulfilling, challenging, and flabbergasting. *Educational Sciences: Interdisciplinary Studies* [Nauki o Wychowaniu. Studia Interdyscyplinarne], *1*, 243–249.

Heidegger, M. (1996/1953). *Being and time* (J. Stambaugh, Trans.). State University of New York Press.

Husserl, E. (1970) [1954]. *The crisis of European sciences and transcendental phenomenology* (D. Carr, Trans.). Northwestern University Press.

Lewin, K. (1943). Psychology and the process of group living. *Journal of Social Psychology, 17*, 113–131. https://doi.org/10.1080/00224545.1943.9712269.

Schrag, C. O. (1994). *Philosophical papers: Betwixt and between.* State University of New York Press.

Schrag, C. O. (2003). *Communicative practice and the space of subjectivity.* Purdue University Press.

8

MASSAGING THE MUSE

Gresilda A. Tilley-Lubbs

I lie on the massage table face down with my eyes closed and my body sur-
rendered to utter relaxation. Julie's fingers knead and push, and I feel her
strength and vibrant energy enter my tense muscles. My spirit infuses my
muscles as she stretches them and slowly pushes out the knots. The soft music
and dim lights carry me to that nether world where spirit and body join as
Julie's hands continue their rhythmic work of freeing my muscles from their
painful frozen state. Every time she kneads a knot, intense pain travels through
my body and into my lungs, causing me to gasp as she holds that spot with
one hand and stretches with the other.

My son Peter suffers from the same anxiety, angst, and painful muscles that I do,
and we often commiserate. He recommended masseuse Julie Yudowitch when I
complained that my back pain required relief beyond the shower's hot pounding
water. Until then, I had only had "relaxing massages" on river cruises—scented oils
and fragranced candles; soft, soothing voices and Eastern music; followed by peppermint tea. I had never experienced massage's pain relief. Since pain was waking me
from sleep and affecting my quality of life, I followed Peter's recommendation.

At first, Julie's perky voice and vitality were discombobulating, but I soon came
to love her bouncy comments and questions: "Your back feels a lot better; last
week your muscles felt solid as rocks."

I smile and mumble through the soft cloth in the chin support, "I've noticed that
I don't *always* have my shoulders hunched up around my ears like I usually do."

"Hunched shoulders are no good," she says firmly, continuing to knead, push,
and pull.

My thoughts float and drift outside my body as I contemplate how the knots
started, first in body, then in spirit. I think about the ways Carolyn Ellis kneaded,
pushed and pulled knots out of my frozen academic spirit just as Julie is massaging
knots out of my frozen back muscles.

First knots form

After a career of teaching middle- and high-school Spanish, English as a Second Language (ESL), and private piano and voice lessons, the discontent that has been brewing for a number of years bubbles over. At the same time, the supervisor for a student teacher I am mentoring presents an opportunity for me to study for a PhD in Curriculum and Instruction at a nearby university. I also can teach Spanish as an adjunct. I immediately resign and start working toward a doctorate with a concentration in Foreign Language Education at age 52.

I feel discombobulated and bored in my education classes. We read studies about teaching the sound system of vowels and consonants, studying the wait time for asking questions, and using literature to teach language. Reading quantitative studies—and facing the thought of doing one—makes me consider resigning, both from the teaching position in the university, which I love, and the Ph.D. program, which I find tedious. The thought of returning to teach public school keeps me going, but I constantly reconsider my decision to get a PhD.

The first muscle knot starts to form on the edge of my right shoulder blade.

As I consider my options, the local immigrant and refugee office asks me to fill in as an interpreter for newly immigrated women at the health department's prenatal, postnatal, and family planning clinics. As I add 20 hours a week of interpreting to teaching four Spanish classes and taking three PhD classes, my spirits rise. I am doing work I enjoy. I design a course on immigration issues that involves partnering with newly immigrated families for whom I interpret. I eventually write a qualitative dissertation using ethnographic methods to study the relationships that did or didn't form between the students and the families. Before beginning the study, I assumed that all my Spanish students and the Spanish-speaking families they visited developed meaningful relationships. However, as I analyze the data, I realize that some students and families have developed friendships, but not all. I discover in some partnerships a lack of cultural understanding and appreciation. I examine the hierarchical thinking that shaped some of the relationships, and I see that Othering was often present in the ways the students discussed the families. I present the findings in portraits (see Lawrence-Lightfoot & Davis, 1997) that illustrate how the relationships developed over the course of a semester.

At that time, I had never heard of autoethnography, but intuitively and organically, autoethnography was my methodology. I knew that I was a participant in the study, not an objective observer. I wrote about being the daughter of a coal miner, and I wondered whether my background might have given me a greater understanding of and appreciation for these families whose lives were shaped by poverty and marginalization. I knew that I had always felt "less than" because of my family circumstances, and I wondered how the families' circumstances would affect their lives in the United States. I shared the cultural and socioeconomic background of my childhood, making connections with participant families.

I don't realize that I am writing autoethnography until many years later, when I encounter *The Ethnographic I: A Methodological Novel about Autoethnography* (2004).

Reading Carolyn's book, I recognize that I have related the personal to the public. Now I have words to think and write about what I am doing.

The knot deepens and spreads

In 2005, when I present my research as part of my interview for a position in the School of Education at the same university, one of the faculty members comments that my study can't be research because it is too easy to read. I am hired as Assistant Professor and Director of Foreign Language Education, but I don't fit in with the other faculty whose research involves data analysis programs and traditional research reports. My background in Spanish literature rebels against the dry writing expected of me.

Well-meaning colleagues and mentors try to steer me to the top-tiered journals appropriate for publishing the 12 articles required for tenure. I try to read articles in *TESOL Quarterly* and *Journal of Teacher Education (JTE),* all presented traditionally. I even have an article provisionally accepted in *JTE,* but I never do the revisions or resubmit the article. I took the minimum requirement for quantitative research while working on my doctorate, but I can't bring myself to do statistical analysis. I am exhausted all the time and worried about tenure.

The knot spreads down my shoulder blade with greater intensity.

During the first semester of my new tenure-track position, I spend most of my time (when I'm not teaching) with my mother, who was hospitalized the day before Thanksgiving. During November and December, she shuttles between hospital and rehabilitation center. As her only child, I constantly feel distraught that I am not spending enough time with her, and I feel equally distraught that I'm not writing the expected articles for my tenure-track job. I can do the math—I have five years to publish 12 articles in top-tier journals. I am already behind. By the time Mom dies in early January, I am an emotional wreck but feel I can take no time to grieve.

The knot has now taken over the entire upper right quadrant of my back.

I stay frenetically busy, attending numerous conferences, doing one presentation after another. I still nourish the impossible dream of getting a position in Spanish, so I attend conferences and write papers in and about Spanish and about education. With every year that passes, that dream becomes more remote, as does any thought of attaining tenure.

As I move through devastating, unacknowledged grief, we sell both our house and Mom's house, buying one we completely remodel. In May, we move into the new house just after our son's graduation from college. He moves out soon after, leaving us as empty nesters. The changes feel overwhelming.

The big knot takes over my entire back

On April 16, 2007, the slow destruction of my inner world comes to a final excruciating explosion. A student on my campus systematically shoots and kills 31 students and faculty members before committing suicide. My office is on the third floor of the building directly across from the one where he begins the final massacre—in the classroom where I taught the previous semester. One of the shot faculty members is a French instructor, a friend with whom I shared many cups of morning coffee during my time as a Spanish instructor. A number of my students in Foreign Language Education were friends of French and German students killed, so the university gives us permission to cancel remaining classes and projects. We all try to regroup.

I sink into a debilitating depression that leaves me sobbing, mostly on the couch, for months. No matter where I go or what I do, I randomly break into uncontrollable weeping. A counselor friend suggests a workbook for stress, and I begin journaling. I realize I am processing not only my grief from the shootings but also the unacknowledged grief from my mother's death and the stress from feeling inadequate and disinterested in my profession. As I fill out a questionnaire, I see that in a short time, I have experienced stress from death, a house move, the last child graduating from college and leaving home, a traumatic event, and a new job. A workbook test evaluates my stress level. Its key states that stress becomes dangerous at 100 points; I score 300.

The knots in my back tighten, and my adrenalin spikes as I read that I need to de-stress or face consequences like stroke and heart attack.

Carolyn as masseuse

The first gentle massage

After I have filled four journals with prompts from the workbook, random comments from kind and caring colleagues happen at just the right time. My former anthropology and ethnography professor suggests that I read the journal *Qualitative Inquiry* (*QI*). He tells me, "I expect this is the kind of writing that would appeal to you." By this time, I am convinced that I can never read or write the traditional research articles my colleagues tell me lead to tenure, so I decide to check out *QI*.

As I search the electronic contents, I find and read "There Are Survivors: Telling a Story of Sudden Death," in which Carolyn Ellis (1993) chronicles her grief over the death of her brother in an airplane crash. I sob all the way through, then search for other articles she has written. I read them all voraciously and next to a box of Kleenex.

In "Grave Tending: With Mother at the Cemetery" (Ellis, 2003), I read about Carolyn accompanying her mother to the cemetery. As Carolyn contemplates the rituals that she assumed after her mom could no longer perform them, I remember standing beside my dad's grave with my mom, helping her to arrange the plastic flowers in the holder next to the simple brass marker. I hear her worry about there being no one to visit her grave when she dies. I realize that not visiting her grave contributes to the constant guilt I carry.

I read "Shattered Lives: Making Sense of September 11th and Its Aftermath" (Ellis, 2002). Carolyn examines how she experienced the horrific event through the lenses of location, since she was on a plane bound for Dulles, and of loss. I realize that I still am trying to process 4/16 and its aftermath. I begin to suspect that my overwhelming grief is not limited to the shootings but is also connected to my mom's death, my guilt about not spending 24 hours a day with her during her last three months of life, and my not allowing myself to grieve.

Carolyn's writing resonates with a place deep inside my soul, and I experience the first cathartic sense of relief I have had since the shootings. Carolyn's articles provide the therapy I have refused, allowing me to process my lived experience. I can see myself floating back to the surface rather than spending the rest of my life lying on the ocean floor (Tilley-Lubbs, 2011a). I exhaust all the search engines as I read one article after another, loving Carolyn's writing more with each. Unlike the other academics I have been encouraged to read, Carolyn is a resonant reader's writer. Learning that it's possible to write for people who enjoy literary reading while tackling tough topics gives me hope and inspiration that I can become a successful, published academic.

Just as my physical massage with Julie loosens the knots in my back, reading Carolyn's work gradually loosens knots in my spirit.

When I next talk to my colleague, I tell him, "I actually stay awake to read to the end. I am sad when the story ends because I want to keep reading."

He replies, "Those folks have a conference in Champaign-Urbana every May. Give it a try."

I am excited at the thought of returning to the campus where I received my first two degrees, and where I began a PhD in Spanish literature. I think about the place where I developed my first notions that a university can be a dwelling place for the mind and spirit. I submit a proposal for the upcoming 2008 conference. I also decide to attend the Autoethnography Workshop to meet Carolyn Ellis.

Carolyn's first deep massage

At the workshop, I first hear the words that become a guiding mantra. Autoethnography is "research, writing, story, and method that connect the auto-biographical and personal to the cultural, social, and political" (Ellis, 2004, p. xix). After the workshop ends, I stand in line to speak to Carolyn. When my turn comes, I tell her, "I've read everything of yours that I can find—I've become your academic groupie! How can I learn to write autoethnography?" Carolyn gives me a hug, probably because I am tearful and gushing.

"In July, I'm doing another autoethnography workshop." Her genuine and caring smile extends to her eyes as she says, "You might want to attend."

The second deep massage

My husband Dan and I make the long drive from Roanoke, Virginia to Long Island, New York. I need to bring a draft of autoethnographic writing, so I decide to write about the campus shootings that continue to haunt and immobilize me. By now I have read a number of Carolyn's articles that have helped me understand the chaos that has me tangled up. I reread "There are

Survivors" (Ellis, 1993), and as Carolyn describes the phone call and events surrounding her brother's death, I remember the day of the shootings and seeing the email, subject line Please stay put: "A gunman is loose on campus. Stay in buildings until further notice. Stay away from all windows."

Just as Carolyn immediately called the airline to find out if the crash was her brother's flight, I dashed to my third-floor office window to look out at police officers crab walking around the Drillfield. I watched as the EMTs carried one body after another to the waiting ambulances. I went to a room with a TV to watch live coverage and follow the growing body count.

I prepare a draft about the shootings to take to the workshop.

While we drive, I read the article Carolyn sent to the workshop participants, "Maternal Connections" (Ellis, 1996), which I had read earlier in my obsessive Carolyn marathon. But this time, I am whisked back to the rehabilitation center where *my* mom spent her life's last days. Carolyn describes helping her mother navigate grab bars in the bathroom and wash, and I remember helping Mom the same ways. I remember her standing at the little sink in her room, trying not to lose her balance as she favors the fractured hip the doctors finally diagnosed. I remember helping her with the bathroom and realizing the reversal of our mother/child roles. I also reread, "With Mother/With Child: A True Story" (Ellis, 2001), reliving the times I went to Mom's house—across the street from our house—to help her get to bed. These memories make me sad, but they are also restorative.

Carolyn's work is easing the muscle knots in my neck as I begin to forgive myself for all the things I regretted having not done.

In this liminal moment, I make the final connections between the shootings and my reaction to my mother's death. I realize my depression has come not only from my reaction to the loss of a dear colleague and the senseless deaths of so many, including the disturbed student who did the shooting. My incapacitating immobilization also relates to the timing of my mother's illness and death, the first year of my tenure track job and its constant refrain of "publish or perish."

Autoethnography provides healing as I face emotions that have coursed through me for several years. I remember reading Carolyn's description of her brother's body in the casket (1993) and envisioning my mother in her light purple polyester suit, lying with her hands crossed. Understanding the relationship between the shootings and Mom's death moves me to think, *Maybe I'm not having my grandmother's nervous breakdown, as my family calls it.*

Dan looks over at me as I cry. "Are you okay?" he asks.

"You know how I feel so guilty about Mom's last three months?"

He nods, and I continue. "I just read the article Carolyn sent for the workshop, about a time she cared for her hospitalized mother. It makes me remember Mom's last months. I remembered that for three months, I stayed with her every day until I had to leave for class, and then I returned every evening to help her get ready for bed. I remember helping her to the bathroom, and helping her avoid getting tangled in the tubes. I had forgotten how much time I did spend with her. In my memory, I was never there because I was always so scared about my job."

Dan responds, "You were there what seemed like all the time. We lived on fast food baked potatoes and chili for those three months. Wendy's was the only place open when we left your mom every night."

I sit in silence, letting the fresh, healing memory fill me with peace. I am finally able to reconcile my memories of the mass shooting and my mother's death.

The knot that had started to progress to the lower right quadrant of my back loosens a bit. Carolyn is a nurturing masseuse. Although I'm not ready to unpack all the details, I am ready to write about the campus shootings and to include some recent self-revelations about Mom's death.

On the massage table as Carolyn massages and kneads

The workshop is comprised of six women with Carolyn as facilitator and guide. We write about trauma and healing. We talk about the ethics of including family and friends in our writing. I have not yet read, "Telling Secrets, Revealing Lives: Relational Ethics in Research with Intimate Others" (Ellis, 2007). Carolyn talks about "act[ing] from our hearts and our minds" (p. 4) when we write about the people closest to us. While she says there are no explicit rules when writing about our lived experiences with family and friends, we can still think through the consequences. She advises that we "seek the good" (p. 23) and, when possible, secure their informed consent. Insights gleaned from conversations around that seminar table became mantras that guide my writing.

As we share our writing, Carolyn proves adept at saying just the right thing to make the story fall into place. I had opened with a bucolic and pastoral scene of my trip to campus through the Blue Ridge Mountains. The day of the massacre was just like any other spring day—until the "Please stay put" email floated across my screen. Carolyn suggests, "Why don't you start with the email? That will hook the reader." Suddenly the story moves from "okay" to "one I want to read." She suggests that I also reread "Shattered Lives" (Ellis, 2002) to help me situate my grief within a larger public tragedy. I later follow her advice and begin to understand my reactions as PTSD (post-traumatic stress disorder).

I publish my first autoethnographic piece, "4/16: Public Tragedy Collides with Personal Trauma" (Tilley-Lubbs, 2011a). By then, Carolyn had massaged out several knots.

The knots return and tighten

During the short workshop, I learned as much as I would have in a semester-long doctoral research course. All the same, the specter of the tenure track continues to haunt me, and I constantly fight immobilization.

I read *The Ethnographic I* (Ellis, 2004), a methodology novel and textbook for autoethnography. I develop a deeper understanding of what autoethnography is and isn't. To help me make sense of the more traditional forms of research I learned in graduate school, I find the "Chart of Impressionist and Realist

Ethnography" useful (pp. 359–364). After reading many articles Carolyn considers exemplars of autoethnographic writing, I see how to include methodological discussion in my own writing.

I read *Revision: Autoethnographic Reflections on Life and Work* (Ellis, 2009). The book resonates deeply. Carolyn describes growing up in Luray, Virginia, only about an hour and a half up the interstate from my home in Roanoke. I realize how similar our working-class backgrounds are and am inspired to write "The Coal Miner's Daughter Gets a Ph.D." (Tilley-Lubbs, 2011b), about leaving West Virginia at age 12 to move with my parents to the Chicagoland area. I unpack the classism and regionalism I experienced as my classmates dubbed me "Hillbilly." In *Revision*, Carolyn uses meta-autoethnography. As she revisits some of her work that has been most significant for me, I see that my perceptions of deeply-affecting events seem different when I revisit them. I draw new connections among the personal, social, political, and historical worlds I inhabit.

When I submit my dossier for tenure in 2011, I have published the required number of articles—a feat I never expected to accomplish and one I never would have accomplished without Carolyn's spirit healing massages. They have eased the pain of the knots in my back and provided the encouragement and guidance I needed to do what was needed to earn tenure.

I should be elated but am struck by a sense of nothingness as I read the letter from the Board of Visitors informing me that I have been granted promotion and tenure. One of my PhD advisees, with me when I open the letter, later says, "I was so shocked that you showed no emotion. I expected you to jump up and down or to cry with happiness. But you looked blank, and then laid the letter aside." Inspired by *Revision,* I later return to and story this experience of non-emotion (Tilley-Lubbs, 2014).

The massages continue

I continue reading Carolyn's work, and her words often resonate with my life and with what I struggle to write about—one of the perks of being near the same age as my mentor/masseuse. In "The Procrastinating Autoethnographer: Reflections of Self on the Blank Screen" (Ellis, 2012), she talks about a 30-year career, and I realize how out of sync my age is with my current career. I am a few years older than Carolyn, but since I started working on a PhD in my early 50s, I will never have 30 years of writing books and articles. In third person, Carolyn talks about writing an article about pro-crastination as she procrastinates writing for a deadline in two weeks. I think about all the times I have faced the computer screen and taken care of everything except writing. After I was granted tenure in 2012, I collapsed into apathy. Once I realize that I am not alone in finding myself in a state of ennui, I am able to write "The Inquisition/ Torture of the Tenure Track" (Tilley-Lubbs, 2014). When I wrote about the shootings on campus, I was able to release the pain that I carried for four years, and with this article about my tenure experience, I am able to heal from the angst of going through the tenure process as a humanities thinker in a social sciences environment.

This time, Carolyn kneaded out a knot beside my upper left shoulder blade.

In 2009, Carolyn published "At Home with 'Real Americans': Communicating Across the Urban/Rural and Black/White Divides in the 2008 Election." She begins the article with the shocking words, "I'm not voting for no nigger," and the pain I feel is visceral. She describes a conversation she and her partner Art had with a neighbor in the Blue Ridge Mountains. I live near the same range and encounter many of the same attitudes. As I read, I think about the first few years of living in Virginia after we moved from California in 1980. We met older people who still referred to their "colored help" and a realtor who discouraged us from looking at a house in a neighborhood he referred to as "salt and pepper." My parents were retiring and moving to Roanoke from Illinois, and they asked us to find them a house as much like the one they were living in as possible. The same realtor found the house. He assured us that, although a Black family lived in a house behind the one we were buying and another lived on the corner, they were "good, clean people."

Carolyn describes visiting New York during that same pre-election time and feeling reassured as she walked down the streets and saw diverse people. As I read Carolyn's article, I remembered how much I wanted to move back to Chicagoland for the first seven years we lived in Roanoke.

As much as the article resonated with me when she published it in 2009, Trump's victory in 2016 brings the full impact of her article to my consciousness. My husband and I have already learned not to have political discussions with our neighbors, so we are not surprised that we aren't invited to the celebration party the night of the election.

I also read "Telling Tales on Neighbors: Ethics in Two Voices," (2009) another story that presents complexities we face living in the Blue Ridge Mountains. She interrogates the ethics of stories "*about* rather than *with* others" (p. 23). I think of this as I write a critical autoethnographic article, "Fear and Silence Meet Ignorance" (Tilley-Lubbs, 2019), about my experience in Spain as a doctoral student who failed to realize, until 33 years later, that I was living under a totalitarian dictatorship. When I returned to Spain in 2013, I talked to older people who had experienced the Civil War (1936–1939) and those who lived through a dictatorship that lasted 36 years, until 1975. Carolyn's article about neighbors inspires me to include a conversation with a woman, originally from Spain, who now lives in my neighborhood in Southwest Virginia. A neighbor had told her that I was doing research in Spain, and she asked about it. I told her I was interviewing people in Catalunya and Galicia to hear their stories about life during those years. Her response shocked me.

"Don't listen to those people," she said. "They're all crazy. Franco was a good man and a good leader."

If I hadn't read Carolyn's article about neighbors, I'm not sure I would have had the courage to write about that conversation. Even though I continue to question the ethics of including her words, another muscle knot loosens a bit.

I read the piece Carolyn and Art wrote about being at ICQI, "Into the Garden of Illini: The International Congress as a House of Being for Qualitative Inquiry"

(2012), and I remember the first year I went to the Congress. The sense of the unfamiliar being familiar rushes back, and I sit down and write about the healing I experienced as we drove onto the campus and I engaged the workshop and conference. The piece I write in response to Carolyn and Art's article becomes part of a chapter in my book, *Re-Assembly Required: Critical Autoethnography and Spiritual Discovery* (2017).

The years following my promotion and tenure bring commitment and busyness. Reading "Jumping On and Off the Runaway Train of Success: Stress and Committed Intensity in an Academic Life" (Ellis, 2011), I realize I am grasping my seat as I sit on the "runaway train." Carolyn talks about taking stock of her academic life and determining her priorities, and I feel a need to do the same.

I am considering retirement. In May 2012, I receive a letter informing me that I am eligible for Social Security; it's the same day I receive the letter informing me of tenure. One letter informs me I can stop working, the another indicates I can start a new position as an Associate Professor. I read Carolyn's conversation with Art when he reminds her that "the academic life is a calling, not a career" (Ellis, 2011, p. 169). The knot loosens a bit more. I realize that I love what I do and that I have made friends and met colleagues from all over the world whose work resonates with mine.

Later, as I write my book, more of Art's words from that same conversation speak to my own experience:

> Things don't really get resolved, but you hope that by reflecting deeply on what is going on that you do come to be smarter about it. You recognize the choices you're making, and you become a bit more willful about committing to what's really important to you.
>
> *(Ellis, 2011, p. 169)*

As I write the book, I mentally move from the role of victim of circumstances to one of resilience, rebelliousness, tenacity, and agency. I didn't accept the path laid out for me by others but rather followed Carolyn's lead to become my own person and scholar. Through Carolyn, I followed Spanish poet Antonio Machado to "make the road by walking" (Machado, 1912/2011, pp. 232–233).

As I write about my friends, family, and experiences, I turn over Carolyn's questions about ethics. A tape of her writer's voice plays: "[W]e constantly have to consider which questions to ask, which secrets to keep, and which truths are worth telling" (Ellis, 2007, p. 29). Because of Carolyn's words, I omit many interesting details in order to keep secrets that are not mine to share. I do this in the book (2017) and other pieces that portray my family, including "The Coal Miner's Daughter Gets a Ph.D." (2011b), which interrogates my sense of class inferiority; "Border Crossing: (Auto)Ethnography That Transcends Imagination/Immigration" (2012), in which I introduce my daughter Eowyn and her Mexican husband; and "The Baptism" (2013), which explores my role in the Spanish-speaking community now that I have a Mexican-American grandson.

Writing the book, I struggle with how to talk about the methodology I had developed organically: autoethnography combined with critical pedagogy as a way of examining my power and privilege as I work in marginalized and vulnerable Spanish-speaking communities. As I read Carolyn's work, I am always captivated by the conversations she and Art have to express ideas in a meaningful, conversational style. I decide to experiment with recalling conversations with my husband, Dan; to my surprise, I find I can explain the most intricate ideas in a way that is engaging and informative.

Carolyn massaged out the big knot beside my left shoulder blade as her voice spoke to me through multiple articles, unlocking my writing spirit enough to finish the book.

Carolyn's massages continue

Listening to Carolyn talk about retirement with other retiring and retired researchers at the 2016 ICQI, I reconsider my decision about retiring. I have coffee with Carolyn and share my thoughts. I feel encouraged by her comments: "You'll be able to keep doing the things you love. You just won't have to do some of the things you don't like." I sign the papers to begin phased retirement, meaning half-time responsibilities in teaching, research, and service, but also half pay! I read Carolyn's article, "A Meaningful Academic Life: Loving, Fulfilling, Challenging, and Flabbergasting" (2019). I remember our conversation when I read, "I no longer feel I have to defend what I do or what I think" (p. 248).

Spiritual and writing massages

Carolyn continues to massage my spiritual and writing muscles as I go beyond autoethnography to write a critical (auto)ethnography that begins with my oblivion to the repression around me as I pursued graduate studies in Spain in 1969 and 1970. After I met the older adults studying literacy in Barcelona, I started following a trail to help me understand the repressive society for all those who opposed the Franco regime. Carolyn's work on the Holocaust (Ellis, 2013, 2014, 2017, 2019) informs my work with people touched by Franco's legacy, which includes hundreds of concentration camps, with a half million people who either passed through or died, and 250,000 disappeared, many of them still missing. I learn the story I never knew I was living amidst when as a graduate student I visited Michener's (1968) tourist Spain of bullfights and flamenco dancers in *Iberia*. I only saw "sunny Spain," the vacationland of Europe. I process the interviews and experiences I have had during this scavenger hunt. Again, Carolyn is my masseuse as I try to organize and document three years of research.

I know Carolyn will massage the knots as they form and deepen while I work through the conundrum of how to write this next book.

Still on the massage table with Julie and Carolyn

I try to visit Julie once a month to work through the knots in my back. Now I relax into the massage table as she and I talk about the coronavirus quarantine. I had texted her to ask if I should still come, and she replied, "Yes, as long as you are comfortable with it and don't have any symptoms."

The soft Eastern music causes me to drift in and out of reality as I contemplate the completion of this chapter. I think about the trajectory of my career and the liminal moments of first reading Carolyn's work, then meeting her at the autoethnography workshop, and finally becoming her friend as well as her mentee. I was never her student in a university class, but I relate to her words about her students, that "[they] respond when you teach to the whole person, providing a loving space, and take into account their emotions, bodies, and spirit as well as their brains" (Ellis, 2019, p. 247). As Carolyn massaged out my doubts and confusion, she massaged the whole person.

Initially Carolyn's massages eased me away from the time I struggled alone, feeling hopeless. She brought me into a community that offers support, whether in person or in writing. As with Julie's massage, there are no perfumed oils or peppermint tea, but the effects are deeper and more lasting than those "relax and feel good" massages. Both offer deep, healing massages that soothe body and soul. Julie's strong fingers ease my back and neck pain as she loosens my frozen muscles so I can sleep at night. Now Carolyn's recent scholarship and emails serve as the strong massage fingers that loosen my frozen thoughts so that I can write and make sense of my world. The knots still happen, and the pain of thawing can still be intense, but I follow the massage of autoethnography to become free again.

References

Bochner, A. P., & Ellis, C. (2012). Into the garden of Illini: The International Congress as a house of being for qualitative inquiry. *International Review of Qualitative Inquiry 5*(1), 73–82. doi:10.1525/irqr.2012.5.1.73.

Ellis, C. (1993). There are survivors: Telling a story of sudden death. *The Sociological Quarterly, 34*(4), 711–730.

Ellis, C. (1996). Maternal connections. In C. Ellis & A. P. Bochner (Eds.), *Composing ethnography: Alternative forms of qualitative writing* (pp. 140–143). AltaMira Press.

Ellis, C. (2001). With mother/with child: A true story. *Qualitative Inquiry, 7*(5), 598–616. doi:10.1177/107780040100700505.

Ellis, C. (2002). Shattered lives: Making sense of September 11th and its aftermath. *Journal of Contemporary Ethnography, 31*(4), 375–410.

Ellis, C. (2003). Grave tending: With mother at the cemetery. *Forum Qualitative Sozialforschung, 4*(2). www.qualititive-research-net/fqs-t\\\

Ellis, C. (2004). *The ethnographic I: A methodological novel about autoethnography.* AltaMira Press.

Ellis, C. (2007). Telling secrets, revealing lives: Relational ethics in research with intimate others. *Qualitative Inquiry, 13*(1), 3–29. doi:10.1177%2F1077800406294947.

Ellis, C. (2009). Telling tales on neighbors: Ethical quandaries in two voices. *International Review of Qualitative Research, 2*(1), 3–27. doi:10.1525/irqr.2009.2.1.3.

Ellis, C. S. (2011). Jumping on and off the runaway train of success: Stress and committed intensity in an academic life. *Symbolic Interaction*, *34*(2), 158–172. doi:10.1525/si.2011.34.2.158?seq=1.

Ellis, C. (2012). The procrastinating autoethnographer: Reflections of self on the blank screen. *International Review of Qualitative Research*, *5*(3), 333–339. doi:10.1525/irqr.2012.5.3.333.

Ellis, C. (2019). A meaningful academic life: Loving, fulfilling, challenging, and flabbergasting. *Educational Sciences: Interdisciplinary Studies*, *1* (8), 243–249. doi:10.18778/2450-4491.08.16.

Ellis, C., Allen, M., Bochner, A. P., Gergen, K. J., Gergen, M. M., Pelias, R. J., & Richardson, L. (2017). Living the post-university life: Academics talk about retirement. *Qualitative Inquiry*, *23*(8), 575–588. doi:10.1177/1077800417716392.

Ellis, C., & Rawicki, J. (2013). Collaborative witnessing of survival during the Holocaust: An exemplar of relational autoethnography. *Qualitative Inquiry*, *19*(5), 366–380. doi:10.1177/1077800413479562.

Ellis, C., & Rawicki, J. (2014). More than mazel?: Luck and agency in surviving the Holocaust. *Journal of Loss and Trauma: International Perspectives on Stress & Coping*, *19*(2), 99–120. doi:10.1080/15325024.2012.738574.

Ellis, C., & Rawicki, J. (2017). Remembering the past/anticipating the future: A professor from the while working class talks with a survivor of the Holocaust about our troubled world. *Qualitative Inquiry*, *24*(5), 323–337. https://doi.org 10.1177/10778004177413

Ellis, C., & Rawicki, J. (2019). The clean shirt: A flicker of hope in despair. *Journal of Contemporary Ethnography*, *48*(1), 3–15. doi:10.1177/0891241617696809.

Lawrence-Lightfoot, S., & Davis, J. H. (1997). *The art and science of portraiture*. Jossey-Bass.

Machado, A. (1995). *Poesías completas: Soledades, galerías, campos de Castilla*. (Edición M. Alvar). Austral.

Michener, J. (1968). *Iberia: Spanish travels and reflections*. Random House.

Tilley-Lubbs, G. A. (2011a). 4/16: Public tragedy collides with personal trauma. *Qualitative Inquiry*, *17*(2), 144–147. doi:10.1177/1077800410392334.

Tilley-Lubbs, G. A. (2011b). The coal miner's daughter gets a PhD. *Qualitative Inquiry*, *17*(9), 720–722. doi:10.1177/1077800411420669.

Tilley-Lubbs, G. A. (2012). Border crossing: (Auto)Ethnography that transcends imagination/immigration. *International Review of Qualitative Research*, *4*(4), 385–401. doi:10.1525/irqr.2011.4.4.385.

Tilley-Lubbs, G. A. (2013). The baptism. *Qualitative Research in Education*, *2*(1), 272–300. doi:10.4471/qre.2013.02.

Tilley-Lubbs, G. A. (2014). The inquisition/torture of the tenure track. *Creative Approaches to Research*, *8*(1), 85–101.

Tilley-Lubbs, G. A. (2017). *Re-assembly required: Critical autoethnography and spiritual discovery*. Peter Lang.

Tilley-Lubbs, G. A. (2019). Fear and silence meet ignorance. *The Ethnographic Edge*, *3*(1), 17–28. doi:10.15663/tee.v3i1.53.

9

CHANGING STORIES

A 20-year autoethnography

Elaine Bass Jenks

Stories change. And we change stories. Though, perhaps most importantly, stories change us. Storytellers age, audiences differ, content shifts. This story begins when I was introduced to autoethnography by Art Bochner and Carolyn Ellis over two decades ago. In 1999, I spent six weeks conducting an ethnography at a day camp for blind and visually impaired children. The "auto" part is that I was the parent of one of the legally blind campers (Jenks, 2002). I've been studying communication and visual impairment ever since.

Since I'm writing about how stories change, I'm going to change where my story begins. My story didn't actually start when I was first introduced to autoethnography by Art and Carolyn in 1997. My story started in my mentor's office that same year when we discussed private versus public research. Only that's not completely accurate either. My story begins even earlier. In 1990. With a dirty diaper. When my first child was ten weeks old, I was changing his diaper and instead of looking at me, his eyes were moving back and forth as if he were following a fly in the room. Except there wasn't a fly in the room. As a new mom, I called the doctor to ask about my son's eyes following a fly that wasn't there.

My family practitioner asked if I could bring my son in for an appointment the next day. After he examined my son, the doctor explained that he'd asked to see my son right away because the symptom I described can be a sign of a brain tumor. But since the doctor's exam determined there was nothing else wrong with my son except for his moving/shaking eyes, my family practitioner suggested I take my son to a pediatric ophthalmologist. It took six weeks to get in to see the specialist, so my son was four months old by then. In addition to his eyes moving as if they were following things that weren't in the room, my son's eyes were crossed. The pediatric ophthalmologist diagnosed my son with strabismus (crossed eyes) and nystagmus (moving/shaking eyes) and said that my son's vision would be about 20/30 or 20/40.

I'm going to stop this story for a moment to talk about measuring visual acuity. Most of us have heard of 20/20 vision. We use that term, as in the saying "hindsight is 20/20," to mean perfect vision. Many people in the world don't have 20/20 vision, but they can get eyeglasses or contact lenses that correct their vision to 20/20. We actually have two types of vision, distance vision referring to things we see far away from us and near vision referring to things we see up close. Usually when we say 20/20, we're referring to distance vision. Think about an eye chart. When you're asked to read an eye chart in a doctor's office, you're positioned 20 feet away from the chart. That's what the first 20 means. The test is examining your ability to identify a letter of a certain size from a distance of 20 feet (American Optometric Association, 2019). If you can read the letters on a particular line of the eye chart, you have 20/20 or "normal" visual acuity. If you can only read the one big fat letter (usually an "E") (now sometimes a row of big letters) at the top of the eye chart, even with glasses on, then your vision is 20/200. The physical difference between 20/20 vision and 20/200 vision is that a person with 20/200 vision has to be ten times closer to an object to see it than a person with 20/20 vision.

The social implication of the physical difference between these two numbers is that the person with 20/200 vision is considered legally blind (American Foundation for the Blind, 2017). Notice that legal blindness is not defined as living in the dark. It's defined as having vision that is approximately ten times worse than normal. People are considered blind starting at 20/200. Visual acuity can actually be measured up to 20/800. After 20/800 visual perception is recorded as the ability, at a certain number of feet, to see hand motions or to perceive light (Texas School for the Blind and Visually Impaired, 2019). Of the ten million people in the United States who are considered blind or visually impaired, only 130,000 of these individuals (1.3%) have no light perception (American Foundation for the Blind, 2019). When sighted people imitate blind people, they close their eyes or put on blindfolds to mimic being in the dark. But that's imprecise because only a very small portion of the blind population can't see anything.

Back to my story. Only before we go back, I need to point out that at the time my son was four months old and I'd been reassured that he would have only slightly lower than perfect vision, I didn't know any of the details about visual acuity that I just wrote above. It's hard to tell a story about who you were then without including who you are now. Now I'm a full professor who researches and teaches communication and disability, specifically blindness and visual impairment. But at this point in the story, I was a new assistant professor with a four-month-old child whose eyes were crossed and shaking.

I remember doing research on strabismus and nystagmus, but the articles I found were written by ophthalmologists for ophthalmologists leaving me with questions. I brought the articles and my questions to the pediatric eye doctor. But instead of answering my questions, he said, "Where did you get this information?" I explained I was a university professor and I got the information through my university's library database. This was the beginning of being both a mom and a researcher.

When my son was eight months old, this same pediatric ophthalmologist performed a surgery to correct my son's crossed eyes. The surgery went well, and my son's eyes were much straighter and shook less. Only when my son was about a year old, I noticed his right eye flicking out sometimes. I accidentally caught this eye movement in a photograph, and I brought the photograph to an appointment. The response I got was not what I expected. The pediatric ophthalmologist looked at the photo, handed it back to me, and said, "Don't take his picture from that angle." That response made me realize that what I'd considered an inquiry was being perceived as an insult to the surgery that had been performed. Moreover, I was now being framed as not only a mom who shouldn't do research, but also as a mom who shouldn't worry so much. And the nervous mother frame is exceptionally difficult to escape.

I escaped by getting a job at a different university in a different state and needing a different pediatric ophthalmologist. I didn't take the new job to change eye doctors. That was just a bonus. Especially because one of the very first sentences the new pediatric ophthalmologist said to me was, "I'm worried about that right eye moving out." I felt like cheering out loud. On the other hand, I really shouldn't have been cheering my intuition because I was very unaware of how low my son's visual acuity was. I had no idea that when I walked ahead of him, he quickly lost sight of me and had to walk toward me based solely on the sound of my voice. I had very few suspicions that my son's visual acuity was seriously different from anyone else's until the day we brought his younger brother home from the hospital. His fully-sighted younger brother, propped up on the corner of the couch, followed me with his eyes—up the stairs, around the room, across the table—highlighting the fact that my oldest son followed me nowhere with his eyes.

It was this second pediatric ophthalmologist who gave my son his first self-report vision test. Infants don't have the language to report what they're seeing, but young children can indicate through pictures what they can see. I didn't just watch my then three-year-old son take his first self-report vision test. I watched him fail that test. I watched my son not seeing what I could see. More surprising was what the pediatric ophthalmologist said to me after that first eye exam. The doctor said, "I'd like you to take your son for an evaluation by a school for the blind." I can't begin to explain how off-topic that sentence sounded to me. It was like someone asking if I wanted fries with my shoes or ketchup on my computer. In fact, when the ophthalmologist first said my son needed to be evaluated at a school for the blind, I actually thought he was sending us to eye doctors at the school. When I realized he meant teachers, I was astounded that a doctor would be recommending we make an appointment with educators, non-medical professionals.

I think part of the reason I had trouble absorbing what the ophthalmologist was saying is that we had already been raising our son for three years. He'd gone through numerous developmental stages, from sitting up and rolling over to crawling, walking, and running. He learned to talk, dress himself, and dance to the *Jeopardy* theme. Plus, my son had participated in lots of activities that involve sight including looking at picture books, watching television, and drawing with crayons. Of course, I didn't know he couldn't see the fine detail in books; or mind that he sat close to the TV; or paid attention to the fact that he tended to draw in dark, bold colors. We had been raising our son. We hadn't been raising a child with an incurable, untreatable vision condition; a child who needed an appointment with educators at a school for the blind.

Besides feeling surprised, I remember feeling worried. It seemed as if the ophthalmologist were eliminating the possibility of medicine ever doing anything to help my son. I think my sensation was heightened by the fact that the ophthalmologist's recommendation was that we visit a school for the blind. The word "blind" had never been uttered in relation to my son before. Blind meant guide dogs, white canes, Braille, and Stevie Wonder wearing sunglasses. Actually, I didn't really know what blind meant. I just had a bunch of negative impressions of the word, none of which I wanted attached to my son.

But my son is blind. It turns out he's always been legally blind. That is, my son's visual acuity hasn't gotten any lower (or higher) since birth. But that line—the one between "Oh, he can't see that far" and "He's legally blind" has changed. The line moved from wearing glasses to needing mobility training. The other side of that line included attending school with an Individualized Educational Plan, an itinerant teacher, and large print. That line, that turning point, that difference, that word "blind," changed everything. Including my story.

On the most basic level, I went from being a parent to being a parent of a child with a disability. I'd always been the parent of a child with a disability. I just hadn't known it. This highlights that fact that we don't know parts of our own stories. And at first, I avoided the language. I said, "visual impairment" or "can't see" instead of "legally blind" or "disability." I learned my son had an underlying retinal condition whose symptoms included strabismus and nystagmus, making that first pediatric ophthalmologist's diagnosis accurate but incomplete. My son was mainstreamed into regular school starting in kindergarten. But at the age of six, he also started attending a summer day camp for blind and visually impaired children.

About this time, in 1997, three things occurred that turned me into an auto-ethnographer of communication and disability, that changed me from a mom who did research into a researcher-mom, that marked the true beginning of this 20-year auto-ethnography. First, I received tenure. Instead of having to produce research, I had a moment to think. Second, I took a National Communication Association (NCA) Preconference called "Interpretive and Narrative Ethnography" that was taught by Arthur Bochner and Carolyn Ellis. Third, I had a series of conversations with my mentor, William K. Rawlins. Bill Rawlins was already part of this story. I just haven't mentioned him yet. Bill Rawlins was one of my graduate school professors and the director of my dissertation in the late 1980s. By the late 1990s, Bill had become my mentor and close friend. The extra connection here is that once upon a time Art Bochner directed Bill Rawlins' dissertation. When my son was three years old and the new pediatric ophthalmologist said my son's vision was never going to be normal or improve, Bill offered to fly across the country and teach my classes while my family and I adjusted to the news. I didn't take him up on the offer, but that gesture is emblematic of his generosity that continues to this day.

In 1997, Bill and I had a series of conversations about what I wanted to study post-tenure. I'd been studying doctor-patient communication. Bill knew I had done a lot of research about my son's visual impairment. Bill knew I talked to my son's ophthalmologist about my research. Bill suggested I consider making my private research public. I was initially resistant to that idea. The research on visual impairment was just for me, not for anyone else. Bill patiently talked through the possibilities of how what I was studying could be useful for others. About how I might enjoy studying a topic professionally that was so important to me personally.

We also talked about how I might protect my son while writing about him. In my early work, I used a pseudonym for my son, but found the fake name jarring to read. The choice I ended up making is that I don't name my son. "My son" is both specific to my life, but also becomes potentially anyone with a disability—perhaps you or someone you know, someone you love, someone you've met, someone you've seen, someone you want to say hello to, someone you wished you'd spoken to, someone you won't be scared of next time.

With Bill's encouragement to make my private research public, with Art and Carolyn's excitement for this new form of ethnography, and with the freedom of tenure, in 1997 I became a researcher of communication and disability, focusing on blindness and visual impairment. First, I read about the topic for two years. Then in 1999, I did my first autoethnographic study at the six-week day camp my son attended. And in 2002, an essay about my experiences of taking fieldnotes at that camp was published by Art and Carolyn in their book *Ethnographically Speaking: Autoethnography, Literature, and Aesthetics*.

While I had made some of my private research public and while I had produced an autoethnography about fieldnotes at my son's day camp, I still didn't completely embrace everything Art and Carolyn had written about autoethnography. In order to explain this more clearly, I'm going to reproduce part of that camp essay here:

> One of the camp field trips was to take a ride on a restored, open-air train. I sat next to Doug (a totally blind camper) and across from two sighted teen volunteers and Patty (a visually impaired camper). At one point during the ride, I saw that we were coming up to a gigantic U.S. American flag that looked to me as if it were painted in a field. The train conductor announced that it was a flag made out of red, white, and blue petunias. My notes read:
>
> It's an amazing sight. I say, "I'm not sure how far you can see, Patty, but there's going to be a big American flag in a field in a minute." She leans and looks. "Is it white?" she asks. "Yes," I say.
>
> In the margin of that page, I later wrote: I wonder why I pointed out the flag to her. If she just saw white on a field, what was the point?
>
> When I reread that portion of my notes, I feel hot with embarrassment. I feel as if I enacted one of the very stereotypes I'm trying to dispel with my research. That is, I, as a sighted individual, viewed a visually impaired individual as missing something. In this case, what she was missing was a flower flag in a field. The unimportance of the object she didn't see just

increases my sensation of humiliation. I could have just told Patty about the flowers in the shape of the flag because, after all, I didn't expect Doug (the blind camper next to me) to even attempt to look at the flag. I could have told her in a way that sighted people appreciate hearing about things in outer space or deep under water even though we've never seen them ourselves.

My point here is that my fieldnotes describe what I saw, heard, and sometimes, thought, but not what I felt. My choice to omit emotions brings me back to my initial hesitancy about calling myself an autoethnographer. Ellis and Bochner (2000) state, "Most social scientists ... are not sufficiently introspective about their feelings or motives. ... Not everybody is comfortable or capable of dealing with emotionality. Those who aren't probably shouldn't be doing this kind of research" (p. 738, 754).

As a newcomer to this perspective, I don't understand why emotionality is so central. I believe the reader learns about sighted people's assumptions about visually impaired people from my flower flag example whether or not the reader knows I felt hot with embarrassment. The main point of my example is that sighted people are often the ones pointing out what blind/visually impaired people aren't seeing and that perhaps sighted people should think twice about their choices. The main point of my example is not my feelings. The goal of my example is to attempt to connect "the personal to the cultural" (Ellis & Bochner, 2000, p. 739).

And later in the essay, I wrote:

Lesson #3:
    Rereading my field notes has shown me that I don't agree with Ellis and Bochner's (2000) statement that "the real work" of autoethnography begins when "you think you can't stand the pain anymore" because I don't believe "connecting the personal to the cultural" has to involve "emotional pain" (pp. 738–739). I do agree with Ellis and Bochner (2000) that auto-ethnography is a place where social scientists can examine "the contradictions they experience" (p. 738). Real life is messy and even those who write about the self's experience change over time.

Much to my surprise, two years later in 2004, Carolyn wrote about a conversation she had with Art in her book *The Ethnographic I: A Methodological Novel About Autoethnography*:

"Lainey Jenks took issue with my association of pain with autoethnography. In her piece on doing research at her son's school for visually impaired kids, she makes a case that autoethnography doesn't have to be emotional and painful."
    "Though Lainey has suffered greatly because of her son's visual impairment."

"I know, but she doesn't talk about that in her piece," I respond.

"Maybe it's too hard for her," Art says, "or she needs to defend herself against the pain."

"Or she just doesn't want to write about that."

"And what she does is still legitimate autoethnography," says Art.

(pp. 110–111)

I've described above feeling hot with embarrassment in 1999 when I reflected on trying to describe that white flower field to a visually impaired camper. But that fieldnote embarrassment was nothing compared to how humiliated I felt when I first read this published conversation between Art and Carolyn that discusses my essay. Why was I being publicly shamed? Why didn't they just say what they thought to me privately? Why were those words not written in an email? Or told to me at a conversation over coffee at NCA that Art generously makes time to have with me?

At first, I was really upset. Let's pause here to note the irony of feeling a lot of emotion over me being called out for not writing about emotion. I was so upset that when I went to write the essay you're reading, I looked back in my computer files and found the drafts of three emails to Art and Carolyn where I ask them why they couldn't have criticized me in private instead of in print? But all of my drafts were unsent. I never said a word to either of them that I'd even read the words in Carolyn's book.

Because here's one of the best parts of changing stories: Reframing is always possible. When I look carefully at Art and Carolyn's published conversation now, I realize that they might not have been trying to embarrass me. They might have been trying to do what they wrote about earlier—connect the personal to the cultural. They might have been using what I said in my essay to point out to others that there are multiple "legitimate" ways to approach autoethnography. That the inclusion of emotion is a choice. And that the exclusion of emotion doesn't make the work any less autoethnographic. Let me highlight here that Art and Carolyn are the people who published my fieldnote camp essay to begin with, the essay that disagreed with what they'd written about emotion. Carolyn and Art had the courage to publish a piece that questioned them at the very time they were articulating, defining, and defending their ideas. This reframing is a perfect example of how stories change.

I find that the continuous nature of studying what I live produces ongoing change. Over the past twenty years, I've moved from just learning about the topic of communication and disability to conducting research and designing a course I teach on the subject (e.g., Jenks, 2005, 2017). I've also changed as a mom as my son has grown. I've moved from the mom of a toilet-training preschooler, who was told by vision professionals to make the water blue to produce a contrast between the white floor and the white toilet, through the mom of a braces-wearing preteen, who had a discussion with the orthodontist about getting a dif-ferent type of dental floss because the thread-through-the-plastic-needle type was impossible for my son to see, to the mom of a non-driving young adult who got a call from the insurance agency wanting to know why my son wasn't on the policy.

Not only is the life I study continuously changing, but the research I conduct is changing my life. The minute I began to reflect on my experience as the parent of a visually impaired child, I was no longer just living my life as the parent of a visually impaired child. I began to continuously analyze my own and others' communicative choices. When I meet blind individuals, their family members, or people who work with individuals who are blind, I ask about their experiences talking about visual impairment in school, work, athletic, social, family, and friendship settings. I'm not certain I wouldn't be having some of these conversations even if I weren't researching the topic. But I find I steer my interactions toward the issues I'm studying, thus, changing the life experiences I'm researching.

To summarize:

Stories change.

- The storyteller gets to choose where the story starts (and where it ends) (and what to include in the middle).
- We don't know parts of our own stories.
- Stories have turning points.
- Some turning points change the whole story.

We change stories.

- It's hard to tell a story about who you were then without including who you are now.
- Reframing is always possible.

Stories change us.

- The continuous nature of studying what I live produces ongoing change.
- The research I conduct is changing my life.

One of the problems with even telling you this story is that as soon as I say my son is legally blind, I have reduced my son to his visual acuity. He is so much more than his eyesight. Besides being an athlete and a saxophone player, my son is currently writing his doctoral dissertation on the intersection of politics and disability. My son is also a member of the 2016 silver-medal-winning USA Men's Goalball Team in Rio de Janeiro, Brazil, making me a mom who has been to the Paralympics, and a mom who has co-authored an article on communication and elite blind athletes with my now 29-year-old son (Jenks & Jenks, 2015). The same son who was an eight-year-old camper during that first autoethnographic inquiry. The son I have written about for 20 years now sometimes writes with me.

Oh, yes, stories change.

References

American Foundation for the Blind (2019). Low vision and legal blindness: Terms and descriptions. Retrieved from www.afb.org/blindness-and-low-vision/eye-conditions/low-vision-and-legal-blindness-terms-and-descriptions.

American Foundation for the Blind (2017). Key definitions of statistical terms. Retrieved from www.afb.org/research-and-initiatives/statistics/key-definitions-statistical-terms

American Optometric Association (2019). Visual acuity? What is 20/20 vision? Retrieved from www.aoa.org/patients-and-public/eye-and-vision-problems/glossary-of-eye-and-vision-conditions/visual-acuity.

Ellis, C. (2004). *The ethnographic I: A methodological novel about autoethnography*. Alta Mira Press.

Jenks, E. B. (2017). Creating a college course on communication and disability. In M. S. Jeffress (Ed.), *Pedagogy, Disability and Communication: Applying Disability Studies in the Classroom*, pp. 11–29. Routledge.

Jenks, E. B. (2005). Explaining disability: Parents' stories of raising children with visual impairments in a sighted world. *Journal of Contemporary Ethnography*, *34*(2), 143–169.

Jenks, E. B. (2002). Searching for autoethnographic credibility: Reflections from a mom with a note pad. In A. Bochner and C. Ellis (Eds.), *Ethnographically Speaking: Autoethnography, Literature, and Aesthetics*, pp. 170–186. Alta Mira Press.

Jenks, E. B., & Jenks, A. B. (2015). An inside look at an invisible paralympic sport: Giving voice to goalball athletes' lived experiences. In D. Jackson, C. Hodges, M. Molesworth, & R. Scullion (Eds.), *Reframing Disability? Media, (Dis)Empowerment and Voice in the London Paralympics*, pp. 218–232. Routledge.

Texas School for the Blind and Visually Impaired (2019). Visual acuity testing/measurement: Making sense of the numbers. Retrieved from www.tsbvi.edu/visual-acuity-testingmeasurement-making-sense-of-the-numbers.

10

A ROSE BY ANOTHER NAME

Zen and the Art of Carolyn

Chris J. Patti

Back to the future of "autoethnography"

Mitch Allen (2020) made some prescient predictions about the future of auto-ethnography during a tribute to Art Bochner and Carolyn Ellis at the Symposium on Autoethnography and Narrative Inquiry in 2019.[1] He offered frank foresight in a shocking question: "What if "autoethnography" isn't used twenty years from now?" This chapter interprets Mitch's forewarnings by going beneath and beyond the labels and disciplinary boundaries of Art and Carolyn's stories and academic art. This chapter is after the eternal, ineffable elements of autoethnography and narrative inquiry: Zen[2] and the Art (Patti, 2012; Pirsig, 1974) of Carolyn.

As Shakespeare (2019/1595) wrote in Romeo and Juliet, "that which we call a rose [b]y any other name would smell as sweet." My sense is that even if the term[3] "autoethnography" isn't widely used years from now (Mitch's *worst case scenario*), the trailblazing legacies and influence of Arthur Bochner and Carolyn Ellis will live on. They are the global godparents of personal scholarship (Adams, Holman Jones, & Ellis, 2015),[4] having mentored generations of students and scholars who all bring their own bents to their teachings and projects; and we—their former-students-now-scholars—are rearing the generations to come, who will adapt, alter, poach (de Certeau, 1984), appropriate (Patti, 2015), and improve upon what we teach them (see, to name just a recent few: Adams, 2011; Arnold, 2020; Boylorn, 2013; Berry, 2008; Dunn, 2018: Henson, 2019; Patti, 2013; Paxton, 2018; Purnell, in press; Roscoe & Tullis, 2015; Tillmann, 2015).

This is our *true vocation*, as professors, in the deepest sense of the term (Bringhurst, 2008). As Gayatri Spivak said publicly when she visited Appalachian State University, the project of higher education is about *the slow cooking of the human soul.* Aesthetically and academically, Art and Carolyn are soul singers (Holman Jones, 2007; Patti, 2015b) helping to slow-cook soul food made from the complexities and challenges of life, love, and loss—for the purpose of raising human consciousness and cultivating compassion (Berry & Patti, 2015; Bochner, 2014; Boylorn, 2013; Ellis, 1993; Patti, 2015a; Tillmann, 2009). Examining the ethic/aesthetic mark of Art and Carolyn involves looking both backward and forward from the standpoint of the present, bringing together a realization of inherent, unstoppable change and the kind of human immortality that comes with sharing one's knowledge[5] (Vico, 1980/1732).[6] But I guess that's the kind of perspective you'd expect from an agnostic Buddhist still reading about Jungian archetypes[7] (Green, 2018; Patti, 2012).

What's in a name?

I must admit, I'm a bit of a recluse, a performing-hermit to be specific. I live on the side of a mountain a half-hour outside of Boone, North Carolina, in the village of Sugar Mountain. The black bears are brave this time of year, preparing for winter, and one likes to walk across our deck in the wee hours of the night. Sometimes the bear knocks on the front door. Bee, my adopted bluenose pit-bull, lets me know when our bear gets too close.

I recently became a tenured professor in the Department of Communication at Appalachian State University. I mention this because living in the beautiful and troubled rural, southern Appalachian Mountains has changed my perspective on a lot of things—including language. I'm from Southern California originally, and even though I'm a Californian at heart, I've never felt more at home than here in the mountains of Western North Carolina. Part of my tenure bid at Appalachian was to note that I look somewhat like our mascot Yosef, and that my middle name is Joseph.[8] I embody the Mountaineers' *ethos* and the warning of the North Carolina state motto: *Esse Quam Videri*, to be rather than to seem. Sometimes, when you're in the right place, things resonate and you are what you seem to be.

Being in the Blue Ridge Mountains of North Carolina and meeting a good variety of folks, I wasn't surprised by the results of the 2016 election. I'm guilty of hanging out more with "blue collar" folks than with other professors. I'm happy to have made a few pagan friends recently. My kind of folks. Take for example my buddy Bluebell (Groome, 2019), who recently self-published what I'd label an autoethnographic book.[9] He made the front page of the local paper for his efforts.[10] My favorite part is, "Chapter 1: Language." Bluebell indexes a beautiful and funny ten-page chapter on the language of the region (pp. 12–22) that reads like an Appalachian dictionary written by Twain. Creatively, Bluebell is a force of nature, and he and I play music together. He sings and plays guitar, while I play drums and sing backup. Our buddy Cas uses my bass rig to round out the group. We call ourselves Bluebell and the Ringers and like to think we sound a bit like Tenacious D. My point is, people—smart, strange, and stellar people—speak differently in different places and contexts. "Autoethnography" is a fine term—in terms of academia, scholarship, and research.[11] It works. But, in terms of the way people speak, it's far from colloquial. Especially 'round these parts.

Bluebell and all these Appalachian pagans remind me of Carolyn Ellis. She too is a creative force of nature. She is from Luray, Virginia and is my academic+ mother. Her husband and soulmate, Art, is my academic+ father. Art, like me, is a coastal guy interested in theory and philosophy as well as a pragmatist existentialist. He even meditates. It's an eclectic and dynamic mix of sensibilities, of complementary and tensional gifts and liabilities, in these intellectual circles, isn't it? So, when I told Bluebell—a well-and-widely-read gentleman about ten years my senior—that I am an ethnographer, I was surprised he had never heard the term. In hindsight, I shouldn't have been surprised. It's a new word for most everybody I talk to around here.[12] I mention this because, while I love the terms ethnography and auto-ethnography, Art and Carolyn's legacies are about much more than specialized terms and contemporary methodological practices. *Apocalypse now* in terms of terms.

Considerations of possible futures

I'm a slow-cooker when it comes to writing, and many of the insights in this chapter come from the conference presentations I have done over the years reflecting on the work of Art and Carolyn.[13] However, it wasn't until I presented "Zen & the Art of Carolyn" and heard Mitch's presentation at the aforementioned symposium that I realized what to do with my thoughts. Allen (2020) makes clear that, even though autoethnography is still at the forefront of the "contemporary qualitative world" (p. 10), with "its own series, handbook, journal, and con-ference[14]" (p. 11), we would be wise to acknowledge "the fluidity of scholarly domains, the centrality of change, and the inability to predict the future of where the research tradition will go" (p. 10). Using his experience and expertise as a publisher and trained archeologist, Mitch forecasts five conceivable scenarios for the future of autoethnography.[15] Here I poach (de Certeau, 1984) insights from across these scenarios and address what Mitch calls the worst-case scenario—*extinction*—from a Buddhist perspective, as a way to situate my interpretation of the timeless and the timely within the art of Art and Carolyn.

It's all universal

Mitch's "Universal" (p. 11) scenarios show the natural appeal of autoethnographic and narrative inquiry exemplified in Carolyn and Art's writing: "It centers the scholar in the research" (Allen, 2020, p. 11). Art and Carolyn's work goes beyond the labels "autoethnography" and "narrative inquiry" because, at its core, it is universal to human experience. As long as earthlings have been telling stories, we've been telling personal stories—even academically. As Mitch (2020) argues, "personal feelings and professional observations were seamlessly blended," even in Darwin (p. 11). I was equally struck by this universality-of-the-personal during Spivak's talk at Appalachian State. Known widely as a critical feminist literary theorist and philosopher of the subaltern, she delivered an autoethnographic story of her fieldwork in a rural village in India. Her story was about the enormous privilege and honor she felt by being entrusted with the poetry of a participant-collaborator (for similar reflections, see Ellis & Patti, 2014; Ellis & Rawicki, 2012; Patti, 2015a).

While Spivak didn't use the term "autoethnography," she didn't need to. Art and Carolyn's work is part of the many waves and turns in the academy that we—students of the humanities and human sciences generally—were forced to read about in graduate school: the narrative, personal, feminist, reflexive, critical, ideological, indigenous, history-from-below, subaltern, postmodern, and post-structural to name a few. Art and Carolyn offered responses and contributions to these debates and contemporary academic developments (Bochner, 2001, 2009, 2012a, 2014; Bochner & Ellis, 1999; Ellis, 1998, 2008; Ellis & Bochner, 1996, 2002). Art and Carolyn are trail blazers (see, e.g., Bochner, 2014; Ellis, 2004; Ellis & Rawicki, 2012). They trampled disciplinary boundaries and became leading voices that helped to legitimize narrative and the personal as having scholarly merit and value. Their work gave us permission to listen to our own voices and share our own stories from our various and relative positions. Whether Spivak uses "auto-ethnography" or not is irrelevant. Because of scholars like Art and Carolyn, the personal, experiential, radically empirical, and narrative are now more widespread and legitimate than ever (see, for example, Pollan, 2018). And the terms and applications of autoethnographies, much like the fungi about which Pollan (2018) writes, are endless and generative.[16] Because of their distinguished careers, we all now get to write our own adventures at a time when listening to different voices is exactly what we need—culturally and academically.[17]

Contemporary nomadism

Mitch's (2020) "Village Raid" (p. 13) scenario identifies the inherent poaching and appropriation that occur in academic culture. This reminds me of de Certeau's (1984) notion of nomadic behavior in everyday life. The metaphor of the intellectual nomad fits well with the work of Art and Carolyn. Their books and articles are a chronicling of their travels, studies, experiences, relationships, transformational moments, and hard-earned insights (see, e.g., Bochner, 2014; Ellis, 1995). They, like the rest of us, are nomads trekking across a rapidly changing intellectual terrain (Bochner, 2014). But, because of their planning and the solid methodological and philosophical applicability of the tools they have given us, we are well equipped to navigate the unforeseeable and inherent changes that lie ahead. It will be a long while before artificial intelligence (AI) makes obsolete human poetry, art, and the humanities. Traditional statistics in the human sciences may not fare well, as narrow AI applications proliferate[18]. It's ever more important to explore humanism in the digital, global age[19]—so we have a chance to figure out how we *best* fit within the ecosystem, rather than how we can *most* dominate the planet (Bringhurst, 2008). Autoethnographic inquiry stimulates such existential and humanist questions, which seek to understand how we—you and I—relate to each other and the world around us—and how we can more compassionately and sustainably do so on a violent, overheating planet.

Regarding extinction: a Buddhist perspective

Mitch (2020) puts "autoethnography's" chance of survival at a conservative 20%. He writes, "All of the above are better options than the *Extinct Civilization Scenario*. Babylonians. Romans. Aztecs. Haven't seen them much on my newsfeed lately" (p. 14, italics in original). Well, as an agnostic Buddhist, extinction scenarios seem natural to me. I'd put our chance of survival at a more conservative 0%. Of course, I'm talking about the long-run. None of us makes it out alive. One day, the sun will swallow our planet. My point is, things fall apart (Chödrön, 1997). This is the nature of existence. And we're still talking about the Babylonians, Romans, and Aztecs long after they're gone. This is the sacred side of communication and what Art and Carolyn have given us—connecting one generation to the next (Ellis & Patti, 2014). Because of their "method," I've been able to share my father, who died of cancer at the age of 39, with hundreds of students and colleagues over the years (Patti, 2012; Paxton, 2018). He lives on in our stories—as will Art and Carolyn and all of us who will shuffle off this mortal coil. Art and Carolyn have done as much as any humans I know to immortalize themselves through the lives they've impacted and guided, both interpersonally and through their writing.

The timeless and timely in art and Carolyn

Quality, it's always hip

One of my favorite musical groups, the Oakland, California soul band Tower of Power, has a classic song called "What is Hip?"[20] In it, they sing: "'cause if you're really hip, the passing years will show." Art and Carolyn meet this definition of "hipness," and their legacy speaks to this kind of lasting relevance. In the spirit of Robert Pirsig (1974), they ask questions of *quality* and *value*—about what is *best* rather than what is *new*. Thus, in the face of change, I want to illustrate what I see as the eternal elements of the narrative and autoethnographic approaches of Art and Carolyn.

That's so meta

Their writing is always self-conscious and meta-aware (see, e.g., Bochner & Ellis, 2016; Ellis, 2004). Their aesthetic is a bit like the character Deadpool,[21] constantly reflecting back on itself and its ethics, breaking the sixteenth wall, telling stories within stories, constructing imaginary workshops from years of real workshops, speaking directly to the audience. This, I believe, is one of the main elements that attracts us self-identified tricksters to the party (Frentz, 2008; Patti, 2012).

Becoming other-wise

Further, I see Art and Carolyn's approach as a kind of contemporary invitation to an ecstatic dance desperately needed in our anxious and divided times (Ehrenreich,

2007). It's the dance between the reader and writer that can also foster a sense of *communitas* (Turner, 1988): the dance of self and other in which we lose ourselves in another's story, reading *with* its authors, getting lost, for a time, in someone else's lives, worlds, and words (de Certeau, 1984). Art and Carolyn's approach to writing the autoethnographic life is a dialogical, relational interplay of self and other, experience and story. Their writing embodies a wholehearted (Behar, 1996; Brown, 2012) ethic of being humane while studying human life and listening *with* an-other's story. In the end, sharing stories is about cultivating compassion with others, a connection with an-other, any-other, becoming other-wise (Conquergood, 1991; Berry & Patti, 2015). It's one of those ecstatic ways we get out of our own abstractions, theories, stereotypes, generalizations, fictions, aggregated models, and heads and come into intimate contact with the particularities of someone else's life as rendered. Through autoethnography, we aim to humanize *each other*. There are few acts more radically human, humane, and humanizing than reading with another's story and writing one's own.

Evoking life's difficulties

Next, their work is often evocative of the messiness of *life itself* (Ellis, 1996; Patti, 2015). Art and Carolyn show us how to write stories that call out and call forth, stories that summon and rouse our curiosities and senses of self and other, that compel us to recognize the difficult and necessary things in life. Theirs are hard-wrought stories of experience that awaken us to the complicated unknowability of life—the joys and sorrows, transformations and traumas beyond the grasp of language (Ellis, 1995). Art and Carolyn's work affects both the heart and the head, allowing the written word to break boundaries within and beyond universities and universes of experience. They bring the specificities of experience to bear on eternal questions of why we're here, why we suffer, how we can suffer well and in solidarity, and how we can understand ourselves and each other a little better, through practicing the simple-but-not-easy art of *listening generously* (Hanh, 2014).

Existentialism in dialogue

Art's story of growing up in urban Pittsburgh contrasts Carolyn's childhood in Appalachia (Bochner & Ellis, 2016). Both of their stories search for belonging, and Art's has his familiar existential tone (Bochner, 2014). What's real in this life, Art and those of our philosophy suggest, is our experience, what we touch and see. "I can see now," he writes, "that Camus was pointing me toward meaning, feeling, and empathy within the concrete human experience of suffering and trauma" (Bochner & Ellis, 2016, p. 32). This ethic is at the heart of their art. Meditating on experience and suffering leads us back to compassion for ourselves and others, and Art and Carolyn call for us to empathize, identify, and feel a sense of solidarity with others. They achieve this through dialogue about the meaning of life.

Critically (self)aware

Their ethic of (auto)ethnography is related to Conquergood (1991) and Boylorn and Orbe (2017):

1. that democratic/dialogic interaction between researchers/participants is sought;
2. that writers share and balance voices of self and other;
3. that we give something back to the communities we study;
4. that we are accountable to each other and those communities; and
5. that readers themselves are co-participants in this process.

Art and Carolyn's work is interpersonal at its core. These interpersonal lessons are not only for those conducting research or writing a particular research story. They extend to readers as well. We often fail to *really listen* to the stories and the people in our lives in the way Art and Carolyn call for (Patti, 2015). We would be wise to ask better questions of the stories we read and hear. "You should be asking," to use Art's (Bochner & Ellis, 2016) words, "How can I get into this story, not what can I get out of it?" (p. 219). Ethical ethnography is about approaching others *on their own terms* and understanding them *in their own terms* as best we can. This ethic applies to both life and method.

Gentle with each other

Art and Carolyn (Bochner & Ellis, 2016) define compassionate, interpersonal research as "researchers and participants work[ing] collaboratively, sharing authority and responsibility. They listen deeply to, speak responsibly with, feel passionately for, share vulnerably with, and connect relationally and ethically to each other with care" (p. 156). As someone who studies compassion and suffering and invites the personal stories of students in my classroom, I appreciate what a delicate business this is. I have seen occasions where this level of vulnerability seems *required* of students by their well-intentioned professors, and it is my firm position that *we ought to always give students **outs and creative options** when inviting them to go personal*. Vulnerability should be encouraged, but not demanded. Each of us and our students are at different places with the suffering in our lives, and not all of us are "ready to go there." We are wise to respect silences, unspeakability, and personal boundaries as much as the stories told (Patti, 2013).

Transformational insights

While there are risks, we also know the transformational potential of such vulnerable inquiry. Through compassionate interaction, writing, and reflection, such work seeks to generate insight, new (re)visions, wisdom, and clarification, planting seeds of transformation and cultivating their fruits (Ellis, 2008). Like Art (Bochner, 2012b) and Leonard Cohen say of life, "like a bird on a wire … I have tried in my way to be free." Art and Carolyn's stories are the sustenance needed for us to become more aware of our own and others' consciousnesses and lives—our quests to know ourselves and each other better, in order to be a light unto ourselves and one another, in order to be free. That's about as classic as existential quests get, and Art and Carolyn are in good company in such timeless pursuits (Vico, 1980/1732).

Hitting home

Theirs are stories for those of us struggling with the myriad hardships, realities, and difficulties of life. As I look back and try to move forward, I find myself calling on my mentors and their stories and the community they have built. Art and Carolyn's work, like a friend, is there for us, especially during the difficult times. Theirs are stories that are alive and enlivening, stories that vivify and inspire. They have the power to exercise ghosts and demons and speak across the generations in the moments we gather to share them. They speak back to and across the divides that are fracturing our society today, putting us in conversation with people who are different from and other than ourselves. They soothe the soul, humanizing us in all our complexity, giving us strength to face what life throws at us.

All that jazz

At its most basic, Carolyn and Art's storytelling exemplifies what John Dewey (1988/1922) calls an "artistic habit" (p. 48). Carolyn and Art are like scholarly jazz musicians. Artistic habits are built over decades of applied, conscious effort, mechanism, and practice. But what makes them *artistic* (rather than merely mechanistic and routine), is precisely that they *continually adapt themselves to the exigencies of the present moment*. In Dewey's (1988/1922) words, "The genuine heart of reasonableness (and of goodness in conduct) lies in effective mastery of the conditions which *now* enter into action" (p. 48). Art and Carolyn's stories—and practices of storytelling—help us to act more reasonably *now*, in the present, in everyday life and interaction. And in that sense, they help us learn and grow and act more morally *now*, in this very moment. They are constantly adapting, updating, reframing, revising, reimaging, rethinking, repurposing, recasting, and recreating in their stories (Ellis, 2008). Each new story further opens us to letting go of the storylines to which we have clung (Chödrön, 1997), because we know there is always more to tell and hear, more to consider, and more to evoke, explore, and unsettle. The writing of Art and Carolyn helps me to cope in the middle of the storm. Their work gets me out of my head and helps me come to my senses, putting things back in perspective. In this sense, their stories provide peace of mind, so I can meet and welcome this moment with greater presence and awareness.

Romeo and Juliet of the human sciences

Art and Carolyn are a *comic* version of Romeo and Juliet in the human sciences (Bochner, 2014), a couple of star-crossed lovers from different disciplines who were somehow able to unite the feuding families of the humanities and social sciences, art and science, body and mind, self and other (Dewey, 1988/1922). By writing about love and loss their work strikes at the core of storytelling and *why* we still tell stories in a changing world. Their scholarship transcends disciplinary categories and boundaries. To my heart and mind, their ethic/aesthetic cares less about labels and specialized terminologies than about making sense of life itself.[22] The art of Art and Carolyn is about creatively facing our struggles and limitations to poetically render the chaos of experience (Langer, 2006; Vonnegut, 2007).[23] Through coming-to-terms with each other as best we can, over and over again, we learn, heal, and make a bit more sense of (human) life in an endless multiverse of vast and senseless unknowability.

Becoming a Laguna Hillbilly[24]

It's been a strange and winding road, getting here to the village of Sugar Mountain, North Carolina, having begun my journey in the city of Laguna Hills, California. The 1970s duplex I have been renting for the past number of years is situated on the side of a ridge at higher than 4,500 feet, almost as high as it gets here in the Southeast. The half-mile unpaved road that ends at my place connects to another half-mile unpaved road, which then connects to the main road. My renovation/ repair-minimalist landlord has neglected to maintain the steep, unpaved road for years, and it's now more of a creek bed than a road. Even with an all-wheel-drive vehicle and snow-and-ice tires, the neighbors and I often have to park our cars a quarter mile away and hike to the apartment during winter months. Sometimes the snow means parking a half mile away. Once, it was a mile. Those January mornings when it is below zero and the wind is howling—when I have to get suited up in full snowboarding attire, with teaching clothes underneath, and hike—are the mornings I feel most alive.

These days, having *gone native* here in the rural south, I sometimes refer to myself as a "Beverly Hillbilly in reverse," or a "Laguna Hillbilly." Southern Appalachia isn't the most likely place for an upper-middle-class, white (Italian-Irish/Puerto Rican), ivory collar dude from Orange County to end up. But, on my first visit, I fell in love with the university and its surroundings. Being here reminded me of visiting Big Bear, California as a kid and brought back memories of being outdoors and camping with my dad and brother–some of my most cherished memories. They are memories of when I first climbed rocks, played in the snow, hiked, tested my limits, and learned to appreciate nature.

Being in the Blue Ridge Mountains brought back a sense of awe and wonder that I experienced growing up. As a professor, I try to bring this awe and wonder, this curious awareness, to my students. Here at home, "at the retreat," I am free to ponder life and the experiences of the Holocaust survivors with whom I have spoken, and to profess in the undisciplined gymnasium of undergraduate education.[25] I get to work directly with passionate and talented students and colleagues, spreading the good word of compassionate communication across difference. And I get to pretend that I am Phaedrus from *Zen and the Art of Motorcycle Maintenance*, a professor of rhetoric at a mountain college who falls down the rabbit hole and comes out the other side. None of this would have been possible without the support, encouragement, inspiration, example, and mentorship of Carolyn and Art.

As an ethnographer, I am drawn to the cultural and environmental richness and complicatedness of life in rural Appalachia. Like Southern California, Southern Appalachia comes with more than its fair share of stereotypes. I came loaded with my own ideas, assumptions, and presumptions—despite my best efforts to practice beginner's mind. In the end, this place stole my heart and shattered my expectations. One of my favorite things about the people I know here is that the usual dichotomies of left/right, so common in the media, don't seem to apply very well. As a particularly Appalachian example of what I'm talking about, on a local farm tour,[26] I once witnessed a politically conservative, many-generations local farmer who lived next to a politically liberal, first-generation sustainable farmer. They were friends, and most nights they broke bread and smoked cannabis together as equals. The farmers seemed to agree a lot more than they disagreed.

There is so much beauty here, and there is so much suffering. Watauga and Avery Counties, where I live and work, have some of the highest income and wealth disparities of anywhere in the United States. According to Census.gov,[27] 21.2% of people in Watauga County live in poverty (compared to 8.59%[28] where I grew up). Watauga County has a per capita/median household income of $24,906/$45,268 (compared to $48,377/$98,168 where I grew up). While the poverty is severe where I now live, so is the wealth. This area (Sugar Mountain and Banner Elk, North Carolina) is also vacation-home to some tremendously wealthy individuals, the class of people who *own* mountains and fly in to the local private airstrip on private jets and helicopters.

I can describe the socioeconomics of where I live in one image. Once again, it's the ridge on which I live. Three socioeconomic classes are stratified along the ridge: the trailers, mobile homes, and small houses at the bottom (some long abandoned and reclaimed by the wild); the lower-middle to upper-middle class dwellings like mine in the middle (in various states of repair, from well-maintained to partially rotted); and the few elite, upper-class vacation properties and estates at the top. All the properties at the top are meticulously maintained, despite being visited only about twice a year by their owners. I enjoy walking around there, through the bizarre and grotesquely opulent ghost town. From that high up, one can see to the other side of the ridge, taking in spectacular views of Profile Trail and Grandfather Mountain.

My landlord tells those who move in stories about the large estate across the valley, atop the adjacent ridge overlooking Sugar Mountain. He claims it's owned by Michael Jordan: "Michael Jordan's fourteenth house in North Carolina," he says. The story goes that Mr. Jordan may have never even been to the property. My landlord does say that he himself has seen the house when it was being built. My landlord tells of an enormous fireplace made completely of dinosaur fossils. From where I sit and type, the house reminds me of one I have seen many times as a kid, "the cocaine mansion," as my friends and I called it—a palatial estate set atop the cliffs above 1,000 Steps Beach in Laguna. 1,000 Steps was my favorite beach as a kid.

Notes

1 I owe a debt of gratitude to Mitch Allen for his presentation at the 2019 Symposium on Autoethnography and Narrative Inquiry in St Petersburg, FL. I'd also like to thank Mitch for sending me the pre-published manuscript of his article, which appeared in the inaugural issue of the *Journal of Autoethnography*. In addition, I cannot offer enough thanks to Tony Adams, Robin Boylorn, and Lisa Tillmann for their mentorship and guidance over the years and for the opportunity to contribute to this collection. Most of all, I am overjoyed to thank Carolyn Ellis and Art Bochner for their academic parentage and for being family+. I love you all and owe my livelihood to knowing you and learning from your teaching, writing, and examples. I know I am far from alone.

2 In loving memory of Art & Carolyn's beloved dog(s).

3 Of course, I am referencing Burke here. T-screens, y'all! #COM1200

4 No reference needed. Google it. Thanks, Deadpool: https://tenor.com/view/blow-kiss-flying-kiss-kisses-kiss-mwa-gif-11696902

5 Shout-out to Dr. Scott Welsh for introducing me to Vico and the specific selections from de Certeau and Dewey.

6 The Dalai Lama too speaks of this kind of human immortality often, in similar terms as Giambattista Vico.

7 My line here is paraphrasing the Vico text, which is about the cultivation of "the heroic mind" for the betterment of humanity and the world. I see Art and Carolyn as exemplars of such heroic pursuits, and the line is meant to refer to them and all those involved in such heroic pursuits.

8 The lineage continues with my nephew's firsts name being Joseph. I'm hoping he'll consider attending Appalachian. Go 'neers!

9 *The Out of Towner's Guide Book to Happy Valley, NC.*

10 "Local artist writes Happy Valley guide" by Virginia Annable. July, 31, 2019. News-Topic: Proud to be Caldwell County's Local News Source Since 1875.

11 To be sure, most all specialized terminologies are cumbersome, colloquially speaking.

12 When I mentioned the term to my then girlfriend, also pagan and a friend of Bluebell's, she replied, "I'm pretty sure you're the only person who knows that term."

13 "Dancing Together: A Meta-meditation on Autoethnography." Part of a panel responding Arthur Bochner and Carolyn Ellis's book *Evocative Autoethnography*, Southern States Communication Association, April 8, Greenville, SC. Other insights in this essay are from my presentation of "Mindful Storytelling: Zen and the Art of Carolyn." Paper presented at the Symposium on Autoethnography and Narrative Inquiry: Reflecting on the Legacy of Carolyn Ellis and Art Bochner, January 4–5, 2019, St. Pete Beach, FL.

14 I poached this endnote from Allen (2020, p. 11), as it's the best, most concise list of Art and Carolyn's writing of which I am aware: "The series *Ethnographic Alternatives* (Alta-Mira, now Rowman & Littlefield) and *Writing Lives* (Left Coast, now Routledge) were both edited by Ellis and Bochner and based in autoethnography. Ellis also coedited with Stacy Holman Jones and Tony Adams (Holman Jones, Adams, and Ellis 2013) the *Handbook of Autoethnography*. The *Journal of Autoethnography* edited by Adams and Andrew Hermann is new in 2020, and a scholarly organization on autoethnography and narrative is being developed at the time of this writing."

15 1. Universal, 2. Isolated Tribe, 3. Village Raid, 4. Ziggurat, 5. Extinct Civilization.

16 I refuse to ramble about Paul Stamets: https://fungi.com/. That's a mycelial rabbit hole I'm no longer willing to ramble down.

17 I see a lot of turf wars in the academy. I think making the best use of personal experience is what the academy needs, and I think of Atul Gawande's book *Being Mortal* and Michael Pollan's *How to Change Your Mind* as examples of this.

18 Narrow applications of AI are designed for the kind of quantitive reasoning used in traditional, largely survey-based social science statistics, which, to my mind, presents a considerable threat to statistics as we know them in the social sciences.

19 www.youtube.com/watch?v=VAPbUXePmig

20 www.youtube.com/watch?v=V2y6yw8ZPPo
21 Or any character in the "multiverse" these days.
22 www.youtube.com/watch?v=Pk8KPdWgAJY
23 Vonnegut credits graphic artist Saul Steinberg for this insight. Kurt calls Saul the wisest person he ever met. Steinberg and Vonnegut suggest that what we respond to in any work of art is the artist's struggle against their limitations.
24 I use this as a term of endearment.
25 As well as some graduate education. My first doctoral dissertation advisee, John Henson, happens to also be my rock-climbing mentor.
26 Shout out to the Blue Ridge Women in Agriculture: www.brwia.org/
27 www.census.gov/quickfacts/wataugacountynorthcarolina
28 www.census.gov/quickfacts/fact/table/lagunahillscitycalifornia/INC110218

References

Adams, T. E. (2011). *Narrating the closet: An autoethnography of same-sex attraction.* Left Coast Press.

Adams, T. E., Holman Jones, S., & Ellis, C. (2015). *Autoethnography.* Oxford University Press.

Allen, M. (2020). The autoethnographer's ball, 2040. *Journal of Autoethnography, 1,* 9–15.

Arnold, A. (2020). Birthing autoethnographic philanthropy, healing, and organizational change. In A. Hermann (Ed.), *The Routledge international handbook of organizational autoethnography* (pp. 209–224). Routledge.

Behar, R. (1996). *The vulnerable observer: Anthropology that breaks your heart.* Beacon Press.

Berry, K. (2008). Promise in peril: Ellis and Pelias and the subjective dimensions of ethnography. *Review of Communication, 8,* 154–173.

Berry, K., & Patti, C. J. (2015). Lost in narration: Applying autoethnography. *Journal of Applied Communication Research, 43*(2), 263–268.

Bochner, A. P. (2001). Narrative's virtues. *Qualitative Inquiry, 7,* 131–157.

Bochner, A. P. (2009). Vulnerable medicine. *Journal of Applied Communication Research, 37,* 159–166.

Bochner, A. P. (2012a). On first-person narrative scholarship: Autoethnography as acts of meaning. *Narrative Inquiry, 22,* 156–164.

Bochner, A. P. (2012b). Bird on a wire: Freeing the father within me. *Qualitative Inquiry, 18*(2), 168–173.

Bochner, A. P. (2014). *Coming to narrative: A personal history of paradigm change in the human sciences.* Routledge.

Bochner, A. P., & Ellis, C. (1999) Which way do we turn? *Journal of Contemporary Ethnography, 3,* 229–237.

Bochner, A. P., & Ellis, C. (Eds.) (2002). *Ethnographically speaking: Ethnography, literature, and aesthetics.* AltaMira Press.

Bochner, A. P., & Ellis, C. (2016). *Evocative autoethnography: Writing lives and telling stories.* Routledge.

Boylorn, R. M. (2013). *Sweetwater: Black women and narratives of resilience.* Peter Lang.

Boylorn, R. M., & Orbe, M. P. (Eds.) (2017). *Critical autoethnography: Intersecting cultural identities and everyday life.* Routledge.

Bringhurst, R. (2008). The vocation of being, the text of the whole. In R. Bringhurst, *The tree of meaning: Language, mind, and ecology* (pp. 46–63). Counterpoint.

Brown, B. (2012). *The power of vulnerability: Teaching on authenticity, connection and courage.* Sounds True.

Chödrön, P. (1997). *When things fall apart: Heart advice for difficult times.* Shambhala Publications.

Conquergood, D. (1991). Rethinking ethnography: Towards a critical cultural politics. *Communication Monographs*, *58*, 179–194.

de Certeau, M. (1984). Reading as poaching. In *The practice of everyday life* (translated by Steven Rendall, pp. 165–176). University of California Press.

Dewey, J. (1988/1922). Custom and habit. In J. A. Boydston (Ed.), *Human nature and conduct: 1922: The middle works of John Dewey, 1899–1924*, Volume *14* (pp. 43–53). Southern Illinois University Press.

Dunn, T. (2018). *Talking white trash: Mediated representations and lived experiences of white working-class people*. Routledge.

Ehrenreich, B. (2007). *Dancing in the streets: A history of collective joy*. Picador.

Ellis, C. (1993). There are survivors: Telling a story of sudden death. *Sociological Quarterly*, *34*, 711–730.

Ellis, C. (1995) *Final negotiations: A story of love, loss, and chronic illness*. Temple University Press.

Ellis, C. (1996). Maternal connections. In C. Ellis, and A. P. Bochner (Eds.), *Composing ethnography: Alternative forms of qualitative writing* (pp. 240–243). AltaMira Press.

Ellis, C. (1998). What counts as scholarship in communication? An autoethnographic response. *American Communication Journal*, *1*, 1–1.

Ellis, C. (2004). *The ethnographic I: A methodological novel about autoethnography*. AltaMira Press.

Ellis, C. (2008). *Revision: Autoethnographic reflections on life and work*. Left Coast Press.

Ellis, C., & Bochner, A. P. (1996). Taking ethnography into the twenty-first century. *Journal of Contemporary Ethnography*, *25*, 1–168.

Ellis, C. S., & Patti, C. J. (2014). With heart: Compassionate interviewing and storytelling with Holocaust survivors. *Storytelling, Self, Society: An Interdisciplinary Journal of Storytelling Studies*, *10*(1), 93–118.

Ellis, C., & Rawicki, J. (2012). More than mazel? Luck and agency in surviving the Holocaust. *Journal of Loss and Trauma*. doi:10.1080/15325024.2012.738574.

Frentz, T. (2008). *Trickster in tweed: My quest for quality in faculty life*. Routledge.

Green, L. (2018). *Jung's studies in astrology: Prophesy, magic, and the qualities of time*. Routledge.

Groome, J. (2019). *The out of towner's guide to Happy Valley, NC*. Amazon (self-published).

Hanh, T. N. (2014). *The art of communicating*. Harper One.

Henson, J. (2019). *Finding Black Mountain: The spirit of progressive education in the 21ˢᵗ Century*. Appalachian State University, Reich College of Education dissertation.

Holman Jones, S. (2007). *Torch singing: Performing resistance and desire from Billie Holiday to Edith Piaf*. AltaMira Press.

Langer, L. (2006). Hearing the holocaust. *Poetics Today*, *27*, 297–309.

Patti, C. J. (2012). Split shadows: Myths of a lost father and son. *Qualitative Inquiry*, *18*, 153–161.

Patti, C. J. (2013). *Compassionate storytelling with Holocaust survivors: Cultivating dialogue at the end of an era*. University of South Florida dissertation. https://scholarcommons.usf.edu/etd/4743.

Patti, C. J. (2015a). Sharing "a big kettle of soup": Compassionate listening with a Holocaust survivor. In S. High (Ed.), *Beyond testimony and trauma: Oral history in the aftermath of mass violence* (pp. 192–211). University of British Columbia Press.

Patti, C. J. (2015b). Hopeful lament: A song in praise of black women/stories. *Departures in Critical Qualitative Research*, *4*(1), 127–130.

Paxton, B. (2018). *At home with grief: Continued bonds with the deceased*. Routledge.

Pirsig, R. (1974). *Zen and the art of motorcycle maintenance: An inquiry into values*. HarperCollins.

Pollan, M. (2018). *How to change your mind: What the new science of psychedelics teaches us about consciousness, dying, addiction, depression, and transcendence*. Penguin.

Roscoe, L., & Tullis, J. (2015). The meaning of everything: Communication at the end of life. *Journal of Medicine and the Person*, *13*(2), 75–81.

Shakespeare, W. (2019). *Romeo and Juliet*. Retrieved from http://shakespeare.mit.edu/rom eo_juliet/full.html (Original work published in 1595).

Tillmann, L. M. (2009). Body and bulimia revisited: Reflections on "A Secret Life." *Journal of Applied Communication Research*, *37*(1), 98–112.

Tillmann, L. M. (2015). *In solidarity: Friendship, family, and activism beyond gay and straight.* Routledge.

Turner, V. (1988). *The anthropology of performance*. PAJ Books.

Vico, G. (1980/1732). On the heroic mind. In G. Tagliacozzy, M. Mooney, & D. P. Verene (Eds.), *Vico and contemporary thought* (pp. 228–245). Palgrave Macmillan.

Vonnegut, K. (2007). *A man without a country*. Random House.

11

BOCHNER AND ELLIS AS TEACHERS, MENTORS, AND FRIENDS

Learning what it means to live a good life

Lisa P. Z. Spinazola

I blink. Fear and hate spill from my red eyes onto swollen, hot cheeks. Ice cubes wrapped in a faded green washcloth do little to soothe welts forming on my thigh and rear, welts from a wooden cooking spoon. I couldn't tell you what set her off; I never am sure.

I could have looked at her wrong or not in the eye. Maybe I didn't answer quickly or loudly or politely enough.

***

I am eating an apple in the living room when she pushes through the garage door leading into the kitchen.

"Get the groceries," she demands from the doorway.

What does she mean? From her arms? I'm caught off guard and hesitate.

Rage flickers across her face; her eyes narrow.

"Eating again?" she seethes. "Get that stupid look off your face and get over here."

"Coming," I squeak. Panic pushes against the bite of apple caught in my throat and threatens to choke me.

The exchange that follows is a blur. All I know is that I end up face down on my bed clenching my teeth and buttocks as she takes aim with a sauce-stained spoon.

***

My childhood was unpredictable and volatile. Books became worlds into which I could retreat and feel safe. I read voraciously, escaping into C. S. Lewis's magical tales of lions, witches, and wardrobes; venturing out to solve mysteries imagined by the ghostwriters who penned Nancy Drew; and learning about what *normal* childhoods could be like through the experiences of Judy Blume's characters. Every spare moment was spent somewhere, anywhere, curled up inside someone else's story to avoid the berating or beating I knew lurked around every corner in mine.

***

"Stop Mommy, stop Daddy,"
In the dark a young girl cries.
"This hurts us more than you," they scream.
She tries to believe their lies.
"It's for your own good," they holler.
As they smack and slice through years.
Believing is no longer an option,
When all they've caused are tears.

***

At 13, I discovered writing and scribbled ideas for poetry, songs, and short stories on napkins and scraps of paper. I wrote about my life as it was and how I wished it could be. I wrote about loneliness, terror, and rare times of delight. Reading books provided a temporary escape, but writing seemed to give me new life.

At 19, I moved from Florida to California with a long-haired, motorcycle-riding artist I'd met a few weeks earlier. I spent the next decade spinning from one catastrophic relationship to the next chasing adventure and unavailable men. I lived in four different states and worked as a receptionist, barmaid, travel agent, and shoe salesperson. Amid the chaos, I became a single mother to two beautiful children and wound up back in Florida living in a remodeled duplex in a part of town known for drug dealing, prostitution, and despair. Peppered with evictions and repossessions, my credit report reflected every poor choice I'd made while simultaneously echoing the desperate state of my depleted self-esteem.

Hopelessness threatened to drag me under and swallow me whole. If I had any hope of finding a way to care and provide for my kids, chaotic living would have to give way to some form of stability and structure. I went to counseling, attended parenting classes, and looked for a full-time job with benefits.

It took me a decade to claw my way out of the trench—the near grave—I'd dug for myself. Step by step, I created a new life, beginning with a five-dollar-an-hour job, to eight dollars an hour, to 15, then 25. Still single, I made my way and was able to afford a new car, purchase a home, and feel a sense of pride and accomplishment. Was life perfect? No. But, I was stable and reliable. Within eight years, I worked my way up from receptionist to general manager of a local, high-end, multimillion-dollar company and was responsible for over 30 employees. I facilitated difficult conversations, helped resolve disputes, clarified expectations, and counseled coworkers in matters of the heart as well as the workplace.

***

All my life, friends would tell me about their lives and ask my advice. Even strangers had no problem sharing their stories of pain, conflict, and deep dark secrets in grocery store aisles, pharmacy waiting areas, and nightclub bathrooms. Established in my new career, colleagues were thanking me for my insight, telling me I was a natural counselor and complimenting my compassion and empathy. This excited me. Intuitively, I found a way to improve my life *and* make a difference in other people's lives. I felt a call to do more—to be more—so I enrolled in my local community college and planned to become a therapist.

I registered for a program called Counseling and Human Services, which featured classes like Behavior Modification, Abnormal Behavior, Interpersonal Skills, and Working with Families. I soaked in every drop of knowledge. My classes provided a filing system of sorts to help me organize and make sense of life experiences. I began to see the role my upbringing played in whom I had once been and how it was within my power to evolve into a better person, for my kids and for myself.

***

A memory from childhood

Vibrant red blood drips down my shin onto a dirty, ruffled sock. My dad's normally deep tone is shrill as he rages, arms thrashing. He's pacing around the living room yelling at me and my mom. She holds her ground, stoic, unfazed. A swirl of white, pink, and silver catches my eye then disappears. My father had flung my tricycle off our second-floor balcony.

"Noooooo," I wail and flop backward into the thick, dark brown shag carpet.

"No more bikes," he bellows and spits through tight white lips, blue angry eyes bulging from their sockets. He moves so close I can feel his hot breath, "They're dangerous!"

***

As I read about Erikson's (1982) stages for a developmental psychology course, I learned how being left to self-soothe as an infant interfered with my ability to trust; how being denied autonomy as a toddler fostered feelings of guilt and shame; how being deprived of social interactions in adolescence contributed to a weak sense of self; and how being subjected to my parents' cycling between violent outbursts and repeated abandonment undermined my ability to have healthy intimate relationships as an adult.

I learned about the ramifications of the ways I had been parented and realized by rooting my own parenting styles in how I'd been raised, I'd unwittingly harmed my own children. I looked for ways to do and be better exercising patience as my own children became self-sufficient. Unlike my parents, I allowed my kids to go to sleepovers and school events to help foster solid senses of self. Instead of resorting to beating and shaming as mechanisms of control, I took deep breaths, counted down, and made efforts to respond with love and kindness as my kids moved from childhood into adolescence. I completed the Counseling and Human Services program and registered at the University of South Florida to pursue a Bachelor's degree.

***

My initial plan was to study counseling or social work but after doing some online research, I discovered the Department of Communication. I took Family Communication, Performance, Interpersonal Communication, and Persuasion. I'd grown accustomed to checking my feelings at the door where I worked *and* where I studied. Self-discovery, contemplation, and personal reflection had not been required for course participation until I took Communicating Emotions with Dr. Carolyn Ellis and Love and Communication with Dr. Arthur Bochner. In their classes we not only had permission but were encouraged to drag our emotional baggage into the room and unpack.

Through impromptu activities, writing assignments, storytelling, memoirs, and relevant articles, we explored topics like grief and loss, aging and death, love and friendship, and the range of emotions experienced throughout our lives. As we aired our dirty laundry and spilled family secrets, I began to understand how writing about our lives as they are lived is a form of learning—one that offers insights into who we once were and are now while providing opportunities to alter what might have seemed like our destined fates.

***

I close my eyes and am transported back into Dr. Bochner's class, Love and Communication. I see him at the front of the room, fingers extended, tips bent at an awkward, seemingly uncomfortable angle. One hand taps then rubs his sternum as he carefully explains,

> Narrative invites others to come along for the ride. Carr (1986) writes that, for a story to make sense, there must be a beginning, middle, and end. And we must decide which characters will figure prominently, who moves the story along, who can be left out.

I scribble furiously, trying to capture every word. *How can something that is new to me feel like common sense knowledge I've possessed forever?*
   He continues,

> If we live our lives narratively and understand our place in the world narratively, then the way to understand our own lives will be through narrative—meaning we must tell our stories with beginnings, middles, and endings they did not seem to have when we were living them. Crites (1986) tells us that a coherent life, a coherent identity, is not readily accessible; it must be made, remade, told, and revised from each new vantage point available to the one doing the living and telling.

Aha! Maybe I survived my childhood because I wrote through it. When I spilled my pain between pages, I stumbled onto a way to confine the hurt and confusion within the words I carved into paper. Writing, storying, helped me make some kind of sense out of my parents' seemingly random and irrational violence; I made beginnings, middles, and endings, scribbling my way through the chaos. Dr. Bochner's class was teaching me how to better organize that chaos into something manageable so the stories that haunted and disrupted my life might hold less power over me (Pennebaker, 2012). Feeling invigorated by these revelations, I hunted down and dug through the box where I kept the scrawls and scraps detailing my early suffering. I set out to make new sense of these stories, of early moments in my life, and contrast them with new writing about the girl I had been and the woman I was becoming.

***

Aimlessly I drifted, thrusting, spinning, twisted, toward some unknown.
Searching, hopeful, blistered, blindly reaching, grasping, yearning for a home.
Like planets all aligned, my family eclipsed, and out of reach and out of mind.

***

Dr. Ellis (2009) required we purchase her book, *Revision*, for her class Communication and Emotions. When she assigned her story about the sudden death of her brother in a plane crash, other students mumbled and complained about having to read something the teacher wrote. *Is she trying to make money off us? Why do we care what she has to say?* But I felt an odd combination of intrigue and curiosity. I'd never read something written about and by a person I knew. What would it be like to get a glimpse into the personal life of my professor?

The night before class, I read "There Are Survivors," and stood by helplessly as Dr. Ellis tuned into television coverage awaiting word of her brother's fate. I could picture her swaying back and forth, eyes scanning news footage of the crash site, heart desperate to spot her brother alive. Several times, I burst into tears needing to take breaks between pages. I wondered if I'd be able to control my emotions in class the next day.

***

We pull out our notes and I glance around. *What do they think now that they've read her work?* I watch Dr. Ellis speaking and wonder if she'll cry when we talk about her brother. She doesn't. We discuss her story and I am amazed at her strength and resilience.

While her voice is soft, she commands attention when she addresses the class,

The past is not concrete or stable. It can be written and rewritten as we age, learn, grow, giving us fresh vantage points from which to examine our memories and the stories we tell (Ellis, 2009). What does all this mean to you?

She searches the room, eyes wide.

I raise my hand and ask, "Are you saying that what we think we *know* happened in the past can be reinterpreted later, after we've learned new things, after we've experienced more?"

She nods encouragingly.

A deep voice in the back scoffs, "How does the past change? It is what it is."

I reply, "The past doesn't literally morph into something different but as time passes we can look back and see our old stories in new ways." I hold my breath. *Am I really getting it?*

"Yes, wonderful," Dr. Ellis says enthusiastically, sliding from her perch on the desk's edge. She moves around the class looking to engage another participant.
Whew.

***

In those early undergrad classes, Dr. Ellis and Dr. Bochner taught us about the healing powers of writing, journaling, and storytelling. Regular journaling quiets the mind, fosters resilience, helps us learn about and accept ourselves, and gives order to chaos (DeSalvo, 1999). Healing can begin once we open up and study the events that have impacted our lives (Pennebaker, 2012). Narratives having the potential to heal are image-laden, vivid, and told in great detail; they include both negative and positive experiences and display insights we've gained through writing and rewriting about the event (DeSalvo, 1999).

Dr. Bochner and Dr. Ellis taught so much more than I have illustrated or was able to glean from my time with them. I absorbed what I needed at the moment, what I knew I could use, and felt myself becoming more alert, aware, and whole. Invigorated, I took the next step and applied to and was accepted into the graduate program where I knew I'd continue to have access to their classes. I took as many as I could with them: Social Construction, Narrative Inquiry, Communication in Close Relationships, Trauma and Interviewing, and Autoethnography.

***

I continued writing and reworking foundational stories from my childhood and newly emerging narratives in my adult life looking for opportunities to heal and grow. In the Master's program, "I wrote my way out of an on-again, off-again, unhealthy, unfulfilling relationship while storying my way into becoming a loving, accepting, supportive, and nurturing mother" (Spinazola, 2019, p. 262). At the Doctoral level, "I narrated my way through the aftermath of a car accident that caused a brain bleed and intermittent crippling pain and began to face the stifling stories I live by regarding body image" (p. 263).

My early lessons in narrative demonstrated the powerful potential of writing and rewriting stories from the past in an effort to find new understandings from which I could learn, heal, and grow. But the stories we write and tell are not ours alone. Once we understand more about ourselves, how do we go about connecting our stories to others' stories? How can we connect our personal narratives to larger cultural narratives and gain even deeper understandings of the world and our place in it?

I started with my personal stories and used autoethnography to tie epiphanies, reflections, and experiences to more general cultural phenomena and practices while being purposefully vulnerable in an effort to compel audiences to engage with and respond to the stories I shared (Jones, Adams, & Ellis, 2013). Autoethnography, a form of narrative writing, is not done solely for personal growth or gain but also to connect the personal to the cultural, a type of autobiographical research that displays multiple layers of consciousness (Ellis & Bochner, 2000). Writing autoethnographically is a way of doing inquiry, interpreting, making meaning and sense of, and sometimes even judging how lives are lived and memories are made (Bochner, 2013).

***

Let's revisit my introductory story. My opening paragraph initially began with the following sentence: *my childhood and early teen years were rife with abuse, abandonment, and neglect.* I included no story, no hook, nothing to compel readers to continue. My opening lacked vulnerability and did little to evoke an emotional response even in myself as I read and reread. Here I am trying to convey the impact of Dr. Bochner and Dr. Ellis on my life but my writing, and my opening did not synthesize, reflect, or engage in any of the techniques I'd learned through my exposure to their scholarship and teachings.

Instead of summarizing my messy childhood neatly in one sentence, how could I honor the lessons learned and offer readers a glimpse into my personal experience that might resonate with or contrast starkly from their own? I realized I was initially "telling" about a time in my life instead of "showing" what it was like to be me in a particular moment in my life (Lopate, 2013). "Telling" comes from the head and is synthesized to give an impression of an event whereas "showing" is an embodied way of describing a moment using rich, evocative detail to allow others to enter our stories and imagine themselves there beside us.

I worked and reworked the opening, dug deep into memories I fought hard to bury, forget, and move past. Is my opening scene exactly what happened on a specific night when I was fourteen? No. It's a patchwork quilt of several moments; a memory conjured from a blurred and once buried collection of vicious, confusing behaviors both my parents exhibited often. It could have easily been my father's black leather belt or a wire hanger instead of my mother's wooden spoon. I could have been watching a show they disapproved of or been up too late. To show who I've become through my time in the classroom with the help of Drs. Ellis and Bochner, I needed a specific story to work with and write through.

***

Once upon a time, I told about my violent upbringing in chaotic, gory detail. I blurted out tales of horror and watched others inhale sharply, cringe, and shake their heads. My wounds still raw and bloody, no words could adequately capture the depth and breadth of my hurt. My stories were chaotic and lacked "narrative coherence" (Bochner, 2014, p. 287) making them difficult to tell, understand, and hear as they were told on the "edges of a wound" and on the "edges of speech" (Frank, 2013, p. 101). Like a flasher showing off his naked body uninvited and for shock value, my rants were unsolicited glimpses into my muddled, frenzied existence. I needed others to understand why I was a girl who spiraled, teetered on the edge, couldn't hold a job, loved recklessly, and wasted "God-given" talents and countless opportunities.

After building a routine and consistent life for my children and me, I was able to put away the tales of horror and instead constructed a quick, tidy, intellectualized synopsis: *my childhood and early teen years were rife with abuse, abandonment, and neglect.* The old ways of telling no longer served a purpose. I did not need others to respond with shock or horror because I had come to terms with my past, was working on mending relationships with my parents, and had become a mother I knew my kids deserved.

Stories we tell become the frameworks for how we understand ourselves and our lives. If I continued to tell the old horror stories, I could have remained trapped in a storyline that no longer served my best interests (Frank, 2013). Detailed, in-depth reminders of my early years would have threatened my recently-attained stability and newly-(re)constructed identity. I no longer needed to make excuses or justify how I lived, coped, struggled because I had moved beyond the broken, violated girl into a capable, contented woman. Like the scribbles and scraps I once collected and stored, I had also stuffed the emotional messiness into a figurative box and put it on a shelf, not sure when or if I'd feel the need to unpack those early memories.

Ignoring the past served a purpose. So why choose to revisit, rehash, dive into, and not just tell but show you the opening story? Because in the classes I took with Dr. Bochner and Dr. Ellis, I learned that merely surviving trauma is not enough, and the key to healing is to deeply feel, explore, and express emotions about events in our past; this links the past to our present and projects us toward a more hopeful future (DeSalvo, 1999). Avoiding or burying the gritty details did not stop those details from taking a toll on/in me and my life. I had to deconstruct and reframe (rebuild) debilitating life narratives to open possibilities of empowerment instead of victimization (Kiesinger, 2002).

Telling, storying, retelling, or (re)storying our lives is how we construct and revise our identities to help benefit our psychological and relational well-being (Koenig Kellas, 2008) as well as our physical well-being. Interpreting and making sense of how lives are lived and memories are made relate to and call on an autoethnographic perspective (Bochner, 2013). As a storyteller, one strives to find "specific meaning of a person's life at a given moment" (Frankl, 1984, p. 110). Using an autoethnographic perspective invites me to look back and ask: what can I remember, learn, expose, and take away from that specific moment when my 14-year-old self found herself caught in the glare of her angry mother?

It wasn't until much later I learned the year I turned fourteen, my mother was contemplating divorce and was trapped in her own violent hell; and that my mother, who just started her first job and got her first driver's license, was about to strike out on her own; and that my mother blamed her pregnancy with me for feeling forced to marry my controlling father. She was most likely in survival mode, and probably felt hurt and angry and alone. Revisiting painful memories from when I was fourteen gave me a chance to unpack the messiness of my life and apply what I was learning. Through looking back, I was able to create new understandings of myself and my mother by reinterpreting events with information I did not have at the time. Potential for new knowledge or perspective did not exist until I was willing to reflect on the past.

Writing reflexively is vital to autoethnography. Reflexivity in living and in writing requires turning the lenses through which we look at the world back upon ourselves (Goodall, 2000). Being reflexive helps us make connections between who we once were, who we are now, and who we'd like to become—between the *what* we know and the *how* we know it. How can I use reflexivity to apply newly-learned information to an old event? Knowing more about my mother—who she was and what she was going through—makes room for new possibilities.

Maybe it wasn't rage or hate that flickered across my mother's face; maybe it was resentment, panic, fear, and/or frustration. Maybe it was guilt because she knew she was leaving. Maybe she used acts of rage and violence as tactics to disengage herself from me so we both might feel relief when she left. Reflecting, writing, and storying give us new ways to see ourselves and the world; allow us to revisit the past; help us invent and reinvent ourselves; and even offer chances to save ourselves (O'Brien, 1990). Making room for forgiveness and understanding of my mother and her actions helps me find forgiveness and understanding for myself and mistakes I've made in parenting my own children.

Dr. Bochner and Dr. Ellis not only write about but also put into practice what it means to live good lives—lives worth living. As teachers, they encourage and guide students to do personally meaningful work. They don't just read students' stories; they try them on, imagine walking in our shoes, and ask impactful questions, inspiring us to dig even deeper. As mentors they demonstrate what it means to be passionate and committed to scholarship and knowledge that has the capacity to improve lives. They embody care and connection, inspiring us to do the same—in the classroom, at conferences, between the pages, and in our lives.

While reading their published stories, they not only taught and mentored me, but became part of me. As if in the room with Art, I learned of his father's passing and struggled alongside him as he grappled with his own mortality (Bochner, 1997). I stood in the doorway while Carolyn cared for and bathed her ailing, aging mother (Ellis, 1996). While Art gazed in the mirror reflecting back his father's face, I joined him as he tried to reconcile the father he wanted with the father he had with the father he himself could have become (Bochner, 2012). As though sitting next to Carolyn, I watched her write about dreaming, aging, and finding ways to make time to do work that matters and feels more like play (Ellis, 2011). I accepted their invitation to use their lives, try them on, and consider what their stories mean to me and my life: how I'll reconcile my mother's image looking back at me in my mirror, or feel about my own aging body, or determine what projects to take on or let go, or prepare to receive news of a parent's passing.

In August of 2018, I sat in the USF Sun Dome with Dr. Ellis and Dr. Bochner by my side. I was one of the last students fortunate enough to have them both as teachers and mentors. When I walked across the stage, graduating with my PhD in Communication, I moved into a new chapter, into a life where I know what it means to have Art and Carolyn as friends. They live within my stories as much as I live within theirs. Our continuing interactions show how my ever-evolving stories resonate within them as well.

***

As I write these words, my mother and I are not on speaking terms. I've danced around estrangement for more than half the years I've been alive. I could blame our estrangement on the fact that when I was 15, she abandoned me and my sisters leaving us alone with our abusive and violent father; or that when I was 16 she and my father signed away their rights to us and sent us to live in another country; or that well into my forties, she continued to belittle me for my inability to control my weight or tame my curly, unruly hair; or that she tried to behave in those ways toward my children; or that she continued to ignore my requests to exercise restraint in all the things I'm mentioning here.

Throughout my life, I've reasoned, plead, begged, put my foot down, ignored, started fresh with both my parents, doing all in my power to make it possible to continue relationships with my mother and father, forgiving old hurts and warning (threatening) them when they scraped at old wounds. My father and I have worked our way into a place of understanding and care, but patience for my mother ran out a few years ago when she renewed venomous tirades against my father for old hurts that were bubbling to the surface of her memory and conscience.

She wanted me to hold a grudge against him with her even though I was no longer permitted to hold my own grudges against her. I was to move on when it came to the hurt she caused me. But I was told to put myself in her shoes, feel her pain with her, and understand her hatred toward him. I explained that I could not side with her. As a mother, I have no understanding available in me for a woman who left her children with a man as brutal and vile as she says my father was to her.

I took a stand and I am sure it felt like I took his side. We went back and forth. I felt attacked by her words; she pushed harder, back and forth, until there was nowhere left to take our conversation. I told her I would no longer respond to her emails until she writes to tell me she is willing to be an asset in my life, a loving force, a shining light, a person who wants to build me up instead of tear me down.

That was almost a year ago.

***

Art and I are seated on the wooden deck of his and Carolyn's North Carolina home. Clouds are nestled between faraway mountain tops. We watch in silence as the sunset takes hold and sets the sky and clouds on fire. Carolyn steps through the open glass doorway carrying a large pottery platter filled with chunks of cheese. A box of rosemary and olive oil crackers is tucked under the other arm. With her free hand, she tosses what's left of a cracker topped with blue cheese into her mouth and searches the table for space big enough for the cheese plate. Art and I shift around our wine glasses, and Carolyn gingerly places the heavy, handcrafted plate at the center of our table.

She settles back into her seat, then leans toward me. Her tender eyes match her careful, concerned tone. She asks, "Lisa, have you heard from your mother since the email blow-up?"

"Well," I say then pause, deciding whether or not to interrupt our peaceful moment with details of estrangement and sadness. "We still haven't spoken. This month marks a full year."

Carolyn gently shakes her head; her eyes do not leave mine.

Art takes in a deep breath and sighs. I know he understands. "How do you feel about her not reaching out to you?" he asks.

I am sitting with two of the kindest, most compassionate people I know who regularly show what it means to care for and love others unconditionally.

I give what I hope is a reassuring smile. "I am okay; I really am."

They both nod and smile back. "Good," they say in unison.

I lean forward to dig into a buttery hunk of aged Gouda and pause to admire the details in the handmade pottery. I am struck by the purple and royal blue specks on the lemon yellow and pumpkin orange swirl at the edge of the platter. It mirrors the view of the sky and mountains I was taking in earlier. Carolyn raises her wine glass and invites Art and I to do the same. We toast and sip and lean back in our chairs. My heart feels full.

References

Bochner, A. P. (1997). It's about time: Narrative and the divided self. *Qualitative Inquiry*, *3*(4), 418–438. doi:10.1177/107780049700300404.

Bochner, A. P. (2012). Bird on the wire: Freeing the father within me. *Qualitative Inquiry*, *18*(2), 168–173. doi:10.1177/1077800411429094.

Bochner, A. P. (2013). Putting meanings into motion: Autoethnography's existential calling. In Jones, S. H., Adams, T. E., & Ellis, C. (Eds.), *Handbook of autoethnography*. Left Coast Press.

Bochner, A. P. (2014). *Coming to narrative: A personal history of paradigm change in the human sciences*. Left Coast Press.

Carr, D. (1986). *Time, narrative, and history*. Indiana University Press.

Crites, S. (1986). Storytime: Recollecting the past and projecting the future. In Sarbin, T. R. (Ed.), *Narrative psychology: The storied nature of human conduct* (pp. 152–173). Praeger Publishers/Greenwood Publishing Group.

DeSalvo, L. A. (1999). *Writing as a way of healing: How telling our stories transforms our lives*. Beacon Press.

Ellis, C. (1996). Maternal connections. In C. Ellis & A. P. Bochner (Eds.), *Composing ethnography: Alternative forms of qualitative writing* (pp. 240–243). AltaMira Press.

Ellis, C. (2009). *Revision: Autoethnographic reflections on life and work*. Left Coast Press.

Ellis, C. (2013). Coming to know autoethnography as more than a method. In Jones, S. H., Adams, T. E., & Ellis, C. (Eds.), *Handbook of autoethnography*. Left Coast Press.

Ellis, C. (2011). Jumping on and off the runaway train of success: Stress and committed intensity in an academic life. *Symbolic Interaction*, *34*(2), 158–172. doi:10.1525/si.2011.34.2.158.

Ellis, C., & Bochner, A. P. (2000). Autoethnography, personal narrative, reflexivity: Researcher as subject. In Denzin, N. K., & Lincoln, Y. S. (Eds.), *Handbook of qualitative research* (pp. 733–768). Sage.

Erikson, E. H. (1982). *The life cycle completed: A review*. W.W. Norton & Company.

Frank, A. W. (2013). *The wounded storyteller: Body, illness, and ethics*. University of Chicago Press.

Frankl, V. E. (1984). *Man's search for meaning: An introduction to logotherapy*. Simon & Schuster.

Goodall, H. L. (2000). *Writing the new ethnography*. AltaMira Press.

Jones, S. H., Adams, T. E., & Ellis, C. (Eds.) (2013). *Handbook of autoethnography*. Left Coast Press.

Kiesinger, C. E. (2002). My father's shoes: The therapeutic value of narrative reframing. In Bochner, A. P., & Ellis, C. (Eds.), *Ethnographically speaking: Autoethnography, literature, and aesthetics* (pp. 95–114). AltaMira Press.

Koenig Kellas, J. (2008). Narrative theories: Making sense of interpersonal communication. In Baxter, L. A., & Braithwaite, D. O. (Eds.), *Engaging theories in interpersonal communication: Multiple perspectives* (pp. 241–254). Sage.

Lopate, P. (2013). *To show and to tell: The craft of literary nonfiction*. Simon and Schuster.

O'Brien, T. (1990). *The things they carried*. Houghton Mifflin Harcourt.

Pennebaker, J. W. (2012). *Opening up: The healing power of expressing emotions*. Guilford Press.

Spinazola, L. P. (2019) Finding heart and soul. *Nauki o Wychowaniu. Studia Interdyscyplinarne*, *8*(1), 261–263. doi:10.18778/2450-4491.08.18.

PART II

Futures

12

TRACES AND SHARDS OF SELF-INJURY

Strange accounting with "Author X"

Brittany Presson, Brandi Barnes, Carol Rambo, and Author X

We attend a panel on arts-based research at the Thirteenth International Congress of Qualitative Inquiry, featuring Arthur Bochner, Carolyn Ellis, and Csaba Osvath. Osvath, a student of Bochner's, is an artist who collects shattered glass from which he crafts large compositions to "create a new whole out of formerly broken parts." Osvath has created a piece in response to Bochner's (2012) paper "Bird on the Wire," which imagines a "purifying conversation" with his deceased father. Many themes are discussed during the conference panel—freeing oneself from one's history, using a story to heal from past wounds, restoration, transformation, and more.

The glass work is difficult. It involves meticulously laying the glass into place one shard at a time, as Osvath "thinks through his hands." A paper copy of "Bird on a Wire" is rendered into bits and incorporated into the piece. The words, though distorted in places, appear through the transparent multicolored glass overlay. Osvath frequently slices his fingertips as he labors over a project.

Ellis comments, "His blood is literally in the piece." Audience members respond with light-hearted laughter. Some of us in attendance who have done research on the topic of self-injury steal knowing glances at each other and fail to repress our smiles. Thematic mischief weaves in and out of our lives, connecting us, one to another. We are all thinking it, "Is Osvath's artwork, in part, a form of unconscious self-injury?"

***

Something skitters across the floor. This chapter's authors collectively track a jewel-toned shard of glass; it lands at our feet, inviting us to pick it up and fashion it into our own hybrid of art and social-science-based inquiry (see Ellis,

Adams, & Bochner, 2011). We know if we pick it up it could hurt us, so we take exceptional care to protect ourselves. Still, we may get hurt.

This autoethnography is a performance text about self-injury and an experiment with *strange accounting* (Rambo, 2016; Rambo & Pruit, 2019) with an Author X. It is performed from the perspective of multiple authors, who have individually taken on multiple identities regarding the topic, such as: researchers, former self-injurers, ambiguous self-injurers, friends of self-injurers, and parents of self-injurers. Those who may not have self-injured provide "cover" for those who may have (unless, of course, everyone did). Some of the authors may not care if readers believe they have self-injured or not. They provide cover for those who do care by *not* outing themselves. We will not indicate who said or did what (glass cuts deep and distorts images at times), though each author claims at least two or more of the identities listed.

Strange accounting, thus far, has been used by solo authors to explore the experience of applying for the chair position in a sociology department (Rambo, 2016) and of being the chair of a communication department (Ellis, 2019). The identities of people and places as well as the meanings of things were left in-play in both manuscripts. In both cases, play created *strangeness* (Simmel, 1950) and distance from harmful specifics.

In the next evolution of strange accounting, two authors used the technique to explore their experiences of marginalization as autoethnographers and qualitative researchers (Rambo & Pruit, 2019), and three authors explored their experiences with toxic masculinity in the academy (Pruit, Pruit, & Rambo, 2021). In situations where multiple authors were involved, each used the other(s) as "cover" to safely tell stories that would otherwise go untold. All the authors were listed on the publication, but the identity of who wrote which sections was left in play, thus creating strangeness and distance for each author.

In this manuscript Author X marks an ambiguous placeholder for the presence or absence of an author. The possible absence creates yet another dimension of strangeness. What the reader takes in may or may not be attributable to one of the authors listed. That space, or pocket of ambiguity, serves as a multiplicative dimension of play, creating more strangeness and distance from harm for authors and others in the manuscript.

***

Can self-injury usefully be conceived as a therapeutic mode of "self" or "ego" destruction, carried out in the spirit of deconstruction/reconstruction/rebirth/renewal? In this chapter, we construct from the shards of our lives a layered account autoethnography (Ronai, 1995) to explore this possibility. We bleed; you read. X will demarcate all the individual authors' identities represented in this paper, identities that remain in flux and under construction. In this way, X serves as a noun. Let X also allude to identity as a process whereby a final meaning never shows up but rather is left *in play* (Derrida, 1993). Readers can guess but they will never be certain whose story is being told. All the authors' individual consciousnesses skim an interconnected surface together through the chapter, across ever shifting rhizomatic synapses of meaning and *associational slides* (Rambo et al., 2019; Rambo & Pruit, 2019). All of us are Author X. None of us is Author X. Author X is something else. Because of the "edgy" nature of self-harm, Author X also serves as a shield behind which we discuss self-injury, collectively protecting one another, and others, from stigma. Or, there could simply be a fourth author who did not want to be named, and the rest is elaborate, obfuscating, postmodern posturing (read that as jargonized "bullshit"). For this to function as designed, Author X stands for a range of possibilities, as a constellation or *strange attractor* (Gleick, 1987) of meanings; meanwhile the status of the authors (who wrote what) cannot be allowed to settle.

***

My hands shake as I staple my paper. The assignment is to write a reaction paper to *The Tender Cut: Inside the Hidden World of Self-injury,* by Patricia and Peter Adler (2011). I am going beyond that. This will be the first time I share my history with self-injury with a non-peer. Why am I doing this? What will my professor think? This is grad school!

***

My classmates take turns discussing their opinions on *The Tender Cut.* As we go around the table, soon it will be my turn to speak. What will I say? Will I be honest? Will I disassociate myself from the topic? I shouldn't share my experience. My paper will be enough; only the professor will read it. But good grief! My classmates are being so judgmental. Self-injurers aren't all "crazy" or "just seeking attention." They don't all *need* counseling, medication, or to be locked up. My "compassionate" sociology grad school classmates are mindlessly labeling and stigmatizing self-injurers. *This* is why people can't talk about self-injury. Nobody understands. Sometimes it feels like others don't even want to try.

***

In the beginner's mind there are many possibilities, but in the expert's mind, there are few (Suzuki, 1970).

***

My classmates' opinions get stronger as they begin to validate each other's perspectives. I become angry. I can no longer keep quiet. To do so would be to allow myself to be bullied. It is my turn to speak. I open my mouth. The words fall out before I can stop myself. "I used to be a self-injurer …"

***

After class, the instructor and the student stay after and gossip.

"He was awesome! He defended self-injurers long before he knew someone in the room had a history with self-injury."

"He was in the minority."

"She has a background in one of the so-called 'caring' social sciences! Yet she could not be convinced that self-injury was anything more than crazy—it is so 'unlike her.'"

"She questioned the wisdom and professionalism of bringing the topic into the classroom at all, 'Some things should not be discussed,' she said."

"Yeah like, should self-injury not be researched at all? She didn't think that through."

"I think they believe we're taking the position that self-injury is 'okay' when we try to look at it as anything but mental illness."

"That is not what we are trying to say!"

"That is *not* what we were trying to say."

We talk at length and exchange confidences about the topic, what we know, who we know, and the "whys" of self-injury. We agree. *There are times self-injury makes good sense; there is a way it can serve the positive function of suicide prevention.* That is a difficult idea to convey in a casual conversation.

The instructor suggests that the student consult the literature. The instructor believes a larger research project could come out of this, though she wonders if they can get their Institutional Review Board (IRB) to approve it. Maybe if the student got University Psychological Services to agree to see anyone who may have been distressed by participating in the project, for free, it might make the IRB happy.

***

Self-injury is a public health concern and a "problematic" social problem. Rates are tracked by organizations such as the Centers for Disease Control and The Institute of Medicine. The International Society for the Study of Self-Injury (ISSS; https://itriples.org) defines it "as the deliberate, self-inflicted destruction of body tissue without suicidal intent and for purposes not socially sanctioned." Examples include self-cutting, burning, branding, bone breaking, hitting, scratching, hair-pulling, and banging one's head. According to the website, "Research … found 12% to 24% of young people have self-injured.… Most studies find 6–8% of adolescents and young adults reporting current, chronic self-injury." They also note that girls and women are slightly more likely than boys and men to engage in the behavior.

Some researchers want self-injury classified as its own disorder (Adler & Adler, 2011). Others document self-injury behavior as a means of diagnosing psychological conditions such as borderline personality disorder (Selby et al., 2012). In the DSM V (American Psychiatric Association, 2013, p. 783), non-suicidal self-injury is not classified as a distinct condition, however, it may be defined as one in the future; it has been listed under "conditions for further study."

Self-injury is also framed in the literature as a rapidly spreading sickness, disease, or as having a contagion status (Matthews, 1968; Ross & McKay, 1979; Taiminen et al., 1998; Whitlock et al., 2006). This proliferation is blamed on the media and more recently social media. In the past, self-injury was thought to be an accidentally learned mental disorder (Adler & Adler, 2008). During the 1990s, according to Ranker.com (2019), Marilyn Manson was known for self-injuring during live performances. People following various music sub-cultures began self-injuring as a gesture of solidarity and a confirmation of group membership (Adler & Adler, 2008). Later, Johnny Depp, Sid Vicious, Angelina Jolie, Lindsay Lohan, Drew Barrymore, Miley Cyrus, Christina Ricci, Fiona Apple, and others, appeared on Ranker's (2019) list of "celebrities who self-harm." Self-injury is viewed by some as "fad" behavior and subculture impression management (Adler & Adler, 2011).

Because of the Adlers' work, research on self-injury has taken a decidedly social constructionist turn. Emphasizing social interaction, rather than individual pathology, Chandler (2012) has framed self-injury as embodied emotion work, where the body was acted on to change one's emotions. Brossard (2014) has shown how self-injury can be viewed as an attempt to maintain the interaction order by managing emotions so that one's outward affect matches what society expects. From a perspective that frames the framers, Bareiss (2014) has examined constructions of self-injury in 78 news accounts. Bareiss noted, "the remedy to the problem is not constructed as redress of contemporary pressures placed upon young people, but rather, as the responsibility of adolescents to conform to the social system that causes them to hurt themselves" (2014, p. 279). Chandler, Myers, and Platt (2011) have examined constructions of self-injury in clinical literature and reached similar conclusions.

***

Each author of this chapter, in their own way, came to question the assumption that self-injury was always harmful. Some of us did so based on our reading of existing literature. Some of us started questioning and remembering our experience with self-injury and started writing.

Claims makers (Best, 1998, 2013), those who define and codify a social problem, describe self-injury as "deliberate" "without suicidal intent" and "for purposes not socially sanctioned." Yet a casual glance beyond the ISSS's webpage (https://itriples. org) reveals that the boundaries of self-injury quickly blur like the edges of a healing wound, leaving in doubt the boundaries of healthy and unhealthy. Depending on time, place, and context, the definition of self-injury is in flux. For instance, eating disorders such as anorexia and bulimia are classified as self-injury in the United King-dom but not in the United States (NSHN, 2019). On-line campaigns such as Pro-ana (pro anorexia) and Pro-cut (pro cutting) have made mainstream news (Castillo, 2012) by advocating for these activities; Pro-ana websites such as myproana.com have even hosted self-injury sub-forums where people supported one another's self-injury.

Some view tattooing, piercing, and branding as forms of self-harm, yet according to other claims makers they do not "count" because they are socially sanctioned forms of body modification (Adler & Adler, 2011). Branding is often accepted as a display of hegemonic masculinity or a symbol of group cohesion in settings such as fraternities, athletics, and the military (Adler & Adler, 2011). However, a Google search of branding and hazing turns up numerous articles where branding is considered a social problem that must be prevented, even though most who get branded do so voluntarily.

Cutting is documented in biblical passages as a way to grieve death and as a practice of those who follow "false Gods." Scarification is found throughout history (e.g., military records from fifth century Greece; see Adler & Adler, 2011) and is still a cultural practice in Sub-Sahara Africa (Ayeni, 2004). Scarification and branding have been banned in some states (Obenschain, 2013) including New Jersey, Kansas, South Carolina, and Oregon.

It is commonly understood in tattooing circles that many who get tattoos have a history with self-injury. One of the authors of this chapter told her tattoo artist the topic of her research. The artist claimed that when she trained, out of a room of 14 trainees, all but one raised their hand when asked if they had ever self-injured (Presson & Rambo, 2015). Another author has been invited to "piercing parties" which take place after hours in tattooing studios. Participants lay on their stomachs and have their backs systematically pierced with hooks. Later the jewelry is removed, and everyone cleans up and goes home (Presson & Rambo, 2015). "Flesh hook suspension" (Forsyth & Simpson, 2008), a practice where participants suspend their bodies from hooks pierced into their skin, further blurs the line between body modification and self-injury.

***

According to Joel Best (1998) "social problem-ing" issues is a social process. He uses the changing definition of toys to illustrate this point. For Best, toys have always been a target for claims makers. Barbie, for example, has been a target of claims makers since 1959. She was first considered a less-than-innocent companion who would "corrupt" the minds of girls. Next, she was guilty of taking a girl's attention away from baby dolls so that she would not want to be a mother. Then she became vapid and anti-feminist, using her sexuality to get ahead in the workplace. Next, she was a promoter of capitalism and the mindless consumption of luxury goods. Later, she was ageist, sexist, racist, and a promoter of anorexia. More recently, some have decided she was a promoter of resistance to parental values.

At first blush (and eyeliner), Barbie appears to have been busy. No 60-year-old ever looked better, occupying girls' toyboxes, adults' curio shelves, Joel Best's attention, and our landfills—a social problem yet to be codified by a claims maker; let us be the first to protest *Trash Heap Barbie*^{TM} and *Ocean Plastic Barbie*^{TM}. We wonder if Barbie can take time out of her busy schedule of hegemonic activities to inform us about self-injury. We think so. Barbie is not busy, but the claims makers have been.

Tokidoki Barbie™, sold with a prickly cactus friend named *Bastardino*, was banned because she had too many permanent tattoos and might encourage girls to want them (Boone, 2014). In 1999, Mattel's *Butterfly Art Barbie*™ was withdrawn from sale in the U.S. after parents had similar complaints. *Totally Stylin' Tattoo Barbie*™ was sold with a "tramp stamp" displaying Ken's name and 19 other assorted tattoos (Boone, 2014). Mattel refused to bow to parental pressure that time, so she sold out. *Babysitter Barbie*™ reads a book called *How to Lose Weight* that advises her inside the pages, "Don't eat!" (Boone, 2014). *Slumber Party Barbie*™ comes with a scale that she takes to her party which permanently reads 110 pounds (Boone, 2014).

We smell burning toxic plastic. Where is *Bodacious Branded Buttocks Barbie*™, with Mattel burned into her gluteus maximus? Or *Self-injury Barbie*™, sold with a soundtrack of Alice Cooper's renditions of "Welcome to My Nightmare" and "Only Women Bleed?"

***

Two psychologists are eventually added to the first project proposal, one on campus, one off campus.

***

Hello,

The University of [X] Institutional Review Board, FWA0000[X], has reviewed and approved your submission in accordance with all applicable statuses and regulations as well as ethical principles.

PI NAME: [X]

PROJECT TITLE: Self-Injury and Identity

FACULTY ADVISOR NAME (if applicable): [X]

IRB ID: #[X]

LEVEL OF REVIEW: Full Board

***

More than one project gets approval, eventually; IRB is, at times, unpredictable. Some of us interview people who have self-injured. More join the project as researchers and/or autoethnographers. Others leave. There is a sense of "churn" as graduate assistants perform work, write theses, present conference papers and publish. Some are informally affiliated with the project; others are concerned about being associated with the project but leave traces in our thoughts on self-injury and in this manuscript.

***

Author X marks (or unmarks) a status and a process. Presence, absence, neither, nor, identities in flux, shifting, rhizomatic associational sliding, strange accounting, strange attracting. We are drawn to one another in this strange process of research and healing.

***

Self-injury has an objective, obdurate, facticity about it. Self-harm is—well—harmful. There is the possibility of injuring oneself more than one anticipates, subsequent infection, or even accidental death. While the Adlers have called for demedicalizing the topic, we suggest claims makers should seek to "de-problematize" the social problem status of self-injury. If we do so and start with lived emotional experience, what other understandings about self-injury might become possible? For those who have self-injured in the past, these vignettes may be "triggering."

***

I am 12. I get off the bus at the elementary school and walk to my parent's house. It is a Friday afternoon. I have my backpack and a silver messenger bag packed with clothes for the weekend. It has been two weeks since I last saw my parent. I let myself into the house, my younger sibling trailing behind me. She/he/they grabs a Hostess cake and eats it while I make a glass of chocolate milk. My parent arrives home through the kitchen door and sees me drinking it. She/he/they becomes visibly angry, her/his/their face straining as s/he/they yells, "You are overweight! You don't deserve chocolate milk. You don't need to eat dinner tonight!"

I successfully hold it together until I can take a shower later in the evening. Only then do I let myself cry. If I were skinny, then maybe I would be loveable. If I killed myself, the only thing my parent would care about would be cleaning up my blood. I pick up the razor and start shaving my legs. I hit another wave of crying; the tears spill out and merge with the shower droplets flowing down my face. Blinded, I quietly sob. I accidentally scrape my shin with the razor and start to bleed. The sobbing stops. I take deep breaths and watch the blood wash down the drain with my tears. I don't think much about it; I just feel better.

***

I am 12 years old. I have been arrested. The police ask why I did it as my guardians stare at me. My guardian comments, with cutting contempt, "You are just like your 'jailbird' parent." I am horrified. My jailbird parent is the personification of evil, tainted genetic material. We all know it. The truth of my existence is exposed; everyone can see me for what I am—a criminal. I am trapped in dread and shame. *Everyone hates me.* There is nowhere to go, nothing to do to repair it. It is untenable. I cannot continue to exist like this, but I can't make it stop. From inside this feeling, an impulse burst through me, overwhelming my mind and body. I repeatedly thrust my head hard, backwards, against the paneled wall of the police station, gripping the arms of the chair as I do so for extra traction. I do not think about it; it just happens, as if someone other than me was making the decision. I wonder how badly I am going to hurt myself, but I can't stop. The police say, "Can't you see she needs help?" My guardian says, "I don't know what the hell's wrong with her."

***

Was that "real" self-injury? Does it count? I still don't know for sure to this day, but I think so. I responded to overwhelming emotion in that manner because my society provided me with no other formulas or schemes through which to process and/or interpret it. I engaged in bodily emotion management (Chandler, 2012). I question it because I did not experience my head banging as an "idea," "thought" or "choice." It felt more like an autonomic process. Often, those who self-injure wonder if their activity "counts" or constitutes "real" self-injury (Presson & Rambo, 2015). Meanwhile, if that wasn't self-injury, then was I in some other way "mentally ill?" The problem with that label is it shuts down further consideration of what was happening to a 12-year-old girl, outside of a jail cell, in a policeman's office.

***

The first time I deliberately cut, I am in my brightly colored room, frantically running around. My favorite band, Saliva, is playing on the radio. It has been a bad, bad day. My family praises my weight-loss, but they fail to recognize that I haven't eaten in a week. If they do recognize, they do not care. My best friend stood me up earlier and has disappeared. I am stranded, trapped, my head swimming, overwhelming me with negative thoughts that won't stop.

Whiplash. I am losing control of my emotions. I can't cry. It is considered weak—a notion conveyed by my parents, friends, martial arts teachers, and media. I can't hit anything. That is considered unladylike; my mom would try to lock me up for sure. Even in Taekwondo our sparring must be levelheaded and void of emotion. I am at a loss for how to deal with my world. The phrase "trust no one" has been drilled into me by my family. I can't talk to them. I can't talk to other adults. I can't speak with a counselor. I tried writing my thoughts down, but my mother hired my sibling to spy on me. He/she/they confiscated my writing. I thought I could turn to my friends, but they were nowhere to be found.

I am in a frenzy. My heart is racing as I search every drawer and surface for a tool. I look over and notice the items hanging on my cork board. There are two photo collages, a beaded necklace from my childhood, a St. Patrick's Day crown, and at the very top left-hand corner, my shark tooth necklace.

The first cut is small, the shark tooth is smooth. My breathing steadies as I dig the point into my skin. I slowly and shakily drag the point along my forearm, trailing behind it a faint red line. My heart rate increases until I officially break the skin. Seeing my blood brings a calming wave that rinses away my panic; I feel my body relax. I am proud of that first little mark. It is roughly an inch long. I eventually make a second with the same necklace before moving on to a better tool.

I am at school, later, when I discover how sharp a soda can is when broken in half. I cut my hips instead of my arm. My friend taught me that the torso area cuts better. We cut together, on occasion, during gym class, sitting along the wall at the start of class until roll is called, positioning our hips against the wall on the side we were cutting, each of us shielding the other. We would each cut for a few seconds— fast—then roll the pant band up and pull the shirt down. Easy-peasy.

***

From an interview:

I lost my virginity and it was traumatic and date rapey and … I don't know. Definitely coerced and vodka and not a good experience. And then my best friends called me a whore that night. I can't really remember what I was feeling at the time which I guess makes sense because it was eleven years ago. I was obviously upset but I know I wasn't crying because I never really cried while self-injuring. That's always been the point for me was to not be emotional. It's the way to feel. It's almost the way to not feel—feeling something physical instead of something mental. So, being able to feel something on my skin—I've never gone deeper than that—it's a reminder. Because once there's a marker there, you can press on it and remember it was there. And I liked [markers]. I liked the visual-ness of [them].

***

The speakers drown out the don'ts. The "don't do this." The "don't think that." The "be perfects." Smile. Breathe. What's the number one rule? Never cry. If you're bleeding, if you're broken, if you're afraid, if you're alone, never cry. Tears are a sign of weakness. Think of other people. You have it better than a lot of kids in this world. Smile.

I'm 14 years old and arrive home from school. My backpack hangs on the kitchen chair. There is no wall separating the kitchen from the living room. I live with my mother and stepfather in a small rental house. The music is blaring from the family desktop computer. I hang up the phone.

I pace the floor. My teeth clench, barring any vocal outrage. Forgotten. She forgot me. A friend was supposed to pick me up to go to the movies, but she ditched me. Left me behind. Stood me up. She would meet up with the group there without bothering to call.

I can feel my breathing quicken. I want to scream, but I cannot. I want to shout and punch things, but I won't. Young ladies don't do that. My heart stings with betrayal. She wasn't supposed to do this. She was supposed to be the one who cared. She was supposed to remember me. I put the song "Always" on repeat. I crank up the speakers even louder.

Abandoned. I am the unwanted child. The mistake. My dad regrets adopting me. My mother didn't mean to have me. She often joked that my name should have been, "Drunken Blackout." My paternal uncle threw a refrigerator at her three months before I was born. My biological father never met me. He signed the go-away papers quickly.

I open the silverware drawer and slam it shut. My fingers squeeze the lip of the counter. I turn on the hot water, washing my hands and forearms. I start to calm down. Supper dishes from the night before are in the sink. It's my job to wash them. My parents don't notice that I don't eat. My stomach feels like it is caving in.

The phone rings. It's my mother. She has a list of chores for me to do before she gets home or I'm grounded. She doesn't hear the strain in my voice. I look at the clock.

A fresh wave of anger hits. I grab a butcher knife from the drying rack. The blade is gleaming. I rinse it with hot water and touch it to my skin. This isn't the first time that I have cut, but I've never used a knife before. I turn this corner.

I typically cut with an aluminum shard peeled from a soda can. Sometimes, I feel emotionally numb and will saw away at my hips until the blood distracts me. The thought of the blood evens my breathing.

I go back into the living room and stand in front of the couch. I hold out my left arm and rotate it, first one way and then the other. I rarely cut on my arm. It's unwise. I don't care this time. I can excuse it away easily. It's still cool enough to wear a jacket, anyways.

I decide on the inside of my arm. It's more concealable. I want to see it bleed. The tip of the blade reaches my skin.

My breath catches. I can't do this. I'm afraid. The knife is so big. What if I go too deep? What if someone sees?

This fear opens the emotional floodgates. I drop to my knees. The mental anguish hurts so much. My hands grab my ribcage, unsure of whether to rip my guts open or hold my torso together before I really crumble. What is wrong with me?! Why am I unwanted? What did I ever do that was so bad? I try to be perfect, but I can't.

Every muscle is tense. Tears blur my vision. My chest heaves with painful sobs. I feel like my sternum is tearing its way out of my chest.

I'm fat. I'm ugly. I shouldn't have been born. I'm not good enough. I'm in the way. My parents battled for custody over my younger sibling. They never fought over me.

For some reason that last thought helps. All I have is myself. I need to be in control. My body involuntarily takes two very deep breaths. I twist my left arm over, exposing the back of it. The tip of the knife pricks the outside of my wrist. I let more of the blade touch. I stop thinking about the "what ifs," the pain, the abandonment. Just me and the blade. I press down. I pull back, slicing my skin, guiding the metal across my arm, stopping when I reach the inner bend of my elbow.

The blood rises thickly. My cut was deep enough. I smear the blood with my fingers. I take the blade and retrace the incision. It's the longest cut so far. I stare at it, no longer feeling anger or pain. I'm in control. I watch myself bleed.

I rub the blood between my fingers. I stretch the sides of my skin back to observe the depth of the wound. It's perfect. It serves its purpose. I don't need stitches. I'm too smart for that. I push the skin back together. I let go. It won't scar.

I know that I don't need to cut on my arms again; knives invite carelessness. I know that this cut is risky. I don't care. I've reached my familiar level of emotional apathy. I decide not to apply pressure or a bandage, letting the wound finish bleeding on its own. I rinse away the evidence, sanitize the knife, sweep the floor, wash the dishes and start the laundry.

***

I search images of self-injury on the Internet, hoping to get grounded and desensitize myself to any graphic material that may come up during my research. My imagination can be quite vivid, and I want to prevent myself from displaying inappropriate reactions with self-injurers. If I am honest, there is curiosity, a voyeuristic component to this. I want to see how extreme is extreme.

I scroll through the images, each row getting bloodier and bloodier. I come across a strange looking picture. "What is that white stuff?" I enlarge it. I involuntarily gag. Someone had cut too deep, beyond just the skin. It looks as if the fat is bubbling out. I feel my own thigh muscle tense in empathy. I place my hand over my mouth and inhale through my nose. I stare at the picture until I no longer feel the urge to gag.

I found my "limit." Perhaps if the image hadn't been a close up, maybe if I had seen the individual's face, or maybe if I had witnessed it in person then my reaction would have been different. Either way, this image of the white bubbling fat is enough for me to complicate my "self-injury is okay" stance. My confidence falters. How powerful are my words? How powerful could they become?

***

The three girls live with their mother, my husband's ex, but visit often. The oldest, the daughter I am most drawn to, is 15 years old and very withdrawn. I see remnants of the little girl inside me, within her. She wears black clothing, thick black hoodies in the middle of summer, and heavy black eye makeup. Her sadness is overwhelming. Though I sense she does not want to be, she is distant and untrusting. As a very small child, there were nights when she would pull her drunken mother out of the front yard and attempt to clean her up while her mother physically fought her. Her dad worked nights and slept all day; she played mom and dad to both of her younger sisters. Her mother degraded her, hit her, and took no interest in valuable things, be it school or extra-curricular activities, that would help her grow as a person.

One day her mother shows up at our house and says, "Now I know why animals eat their young. Take the little bitch; maybe you can do something with her. I'm finished. She'll be a pregnant little whore running around here in another year or so anyway, and I'm not taking care of some n***er's baby. See if you can take her and teach her how to love something, anything. I don't have the capacity."

I want to harm this woman—physically harm her. I ball my fist at my side, trying to contain the contempt I feel towards this so-called mother. I have no idea what to do with a teenage girl, but I take her. There is never a question. I coax her out of the car. She stands up with her head down, that black hoodie hiding her face. She slowly looks up at me, wide-eyed and scared. I softly tell her, "It's okay" and lift my arms in her direction. She throws herself into me, sobbing uncontrollably. *This little girl is so messed up*, I think, *God, how am I ever going to be able to help her?*

As time moves on, it is clear she is lost in a dark place within herself. For one four-day span, she routinely comes home from school and disappears into her room, not interacting with anyone. If I happen to catch her when she decides to go to the kitchen, my questions are responded to with a short answer or no answer at all. I try to respect her space as much as I can, but I have had enough of her attitude and follow her into her room. As she tries to shut the door, I push her out of the way and go in.

In that moment, time stops. Her room is dark; the only light emanates from a tiny desk lamp pointed downward. Her little stereo pulsates with screaming vocals that sound like people being tortured in hell; the music is by a screamo band called Brokencyde. As I turn, I see lyrics from this band written in black sharpie covering the back of her door; they are horrible words that speak of death, destruction, and hatred. As I turn to my left, a wall is covered with more lyrics, this time from Linkin Park and in the same black motif. I turn a little more to see the lyrics from Rihanna's "Russian Roulette" covering another wall. I think, *What the fuck is wrong with this kid?*

And then I see "them"—the cuts, the open lines on her arms that attest to her suffering. I am mortified. There are so—fucking—many—of them. One line, two lines, three lines, four, five. Fuck! Her other wrist tells the same story. She cuts everywhere on her body, not one piece of flesh left sacred. She is crazy, legitimately DSM-diagnosable crazy. Her room, the walls, the music, the self-mutilation are too much. I explode and rage at her, "Are you fucking stupid? You whine that no one sees you but resent when I try to help you! Do you want to die? Because if you really want to make the point, you are cutting your wrists in the wrong direction—try vertically. You want my attention? You got it. You are not the only one in this house, and it is not all about you. Why are you doing this? What the fuck is wrong with you?" I have no idea what this cutting stuff is about, but I am terrified. And angry.

I walk out and slam her door, leaving her alone in the aftermath. I talk to her dad, who is completely clueless as to what has been going on. She has been cutting since she was 12 years old. My anger turns on him. "This is your child; how could you not know?"

I cry. I cry for her pain, for the total neglect she has been subjected to, and for the overwhelming feeling that I have failed her. I am the only one, at this point, who has even cared to notice that she hurts herself. I'm trying to love her and desperately want to save her, but I'm realizing that it's not enough. Why isn't my love enough? I am alone in this struggle with her. I want to scoop her up and hold on to her, tell her that everything is going to be okay. But I don't know if everything is going to be okay and anyway, my anger bars me from reaching out to hold her.

After that night, I try talking to her, but she tells me what she thinks I want to hear and then cuts herself again. I become angry, and the cycle repeats. Most of the time she just stares at me, blank, empty. When she talks, she cannot articulate how she feels, only that she "hates herself" or that "she can't feel anything" or worse, "this [the cutting] is why I am not dead." What the hell does that even mean? Sometimes she opens up a little, and just when I think progress is being made, she cuts again. Only she cuts in a different place, somewhere that we cannot see. Eventually it comes out when she forgets to be cautious around one of her sisters. They always tell. I yell at her, "Stop lying to me about everything. You'll lie when the truth is easier." I learn much later that the truth is never that cut and dry, and sometimes the truth is the hardest thing in the world to face, especially when you feel alone.

We decide to put her in Parkwood, a mental health facility, thinking that they might "fix" her. Her dad takes her to check in; I stay home. I cannot bear to watch her walk into that place. I do not have the strength to be the one to leave her there, though I feel like it is the right decision. I do not want her around the other kids; I am not interested in the lessons that might be learned from her teachings. She is not healthy, and I do not want them tainted by her darkness. I love her though. From her perspective, my love must seem conditional. That is not true, but I cannot tell her. Or is there a little truth in that? Why can't I tell her how much I love her and just want her to feel better? She blames me for Parkwood, even though it is jointly decided by her father and me. I am in this role of "disciplinarian" for many years, set up to fail; everything is my fault because I am, after all, the evil stepmother. My "role" makes life much more comfortable for those around me. At least she might get help, and ultimately, I just want her to be safe.

The hatred spews from her eyes when she leaves the house. According to her father, she does not say a word in the car on the way there, nor does she tell her dad "bye." She cuts the entire time she is there; she uses door hinges, bed frames, or anything else her creative mind can conjure to carve her work on her canvas. Later, she is told by her roommate that if she ever wants to get out of there, she better start talking in group. Our girl knows exactly how to play that game; just say enough of the right things to be "miraculously healed" and discharged quickly.

The same girl comes right back home; only she has honed her acting skills while locked up, playing out her role with absolute perfection. I have no idea how to handle her. Sometimes I cry, sometimes I rage. To say nothing risks the perception that I don't care, and frankly, she has had enough of feeling like that. To say too much risks complete alienation and I might lose her.

***

In hindsight, I did not handle anything correctly. Recounting those instances as I write this, I understand why she could not or would not talk to me. She must have felt like I hated her. I wasn't equipped to know how to handle her. It felt like continually beating my head on a brick wall. We did this for the next year and a half. Shortly after her 18th birthday, she waited for me to go to work and left home—for good.

"Good, let her go. I had a fucked-up childhood, too, and I wasn't hell bent on a path of self-destruction." Was I? "She can't deal with her problems, and I sure as hell can't fix them for her. She doesn't want help, and I'm tired. Maybe she'll find the attention she so desperately seeks out there."

Yeah. Wow. That was me. I didn't mean it. I didn't mean a lot of things. More than anything, I just wanted her to come home. She never did. God, what have I done?

***

The authors chorus together, "How could you know, Mom? No one ever talks about this." If no one talks, no one heals.

***

We were estranged for several years after she left. I kept tabs on her through social media and word of mouth but never by direct contact. That is, until the night I walked into Domino's Pizza where I was told she was now working as a shift manager. I saw her in the back of the store, and I couldn't do anything except stand there and watch her. She was so confident in her abilities and had taken the reins as a leader. A small smile crept across my face. *What do I say? I've missed her so much*; I think to myself.

"Ma'am, can I help you?" The cashier's voice interrupts my thoughts.

"No, thank you," I respond, "I'm here for my daughter." Recognizing my voice, my daughter looks up and freezes. I'm afraid this isn't going to go well. It's been too long.

"Are you okay?" one of the employees asks, noticing the shock on her face. "Who is that?" A smile slowly lights up my daughter's face as tears begin to roll down her cheeks.

"That's my momma," she replies as she runs to me and collapses in my arms. "I'm so sorry, momma. I love you so much. You were right about everything," she says as she sobs into my chest.

The truth is, I wasn't right about everything. The social sciences have taught me that there is no capital 'T' truth about anything, only belief systems influenced by social constructions of right and wrong. Arguably, her cutting could be viewed through the same lens as my tattoos. They could both be seen as self-mutilation or as therapy, depending on the value system of the one holding judgment. I now understand that cutting was a way for my daughter to manage emotions that were otherwise out of her control.

She talks openly with me now about her cutting and confides in me how it kept her from suicide. She describes the darkness, the place inside her that would not allow her to feel, as the absence of everything—*dead*. Humans are innately predisposed to feel certain things. Pain. Pleasure. Happiness. Sadness. She felt none of these things naturally. Cutting gave her permission to be human, to *feel* human. Cutting gave her power to control the extent of what she felt in those darker moments—the ability to feel *anything*. She tells me that when the razor slit her skin, it was cathartic, empowering, almost euphoric. She dictated how far to allow this ritual to go and when to stop. It quieted the chaos inside her. She felt control over nothing else. I finally understand what she meant when she said, "This is why I'm not dead." She now wears rubber bracelets to hide the scars on her wrists. She pops them on her scars when she's triggered, a reminder that she can choose how to cope in moments when the darkness creeps in. So far, she continues to just pop the bracelets. We have both let the guilt and the blame go; there's no room for them here. I listen to her with a heart that wants to understand rather than anger that seeks to judge. She listens to me with the full understanding that my anger came from a place of fear and love. She says that she always knew that; no one else had ever cared enough to be that angry with her. Forgiveness and love have opened the door to many conversations about cutting since that time. The fact that she cut may not have been the ideal coping method, but in hindsight, it probably did save her life. She knew what she was doing, in her way. I just wish that during that time, I had known what I was doing as well.

***

From an interview:

It wasn't just heartbreak, it was shattered. Everything was just shattered. And in order to get the pieces back together, I had to break 'em up a little more because they weren't fitting together anymore. Self-injury was very much, like, this is me chopping the pieces. Only it wasn't chopping. It was cutting and all of that.

***

Self-injury can be viewed as a technique for managing both embodied emotions (Chandler, 2012) and internalized self-dialogues (Blumer, 1969). The physical injury "grounds" the self-injurer in their body, turning attention away from the incessant, destructive, chatter of old stories of self and other. In shutting off the dialogue, the self-injurer therapeutically shuts down negative constructions of self, creating space for peace or other more useful and positive dialogues to emerge, even if only temporarily. Self-injury, interpreted in this way, is both narratively deconstructive and "self"-destructive. By interrupting the internal dialogue that constitutes the self (Blumer, 1969), reconstruction, rebirth, and renewal become possible. We know this is a ridiculously positive interpretation of self-injury for some folks. We stand by it.

***

Our blood is in this piece.

***

Self-injury can be thought of as a built-up response to self and others; a negotiation of both internal pain and external social pressures which are at war in the individual. There are too many "experts" or claims makers (Best, 2013)—who medicalize, pathologize, and "social problematize" self-injury—all while creating more negative discourses and social pressures that self-injurers must navigate (Presson & Rambo, 2015).

In this chapter, instead of examining self-injury as a deviant process or social problem, we framed it as a social practice and, for some, a normalized everyday practice. Via strange accounting, we openly approached the topic with "beginners mind" (McGrane, 1994) and made self-injury "anthropologically strange" (Garfinkel, 1967). From that position of understanding, we were situated to apprehend our experiences of self-injury; to first feel them, and then later comprehend why self-injury could "make sense." In this way, emotional experience centered the analysis.

This method and mode of representation featuring Author X is inspired by and epitomizes Ellis's (1991) emotional sociology. Some ideas are difficult to get across in conversation, discussing them is not enough—they must be shown—lived by writers and embodied by readers. In this chapter, mothers speak to daughters and researchers; daughters speak to mothers, researchers, and friends; researchers speak to colleagues and more. With Author X in play, multiple writers give voice to multiple intersecting emotional perspectives on self-injury while cultivating compassion for a way of being that may otherwise seem alien or even be untellable.

Throughout the stories, common emotional themes emerged regarding self-injury: alienation, isolation, anomie, over-socialization, and unbearable somatic sensations that feel as if they *must* be managed. The pressure to conform is emotionally overwhelming. Claims/policy makers should take into consideration the socially embedded nature of the phenomenon of self-injury. Disregarding emotional experience could, unintentionally, fly in the face of effective "treatment," via the formulation of half-baked solutions that only focus on the individual who self-injures. One might conclude from this chapter that one must "treat" not just the patient but the whole culture (Brossard, 2014).

***

Without the groundbreaking work of Art Bochner and Carolyn Ellis in autoethnography (1992), the strange accounting with Author X would not be possible. Given Ellis's (2007) call for autoethnographers to take responsibility for our actions and their consequences, an "ethic of care" compels us to seek out and *codify* new, protective, compassionate ways of writing about our lives and the lives of others. Autoethnographers may be morally and ethically challenged when writing about difficult topics. Our personal identities may become stigmatized and/or events in our lives may involve risks and secrets that may endanger ourselves and others. Strange accounting as a mode of representation with Author X facilitated this "edge ethnography" (Ferrell & Hamm, 1998; Miller & Tewksbury, 2010), where the issue under consideration was liminal, seemingly beyond the margins of society; and where there might be risk-taking and physical, legal, or social danger involved in the research (Rambo, Presson, Gaines, & Barnes, 2019).

The reader was never sure who a storyteller was; the authors' identities were unsettled and "in play" with one another. In all cases with strange accounting, it is our hope, as one reviewer put it, that "there are no 'giveaways' in terms of distinguishing voices, only takeaways about the shared (and interconnected) experience and an opportunity to highlight self-injury in a way that humanizes participants and informs readers."

***

Traces and shards of self-injury—creating a new whole out of formerly broken parts. Connection. Strange attractions. We love you Art, Carolyn, and Csaba.

***

By making it safe to talk about, we hope that at least some facets of self-injury no longer appear "crazy." We are not saying self-injury is okay. We are saying that self-injury often makes sense, given that we live in a society that has few scripts and offers few options for managing extremely negative emotional affect.

References

Adler, P., & Adler, P. (2008). The cyber worlds of self-injurers: Deviant communities, relationships, and selves. *Symbolic Interaction, 31*(1), 33–56. https://doi.org/10.1525/si.2008.31.1.33.

Adler, P., & Adler, P. (2011). *The tender cut: Inside the hidden world of self-injury.* NYU Press.

American Psychiatric Association (2013). Section III: Emerging measures and models, conditions for further study. In *Diagnostic and statistical manual of mental disorders, 5th edition* (pp. 733–783). Author.

Ayeni, O. (2004). *Observations on the medical and social aspects of scarification in Sub-Saharan Africa.* Manuscript. University of Ottawa. Retrieved from www.medicine.uottawa.ca/historyofmedicine/hetenyi/ayeni.htm.

Best, J. (1998). Too much fun: Toys as social problems and the interpretation of culture. *Symbolic Interaction, 21*(2), 197–212. https://doi.org/10.1525/si.1998.21.2.197.

Best, J. (2013). *Social problems* (2nd ed.). Norton.

Bareiss, W. (2014). "Mauled by a bear:" Narrative analysis of self-injury among adolescents in US news, 2007–2012." *Health, 18*(3), 279–301. https://doi.org/10.1177/1363459313497608.

Boone, J. (2014). *The 14 most controversial Barbies ever.* Retrieved from www.etonline.com/news/154308_the_14_most_controversial_barbies_ever.

Bochner, A. P. (2012). Bird on the wire: Freeing the father within me. *Qualitative Inquiry, 18*(2), 168–173. https://doi.org/10.1177/1077800411429094.

Bochner, A., & Ellis, C. (1992). Personal narrative as a social approach to interpersonal communication. *Communication Theory, 2*(2), 165–172. https://doi.org/10.1111/j.1468-2885.1992.tb00036.x.

Blumer, Herbert. (1969). *Symbolic interactionism: Perspective and method.* Prentice-Hall.

Brossard, B. (2014). Fighting with oneself to maintain the interaction order: A sociological approach to self-injury daily process. *Symbolic Interaction, 37*(4), 558–575. https://doi.org/10.1002/symb.118.

Castillo, M. (2012). Despite social media bans of "Pro-Ana" websites, pages persist. CBS Interactive Inc. Retrieved from www.cbsnews.com/8301-504763_16257405463-10391704/despite-social-media-bans-of-pro-ana-websites-pages-persist/.

Chandler, A. (2012). Self-injury as embodied emotion work: Managing rationality, emotions and bodies. *Sociology, 46*(3), 442–457. https://doi.org/10.1177/0038038511422589.

Chandler, A., Myers, F., & Platt, S. (2011). The construction of self-injury in the clinical literature: A sociological exploration. *Suicide and Life-Threatening Behavior, 41*(1), 98–109. https://doi.org/10.1111/j.1943-278X.2010.00003.x.

Derrida, J. (1993). Structure, sign, and play in the discourse of the human sciences. In J. Natoli & L. Hutcheon (Eds.), *A postmodern reader* (pp. 223–242). State University of New York Press.

Ellis, C. (1991). Emotional sociology. *Studies in Symbolic Interaction, 12*, 123–145.

Ellis, C. (2007). Telling secrets, revealing lives: Relational ethics in research with intimate others. *Qualitative Inquiry, 13*(1), 3–29. doi:10.1177/1077800406294947.

Ellis, C. (2019). Failing to communicate in a communication department: A former chair calls her spirit back. In W. Benjamin Myers & J. Brower (Eds.), *Critical leadership in higher education: A communication perspective* (pp. 49–76). Lexington Books.

Ellis, C., Adams, T. E., & Bochner, A. P. (2011). Autoethnography: An overview. *Forum: Qualitative Social Research, 12*(1). doi:10.17169/fqs-12.1.1589.

Ferrell, J., & Hamm, M. S. (1998). *Ethnography on the edge: Crime, deviance, and field research.* Northeastern University Press.

Forsyth, C. J., & Simpson, J. (2008). Everything changes once you hang: Flesh hook suspension. *Deviant Behavior, 29*(4), 367–387. https://doi.org/10.1080/01639620701588305.

Garfinkel, H. (1967). *Studies in ethnomethodology*. Prentice-Hall.

Gleick, J. (1987). *Chaos: Making a new science*. Penguin Books.

Matthews, P. C. (1968). Epidemic self-injury in an adolescent unit. *International Journal of Social Psychiatry, 14*(2), 125–133. https://doi.org/10.1177/002076406801400206.

McGrane, B. (1994). *The un-tv and the 10-mph car: Experiments in personal freedom and everyday life*. The Small Press.

Miller, J. M., & Tewksbury, R. (2010). The case for edge ethnography. *Journal of Criminal Justice Education, 21*(4), 488–502. https://doi.org/10.1080/10511253.2010.516566.

NSHN (National Self Harm Network). (2019). Retrieved from www.nshn.co.uk/index.html.

Obenschain, P. (2013, August 21). Arkansas state legislature passes bill to ban certain body modifications, tattoo procedures. Alternative Press. Retrieved from www.altpress.com/news/entry/arkansas_senate_passes_bill_to_ban_certain_tattoo_procedures_nontraditional.

Presson, B., & Rambo, C. (2015). Claiming, resisting, and exempting pathology in the identities of self-injurers. *Deviant Behavior, 37*(2), 219–236. https://doi.org/10.1080/01639625.2014.1004036.

Pruit, J., Pruit, A., & Rambo, C. (2021). "Suck it up, Buttercup": Status silencing and the maintenance of toxic masculinity in the academy. *Studies in Symbolic Interaction, 51*.

Rambo, C. (2016). Strange accounts: Applying for the department chair position and writing threats and secrets "in play." *Journal of Contemporary Ethnography, 45*(1), 3–33. https://doi.org/10.1177/0891241615611729.

Rambo, C., Presson, B., Gaines, V.L., & Barnes, B. (2019). Autoethnography as a methodology in researching social problems. In A. Marvasti & A. J. Treviño (Eds.), *Researching social problems* (pp. 122–138). Routledge. doi:10.4324/9781315107882-7.

Rambo, C., & Pruit, J. (2019). At play in the fields of qualitative research and autoethnography: A strange account. *International Review of Qualitative Research, 12*(3), 219–242. https://doi.org/10.1525/irqr.2019.12.3.219.

Ranker. (2019, September 27). Celebrities who self-harm. Retrieved from www.ranker.com/list/celebrities-who-self-harm/celebrity-lists.

Ronai, C. R. (1995). Multiple reflections of childhood sex abuse: An argument for a layered account. *Journal of Contemporary Ethnography, 23*(4), 395–426. https://doi.org/10.1177/089124195023004001.

Ross, R. R., & H. B. McKay. (1979). *Self-mutilation*. Lexington Books.

Selby, E. A., Bender, T. W., Gordon, K. H., Nock, M. K., Joiner Jr., T. E., & Thomas, E. (2012). Non-suicidal self-injury (NSSI) disorder: A preliminary study. *Personality Disorders: Theory, Research, and Treatment, 3*(2), 167–175. https://doi.org/10.1037/a0024405.

Simmel, G. (1950). *The sociology of Georg Simmel* (K. Wolff, Trans.). Free Press.

Suzuki, S. (1970). *Zen mind, beginner's mind: Informal talks on Zen meditation and practice*. Shambhala Publications.

Taiminen, T., Kallio-Soukainen, K., Nokso-Kovisto, H., Kaljonen, A., & Helenius, H. (1998). Contagion of deliberate self-harm among adolescent inpatients. *Journal of the American Academy of Child and Adolescent Psychiatry, 37*(2), 211–217. https://doi.org/10.1097/00004583-199802000-00014.

Whitlock, J., Powers, J., & Eckenrode, J. (2006). The virtual cutting edge: The Internet and adolescent self-injury. *Developmental Psychology, 42*(3), 407–417. https://doi.org/10.1037/0012-1649.42.3.407.

13

TANGIBLE AUTOETHNOGRAPHY

Merging autoethnographic writing and artmaking

Csaba Osvath

The reader's vocation

In September 2011, Terry Gross interviewed 83-year-old Maurice Sendak. During their conversation, the beloved children's author and illustrator shared a charming story about a little boy named Jim, who sent him a fan letter with a drawing on it. Sendak loved Jim's drawing so much that he sent back a letter with an original drawing of a wild thing. A few weeks went by, and Sendak received a reply from Jim's mother. She wrote: "Dear Mr. Sendak, Thank you for your letter and the original drawing. Jim couldn't be happier. He saw it, he loved it, he ate it." Then Sendak told listeners that, for him, this was the highest compliment he had ever received. "The boy did not care that it was an original Maurice Sendak drawing probably worth thousands of dollars. He saw it, he loved it, he ate it" (Gross, 2011).

This story reveals an intimate exchange between author and reader, and I find the little boy's instinctual and primordial engagement with text and image profound and original. The physical consumption of Sendak's letter is like taking sacred communion. The literal ingestion of the author's work signifies love, delight, and the desire to be nourished by another person's creation.

In this chapter, I explore how the readers/audience of autoethnography may utilize artistic media and processes to creatively engage and respond to autoethnographic narratives. For me, art-making and the creation of aesthetic objects have been instrumental in deepening my reading experience, developing intimacy with a story, and being transformed by someone else's story. Drawing insights from my maker-centered aesthetic engagements with existing autoethnographic writings, I expand the horizon of the reader's role, calling, and potential contributions. Cultivating active and engaged readers of autoethnography is as vital for the future of the field as training skilled autoethnographers.

If I liken existing narratives to a nourishing meal, what does it take to enjoy, digest, and draw life-sustaining energy? What does it mean to move beyond consuming and to *commune* with autoethnography? What does it require from the reader to inhabit or embody someone else's story (research) so it may transform readers and, by extension, their worlds? What are the potential tools and methods available for readers that may lead to deeper engagements with research narratives?

Specific methods, tools, and philosophical perspectives guide the composition of autoethnographic narratives. The practice is engaged and structured. I believe the act of reading and readers' engagement with autoethnographic narratives should be similarly guided, informed by principles and rituals that deepen and broaden the exchange between authors and readers. These practices of close, deep reading maximize engagement, resonance, and intimacy with stories. Close reading techniques enhance the meaning-making process and any resulting inner transformation.

Traditional close reading techniques emphasize the exchanges between readers and text as a cerebral or cognitive engagement. Thus, the reading experience often remains a stationary or sedentary activity, where the reader's eyes and intellect are given prominent roles but the rest of the body remains at rest. As a maker, I am aware of the epistemic dimensions of the body, especially the hands. Knowing, understanding, feeling through crafting objects has been an invaluable part of my existential journey. Art making is a deliberate process through which I can explore ideas, stories, events, feelings or phenomena mediated by a skillful interaction and reliance on artistic media, tools, and methods. This embodied, ritualistic process of creating and crafting often generates a new or different layer of understanding and inner transformation that I would not gain from simply reading or writing a story. This is why I experiment with an engaged, aesthetic reading and writing practice involving the creation of tangible objects.

Communing with stories

The holy communion in the Christian tradition is a profound ritual. It is a somatic, multi-sensory engagement with a story (the last supper) and sacred substances (bread and wine). The ultimate goal of this ritual is to incarnate or embody the teachings of Jesus of Nazareth, who sets an example of unconditional love and forgiveness to be emulated by his followers. In this religious rite, the physical participation in the liturgy (i.e., eating, digesting, and absorbing nourishing substances) is essential to make a sacred story into energy and flesh—a lived experience. The phrase, proclaimed aloud during the liturgy, "Do this in remembrance of me," stresses the importance of re-collection. It is an ordering, healing act. It pieces together what has been injured or dismembered. Remembering is the antonym of dis-membering. Thus, remembering is an active re-making of order out of chaos through full participation in the sacred liturgy. Also, the physical acts of eating bread and drinking wine serve as powerful reminders. Like the body of Christ was injured (dismembered) and killed, the grape has been crushed and the grain ground into flour.

However, through the ritual of holy communion, everything becomes whole again. Through transformative processes (i.e., fermentation, kneading, baking), the crushed grapes become nourishing wine, and broken, pulverized seeds become bread. Similarly, as we consume these substances, all elements of the bread and wine integrate into our bodies. Since Jesus identified himself with these elements ("Take and eat; this is my body"), devotees believe that, through communion, Jesus himself will become an integral part of their existence.

Inspired by this ritual, I try to approach and engage with evocative narratives and scholarship as sacred stories, as substances requiring my full attention and participation. For me, "reading or listening to a story [is] a powerful stimulus to re-materialize [it] outside of the pages, outside of my bodily confines" (Osvath, 2018, p. 2). In this way, I couple the traditional practice of reading narratives with creating aesthetic objects—materialized, tangible responses.

I aspire to a reading practice that requires full-body engagement. My goal is to bring into existence something new, an extension to or continuation of the author's work. For me, transformation through a story happens most vividly when reading culminates in a creative process of contemplative making, of active engagement with tools and artistic media. I often approach stories as the author(s)' shared harvest, which requires participation, celebration and transformation. "Completed" or published works do not signal closure. Rather they begin a new cycle of harvest and life.

What if we approach published research as seeds requiring mindful tending and prolonged caring? Of course, seeds can be consumed as they are, as highly concentrated nourishing substances. Some readers will choose this approach and simply consume stories in order to serve their individual existence, to fulfill a particular need or desire. Often, especially in academia, people read others' work to inform, guide, or enhance their own scholarly output. My intention here is not to diminish the importance of promoting the publication of more works, including autoethnographies. However, I offer an alternative path, taking on the role of artist or gardener. In this scenario, existing seeds or raw materials are tended into new forms. Instead of turning scholarship (text) into more scholarship (text)—a kind of monoculture of scholarly output—I propose a new engagement in which readers transform the text into new or different manifestations, in my case, aesthetic objects.

Creatio ex fabulae: creating from stories

Even as a preliterate child, my encounters with stories often sparked creative acts, like building my version of Narnia from Lego blocks or designing shadow puppets for my reenactment of Captain Nemo's adventures. I consider these reading responses as valuable forms of engagement through which an author's content is re-materialized in new ways and forms through my enactments.

In 2001, when I began my graduate studies in theology in the United States, this kind of artistic resonance with stories undoubtedly saved my academic career. Though I was competent in Hebrew and hermeneutics, my English language skills were inadequate to communicate my full knowledge and understanding of biblical text. I found it difficult to engage in seminar discussions. My peers often grew impatient with my heavily accented utterances as I slowly and arduously articulated my responses. My growing sense of failure and inability to communicate and connect shifted when I encountered an abandoned bag of clay in the seminary's basement art studio. Though I'd had no training in sculpting, one day after class I decided to express my understanding of the stories we studied in a series of clay sculptures. Besides the therapeutic benefits of interacting with clay, I suddenly realized how this malleable, forgiving medium could serve as a powerful tool for expressing ideas and feelings. I began scribbling in my notebook while working on the sculpture, naming the objects, describing visual clues, all of which fed an emboldened desire to show and share my work, to use it as an intermediary to speak on my behalf.

I will never forget the first time I brought a sculpture to class: the pregnant initial silence of fellow students and my professor, how everyone walked over to my table to look at and touch the sculpture. Creating and sharing afforded not only membership into the group, but it also set me on a path of deliberately making aesthetic objects to engage with and respond to stories.

Over time, my goal became to promote *tangible* scholarship where "knowledge production" is not confined to a rigid and formulaic modus or scheme, where publication in scholarly journals is not a terminus or expected norm. What now

FIGURE 13.1 "The Sacrifice of Isaac" from the Genesis series

most interests me is the *afterlife* of stories—how readers may give narratives created by others new shape and meaning. This is why I propose a "tangible" auto-ethnography, where readers' engagement with stories results in material creations through repeated interactions with stories and their authors. If we want to nurture a vibrant, spirited autoethnographic community, purposeful and creative engagements with each other's work are just as important as publishing new research.

For me, autoethnography is inseparable from and central to everyday life. It is an existential scholarship that aims to promote equilibrium, eudaemonia, social justice, and the possibility of wise living. Bochner (2012) suggests that autoethnography

> in practice … is not so much a methodology as a way of life. It is a way of life that acknowledges contingency, finitude, embeddedness in storied being, encounters with Otherness, an appraisal of ethical and moral commitments, and a desire to keep conversation going.
>
> *(p. 225)*

This statement serves as an invitation to reimagine the possibilities both as authors and audience of autoethnographic scholarship.

Shifting priorities

When I began taking formal art classes as a young adult, I dreamed about life as a successful maker/creator. I was overwhelmed by the desire to become prolific. One day, when I presented my weekly portfolio with a few dozen new sketches, my wise instructor said, with kindness and certainty, "The world does not need more art." As an aspiring artist, I so resented her statement that I did not pay attention to what came next, that our world "desperately needs more artists and creators." I was caught up in my ideas of making lots of art and making it big in the art world. It took years to realize that maybe she was right. Indeed, there is already enough art in the world from which to learn and draw inspiration. Making fewer new works while engaging more—and more deeply—with what we already have came to seem like the most meaningful, fulfilling path.

Perhaps some readers would be offended if I suggested the world doesn't need more autoethnographies. However, the statement provides a valuable thought experiment. It doesn't mean we should not write/publish autoethnographies. I did not abandon making art even as I discovered the truth in my mentor's suggestion. But by coming to take her suggestion seriously, I found that my art was no longer created out of desire for fame. Taking on each new piece became a deliberate choice. Applying this lens to autoethnography, I wonder: What would happen if we could only interact with, read, play with, build on, transform already existing autoethnographies?

Bochner and Ellis (2016) question how readers ought to interact with auto-ethnography. As mentioned, I often approach published research as seeds to cultivate; my role as a reader entails prolonged, creative, mindful engagement.

But is it feasible or even possible to promote an engaged, maker-centered reading response in an academic culture that values mainly the production and dissemination of "original" research? I believe it would bring more balance to academia if faculty and students were not only rewarded for the fruits of their own research but also for the cultivation and tending of the research created by others.

Moreover, I yearn to witness more engagements with autoethnography beyond the boundaries of academia. How would a dancer tend, cultivate, creatively engage with an autoethnographic story? What about a veteran, a composer, a jazz pianist, a migrant worker, or a group of preschoolers?

In addition, it is worthwhile to reflect on the need for autoethnographers in our world. Like my art teacher suggested, we do not necessarily need more art (autoethnographies), but we desperately need more artists (autoethnographers). Reflecting on my encounters, collaborations, and friendships with auto-ethnographers, I often find that their embodied existence in my life and the time I spend with them brings the most joy, restoration, and meaning. I believe that autoethnographic writing is fundamentally a transformative medium, a powerful catalyst that (re)shapes our humanity, the heart, the body, and the intellect. Thus, it serves us well to be mindful about how we approach and engage with autoethnography.

Restoring harmony and freeing my father within me

As a mixed-media artist, I actively search for new ways to respond to, embody, and cultivate existing autoethnography. My first tangible response to a series of auto-ethnographic narratives was a mixed-media glass mosaic, "Restoring Harmony" (2016), which became the cover art for *Evocative Autoethnography: Writing Lives and Telling Stories* (Bochner & Ellis, 2016).

Metaphorically, the book offers a plentiful harvest and nourishing substances. I approached the book as seeds to cultivate, as a calling to become more than a reader by adding a physical layer to the stories. I engaged in the slow, ritual process during the aftermath of a retina surgery that resulted in drastic changes to my visual perception. The process offered a contemplative, healing space for examining my pain, fears, and the uncertainty of my recovery.

Though temporarily losing the ability to read shook my world, using my hands and fragmented glass to create a tangible object became a restorative act, a new kind of reading experience. A more detailed narrative of my experience of creating this work can be found in the *Coda* section of *Evocative Autoethnography* (Bochner & Ellis, 2016, pp. 257–269).

Similarly, my piece "Freeing the Father within Me" (2016), based on Art Bochner's (2012) narrative, "Bird on the Wire," offers another example of culti-vating an existing story.

My artistic response to Bochner's story allowed me to slow down radically, to stay with a story until it became part of me. The process began as a classroom exercise in which I was assigned to critique the story using a qualitative research

FIGURE 13.2 "Restoring Harmony"

rubric. Engaging with Bochner's work, I realized that "Bird on the Wire" demanded more from me as a reader than rubric-based criticism.

At the time, my own relationship with my father was in crisis. I heard Bochner's story as an invitation to reenter my own stories and memories, to deal with ambivalence, and to seek "purifying conversations" with my father. But this task required more than reading and critiquing the article. What afforded change and transformation was the long, arduous process of creating the artwork out of tiny, broken pieces of glass. The daily ritual of working on the piece expanded time; the slow progress became a source of discoveries and epiphanies that I could not have received from reading alone. The symbiosis of reading and making resulted in a seismic shift not only in my understanding and communion with Bochner's story, but it also created an entry point to re-connect with my father. Later, I added another layer to my reading response by making a film about this creative process (Osvath, 2017).

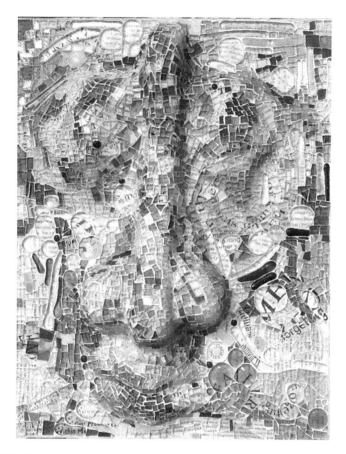

FIGURE 13.3 "Freeing the Father within Me"

"The Clean Shirt" and *Final Negotiations*

I first encountered Carolyn Ellis' and Jerry Rawicki's story, "The Clean Shirt: A Flicker of Hope in Despair" (2019), during a graduate seminar in grief and loss. Jerry attended Dr. Ellis' class one evening as a guest speaker. Moved by Jerry's presence and story, I wanted to create an aesthetic response, an offering to Jerry. Though I did not have a concrete idea about what this artwork would look like, I repeatedly read the story and watched Carolyn's documentary film about visiting Treblinka with Jerry (Ellis & Schoen, 2016). I then created a kiln-formed glass panel.

The work symbolizes the encircling wall of the Warsaw ghetto and the small opening through which Jerry crawled, escaping imminent death. The layered, hand-carved red glass is not simply my representation of the bricks and the wall but also of the lives lost. The overall design evokes the memorial site at Treblinka, which consists of thousands of stones inscribed with the names of the Jewish

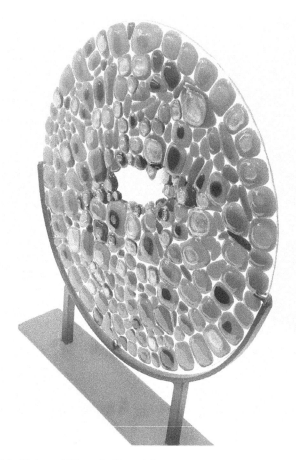

FIGURE 13.4 "A Flicker of Hope in Despair"

villages and communities that were obliterated during the Holocaust. During my creative process, I printed the names of those places and the names of Jerry's family members who perished. While I hand-carved each piece of glass before firing it, I offered a silent prayer. Reciting the names of villages, towns, and people became an active and restorative re-collection.

Inspired by the Jewish concept of Tikkum Olam (reparative acts of kindness), I seek new, creative, tangible ways to mend/heal the world. I long to create in response to my reading experience and to share my work not necessarily as "new" scholarly output but rather as an expression of reciprocity or grateful recompense. Handing the piece to Jerry in his home and seeing the surprised joy and gratitude in his eyes and face meant so much more than a line on my vita or an acceptance letter from a journal.

Working on the cover art for *Final Negotiations* in collaboration with Carolyn Ellis also was an undeniably transformative and meaningful experience.

FIGURE 13.4 (Cont.)

Book covers stand as potentially powerful entry points to stories. Thus, creating cover art offers a meaningful challenge to both artist and writer: to design a work that evokes the message of the book.

Carolyn tried to remain a good ethnographer and conscious qualitative researcher by recording interview conversations after each work session. In retrospect, however, what was most transformative about our collaboration was the silence, the mundane but *deep work* of progressing slowly, and those moments of *flow* we experienced together (Csikszentmihalyi, 1990; Newport, 2016). This project is also an example of autoethnographic collaboration where autoethnographer and artist co-create, adding a visual layer to a textual work.

"Maternal Connections"

Currently I am working on a visual response to Carolyn Ellis' "Maternal Connections" (1996). Though the artistic processes involved in the creation of my art often

FIGURE 13.5 "Final Negotiations"

change, I embrace methods and techniques that deepen my engagement, both with the story and with making the corresponding art. To enliven the reading experience of Ellis' story, and after repeated readings of the text, I copied the text by hand, word for word. For me, copying text or images by hand is a valuable practice and a form of engaged reading. Feeling the words through hand and body and listening to the sounds of pencil on paper help me pay closer attention. There is an intimacy in copying. Next, I took my handwritten script and typed the story to gain more familiarity, more intimacy. I aim to learn a story by heart, as this process often leads to epiphanies regarding the idea or vision for the art. With "Maternal Connections," I continued to play/experiment with the text by turning it into a medieval form of writing, called *scriptura continua* or continuous writing. Through this ancient form of representation spaces and punctuation are eliminated and the entire story becomes a continuous text with capital letters:

WITHONEHANDSHEHOLDSTIGHTLYTOTHESUPPORTBARALON
GTHEWALLOFTHEBATHROOMITAKEHEROTHERHANDGENTLY
INMINEWASHEACHFINGERNOTINGTHESMOOTHNESSOFHERSK
INTHEBEAUTYOFHERLONGSLENDERFINGERSMYFINGERNAILS-
SHESAYSTHEYAREDIRTYWITHOUTSPEAKINGIRUNMYINDEXN

AILCOVEREDWITHAWASHCLOTHUNDEREACHOFHERNAILSSYS
TEMATICALLYSNAPPINGOUTTHEDIRTASIGOITSAGOODSIGNTH
ATSHECARESUNTILNOWSHEHASNTBEENTHATCONCERNEDEV
ENABOUTURINATINGINBED

Reading a script like this requires rehearsing and reading it out loud. I also plan to use *scriptura continua* in my collage, inviting readers to wrestle with the text.

Tangible autoethnography is not limited to aesthetic objects created as responses to autoethnographic narratives. As I continue to engage with "Maternal Connections," I also write autoethnographic vignettes:

> I will never forget my first reading of "Maternal Connections" in Carolyn's autoethnography class. It transported me into a bizarre, symbolic, imaginary place where my recollection of past memories and events presented themselves in the shape of my mother, pleading for my touch. I still see myself in this dreamlike vision, holding a soaped washcloth (as Carolyn did) but unable to touch my mother's body, which is covered with dirt and bruises. I still fight this childhood memory, resenting my mother's alcoholism, finding her naked in the bathroom, collapsed over the toilet, covered with vomit and feces. But reading Carolyn's story alters this memory. Her story places the soaped washcloth into my hands. It is Carolyn's story that wakes up my mother, who says in a clear and kind voice, "I'm sorry about last night."
>
> Before my birth, before the drinking, before the divorce, there was a slender, youthful body radiating pride with an unashamed display of her long legs. There's a black and white photo I found between the pages of a dusty encyclopedia. It's a young woman in her late teens in a miniskirt and white blouse.
>
> I watch the rising smoke from her long cigarette, frozen in mid-air, a ghostly reminder of the transience of her youthful body. This young woman will become my mother whose body pushes me away. However, reading "Maternal Connections" creates a space that continuously asks for my touch, for my love, and for my forgiveness. I also realize that I need an added dimension of making a work of art. I must find ways to deepen my communion with Carolyn's story, so it may go further, transforming me on an even deeper level ... I want to make sure that one day, the touch, the love, and the forgiveness toward my mom will be more than a thought experiment.

Calling on readers: an invitation

My intention with this chapter is to promote new engagements with autoethnographic narratives. I call on readers to consider making and creating as vital forms of engagements with existing stories. We should not limit the scope of these tangible responses to objects or artistic media like collage, paintings, and sculptures. Dance, music, and other forms of performance also should be championed and cultivated as aesthetic responses to autoethnography. I envision tangible autoethnography as a sub-genre where autoethnographic writing and non-textual objects are presented together as performance, exhibit, or publication.

I realize that, for me, reading without making will often short-circuit the process of embodying a story. As an advocate for tangible autoethnography, I want to embody the text on the page, to make change both necessary and palpable. As a maker and autoethnographer my calling is not "to resolve or exhaust … the mysteries and complications of being alive," but "to artfully arrange" those in ways that help people to cope and to feel less alone and more empowered (Bochner, 2017, p. 2).

Finding and creating new ways to share stories through writing and making merges the processes of art-making and autoethnographic writing. I envision publications that pair autoethnographic stories with visuals—like picture books for adults where writing and art play equally important roles. The art gives a new layer to the writing. It is not subservient. It is not decorative or simply an illustration of the text. Nor does the writing have lesser value than the art. It would be a perfect symbiosis, a new platform to share our work as nourishing substances, like a shared and sacred meal.

References

Bochner, A. P. (2012). Suffering happiness: On autoethnography's ethical calling. *Qualitative Communication Research*, 2: 209–229. https://doi.org/10.1525/qcr.2012.1.2.209.

Bochner, A. (2012). Bird on the wire: Freeing the father within me. *Qualitative Inquiry*, *18*(2): 168–173. https://doi.org/10.1177/1077800411429094.

Bochner, A. (2017). Heart of the matter: A mini-manifesto for autoethnography. *International Review of Qualitative Research*, *10*(1), 67–80.

Bochner, A. P., & Ellis, C. (2016). *Evocative autoethnography: Writing lives and telling stories.* Routledge.

Csikszentmihalyi, M. (1990). *Flow: The psychology of optimal experience. Steps toward enhancing the quality of life.* Harper & Row.

Ellis, C. (1996). Maternal connections. In C. Ellis & A. P. Bochner (Eds.), *Composing ethnography: Alternative forms of qualitative writing* (pp. 240–243). AltaMira Press.

Ellis, C. (2018). *Final negotiations: A story of love, loss, and chronic illness.* Temple University Press.

Ellis, C., & Rawicki, J. (2019). The clean shirt: A flicker of hope in despair. *Journal of Contemporary Ethnography*, *48*(1): 3–15. https://doi.org/10.1177/0891241617696809.

Ellis, C. (Producer), & Schoen, S. (Director). (2016). *Groaning from the soul* [video]. Retrieved from https://vimeo.com/158748870/3851d85549.

Gross, T. (2011, September 20). This pig wants to party: Maurice Sendak's latest. *Fresh Air* [podcast]. Retrieved from www.npr.org/2011/09/20/140435330/this-pig-wants-to-party-maurice-sendaks-latest.

Newport, C. (2016). *Deep work: Rules for focused success in a distracted world.* Grand Central Publishing.

Osvath, Cs (2017). *Tending bird on the wire* [video]. Retrieved from www.youtube.com/watch?v=yksY1VtXIJw&t=13s.

Osvath, Cs (2018). Ready learner one: Creating an oasis for virtual/online education. *Journal of Language and Literacy Education*, *14*(1): 1–20.

14

SEARCHING FOR UTOPIA IN RURAL QUEER NARRATIVES

Darren Cummings

A snapshot[1]

    I was 13 years old and sitting on my mother's Pepto-Bismol pink throw-covered sofa. I was working on some kind of school project because I had a piece of paper and a book on my lap. I do not know where the thought came from, and I can remember at the time wondering why I was just now able to put into words what I had known for a long time: "I am gay." I wrote it over and over again on the paper, wondering what it really meant. My only instruction at school about the existence of gay people came from negative words directed at me by my peers. I do not remember any specific teaching or discussions about being gay in any other context. This was the early 1990s, when Oprah wasn't yet talking about queer topics and Ellen had yet to come out. My conceptualization, therefore, was that, yes, I was gay, as I had frequently been called, and that meant I was attracted to boys. It also meant it was wrong and that I could not tell anyone. I rushed out to the woodstove and burned the piece of paper so my Mom wouldn't see it.

This story brings forward questions. Could a similar story be written today? If so, what does it say about the value placed on queer youth and the value with which they see themselves? What does this kind of story do, and what can one do with a story like this?

    Autoethnography is a methodology that utilizes personal experiences to bridge the connection between the self and the culture that produces the self, demonstrating how power works to dominate and marginalize particular groups within society. Like autoethnography, queer theory seeks to point out social conventions that cause harm and disrupt them. This chapter demonstrates the process and possibilities inherent in using queer autoethnography to interrogate compulsory hetero-normativity and cisnormativity. It shows how gender and sexual norms restrict us and how queer autoethnography can be used to investigate future queer possibilities. I tell stories of what it was like being a queer child and teenager in my community and school in the 1980s and 1990s in rural Nova Scotia, Canada. I also document my experiences of moving back from University and working in rural towns for 15 years. I then explore how queer autoethnography can counter deficit discourses that surround queer individuals, particularly the discourse of the suffering rural queer. I end by asking what the possibilities are in telling ordinary stories of queer love, friendship, and belonging as a way to imagine a queer utopia.

I have included various remembered moments throughout this writing, which I refer to as "snapshots." My method of writing is similar to Adams and Holman Jones (2008, 2011; Holman Jones & Adams, 2010) who present narratives in a non-linear fashion alongside theory; the theory validates the stories, and the theory is validated by the experiences in the narratives. Telling stories in this way interrupts the need for a traditional plot, with a beginning, middle and end. As Heckert (2010) notes, queer research need not involve the telling of "linear stories and their (continually postponed) happy endings (p. 43). Rather, he states queer:

> [M]ay refer to the erotic potential of everyday life, to the ongoing joyful awareness of being alive, even when it hurts; an awareness that life itself is exuberant and *always* escapes, overflows, undermines or disregards all attempts to impose categories, to discipline.
>
> *(p. 43)*

This writing is not meant to be a complete account. Choosing what to include and not about my life is a subjective and personal act. This account reflects moments in time, frozen once in print; the text cannot encapsulate the whole of my experience (Adams & Holman Jones, 2008, p. 382). Adams and Holman Jones (2008) caution that "a written text can function as a permanent representation, a lifeless, uncompromising snapshot of culture" (p. 382). The moments I write about are like a photograph, a "snapshot," that presents a picture of my past and my current thoughts, but like a photograph they cannot tell the complete story. The snapshots cannot display how my thinking may change after publication. Because the author will continue to evolve after the writing has ceased, autoethnography is always unfinished; questions always remain unanswered (Adams & Holman Jones, 2011, p. 109). There is no ending. I may come to new interpretations or remember other memories, and I will hopefully go on to make more memories, which may change my interpretations. Even when I am gone, this text and my life can be remade by the reader and also by my loved ones who have their own versions of my life.

We all carry incomplete accounts of our loved ones' lives, and therefore, Ellis et al. (2011) advise that it is important to understand how we frame ourselves in relation to others. Researchers are connected to many social networks. I write about classmates, friends, and family in the vignettes that follow. It is not my intent to pass blame or judgment on anyone mentioned. The events I write occurred in the past and are my subjective remembrances. My memories may not be the memories held by the people mentioned. In addition, people and their conceptualizations, including my own, continually change. I am aware that the actions of someone 30 years ago may not reflect who they are today.

These stories are constructed as best as I can remember. Bochner and Ellis (2016) discuss how writing vividly about feelings, emotions, and sensations can assist the autoethnographer in accessing the memory and also provide a rich narrative for the reader. These stories are personal, and by sharing I am forced to make myself vulnerable. I want readers to identify with my experiences as a queer person within their own frameworks, which may not be queer. By making the stories personal I am inviting readers to identify the human experience common to us all. As Pelias (2004) states in *Methodology of the Heart,* "being emotionally vulnerable, linguistically evocative," while using a "poetic voice can place us closer to the subjects we wish to study" (p. 1).

I wish to present a picture in these stories of a fully human life. As I wrote, I laughed, cried, longed for, smiled, reflected, hurt, and felt love. Thus, I tell the following stories to give the reader insight into what my queer life has been like, to make the reader feel and reflect, and to educate. As Ellis et al. (2011) remind, autoethnographers seek to create "meaningful, accessible, and evocative research grounded in personal experience, research that would sensitize readers to issues of identity politics, to experiences shrouded in silence, and to forms of representation that deepen our capacity to empathize with people" (p. 274). The power of queer autoethnography is to tell stories that need to be heard (Adams & Holman Jones, 2011).

Part 1. Home

A snapshot

I always loved soap operas. I remember in Grade 3 writing about the eight different "soaps" that I watched at the time, their plots and their characters. I shared this writing with the class, to Mrs. J's shock and probable dismay. Likely because of this daily foray into the "dramatic," and because children are often imaginative, I would often role play at home that I was a cast member in one of these soap operas. However, I had no desire to be the man in these re-enactments; no, I had to be the heroine! At home, these role plays consisted of taking one of my mother's aprons and wearing it over my clothes, as a dress, along with the longest towel I could find. I would centre this on my head and tuck its edges behind my ears, pulling it down so that I had a straight set of bangs, with the rest of my "hair" flowing down my back. I would put on a pair of my mom's shoes to complete the ensemble. My only real playmate at home was my cousin, Molly, who was 1 year older than I. Because our parents were close, we were always at each other's houses. We would often act out scenes together (I say "act" here, but it is important to note that I remember not just wanting to play these women, but to actually "be" one). I don't remember any initial judgment from Mom and Dad about this play, and maybe that's why I figured I could reproduce it at school.

One Halloween, I decided that I would dress up as a girl, so I donned my mom's dress and shoes, foregoing the towel-as-wig look, and went off happily to school. When I arrived, many peers were laughing and snickering at me, saying things like,

"Nice dress, Darren!" in the sarcastic, judgmental tone to which I had become accustomed. What I found ironic was that some of the boys who usually presented themselves as "typically," masculine also chose to dress up as girls, but the reactions to them were much different. Peers looked at them with amusement and applauded their sense of humour, because who could imagine that these boys would ever really want to be a girl? The looks directed at me were scornful—a laughing at, rather than a laughing with, the boy in the dress alone on the swings.

A snapshot

I loved watching *Dukes of Hazzard*. I remember Molly and I watching and role-playing it. Her favorite character was Bo and mine was Luke. I thought he was so good looking. Molly was always good enough to let me be Daisy Duke, and she would reluctantly be one of the boys. The show was popular at the time, so when I went to school I would ask classmates if they wanted to play *Dukes of Hazzard*. I can see myself screaming, "I'm Daisy Duke" and running away from some imagined "bad guy." The other children picked up on my desire to always "play" the girl part, and eventually they created a new name for me. It was the beginning of many names that would be leveled at me over the next decade and the beginning of my subjectification: "Daisy Duke Darren."

A snapshot

I was in Grade 1, my cousin Molly in Grade 2. I know this because I couldn't write very well yet and she could. The cutest boy at school was in the same grade as my cousin. One of the things that seemed popular at the time, in my mind at least, was that one should write the person on whom you had a crush a "love note" to express your undying love so he could reciprocate it; then you could hold hands on the merry-go-round. How romantic! So, because I couldn't write very well, and Molly could, one of us decided that the best course of action would be that she would write this boy a note telling him of my undying love and that if he felt the same way he should meet me out by the swings at recess the following day.

The next day I waited in anticipation all morning until recess finally arrived. I bounded out to the playground to see if he was waiting, but he did not show up. What did show up were other children; laughing and pointing and shouts of "Darren Loves Bill." From that point on, he avoided me, and throughout that year my transgression would be brought up repeatedly by those who didn't appreciate my courage. I never again made that same mistake.

A snapshot

I feared walking home after school through much of my middle school life. It was not a long walk. The school was at the top of a steep hill, our house at the bottom. The quickest way home was to take a wooded path that began just off the school property. I would always ask my friends if I could get a ride with their parents after school, but if I had to walk, I would try to walk home with a friend. I ran through the woods as fast as my moderately overweight body could take me on many occasions. One day I was walking down the path when a boy I knew, of whom I wasn't particularly afraid, asked me why I always hung around with girls. He asked me if I was a girl because I sure acted like one. He then reached out and grabbed my flabby chest. Nature was not a safe space. I would avoid going in nature alone until my 30s.

A snapshot

Every Christmas my mom and I get together with close friends who are like family. We pick a day and meet for dinner. Recently we went to a restaurant that had a long line at the door. As we stood there, a group of loud men entered behind us. My mom was waiting in the car because she has chronic leg pain. The host approached us to say that we should have a table soon. I decided to get Mom. I turned around and said, "Excuse me," and the men parted like the Red Sea. As I walked through their stares and snickers, I recognized danger on either side of my body. In a small community, I am (usually blissfully) aware that my shoulder-length hair, foundation-ed face, and long scarves are not considered masculine.

When I came back, walking past the men with my mother, the snickering continued. I saw one of them pretend to kick a cane out of the hand of one of my elderly friends. Then one of them pushed himself into my back, hard. I continued to face forward. One of my friends saw this happening and gave them dirty looks. I felt terrified she would say something to them. I knew what a confrontation could bring, and I had no plan to get bashed on that day. I felt relieved when we were finally brought to a table. However, I also felt embarrassed that this had happened in front of my loved ones, as if it were my fault. I tried to pretend like nothing had happened, but for me, the encounter hung in the air throughout the dinner.

A snapshot

As I look back on Grade 9 I can remember being awake many sleepless nights when I knew I had Physical Education the next day. I would get up in the morning and wonder if I could pretend I was sick one more time, or get myself to school and then cut the class. I knew the latter would result in a call home, and it was easier to go to gym than to explain to my Mom why I didn't want to.

The gym was segregated with a curtain down the middle, girls on one side, boys on the other. Away from the girls I would often find myself alone and dealing with name calling, harassment, balls thrown purposely at me, one time hitting me square in the face. The Phys. Ed. teacher was a nice person, but he knew neither how to address the behavior nor how to deal with me. We had no meaningful relationship. Then there was the locker room! I would try to avoid the space by wearing my gym clothes to school or changing in a bathroom stall. After two years, I told my mother that I was not going to participate in Phys. Ed anymore. I said I didn't like it and I wasn't good at it, which was true. I did not tell her, or anyone, how unsafe I felt in the space. I went to school the next day and sat on the bleachers telling the teacher I wasn't participating.

After a week, I was sent to the office, and the principal asked why I wasn't participating. I told him the same answer I gave my mom. He called home, and Mom said she would talk to me. I continued to insist that I wasn't doing it. Every day I would go into the gym and sit on the bleachers, and for a while the response from the teacher was for me to just go directly to the office and sit, which I happily did. Eventually, both the principal and teacher allowed me to sit out. At the end of the course I had a 20%. For attendance, I guess.

A snapshot

It was wintertime, and I had stayed over at my boyfriend's apartment, as I had many nights, because I didn't want to drive home in the snow. His apartment was in a house with a couple of units downstairs and two upstairs. He didn't talk to his neighbours, and I hadn't met them before but would see them often. That morning it was cold and frosty. I was going to leave early because I hate driving on slippery roads. I went back to the car to get the window scraper and stopped, frozen, by the three-letter word written in the frost on my windshield.

Why am I sharing these stories about how I, even as a small child, did not fit within the normalized category of what it meant to be a "boy" and in particular a "straight boy"? It is my hope that, by offering my "retrospectively selected epiphanies" (Ellis et al., 2011, p. 276), the reader can see how the heterosexual and cisgender hegemonic social and cultural world affected me and continues to affect me in adulthood. In this way, as Grace (2006) reminds, queer autoethnography is an educative act, as "readers have opportunities to understand how hegemony and the culture-language-power nexus work to demonize queer, to silence it, to make it invisible" (p. 827). In addition, by sharing how my queer body has been affected by queerphobia, I ask the reader to move beyond a simple understanding of my experiences toward a consideration of how we might change the future for other queer people.

A return to one of the questions posed at the beginning of this chapter might be helpful: "What does this kind of story do?" I have shared stories that describe the moments I have suffered because I did not perform within traditional, rural norms associated with sexuality and gender. In sharing these stories, I am also perpetuating a dominant narrative about the suffering rural queer. Much of the discourse around rural queer life equates rurality with homophobia and harassment (Baker, 2011; Crawford, 2008; Detamore, 2013; Gray, 2009; Halberstam, 2005). Following this storyline, queer people must leave the "homophobic" countryside and head to the city to find a "home" and, therefore, acceptance (Schweighofer, 2016). This story is reinforced by a metronormativity in scholarship where rural queer stories are often ignored, and when they are told they frame the social world through a lens of deficit (Stone, 2018). However, this familiar narrative forgets, and thus, diminishes, the experiences of rural queer people who stay and have successful and fulfilling lives in their communities. Despite the above stories, I consider my time living and teaching in rural Nova Scotia as a success. The problem with queer deficit discourses, and the stories I told above, is that they do not present a nuanced and comprehensive picture of queer life.

The narrative of rural queer deficit fits within larger discourses that equate queer sexuality and gender identity with homophobia, transphobia, and harassment (Payne & Smith, 2012). The world, urban and rural, can be a hostile place for queer people, particularly queer youth. As a rural public school teacher for many years, I am aware of the statistics regarding the levels of homophobia, transphobia, and queer bullying that exist in schools. I have also experienced it first-hand. The way districts and educators have attempted to address the harassment of queer students has been a doubled-edged sword. Homophobia has become the main way queer topics are approached in schools. Students are taught that homophobia and homophobic harassment and bullying are wrong, yet discussions around queer identity largely end there (Schmidt, 2010). Queer lives become associated with vulnerability and victimhood (Fields et al., 2014). Missing in this dialogue is any talk of queer love, joy, community and belonging. The message this sends to queer youth, as they consider the possibility of a queer life, is that it is going to be a life of struggle.

Colin Johnson (2013), in his work on rural gender and sexuality, tells us that history suffers from amnesia, where some stories make it into the official narrative and others are ignored (p. 1). When LGBTQ life is reduced to narratives of suffering and violence, what is left out? What are we forgetting, and how might we remember? Queer theorist José Muñoz (2009) offers an answer. To counter this amnesia, Muñoz suggests that we look for instances of utopia found by remembering forgotten moments of pleasure from the past. He writes, "A posterior glance at different moments, objects, and spaces might offer us an anticipatory illumination of queerness" (p. 22). For Muñoz, utopia can be found by searching for the "no longer conscious" (p. 20) of the past. There we can critique the present and work towards future utopian possibilities. Cvetkovich's (2012) writing on depression is also fitting. Cvetkovich urges us to investigate not only the conditions that create or contribute to depression but also those that bring us pleasure and joy. She calls this the search for the "utopia of ordinary habit." (p. 189). She continues:

> Using the term *habit* in connection with utopia … suggests that habit can be a mechanism for building new ways of being in the world because it belongs to the domain of the ordinary, to activities that are not spectacular or unusual but instead arise from everyday life.
>
> *(p. 191)*

Placing Muñoz and Cvetkovich in conversation, I wonder if memories of love, friendship, and community occurring in "daily life in all its ordinariness" (p. 191) can be used as a utopian vision for the present and future? Searching for utopic memories certainly does not discount the stories of suffering I shared previously, nor does it seek to present sentimental and idyllic stories that mask negative experiences. Cvetkovich calls us to view depression as an "ordinary" affect that pervades our lives, much like compulsory heterosexuality. Her solution is to illuminate the problem but then search for utopic moments in the everyday that help us survive and thrive (p. 191). Thus, within Cvetkovich's work, she "fully recognizes the sorry state of the world and maintains plenty of room for unhappiness, melancholy, depression, and other bad feelings" (p. 190). We must *both* explore the conditions that cause harm and tell other narratives, ones that are potentially reparative (p. 202).

Remembering past everyday and "ordinary" moments of joy, love, and belonging that may have been forgotten by a world that would rather look at queers as suffering, creates possibilities for queer worlds in the present. Muñoz calls this work "queer utopian memory," which becomes a political act when attached to a medium like art, video, performance, or writing (p. 35). According to Muñoz, when we engage in such memory work we are engaging in "queer world making (p. 37), which occurs when remembering utopic moments in the past becomes more than just nostalgia or a projected hopeful future, but creates a "utopia in the present" (p. 37).

This brings me to the possibility of searching for memories that go beyond the traumatic— not to erase them but to un-mire a self, or perhaps a collective queer consciousness, from negativity. I now ask how one might undermine the historical amnesia of the rural queer by looking to the past for ordinary and everyday moments of utopia?[2]

Part 2. Home

A snapshot

It was the first Easter with my new boyfriend. It was only a few months into our relationship, so I decided to get him something small. I bought a chocolate bunny and wrote on the package, "To Sam, From the Easter Bunny." I put it in the living room for him to find the next morning. When he woke up, he went into the kitchen to make coffee and found the bunny. He brought it back into the bedroom, smiling, and laid on top of me with his head on my chest saying how much it meant to him that I would give him something for Easter.

A snapshot

I was walking home from a party with my boyfriend who was "out" to his family, but not to his co-workers. It was two in the morning, the snow falling gently. We were walking side by side, still intoxicated by the fun of the night. We turned the corner to the back road to my house. I took his hand. He let me take it, even though we were out in public, and we walked the rest of the way home together.

A snapshot

I had been dating someone for a couple months. It was a nice, sunny Saturday, so I asked him if he wanted to go for a drive to my hometown and meet my mother—for me, a first. My apartment didn't have a washing machine or dryer at the time, so like many 20-somethings, I would frequently drive to Mom's to do a wash and have a good home-cooked meal. Surprisingly, my boyfriend agreed to go, and off we went.

Upon arrival, I was surprised to find that my brother, his wife, and their two small children were there. Immediately I thought, "What have I gotten us into?" Introductions were made and everyone was quiet. My boyfriend, feeling uncomfortable, decided he would go to the kitchen and put my clothes in the washer. I went with him to ask how he was doing. From the living room, I heard my 11-year-old niece ask her dad, "Why is Mark out there doing Uncle Darren's laundry?" He replied, "Well, who else is going to do it?" This was probably a dig at my laziness, but it felt like acceptance.

The above vignettes are seemingly "ordinary" (yet, arguably monumental) memories of queer love and belonging. To me they offer utopic possibilities. Of course, to characterize these narratives as significant or ordinary is subjective. For some, the above vignettes about my boyfriend laying his head on my chest because I gave him a present, or walking down a country road hand in hand, or my boyfriend doing my laundry at my mother's house, may seem as the epitome of mundanity. But for those who cannot imagine these stories as *their* stories, they may be monumental.

A snapshot

I got a phone call one evening in middle school. It was a classmate that I had known since the first day of elementary school. She called herself "Jake." I was shocked that Jake was calling me because we hadn't gotten along in the past. I cannot say why she called me that evening, but it would be the beginning of a nightly call that would continue for many years.

We became best friends. Jake was loud, opinionated and generally outrageous. I was quiet, sometimes withdrawn, but also opinionated. I think we grew into ourselves together. Life became better because I began to make friends with her friends, offering me my first solid friend group. We went to prom together. Before I went off to University, she told me she loved me. I loved her too, but not in the same way. I wondered if I could and wished that I did. I didn't come out to her until I was in my early 20s, but she was not surprised. I think I was the surprised one when a few years later she introduced me to her girlfriend. Although we didn't talk about it for many years, we were both queer from the start. Maybe that's what drew us together.

A snapshot

By the time we were in our early 20s, Jake and I frequented the two local bars in town. Jake would eventually attend with her then-girlfriend. I had begun to come out, and most people knew that I was gay. In my mid-20s I began experimenting with foundation and eyeliner. I would wear this to the bars in my hometown. Sometimes I would end up in the "Women's" washroom using the mirror or Jake would end up in the "Men's." No one ever bothered us.

A snapshot

I became friends with another community member, Barb, that I met through work. When I met Barb, I thought she might be queer, based upon stereotypes of femininity that we all have been conditioned to hold. But Barb also had a male partner. As we became better friends, we began a lengthy online relationship. We slowly disclosed more and more about ourselves, and eventually, she talked about her attraction to women. She met a woman, Judy, and began to see her. Barb introduced me to Judy, and the three of us began to spend time together. We would go for drives, eat at restaurants in our small community, and even spent a weekend together at Barb's cottage. Eventually, gossip circulated about the two women, and this made its way back to Barb, who decided it was best to stay with her male partner. Both women were devastated.

Judy and I became great friends over time. She began to attend a monthly "queer dance" held in a public hall a few communities away. Judy asked if I wanted to go. Another great friend of mine, Katie, who identifies as bisexual, and I decided to drive up.

Katie and I went to many of these dances. One October we planned to attend a Halloween dance. Katie decided she would be, and I quote, "Fairy Mary, the Bisexual Fairy" complete with wings and tiara. I decided I would create Barbra Streisand's "Owl and the Pussycat" costume—a little black dress with hands of purple fabric holding up the bosom. I got a pair of purple gloves and sewed them onto the dress. I found a long blond wig and some size 12 heels from the costume department at our local theatre. I looked good. I got compliments, and remember that someone told me I was a good-looking woman. I guess it was a full-circle moment from that time in elementary school when I sat, dejected and rejected, on the swings. One of my favourite memories of these dances was watching Judy and her new partner waltz across the dance floor, as if they were a couple from out of the 50's. I would eventually go to their wedding. These dances held such possibilities.

What is most striking to me about these memories is that they have motivated me to reflect upon the number of queer-identified friends I made in my rural communities. I am reminded of Kath Weston's (1997) early work on "families we choose." Her book explores notions of kinship beyond the heterosexual family, where a group of queer friends might become like kin (Weston, 1997), something novelist Armistead Maupin calls one's "logical family." (Maupin, 2017). I have many utopic memories of belonging with my rural queer kin.

But, what does it mean to "belong" in rural communities that are heteronormative and sometimes unfriendly spaces? Mary L. Gray's (2009) extensive study of queer rural life found that the priorities in rural communities are familiarity and solidarity, not standing out as "different." Thus, "one's reputation as a familiar local is valued above all other identity claims" (p. 31). People are considered, first and foremost, members of particular families. This fosters an impetus to blend in, as the family is what ensures survival. Gray argues that "LGBTQ-identifying people use their stories as 'familiar locals'" to "rework the boundaries of public recognition and local belonging" (p. 4).

Gray refers to rural queer landscapes not as bound places but "boundary publics" which are "iterative, ephemeral experiences of belonging that circulate across the outskirts and through the center(s) of a more recognized and validated public sphere" (p. 93). Similarly, Mathias Detamore (2013) discusses many instances of queerness in rural Kentucky. He questions how rural queer space is made and names his investigation as one into "counterpublics" (p. 84). For Detamore, counterpublics are "understood to be those queer zones that exist outside of normative representations of sexual otherness [i.e., rural locations,] which often exceed the borders and typologies of metropolitan gay sex/life/politics" (p. 84). Like rural boundary publics, counterpublics may be found at unexpected intersections of queer and straight worlds. At such intersections, queer space transforms public space, even if only briefly (p. 85). When Jake, our friends, and I went out together in public I never worried about my safety. Nor did I feel unsafe at the country queer dances we attended. Gathering at the bar, eating at restaurants with a same-sex couple, and attending country dances exemplify "boundary publics" where we injected our queerness into public places.[3] We protected each other, and we were also protected by family and a community who knew us, and who, for the most part, accepted us.[4]

A snapshot
    I met my next-door neighbors, Leo and Meredith, when I was 5 years old. I was a precocious child and had no fear of new people, so one day I walked over and

introduced myself. It would be the beginning of a deep friendship with both, particularly with Meredith, because I tended to feel most comfortable with women. They used to take me camping and on road trips, and Meredith and I bonded over our love of primetime soap operas. I went to Meredith's and Leo's almost every day. We had sleepovers all the time; they would barbecue or cook me a nice meal and serve a typical bed-time snack of ice cream. They became my second parents.

I can only characterize Leo as masculine, kind and gentle. He had boxes of jokes, many inappropriate, written on cue cards. He tried his hand at repair work, electrical work, and small business ownership, selling electronics out of his basement. I did not tell Leo or Meredith that I was gay. I told no one in my teenage years.

When I left for University, I had come out to Meredith's sister, and we had a conversation about my concern of coming out to Meredith and Leo. She told me that Leo had talked to her about my masculinity, saying that he was concerned about how I would be treated because I didn't act masculine. She said to Leo, "Do you love him the way he is?" and he replied, "Of course, I do." She replied, "Then why would you want him to change?" That spring I arrived home for March Break and went over to surprise Leo and Meredith. As soon as I opened the door and Leo saw me, he bounded up from the chair exclaiming, "Darren, you're home!" He gave me a huge bear hug. It is my favorite memory of him.

A snapshot

My mother was the last close family member to find out I was gay. I was 25 years old. I was fearful she wasn't going to understand and that she wasn't going to accept me, after hearing so many stories from the media, particularly talk shows, where families disown their children if they are queer. I began to tell people slowly. First, I told my friends, and then I told an aunt who was good friends with my Mom, and then my two brothers. I told my aunt because I wanted Mom to have someone to talk to about it once I told her. My aunt's response was acceptance. She said she would be there for my Mom. My brothers were also accepting; one of them was not surprised at all, and the other didn't know but was fine with it.

I was living in another province at this time and decided that when I returned home for the summer I would finally tell Mom. It was about two weeks before I was to return home and I had disconnected the phone in my apartment building in preparation for leaving. I would go down to the lobby and use the pay phone if I needed it. One evening I went down and called home and Mom answered crying and upset. She said that she had received a letter in the mail that afternoon and she read it to me over the phone. "Dear Laura," it began, "I am writing to tell you that Darren is gay, and he does not know how to tell you. Everybody knows and is talking about it." It was signed "Anonymous." My Mom asked me if it were true and I started to cry and told her it was and we should talk about it in person when I arrived home.

The way she learned the news was upsetting for both of us—for her because it was a shock to hear the news in that manner, and for me because I was not prepared to come out to my mom over a payphone in a public lobby. When I arrived home, things were strained. I tried to explain to her what it meant and that I hadn't changed at all. I told her that if I weren't gay, I wouldn't be the person sitting in front of her. She struggled because she felt like she didn't know who I was anymore, as I had kept such a large secret from her. She was also upset that she was the "last" person to know. I tearfully sat down beside her and said, "Mom, you were the last person to know, because I was so afraid of losing you. I thought you wouldn't love me anymore and would disown me." She started to cry and hugged me, "Darren, you know that I would never disown you! I love you." This moment was the beginning of a new, more open, relationship between Mom and I, one that would make us closer than ever.

A snapshot

My dad was the kindest man I have ever met and probably the only man I have ever truly loved. I loved spending time with dad. He was an affectionate man. My earliest memories are of him holding me and rocking me in his favorite rocking chair. He was always up for hugs and for me sitting on his lap while we watched television.

For many years he was a fisherman, but he eventually stopped fishing and got a job driving the chip truck for Humpty Dumpty. He would often come into the house with boxes of expired potato chips. I remember being so excited when he would come in the door at the end of the day that I would run out to him to get a hug and see what he brought me. I can still picture the plastic pen protector that he wore in his shirt pocket as he lifted me up for a hug.

With this new job I would get up in the morning and drive with him in the chip truck. I thought it was fantastic. We would go to small local community stores where he would take inventory of what was needed and then I would help him bring the boxes in. My fondest memories involve these trips. A Hank Williams cassette would invariably get put into the tape deck, and we would begin to sing. As we drove, I would lean out the rolled-down window, taking in the green fragrance of the countryside. Or if I were tired, I would lean into him and fall asleep.

A snapshot

There were two older teenage boys who would frequently walk up and down the street on which I lived. They were mean and snarly, and for some reason they did not like me. One day I was riding my bike down the road, and I saw them walking towards me on the other side. I picked up speed so that I could quickly get past them. I saw one of them reach down and knew that he had a rock in his hand. As I sped past, he threw the rock and it flew over my handlebars removing the skin off my fingers on one hand. I ran into the house crying and told my mother about them. When my father came home, she told him. Later I was sitting out on the front step, and they went by. I ran in and told my dad that they were the boys. My mild-mannered dad ran out the door lambasting these boys that they were to leave me alone. I stared in amazement as dad proceeded to raise his leg and kick one in the backside as he was walking away. From then on, they would always scowl at me, but they never bothered me again. Dad was an ally to me. His space was a safe one.

A snapshot

As a child I spent a great deal of time at my Great Aunt Sweet's house who was well into her 70s. I remember not liking her when we first met. She had no time for misbehavior. Her knobby wooden cane was enough to instil the fear of God in any truculent child, and I was one. But our relationship would change. Maybe it was the card games we would play, where she was not against cheating, or the date squares, chocolate chip cookies, and banana bread she would make. Or perhaps it was the chocolates she always had on hand to give out to the neighbourhood kids who would also visit her, or her mischievous laugh, and her often foul language. Somewhere along the way I realized what a character she was—strong, strict, no-nonsense, yet kind, caring, and generous.

Most of all, I remember stories of her life that she told mirthfully. We would sit for hours while she crocheted afghans, and she would recount stories from her past, stories of survival, stories about her character. Over freshly baked sweets, she would tell these stories repeatedly to any company that would come visit. I still smile as I remember them. In a Loyalist community that had its share of racism, Sweet had no time for it. She befriended any newcomers to the community, and she would offer her home to any of her friends who fell on rough times. One of her great friends was her neighbour and hairdresser, who was her age, and always had a fantastic tan to offset his poufy blond wig. I would learn, or figure out, later, that he was gay. I didn't have to pretend at Sweet's. She never asked me change.

A snapshot

Jake and I got our driver's licences when we turned 16. I didn't have a car, but Jake would often borrow her mother's truck. She was a terrible driver. We had our share of accidents; some she told her mother about and some she did not. Jake would often call in the evenings and ask if I wanted to go for a drive. Undeterred by her driving history, I would go. I cannot recall the number of times we would just drive around "downtown," which consisted of one street that looped back around on itself, and then drive up the hill and into the mountains. Sometimes we would pick up friends along the way. We would blast music and sing along. We travelled down the back roads and out into the countryside. I saw the beauty of the town: the rolling landscapes and hills looking out over the ocean. We sat at the lighthouse and watched the boats come in. We went into someone's expansive field where she photographed me sitting in a wooden chair, smiling. We had each other. And when Tracy Chapman's "Fast Car" would play on the radio I finally believed that I could "be someone" (Chapman, 1988).

A snapshot

(I wonder how the lives of two men I once knew have become intertwined in my memory so that it is not easily discernable with whom I did what: my father or my brother? I remember doing the following with both my father, before his death when I was ten years old, and my brother after.)

I got up at 5 am to go lobster fishing. I remember my excitement as we drove out of town to a cove, partially enclosed by a dilapidated wharf, and I remember being frightened when I saw that it was low tide and I would have to descend the precarious, rust-covered ladder. "I can't do it," I cried, and I stood there, until someone, my dad or my brother, came up the ladder and said, "I'll go down first and make sure you don't fall."

Shortly after, we were out on the open water. I loved the salt-water smell as the wind whipped through my cow-licked hair. My lungs couldn't get enough of the exhilaration and freedom. As the land departed, the captain might then say, "Darren, come up here and steer the boat while I eat," and the nervous boy would step up on a wooden ledge, barely tall enough to peer over the wheel, and become the captain for a few moments. "Am I doing OK?" became my every-minute refrain.

I learned how to be a lobster fisher and what that meant. I learned how to pull the buoy out of the water using a wooden gaffe, and how to wrap the rope attached to the buoy around a pulley that would extract the soaking trap out of the water. I would grab onto its side and pull it onto the boat. I remember how the captain would throw back any fish or crabs caught. I watched with awe how the experienced fisher could extract the lobster without getting his fingers crushed in the powerful front claws. I was then given the job of banding the lobsters, where a small rubber band is placed upon a wrench-like apparatus and then stretched over the lobster claw. All was well until one of these terrible pincers wrapped around my finger and I screamed and flailed until it was removed.

Fearful now of that job, I was then given the task of baiting the bags, which involves stuffing dead and rotting herring into twine bags that I watched my father and brother make themselves at home. They would attach a piece of twine to a kitchen drawer knob and begin to weave. I thought it was beautiful.

But the smell and feel of the slimy fish on my scaly hands was enough to bring on the first waves of seasickness, until finally overcome, I rushed to the side of the boat to hang my head over. The early morning exhilaration would soon be gone, eclipsed by the knowledge that this was probably not the life for me. I would not follow in my father's and brother's footsteps.

These ordinary moments speak to the utopic memories of relationships forged with family members and friends as well as between myself and the rural landscape.[5] The fact that I knew that fishing was not for me does not erase the feeling of connection I felt when I was on the water with Dad. I could have ignored my father's connection to the water and a familial connection to the land; my mother's parents and her grandparents were all farmers. Additionally, I could have continued to fear nature, or more succinctly to fear being attacked in nature. But I did not. I could focus on the many negative, queerphobic encounters that I have had while living in the rural, and for many years I did. Perhaps it is much easier for all of us to focus on moments in our lives when we have been harmed. When I started composing the vignettes, memories of such harm came to mind first. We must tell stories of violence so they might be heard and used in service of personal, relational, and cultural change. But maybe it is also necessary to tell them so that we can begin to let them go, to create a space for new narratives to emerge. The everyday stories of utopic moments that I have shared perhaps serve as an antidote to an historical amnesia regarding, for the purposes of this work, rural queer life, but also queer life in general. Perhaps, I have made us think about what happens when we only tell and hear stories of despair and, how perceptions of queerness might be reimagined through stories of love and belonging. It is the latter memories that draw me home.

A snapshot

When I return home nowadays, I am drawn to the old wharf that sits broken and abandoned. I walk on the rocks upon the shoreline, taking in the debris from the past: a beached boat falling apart near the road, pieces of old rope scattered across the landscape, the skeleton of an abandoned bait shed. I look to the wharf, where my dad's and then my brother's boats were moored. I remember the moments we shared. Amid the sadness I feel as I search for my father's ghost, I relive the joy, the utopia found in my memories. It is peaceful. I can almost see a little boy from the past skipping along the rocks. He looks at me with curiosity. I look at him with hope. I am alone and I do not fear.

Notes

1 Some vignettes appeared in, and some parts of this writing have been revised from, my masters' thesis, *Desirable Queerness: A Critical Queer Autoethnography of Being and Becoming.*
2 I am aware of a possible criticism whereby looking for moments of love, joy, and belonging in a heteronormative environment may be construed as embracing that environment and as a homonormative endeavour. Indeed, both Muñoz and Cvetkovich speak against homonormativity in their writings on utopia. Muñoz states that LGBTQ people engaged in the politics of equality seek to have the same rights as heterosexuals, such as marriage and access to other heteronormative family structures, rather than critiquing such institutions. The version of utopia in his book is to seek for the "no longer conscious" memories of queer life around the time of Stonewall, and the dreams and desires that existed there. To uncover such utopic moments, Muñoz offers examples of art, theatre, stories of cruising, and photography, the lesser known accounts of queer worlds from this time period. Unfortunately, separate queer worlds do not exist as readily in the rural. They are tied up with heteronormative traditions and customs that must be navigated and challenged. The purpose of writing rural utopic memories of joy and love is a way to reimagine the rural queer experience, not to uphold heteronormativity.
3 It certainly does not escape me that the insertion of queerness into any public space holds the possibility for danger. The gay bashing of Scott Jones (See film *Love, Scott,* 2018) from rural Nova Scotia is a prime example of what can happen after someone leaves the safety of their friends after a night at the bar. It frightens me to think about what might have happened had I encountered the men at the restaurant, outside and alone, after an evening out.
4 Once again, talk of my boyfriend doing my laundry and feeling accepted by my family as well as my lesbian friends getting married seem like very homonormative enterprises. However, in her research on LGBTQ lives in the small city of Lethbridge Alberta, Tiffany Myrdahl (2016), notes that we must be aware of the dominant norms of a geographical location when considering homonormativity (p. 43). She provides the example of a participant who interjects her life with her partner in heteronormative conversations. Myrdahl states that this encounter "may be identified as homonormative in its unwillingness to interrogate liberal rights and privileges, but in Lethbridge, at this particular moment, it also counts as queer activism that disrupts the work of heteronormativity" (p. 43). In the rural, queer boundary publics and the appearance of queerness within the traditional, creates a queering effect.
5 With this said, I am very much aware that when queer people recount their pasts, they may not have as many positive experiences with family and friends as I speak of here. For some, "home" is not a refuge.

References

Adams, T. E., & Holman Jones, S. (2008). Autoethnography is queer. In N. K. Denzin, Y. S. Lincoln, & L. T. Smith (Eds.), *Handbook of critical and indigenous methodologies* (pp. 373–390). Sage.

Adams, T. E., & Holman Jones, S. (2011). Telling stories: Reflexivity, queer theory, and autoethnography. *Cultural Studies⬛Critical Methodologies, 11*(2), 108–116. https://doi.org/10.1177/1532708611401329.

Baker, K. (2011). Conceptualizing rural queerness and its challenges for the politics of visibility. *Platform, 12*(30), 38–56.

Bochner, A. P., & Ellis, C. (2016). *Evocative autoethnography: Writing lives and telling stories.* Routledge.

Chapman, T. (1988). Fast car [song]. On *Tracy Chapman* [album]. Electra.

Crawford, L. C. (2008). Transgender without organs? Mobilizing a geo-affective theory of gender modification. *Women's Studies Quarterly, 36*(3/4), 127–143. Retrieved from www.jstor.org/stable/27649790.

Cummings, D. (2016). *Desirable queerness: A critical queer autoethnography of being and becoming.* [Unpublished master's thesis]. University of New Brunswick. Retrieved from https://unbscholar.lib.unb.ca/islandora/object/unbscholar%3A7638/datastream/PDF/download/citation.pdf.

Cvetkovich, A. (2012). *Depression: A public feeling.* Duke University Press.

Detamore, M. (2013). Queering the hollow: Space, place, and rural queerness. In A. Gorman-Murray, B. Pini, & L. Bryant (Eds.), *Sexuality, rurality and geography* (pp. 81–94). Lexington.

Ellis, C., Adams, T. E., & Bochner, A. P. (2011). Autoethnography: An overview. *Historical Social Research/Historische Sozialforschung, 36*(4), 273–290. Retrieved from www.jstor.org/stable/23032294.

Fields, J., Mamo, L., Gilbert, J., & Lesko, N. (2014). Beyond bullying. *Contexts, 13*(4), 80–83. https://doi.org/10.1177/1536504214558226.

Grace, A. P. (2006). Writing the queer self: Using autobiography to mediate inclusive teacher education in Canada. *Teaching and Teacher Education, 22*(7), 826–834. https://doi.org/10.1016/j.tate.2006.04.026.

Gray, M. L. (2009). *Out in the country: Youth, media and queer visibility in rural America.* NYU Press.

Halberstam, J. (2005). *In a queer time and place: Transgender bodies, subcultural lives.* NYU Press.

Heckert, J. (2010). Intimacy with strangers/intimacy with self: Queer experiences of social research. In C. J. Nash & K. Browne (Eds.), *Queer methods and methodologies: Intersecting queer theories and social science research* (pp. 41–54). Ashgate Publishing, Ltd.

Holman Jones, S., & Adams, T. E. (2010). Autoethnography and queer theory: Making possibilities. In N. K. Denzin & M. D. Giardina (Eds.), *Qualitative inquiry and human rights* (pp.136–157). Left Coast Press, Inc.

Johnson, C. R. (2013). *Just queer folks: Gender and sexuality in rural America.* Temple University Press.

Maupin, A. (2017). *Logical family: A memoir.* Random House.

Muñoz, J. E. (2009). *Cruising utopia: The then and there of queer futurity.* NYU Press.

Myrdahl, T. M. (2016). Visibility on their own terms? LGBTQ lives in small Canadian cities. In G. Brown & K. Browne (Eds.), *The Routledge research companion to geographies of sex and sexualities* (pp. 61–68). Routledge.

Payne, E. C., & Smith, M. J. (2012). Safety, celebration and risk: Educator response to LGBTQ professional development. *Teaching Education, 23*(3), 265–285. https://doi.org/10.1080/10476210.2012.699520.

Pelias, R. J. (2004). *A methodology of the heart: Evoking academic and daily life.* Altamira.

Schmidt, S. (2010). Queering social studies: The role of social studies in normalizing citizens and sexuality in the common good. *Theory and Research in Social Education, 38*(3), 314–335. https://doi.org/10.1080/00933104.2010.10473429.

Schweighofer, K. (2016). Rethinking the closet: Queer life in rural geographies. In M. Gray, C. R. Johnson, & B. J. Gilley (Eds.), *Queering the countryside: New frontiers in rural queer studies*, (pp. 223–243). New York University Press.

Stone, A. L. (2018). The geography of research on LGBTQ life: Why sociologists should study the South, rural queers, and ordinary cities. *Sociology Compass, 12*(11), e12638. https://doi.org/10.1111/soc4.12638.

Wayne, L. M. (Director). (2018). *Love, Scott* [film]. National Film Board of Canada.

Weston, K. (1997). *Families we choose: Lesbians, gays, kinship*. Columbia University Press.

15

KINDRED SPIRITS

Narrative, art, life

Mark Freeman

Finding one another

July 19, 2006

Dear Professor Freeman:

I don't know whether you remember me. We were on a panel on narrative (that you chaired) together several years ago at a National Communication Association convention. I admire your work tremendously and have used and cited most of your essays (quite liberally) in my published work. Indeed, in reading your essays I often feel the presence of a kindred spirit. Though I tend to write narrative more than analyze it—to the extent that is a useful distinction—our sense of the issues at stake seems very much alike.

I am currently working on a book that will feature a discussion of the narrative and identity literature. This morning I ran across a reference to the forthcoming *Handbook of Narrative Inquiry* and saw that you were contributing a chapter on "autobiographical understanding." I was wondering if you had an advanced copy of your chapter that you might share with me. I'd greatly appreciate seeing your most recent thinking. I found your concluding essay in the *Narrative and Identity* volume right on target and very heuristic.

Cheers,

Art Bochner

July 20, 2006

Dear Art,

Thanks for your note. Sure I remember you! And I also know a good deal of your work, which I've admired for some time. Yes, it does seem that we're kindred spirits …

Perhaps more kindred, in fact, than that line about my "analyzing" rather than writing narrative might suggest. And so, I continued,

The autobiography chapter is just in draft form, but the printed version will be pretty close to what I'm sending along. I'm also taking the liberty of sending along two other pieces, both of which are "semi-autobiographical" that you might find relevant to some of your concerns: one called "Charting the Narrative Unconscious" (from the journal *Narrative Inquiry*) and another called "Beyond Narrative: Dementia's Tragic Promise." The second one is largely about my mother, and it will be published in a volume on *Broken Narratives* sometime this year. Please don't cite this one; it may still need some editing, and I haven't quite "let it go" yet. But given your own angle on things, I figured I'd send it along.

I hope our paths will cross again sometime soon. Let's be in touch.

All the best,

Mark

I can't recall how much I knew then about autoethnography. Did I really know "a good deal" of Art's work at the time? I'm pretty sure I did. But I probably didn't know the whole "aura" surrounding it or the kind of following Art and Carolyn had—and continue to have. Knowing now what I didn't know then, it seems kind of audacious to have spewed forth as much of my own work (and soul) as I did. But maybe there was something about the vibe of Art's letter that moved me in that direction.

July 20, 2006

Thanks so much, Mark. I'm really looking forward to reading these, especially the one about your mother. My mother died in 2001, 10 days after 9/11. I was her primary caretaker for the last five years of her life during which she suffered from dementia. I started a book that I called *Minding Mother*, which is written in an autoethnographic/autobiographic mode, but I've never been able to finish it. I've presented various portions at conferences but have never submitted any for publication, partly because of ethical concerns that run deep within me and partly (I guess) because working on it drains me emotionally. I did publish a short piece (story) in a special issue of *Qualitative Inquiry* on 9/11. It's called "Love Survives" and parallels my struggle to let go of my mother with the terror and fear experienced in the aftermath of September 11.

I have used your piece on Tolstoy's *Death of Ivan Ilych* many times (and in many classes), and your use of "narrative integrity" in that piece was a source of inspiration and moral guidance for me during the darkest days of my mother's illness. We social scientists often get hung up on how much influence we may have on our colleagues and on our field(s), but to me the really important thing is what difference what we do can make in our lives and the lives of the people who hear our stories (theories). I look forward to seeing you sometime, somewhere in the future.

Sincerely,

art bochner

How cool. Our relationship was now officially two days old, and we were talking about our mothers, dark days, Ivan Ilych, and more.

It would be two years before Art and I were in touch again, this time to swap some new pieces and discuss the possibility of my speaking at the International Congress of Qualitative Inquiry (ICQI) at the University of Illinois.

December 1, 2008

Thanks for your note, Art. I really ought to attend one of the congresses; they've been on my radar, but I haven't quite pulled it together to attend. As for the "qualitative revolution," which you pursued with Ken and Mary Gergen, I'm actually in the middle of an interesting—if somewhat puzzling—enterprise with Ken and Ruthellen Josselson. At one point there was a movement afoot to establish a new division of the American Psychological Association (APA) on qualitative inquiry. Lots of signatures (~900) were gathered, and it was eventually brought before the APA Board (or whatever it's called); a majority voted in favor, but 2/3 was needed, so it didn't pass. But then a strange and unanticipated thing happened: An invitation was put forth by APA Division 5, which is Evaluation, Measurement, and Statistics (!), asking us to consider joining forces with them and forming a new division called something like "Psychological Research Practices." What a strange possibility! At first, I was quite resistant; in fact, I'm still somewhat resistant. But a number of folks—Ken especially (who, through it all, really is something of a utopian thinker)—convinced me that this really might be worth pursuing, particularly owing to the possibility of it transforming the discipline. Anyway, I'm currently on a three-person qualitative team with Ken and Ruthellen, and we're planning to meet with a Division 5 team at the next APA to see what can be worked out. Curious, don't you think? What's also curious is the moderating effect Ken's had. He really does seem to have a dream of unity here, a dream that we'll be able to find common ground—or at least coexist in more benign fashion than we have. Only time will tell.

Anyway, yes, let's find a way to get together sometime soon. If you find any extra interesting conferences, please do let me know. I'll do the same. And maybe between us, we'll come up with one.

Best,

Mark

That I was asked to be part of Gergen and Josselson's team had taken me by surprise. I knew both of them fairly well—but not so well that I saw this sort of thing coming. In fact, I had tangled with Ken off and on for years about his relativism and what had appeared to me at times to be a kind of nihilism. As a staunch social constructionist, he would sometimes say things that simply struck me as flat-out loony. "Do you really think our interpretations of the world aren't at all constrained by what's actually in it?" I might ask. Our exchanges had always been respectful, but we were hardly on the same page when it came time to considering foundational philosophical issues. I can recall a panel we were on together at APA back in 1995. It was called "Postmodernism and Its Malcontents." I was one of the malcontents. Ken was the discussant, there essentially to proclaim to those of us still holding on to the remaining shreds of reality that we needed to let it all go and thereby be liberated to remake the world. Fun! As for my relationship with Ruthellen, she and I seemed more compatible owing to our shared interest in narrative, but we too had somewhat different images of what the enterprise was ultimately about. She was much more the social scientist, committed to ideas and ideals like the accumulation of knowledge and the importance of locating ourselves under the umbrella of science. I was more ambivalent about it, and found myself more interested in linking up with the arts and humanities. In the end, I'm pretty sure I was brought on board as a kind of referee. The situation was a curious one. Although Ken's work was certainly more radical than Ruthellen's, he was the one most excited about the prospect of forging an alliance with Division 5; for him, this was the proverbial "foot in the door" of mainstream psychology, and he was surprisingly willing to work with people whom he undoubtedly found intellectually, and perhaps personally, loathsome (and they him). As for Ruthellen, she was something of a firebrand in this context, ready and willing to blast forward in whatever way she could. If Ken wanted to get his foot in the door, she wanted to kick that door down. I was the go-between, not quite the utopian dream-of-unity person Ken was but not quite the door-kicking hell-raiser Ruthellen was.

I should note that, flattered though I was to join the two of them, I did so with no small measure of trepidation—partly because the alliance seemed bizarre, partly because I didn't see myself as an "organizational" type, and partly because I wasn't really a qualitative researcher, in the sense of someone who goes out and does studies and is trying to lay claim to their scientific legitimacy—which, rhetorically speaking, was the most appropriate way forward. "We're scientists too!" had to be the rallying cry, whether we believed it or not—only then would there exist the possibility of our joining forces with these scientists-to-the-core methodologists, most of whom were firmly and exclusively committed to quantitative methods and some of whom positively despised the idea of people like Ken Gergen becoming part of their club. Among the three of us, Ruthellen was the most comfortable wearing the "scientist" mantle, but because she had a tougher time suffering fools gladly than either Ken or me, I would also assume the role of quasi-scientific mediator, not only between Ken and Ruthellen but, on some level, between these two radically different camps. It was weird, and frequently quite uncomfortable. I remember the first time Ruthellen and I were to attend one of the Division's business meetings, mainly to make our case for the virtues of this unlikely marriage. We were instructed to wait outside, which we did for a good long while—it seemed intentional to both of us. And when we finally entered the room, saw who was there and felt the vibe, we both immediately knew that this was destined to be one wacky process. They were our inverted images, and we theirs. And everyone knew it. Freaky, and scary. *I want to go home.*

But onward we trudged, through the dense, frequently hostile, thickets of additional "bridge-building" exchanges, large divisional meetings where crusty old men stood up and shouted, "This will be the end of Division 5!", and APA-sponsored social gatherings, where we all would suffer over forced niceties and $12 glasses of mediocre wine, which I, for one, would gulp down with abandon if only to cushion the blow of reality. *Where was I? And who?*

As it turned out, the Society for Qualitative Inquiry in Psychology did become an official section of Division 5, which, remarkably enough, would be renamed "Division of Quantitative and Qualitative Methods." Not surprisingly, there was a lot of fuss over both. For some of the Division 5 old guard, it no doubt felt not only like the end of the division but the end of civilization. As for us barbarous interlopers who'd launched it all, we basked in our great good fortune, celebrated over high end food and drink, and, speaking for myself, occasionally asked, "Now that I'm a card-carrying member of this club, do I actually have to act like one?" The divisional business meetings were reminiscent of divided-by-gender orthodox synagogues, with the stalwart quantitative methodologists on one side of the room and us upstarts on the other, alternating between snickering like wise-ass teenagers and shivering with horror.

What place stories?

January 23, 2009
Hi Mark:

Thanks for your note about the APA struggle to legitimate qualitative inquiry through the establishment of a division or section. Ken Gergen had told me a little about it, but it was quite intriguing to hear your version, which included more detail. I recall one of my professors in graduate school saying that "academics talk like liberals and act like conservatives." That statement has stuck with me for a long time. How true!

I've been meaning to send you the brief review I did of your proposal to Oxford. They contacted me in November and asked for a review, which I delivered in December. I don't know if they sent you all my comments. They seemed in a hurry to make a decision, which I assume was positive. I would love to have published your book in our series for Left Coast Press, but of course, we're not Oxford. They wanted a pretty quick turnaround, so I kept my comments rather brief. I'm sure you're not surprised that I wanted more stories, but that's just the way my tastes run these days. It's a brilliant project and I can't wait to see it in press. I hope my brief commentary was/is beneficial to you. Let me know how it's going.

Cheers,
Art Bochner

It was good to hear from Art again; he really seemed to "get" the dynamic of the APA venture. More important, though, was his review of my proposal for what would eventually become my book *Hindsight* (2010). It sounded by his email that he really liked it. Great! But what about that whole "I wanted more stories" thing? Hmmm … And what about the review itself? This was his first foray into feature-length Freeman. What did he think?

Art had some wonderful things to say about both me and the work in his initial words—in the interest of (some semblance of) modesty, I'll refrain from sharing the gushier words, gratifying though they were. After an introductory gush, and by way of "testifying" to his readiness to assume the role of reviewer, he wrote,

> I have read virtually all of Freeman's work. He and I appeared on a panel together once and we have corresponded over e-mail on a number of occasions. I wish I knew him better, because he appears to me, at least through his published work, to be a kindred spirit.

Truthfully, I doubt whether he had read virtually *all* of my work. But whatever—I wished I knew him better too, kindred spirit as he appeared to be. Later in the review, he had some challenging things to say—as well he should have. I spent too much time addressing the issues of narrative distortion and of "the discontinuity between living life and telling about it." These issues were already well traveled, and it didn't seem that there was a whole lot new to say about them. For seasoned narrativists, Art suggested, I should have done more to engage the narrative-and-identity literature over the past 30 years or so. I ought to have capitalized more on my own thinking about "the project of self-understanding," which Art saw to be central to my work. And, not least, I ought to have "broadened the scope of [my] treatment of 'life as literature' by pointing to exemplars of the work of social scientists who have been doing just that, say Ruth Behar in Anthropology and Carolyn Ellis in Sociology/Communication." He also mentioned Carolyn's (then) new book *Revision* (2009), seeing it as

> a particularly compelling exemplar of where a lot of social science "life writing" is headed, not only in the direction of "autoethnography" but also toward revising what one thinks things that happened earlier in life mean now … a direct exemplar of hindsight used as a social science methodology.

Hmmm … That sounded pretty relevant. I really ought to know more, and say more, about what's been going on out there, especially in autoethnography quarters. Carolyn's book landed on my shelf shortly after, as have a number of others since that time (Bochner, 2016; Bochner & Ellis, 2016; Ellis, 2018), all of which speak, cogently and indeed poetically, to the issues Art's review highlighted.

So, where did Art actually land in terms of his overall assessment of the book? Happily, he went on to do some more gushing, spoke about how some of the ideas I had addressed had been "critically important" in his own thinking, and "strongly" recommended that Oxford publish the book. (Whew!) What about revisions? "This draft," he wrote,

> is in fairly good shape, but I would advise Professor Freeman to consider a few significant revisions. In my opinion, his own personal narratives—the story about the ride with his father, his daughter's illness, and his trip to Germany—are the

most compelling materials in the book. These aren't as poetically expressed as one might like, but they are written from the heart (as well as the mind) and they evoke strong responses and identification. Yet repeatedly he says, "I'll spare you the details" and other remarks that express his discomfort with personal writing. I found these asides annoying and my own preference would be for more rather than fewer personal stories (and more detail where possible).

Art went on to say a few other things too, but this was the core of his suggestions. It made sense that he wanted more personal stories—that was clearly his and Carolyn's thing. But what about the idea that I might have been more poetically expressive in the work? Was he right about that? What exactly did he mean by it? And how might I go about making it happen? And did I really have "discomfort" when it came to personal writing? Gee, I didn't *think* I did. But then why all the "annoying" disclaimers?

Hmmm …

At the end of my first book, *Rewriting the Self* (1993), I concluded with an Epilogue titled "Toward a Poetics of Life History." Subsequent to that, I wrote a number of pieces that sought to deliver on the promise (see, e.g., Freeman, 1999 , 2000, 2001, 2002). So, hadn't I been doing some poetically expressive stuff? Well, not a whole lot, actually. Of all of those pieces, there really was only one—"The Presence of What Is Missing: Memory, Poetry, and the Ride Home" (Freeman, 2002)—that truly embodied the promise; the rest, for the most part, remained largely programmatic and theoretical, urging psychology to do this or that in service of crafting a more humane discipline. Was Art on to something here? There is no question I was attracted to the *idea* of doing more personally storied work—I had even developed some pretty funky philosophical rationales for doing so. But was I up to actually *doing* it?

I'm still not sure whether "discomfort" is the term that best fits what was going on at the time. But looking back, I can see a definite tension between my stances as theoretician and writer and between being assimilationist vis-à-vis the discipline of psychology (especially as embodied in the movement to institutionalize qualitative inquiry within the APA) and being radically subversive, precisely by doing the more artful work that narratively exploring human lives seemed to require.

January 24, 2009

Hi, Art

Thanks so much for your note. Oxford did indeed send along your review a while back. I did know it was yours—not because they told me but simply because it bore your "signature." I thank you for it—and not only for the laudatory comments but also the critical ones, just about all of which were right on. Out of the six reviews Oxford gathered, yours and one other really got me thinking about some things: what's focal and what's peripheral, what's simply a repeat of what's already out there, and so on. I'm actually in the process now of reordering some of the chapters, beginning, for instance, in a more autobiographical mode, partly for the sake of introducing myself to the reader, partly for the sake of tone. In any case, I found your comments really helpful. They help incite the kind of reflection that's part and parcel of hindsight— looking back and seeing things that simply weren't visible, or as visible, at the time.

Anyway, I'm going to continue right now with my own revision. Tedious though the process can be, it's also exciting to get closer, by degrees, to what the book ought to be.

All the best,

Mark

Narrative

What did I mean when I spoke of "getting closer, by degrees, to what the book ought to be"? What *ought* it be? More generally, where should we narrativists, autoethnographers and performative whatevers be going with our work?

Eventually, there would be a symposium at the 2012 ICQI devoted to just this question. It involved Art and Carolyn, Ken and Mary Gergen, Michael Bamberg, Norman Denzin, Kristen Langellier, and me. Titled "Dilemmas and Challenges of Narrative Practices and Narrative Inquiry," this mega-exchange basically seemed oriented toward all of us confessing our respective troubles in carrying out our work and navigating our respective disciplines. Serious company. Important topic. The pressure was on.

I decided I would give a talk on "Narrative Inquiry and the Mainstream: Assimilation or Revolution?" In it, I would try to work through some of the aforementioned tensions I had felt between serving the discipline of psychology in some scientifically "respectable" way and exploding the whole enterprise in favor of the sort of work that, in my heart of hearts, I wanted—and felt I *ought*—to be doing. To set the stage for the talk, I told two brief stories that eventually found their way into a piece I did for *Qualitative Inquiry* (Freeman, 2014a). In the first one, the year was 1996, and I was asked to speak at the induction ceremony of Psi Chi, the psychology national honor society. Now that tenure was a few years behind me and I had become a semi-respected member of the department, I figured I could lay my cards on the table and tell everyone how I thought our curriculum should change so as to better include actual human beings. Titled "Narrative Psychology and the Study of Human Lives," the talk was a somewhat daring proclamation of what I really thought about things, sprinkled, as had become my custom, with enough literary flair and (what appeared to be) intellectual humility to reel everyone in. The inductees seemed psyched; the vision of the discipline I was putting forth was what many of them had (mistakenly) thought psychology actually was. Some of my colleagues seemed (moderately) enthralled too—even the one who came up to me after my talk, told me she very much appreciated what I had to say, and then asked, "Why do you call yourself a psychologist?"

Then there was the time I was going up for full professor and was to receive my departmental report. I wasn't all that worried about the outcome. In fact, I can recall jokingly saying to some people (outside my department) that, knowing my colleagues probably hadn't read most of the work I'd done but seeing that it landed in what appeared to be legitimate venues, I would be fine. It therefore came as a shock when I read the cover letter to the report, which essentially said that, despite enjoying reading fiction (as one person, in particular, would put it to me sometimes when reading my work), they had no idea whatsoever what this work had to do with psychology and were consequently sending my dossier on to the English Department, which would no doubt appreciate what I had to say much more than they possible could. *WTF?!* Only kidding, Mark … (Yuk Yuk!)

As the saying goes, many a truth is said in jest. It was good, I suppose, that my department colleagues could rib me about the weird stuff I did, but it was unsettling too, and led me to pose some questions at ICQI that, perhaps owing to the drive for tenure and then promotion, had been concealed. I wrote:

> How much do I really *care* about the discipline of psychology, its methodological commitments, its theoretical inclinations, its philosophical foundations, and so on? What exactly do I *owe* the discipline? *Anything?* Is it a *moral responsibility* to be part of, or at least enter, the mainstream—if only to transform it in some small way, so that my students and the students to come can have a more habitable space for carrying out their thinking and their passions? Or does it make more sense to just do the best possible work, the work that's closest to my heart and soul, discipline be damned? Now, on the face of it, this second stance might appear selfish, amoral if not immoral. But I think of it a bit differently. There's still a moral commitment at work here. But it's not to the discipline per se; it's to a set of ideas and ideals that transcends disciplinary concerns, disciplinary boundaries.

And so, I eventually asked: "Assimilation or revolution? Or something else entirely?" As I went on to acknowledge,

> There are of course political realities at work, unofficial and at times official demands and "requirements"—that work be published in the "top" journals, that it's recognizable as "science," that it can be situated somewhere, somehow, in "the discipline," as it's generally known. In this sense, it might be argued, the main question I've posed here today may be considered something of a luxury. Some people, lots of people, have no *choice* but to assimilate—at least if they want to have a job, put food on the table, and so on. It's also the case that some people really *want* to assimilate—that is, they're either true pluralists or psychological "multiculturalists" or they see a deep continuity between qualitative and quantitative inquiry, such that it's all of a piece. Some folks who do mixed methods work seem to inhabit this sort of space, and on some level it's an enviable one. Others still are more reluctant to inhabit this space but feel the need to do so anyway. What often happens, in fact, as some of you probably know, is that people split themselves in two, one part

mainstream, or close to it, and the other part more qualitative, humanistic, literary, performative, or what have you. This way, they can live with their colleagues as well as with themselves. But it can be a high wire act too, one that requires a kind of caution and vigilance, lest others come to know too much about one's secret interests and desires.

But what *about* these secret interests and desires? Given the aforementioned alliance-in-the-making between qualitative inquiry and mainstream quantitative inquiry, they would, it seemed, have to be set aside for a while. "Is this alliance a good thing?" I asked. "Many think it is. For the most part, *I* think it is—not least because it presents the opportunity to transform the discipline in a way that more 'separatist' endeavors don't." But it wasn't easy for me to be too gung-ho about the endeavor either. Some of my more radically philosophical colleagues thought this alliance was absurd and implied that I had somehow been "coopted" and sold out. Rumor has it, in fact, there was a fairly drunken night a few years back when some of them had wondered aloud what the hell I was doing getting involved with all this stuff. Fortunately, one or two people apparently slurred a defense on my behalf and tried to reassure their more cynical cronies that I was in it for good and noble reasons. Was it so? "Only time will tell," I said at the ICQI. "The jury is still very much out."

As indeed it was—and remains. I therefore set aside these more institutional concerns and went on to address "a somewhat deeper and more substantive set of questions and issues," having to do with the idea that, through it all,

> those of us who've been carrying the narrative torch for the last 30 or so years generally believe, still, that there's something … and I say this cautiously … *revolutionary* about the enterprise. I've even suggested that it provides a *truer* portrait of the human condition than what we often find in mainstream work. People are more recognizable as *people*, living, loving, suffering, dying. Bearing this in mind, I've also suggested, at this very congress, last year, that in a very real (if paradoxical) sense, narrative inquiry is *more* scientific than those more reductive, objectifying approaches that are so often held up as the very models of science. For insofar as the first and most basic responsibility of science is to be faithful to its object—in this case, the living, loving, suffering, dying human being—what we ultimately have, in narrative inquiry, is the very self-realization of psychological science. That, at least, is the story I've tried to tell in recent years.

But what, I ultimately had to ask, did I actually *make* of this story?

> Is it true? Or is it just fancy BS? More to the point, for present purposes (and this, as I recall, is one of the questions Art was interested in having us address): Can narrative inquiry be a discipline of its own? What exactly would this mean? What *kind* of discipline? And in which sector of the university or

college would it be housed? The social sciences? The humanities? Something in-between—a hybrid, or amalgam, of the two? What would its foremost aims be? Truth? Goodness? Beauty? Would it aim to amass cumulative knowledge, or something akin to it? Or would its aims be rather more transient and ephemeral, "poetic"—a kind of counter-discipline, as it were, filled with a vast plurality of exemplars, but not really heading *anywhere*, in particular? What *are* we doing, anyway? Thank you.

I guess I was confused at the time—certainly about the institutional dimension and the role I might play but also, and more importantly, about those "secret interests and desires" I mentioned earlier. My "solution": "poetic science" (Freeman, 2011) of the sort that would culminate, triumphantly, in the very "self-realization of psychological science" (Freeman, 2014a). (Yay!)

Art

Over the years, Art and I had several more exchanges, many involving our writings focused on issues ranging from narrative, first and foremost (Bochner, 1997, 2001), to fathers (Bochner, 2012) and mothers (Freeman, 2014b), to the meaning of science (Bochner, 2017; Freeman, 2014a), the nature of catastrophe (Freeman, 2014c), and the horror of election night, 2016 (Bochner, 2018). These exchanges were inspiring and wonderful and would conclude with words like "fondly" and "love" and "hugs." From my perspective, the most important ones, in the sense of being formative for my own work, have been those that pushed me toward reimagining the very nature and purpose of inquiry into the human realm— including, especially, those early ones that tweaked my own "analytical" proclivities. For a time, I continued to fly the banner of poetic science. It seemed like an interesting move—it was kind of catchy in an oxymoronic way, and people I admired, like Art and Carolyn, seemed drawn to it. The only problem was that I was slowly but surely beginning to question whether I actually believed what I was proposing. So it was that I would eventually "confess" (Freeman, 2015, 2019) that I had begun to find some of my own commitments "disingenuous" in a way. Was the work I had been doing on my mother really "science"? Sure, I could render the meaning of science so elastic as to include just about anything, including poetically inspired musings of the sort I had been pursuing. No one had definitively established the meaning of the term, I was firmly convinced that the prevailing conception was problematically narrow and parochial, and it was high time, I had believed, to offer a conception that better fit this more artful work. I had even conjured an oxymoronic slogan to capture the spirit of the project: *the more art, the more science*. But why? Why, besides the political realities referred to earlier, did I have to couch all the things I and others were doing as science anyway? Why did any of us would-be "revolutionaries"?

Let me leap ahead to some words Art and I shared in the fall of 2018, around the time I told him and Carolyn that was I hoping to join in the celebration of their work at St. Pete Beach in January 2019. Art had started this one off, sending me some lovely words as well as a couple of new pieces.

> October 3, 2018
>
> Dear Mark:
>
> Sorry that I've been out of touch for so long. I do think about you often and long for the kind of conversations we had on several occasions at ICQI. As I recall, you were chairing your department last time we exchanged messages. So fortunate for your department. These days few people like you are drawn to these administrative positions. Of course, Holy Cross may be an exception, but in my experience chairing a department has become exceedingly demanding, political, and too often not very humane.
>
> Carolyn and I have now been retired for two months. I miss the teaching—a lot—but I'm loving all the reading and writing time (and hiking too). We'd love to have you visit and stay with us sometime at our mountain cabin. That would be a real treat for us. I hope you can make it to our symposium in St. Petersburg in January. Your influence has been profound and though much of our work continues to be situated in "evocative autoethnography," the community of writers and researchers immersed in this work are very much oriented toward your vision of poetic science. That group's size and passion for this kind of work is greater than you might think (though largely outside psychology). We have a fairly wide net of former students and most of them know and admire your writings.
>
> When you get time, please send me any of your recent work. I'm attaching a couple of things that I've recently published.
>
> Love,
>
> art bochner

Interesting that after all these years, and even along with words like "love," Art continued to include his last name! Have I *ever* concluded a letter with "Love, Mark Freeman"? It was a precious letter nonetheless, and extremely gratifying, to say the least. For the most part, Art and I were the ones who had been in contact through the years. But Carolyn had come to be there too—another kindred spirit and another beautiful person. What an extraordinary gift to know them both.

What might I say about poetic science, though? It wasn't that I had come to find the idea invalid, it still had its place. But the fact was, I had grown somewhat less comfortable with it and had found myself wanting—needing, actually—to break some new ground.

> October 3, 2018
>
> Great to hear from you, Art. (…) I'd been on the fence about St. Petersburg, but got off it just last night and sent in my registration. The bottom line: Seeing, and honoring, you and Carolyn was more important than any uncertainties (mainly travel-related; been doing a lot of it) I had. Really looking

forward to seeing you both, catching up. I'm trying to convince my wife to come along too. I'd love for you to meet her and her you.

I don't have access to any of my recent stuff out here in the wilds of Michigan. But I'll be glad to send you a couple of things when I return home in about a week. Suffice it to say for now that I'm still doing lots of thinking about interests we share. I'm also moving more squarely into arts-related work owing to a campus initiative at Holy Cross called "Arts Transcending Borders." Cool stuff; broadening and deepening my palette. Will fill you in sometime soon.

(…)

Love to you and Carolyn. Looking forward to seeing you in a few months! Mark

In his next note to me, Art told me that he looked forward to hearing more about what I was doing with the Arts Transcending Borders initiative. He too had been "concentrating [his] energies on the poetics/science interface," he told me. In fact, he had been working collaboratively with a local artist, whose medium is collage and mosaic, who had contacted him after he read "Bird on the Wire: Freeing the Father Within Me" (Bochner, 2012) and had given a joint presentation with him in Santiago, Chile, using one of the videos they had made together (Bochner & Osvath, 2018; see Osvath, this collection). Cool. Great video. And how interesting that Art and I seemed to be moving into some of the same territory.

December 27, 2018

Thanks so much for your note, Art. I look forward to seeing you and Carolyn too; been too long …

Last time we communicated, I told you I'd send along a few pieces of my own (which I neglected to do; sorry). One is a piece on Trump I did a while back; like you, I find that particular topic hard to resist—abhorrent though the situation is. I'm also passing along a few others that you may find interesting and/or relevant. Two are talks I presented not too long after my mother's death: "The Gift of Giving" and "The Sacred Beauty of Finite Life" (an audacious title, I realize!) For that one, I'm also attaching a "slide show" [featuring 16 photos of my mother, from her early twenties until the day before her death] that I presented before launching into the talk. I was silent in presenting it; took about two minutes. And then it was on to the words.

Finally, I'm attaching a recent piece dealing with the poetic: "Toward a Poetics of the Other," which remains in manuscript form and will be coming out in a volume edited by Thomas Teo, *Re-envisioning Theoretical Psychology*. As you'll see, the poetic is there in full force, the science, not so much …

I feel like I'm deluging you with all these! My point in sending them is just to share some of the directions in which I've been moving. The other thing I've been doing, by the way, is playing lots of guitar. Been screwing around with guitars for 40+ years. Figured it was time to get a bit more disciplined about it, so I've been taking lessons from a local guitar hero, mainly playing blues. Fun. Looking forward to hearing some tunes down in St. Pete. Cool that a band will be there.

Lots to talk about, my friend. Looking forward to it.

For now: Happy (almost) New Year!

Love to you and Carolyn,

Mark

I had some uncertainty about going to the conference. I had never been a student of either Art or Carolyn, and I hardly knew any of the people that would be there. In some ways, I hardly knew Art and Carolyn. A couple of conferences, lots of email exchanges, mainly with Art, and lots of sharing of our work. That's it. I don't mean to make any of this sound insignificant. It's not. But the reality is, we really hadn't spent much time together, in the flesh. And yet, I found myself drawn to the celebration in a big way. In fact, I cannot think of another "intellectual relationship"—if that's the proper term—that would have drawn me in this way. There was—there *is*—something unique about this one, something special. I wanted them to know that.

I also wanted to share with them what felt like a critical transition in the direction of doing arts-based work. There were a number of inspirations for this transition, both near and far, recent and distant. Art and Carolyn were at the top of the list, partly because of their work, but more because of the spirit that infused it: the generosity, the wide-openness, and, even amidst the personal stories and the play and the sheer joy with which they carried out their work and their lives, the seriousness of purpose. Some people don't get this, they think of autoethnography as some sort of self-indulgent substitute for serious inquiry. But it's not that. Or at least it's not that for Art and Carolyn and the people who have been truly, and not superficially, inspired by them. I am one of them.

Eventually, I would share with them some details about the transition I was in the midst of making. A few years before, I had become part of a team of eight faculty, including a novelist, a composer, a sculptor, and a couple of people from theatre, for a class called "CreateLab," which brought some 70 students together twice weekly basically to make cool stuff. The theme for the year was "Time, Memory, and Identity," which was a great fit given the nature of some of my own work. Among the events taking place that semester was a kind of performance/lecture I gave on my mother's dementia. I would also do some collaborative work with a visiting artist, a classical pianist and Galician bagpipe (*gaita*) player from Spain, who is a member of the Silkroad Ensemble, an extraordinary group of musicians from all over the world that had been established by the renowned cellist Yo-Yo Ma. Her mother had dementia too, and we shared a lot about ourselves, our families, and how art might serve to articulate and express dimensions of our experience that went beyond words, however well-chosen and well-crafted they might be.

I brought this set of ideas and possibilities to a new seminar I offered in fall 2019 called "Psychology and/as Art." There were some terrific words in that course. There were also drawings and paintings, videos, musical and dance performances, and more. I even invited my guitar teacher to class, and I joined him on some improvisation, the course theme that particular week. After he and I played, a student who'd brought in his own guitar joined us, and the three of us made some music together. I'd fantasized doing something like this years ago, but never did. It was time. And I had a reason for doing it that I could only glimpse years ago, tethered as I was to more standard classroom fare. It was pretty wonderful. I'll be heading up CreateLab in spring 2020, working with a great group of colleagues (from English, Music, Sociology, and Theatre) and some 45 students, focusing on "Originality and Its Origins." We'll be working again with members of the Silkroad Ensemble as well as a number of other visiting artists, mainly musicians and dancers. I'm also at work on a book on my mother, who died at age 93 just about four years ago, and will be complementing the book by working with a composer and pianist I've known since high school. "The Dementia Suite," it will likely be called.

Life

I needn't go any farther in describing these activities. They're in keeping with those interests and desires that have been there for years. The difference now is that I'm finally setting them in motion. I'm not going to completely give up "analysis" or "theory"—both seem to be pretty well a part of me. But this other side has been calling out for some time, and it's come to feel imperative that I honor it.

The 2019 conference in Art's and Carolyn's honor turned out to be a real treat. It was wonderful to spend some quality time with Art and Carolyn and also to meet some new people, virtually all of whom I found warm and welcoming. I was especially glad to spend some time with Laurel Richardson—she was one of the people whom I'd been hearing about for years but had never met. As it turned out, we too seemed to be kindred spirits and have been in touch since that time, exchanging work, exchanging ideas, and just being in touch. Being at the conference—with its talks and performances, the great band that played closing night, the whole vibe—leads me to think that the kinds of interests and desires I have been referring to in these pages had found their way into a lot of the people there—people who may not have been trained as artists or see themselves as artists but who are drawn, viscerally and spiritually, to those modes of expression and communication that allow us not only to think but also to sense and feel, to get closer to the pulse of life. I certainly saw this in Art way back when—I saw it in Carolyn too—and I saw it, and felt it, in lots of others in St. Pete Beach. They, we, are seeking and reaching, finding new ways to speak the language of the heart and soul. For me, it's hard to say where it will all lead—besides retirement! Wherever it will be, it will be good to know I'll be among kindred spirits.

References

Bochner, A. P. (1997). It's about time: Narrative and the divided self. *Qualitative Inquiry*, *3*, 418–438. https://doi.org/10.1177/107780049700300404.

Bochner, A. P. (2001). Narrative's virtues. *Qualitative Inquiry*, *7*, 131–157. https://doi.org/10.1177/107780040100700201.

Bochner, A. P. (2012). Bird on the wire: Freeing the father within me. *Qualitative Inquiry*, *18*, 168–173. https://doi.org/10.1177/1077800411429094.

Bochner, A. P. (2016). *Coming to narrative: A personal history of paradigm change in the human sciences*. Left Coast Press.

Bochner, A. P. (2017). Heart of the matter: A mini-manifesto for autoethnography. *International Review of Qualitative Research*, *10*(1), 67–80. https://doi.org/10.1525/irqr.2017.10.1.67.

Bochner, A. P. (2018). The night of and the mourning after: Truth and transference in the election of Donald Trump. *Qualitative Inquiry*, *24*(5), 309–317. https://doi.org/10.1177/1077800417745428.

Bochner, A. P., & Ellis, C. (2016). *Evocative autoethnography: Writing lives and telling stories*. Routledge.

Bochner, A. P., & Osvath, Cs (2018). Autoethnography and purifying conversation. www.youtube.com/watch?v=a8ISggR6u8g.

Ellis, C. (2009). *Revision: Autoethnographic reflections on life and work*. Left Coast Press.

Ellis, C. (2018). *Final negotiations: A story of love, loss and chronic illness*. Temple University Press.

Freeman, M. (1993). *Rewriting the self: History, memory, narrative*. Routledge.

Freeman, M. (1999). Life narratives, the poetics of selfhood, and the redefinition of psychological theory. In W. Maiers, B. Bayer, B. Esgalhado, R. Jorna, & E. Schraube (Eds.), *Challenges to theoretical psychology* (pp. 245–250). Captus.

Freeman, M. (2000). Theory beyond theory. *Theory & Psychology*, *10*, 71–77. https://doi.org/10.1177/0959354300010001601.

Freeman, M. (2001). Worded images, imaged words: Helen Keller and the poetics of self-representation. *Interfaces*, *18*, 135–146.

Freeman, M. (2002). The presence of what is missing: Memory, poetry, and the ride home. In R. J. Pellegrini & T. R. Sarbin (Eds.), *Between fathers and sons: Critical incident narratives in the development of men's lives* (pp. 165–176). Haworth.

Freeman, M. (2010). *Hindsight: The promise and peril of looking backward*. Oxford University Press.

Freeman, M. (2011). Toward poetic science. *Integrative Psychological and Behavioral Science*, *45*, 389–396. https://doi.org/10.1007/s12124-011-9171-x.

Freeman, M. (2014a). Qualitative inquiry and the self-realization of psychological science. *Qualitative Inquiry*, *20*, 119–126. https://doi.org/10.1177/1077800413510270.

Freeman, M. (2014b). From absence to presence: Finding mother, ever again. In J. Wyatt & T. E. Adams (Eds.), *On (writing) families: Autoethnographies of presence and absence, love and loss* (pp. 49–56). Sense Publishers.

Freeman, M. (2014c). *The priority of the Other: Thinking and living beyond the self*. Oxford University Press.

Freeman, M. (2015). Narrative psychology as science and as art. In J. Valsiner, G. Marsico, N. Chaudhary, T. Sato, & V. Dazzani (Eds.), *Psychology as a science of human being: The Yokohama Manifesto* (pp. 349–364). Springer.

Freeman, M. (2019). Toward a poetics of the Other: New directions in post-scientific psychology. In T. Teo (Ed.), *Re-envisioning theoretical psychology: Diverging ideas and practices* (pp. 1–24). Palgrave Macmillan.

16

FRIENDSHIP, MUSIC, AND LIVING LEARNING

The story of a song

William K. Rawlins

Having devoted much of my career to studying dialogical and narrative practices and unpacking dialectical aspects of friends' communication across the life course (Rawlins, 1992, 2009), over the past several years I have become increasingly interested in aesthetic and performative conceptions of interpersonal communication. Since 2010 I have sung and performed songs on guitar as a regular part of my scholarly participation at professional conferences and as a visiting scholar at educational institutions, as well as in my classroom teaching. At the same time, I have been involved in performing music as a professional drummer and as a singer/songwriter on guitar. I continue to draw upon all of these experiences in developing my latest contributions to interpersonal communication theory and teaching.

In this chapter I will interweave my experiences living, seeking to understand, and teaching about the communication of friends with my moments making music with and for others. In doing so, I will dramatize the animating interplay I perceive among storytelling, growing older, making music, and co-learning. As we create stories, conversations, and melodies with others, we reflexively undergo the incremental and dramatically fulfilling consequences of our efforts. In creating something new, we remake our own thoughts, feelings, bodies, and relationships with others, as well as our worlds.

My chapter hopes to embody the spirit of Art Bochner's and Carolyn Ellis's generative scholarship through exploring intersections of aesthetic, narrative, and musical modes of expression to convey and probe my concrete lived experiences as a scholar/teacher, musician, friend, and being-in-the-world-with-others. Several emphases across their work inspire me to share this story about making music with my friends (see e.g., Bochner 2001, 2014; Ellis & Bochner, 2000). First and foremost is their sustained encouragement of scholars to voice their understandings of lived experience as a personal narrative, that is, to tell one's own story. Doing so allows us to express in detail how we address the emerging contingencies of our lives in fashioning meaningful moments with others across time. And while significant in their own right, personal stories also shed light on broader themes. As Carolyn has observed, "By exploring a particular life, I hope to understand a way of life" (Ellis & Bochner, 2000, p. 737). Moreover, abstract rational accounts have dominated social inquiry but tell us little about how it *feels* to live in particular ways. What emotions and sensibilities drive and shape the depicted events, and what is their existential pulse? In portraying such matters, Art and Carolyn, in one of their most vital legacies, embolden scholars to experiment with different types of writing and performing understandings. Throughout their oeuvre, they celebrate the virtues of *showing not merely telling about* the meaningful, emotional, aesthetic, and morally freighted activities composing the stories of our lives. The point of such work is not to lecture, qualify, or stipulate what is the case. Rather, the goal is to perform versions or instances of human meaning-making in ways that invite witnessing and consideration, summon reactions, provoke questions, and evoke embodied participation.

Art's and Carolyn's works across the years embody a coming-to-consciousness and an expressively enhanced self- and other-recognition for scholars of communication. I've always admired the courage and erudition that Carolyn and Art have displayed in pursuing together their projects. Partly due to their efforts, I am encouraged by the blossoming work in our discipline narrating, addressing, critiquing, co-authoring, and performing diverse lived experiences and discursive practices of human communication inquiry. Such work embodies the motivation to learn from and with others through respecting their own words and worlds. We must embrace continually the *radical inclusion* of diverse and alternative discourses, and of ways of knowing and performing inquiry. These endeavors should be presented on their own terms and not encapsulated by narrow conventions of social science or pious assumptions about what it means to represent or warrant knowledge claims.

Inspired by such convictions, I want to tell you a story that portrays how my experiences learning and teaching about friendship connect with me making music with lifelong friends. In preparing this chapter, I realized that while I have spent my entire career studying friendship and routinely tell stories about my own friends to illustrate issues of communicating and relating in my undergraduate classes and seminars, I have rarely done so in print. Accordingly, I decided to recollect here a recording session with my old friends to celebrate an array of shared features and dedications that I recognize in storytelling and making music together (Rawlins, 2018).

For me, the musical punctuation of lived experience is a vibrant complement to narrative punctuation. Activating an ongoing integration of past, present, and future melodies and meanings, the involving temporality of music embodies a pleasurable combination of memory, surrender, and anticipation. The distinctive alchemy of rhythm, melody, and (when present) the poetry of lyrics interweave as music creates a dwelling for its players, singers, and audiences. Music is a form of aesthetically bound time, structuring the experience of everyone within earshot. Making music indeed fashions a sturdy dwelling, a place to grow older together in purposively shaped and rhythmically arched time; yet the process also molds moments we share that seem to transcend time.

Music is a conduit, an emotionally charged escort to memory. Musical memories have a visceral quality, calling out to be heard, moved with—felt. Sound waves, undeniably physical disturbances, actually enter our bodies. Musical moments are engulfing, atmospheric, respiratory, breezy, yearning, fist-pumping, sensual. Recall some of the most heart-warming and heart-wrenching moments of your life. What is music's place in them? When we return to a favorite song, what we are feeling now is enriched and complicated by times, places and people summoned vividly by this memorable tune we have experienced before. Past and present moments are telescoped into emotionally contoured pieces of music—part cognitive recognition, part muscle memory, part achingly sad or ecstatic gut feelings—mysteriously uncontrollable associations.

In my experience, playing music with others and listening to music are part of lifelong learning—they attune us to the musicality of life and help us find the rhythm to share with others. I live for music's distinctive potential for summoning and activating consciousness. Music and narrative intermingle in my life to co-produce uniquely musical memories. I believe that songs serve as bookmarks in our lives, taking us back to favorite and challenging parts, continually charting our unfolding stories as melodies. I am thrilled by the simultaneous generosity of music—how it gives meaning to our moments— *and* by its eager receptivity—the way it sponges significance from all that surrounds it.

What follows explores making music with friends as a particular "way of life" and gives readers a glimpse of the communicative practices and practical details involved in recording a song. Yet as the story unfolds you also witness the relational history and nuances shaping how these friends accomplish this creative endeavor together. In doing so, I hope you feel invited to reflect on the activities that you pursue with your own friends and loved ones, like cooking, planning a gathering, writing together, or building a swing set for your children. How do these activities resemble making music? Further, I hope it registers the vulnerability each of us may feel in the throes of trying to create anything—be it a song, an essay, an application letter, or some other demanding communicative performance. Aesthetic creations like music require consummation through others' responses. Understanding art as communication, Dewey (2005) insists, "The hearer is an indispensable partner. The work of art is complete only as it works in the experience of others than the one who created it" (p. 110). Accordingly, this story of music-making also emphasizes the vital role of listening carefully and responding in supportive ways to others.

Notice as well the number, variety, and depth of relationships that call for recognition in telling the story of this song. We witness how my life as a scholar and musician interweaves with that of my advisor Art and other teachers, my parents, wife, children, brothers, other family members, close friends, fellow musicians, and quoted authors I've read—the assorted persons populating anyone's biography in the course of a lifetime. It is humbling and gratifying to realize our debt to others in becoming who we are. The sweetness of shared moments with friends, the contingencies and press of aging, coupled with the interconnections across time of numerous relationships and multiple generations in composing a life are dramatized here. Meanwhile, it also is a story about what it feels like *now* to age with old friends, to cherish those years of interlaced unfolding and to try to create something together that captures that passage of time.

***

I quit a really good band called National Pastime to start graduate school in the fall of 1976. Recommended by C. Jack Orr, my college teacher of interpersonal communication and an inspiring thinker and scholar in his own right, I went to Temple University to study social movements with Herb Simons. But since he was away on leave, I was assigned to an intense young professor named Art Bochner. Half hippie, half polymath, he was intimidating to many folks. But Art and I completely clicked from the first moment we met in the Weiss Hall mailroom. We both loved ideas, found joyful reading and learning, and were each fearless in our own ways. Even so, I kept my identity as a musician on the down-low. I feared Art might think I wasn't serious about grad school—which I actually wasn't until the spring semester of my first year when I took his course on relational communication. His seminar enthralled me, and the readings and research I did for the course launched my life's work addressing friendship. After noticing from gatherings in his home how much Art enjoyed music himself, later that first year I told him I had played music professionally since 8th grade. He said he figured as much based on what I said in class, and he wondered why I wasn't still performing. Soon after, when their drummer died tragically in an automobile accident, I was asked to join a six-piece jazz-rock band, Kickback, composed of folks I had known and gigged with since early high school. The experience gave me joy, friendship, and additional income for the duration of grad school. Art's affirming response at that time is just one in a still-unfolding stream of consequential moments when he has listened carefully to what I say and play and encourages me to follow my lights.

My first formal attempt at qualitative research occurred in a course on field research methods a couple years later in the fall of 1978. Instead of playing our usual touch football one crisp Sunday afternoon, I recorded my musician friends and me shooting the shit over beer. Their turns at talk were so unique, and their stories were so vivid, that after speaking with and interpreting them in my final paper, I earned an A in the course and was informed that I had a knack for qualitative inquiry and field research.

Fast forward four decades to the summer of 2018. I decided to record a song for posterity with three cherished musical soulmates, Sherman, John, and Ed (the first two of whom participated in that fledgling study of friends' discourse so many years ago).

Sherman Ward is the most colorful, engaging, larger-than-life person and performer you'll ever encounter. I've known him since 9th grade. He's brightened my world more times than I can count, and he makes me laugh so hard that I've had to get angry at him to make him stop so I can breathe again. I remember one of my undergraduate students secured an internship working as a grip on a video Sherman was directing in Philadelphia. The student asked me incredulously, "Is he for real? He took over an entire city block by himself so that we could shoot a scene for the hospital commercial we were making!" I said, "You better count your blessings working with him. He's one of the most dynamically real persons I have ever known. And he's forgotten more than most people know about staging and shooting videos!" Once, the entire Penn State Reserve Officers Training Corp (ROTC) platoon was standing at ease in combat gear on the large shaded mall outside of my office in Sparks Building. Ever the fan of westerns, Sherman strode out onto the marble steps and barked loudly in his most commanding, mock John Wayne voice, "Okay men, MOUNT UP!" I doubled over laughing as a significant portion of the regiment actually began forming into units and helping each other shoulder backpacks.

One of the best kept secrets in my family was that my mother was once a singer in a dance band. I can only surmise that this identity was somehow considered incongruous with her roles as a genteel housewife and mother, just as I now realize I had initially thought being a rock and soul musician would be perceived as at odds with my being a dedicated graduate student. I am thankful I was able to speak with her at length some months before she passed away about her singing in public. During our conversation, I learned about even deeper musical connections in our family. She recalled:

> The first time I sang in Lewes for my dad's Lion's Club: "I Double Dare You" and "Smoke Gets in Your Eyes." My dad was real proud of me that night. Mother played piano for me. She played for "silent" movies with music in the background. Scary or happy; she'd be the one on piano giving that atmosphere.

I had no idea that my Mommom Baker played piano, let alone in this narratively attuned and evocative capacity! Yet I've always known that my parents loved music. They saw Frank Sinatra sing with The Harry James Orchestra on the Steel Pier in Atlantic City and always loved dancing whenever they got the chance.

Just a couple years before they died, I took my parents, then in their late eighties, to see Sherman perform with his wife and jazz singing partner Peggy at a nightclub by the boardwalk in Rehoboth Beach. Their repertoire included classic tunes from the Great American Songbook that I knew my parents enjoyed so much. Sherman made a big deal about their arrival, crossing the ballroom to hug them both, and I could tell they felt quite honored and welcomed. After the show Sherman cajoled and charmed my always-lovely-yet-shy mother June onto the stage to sing a duet of "I Double Dare You" with him. It warms my heart to recall them crooning together the very song my mother sang at a dance the night my parents first met. Her brown eyes sparkled and Dad's were brimming as her dulcet voice softly wavered over the sound system in perfect harmony with that of my lifelong friend and big-hearted bandmate.

John Render and I started a band called The Dynasty in 9th grade. I can't do justice here to his sustained presence as a friend in my life. Rehearsing in bands with him, I learned how to learn songs by listening closely to artists' records. We also played high school football together and basketball in my home's driveway until the rim broke off. Together we filled and stacked on pallets eight hundred 65-pound bags of barley and wheat seed each day in a feed mill for two summers at $1.60 an hour. He was Best Man at my wedding. John was always the musical leader and arranger in our bands; he could make a Hammond organ growl and riff his ass off on a Fender guitar. But he hung up his rock-n-roll shoes in the 1970s to become an accomplished lawyer and a preacher. A man of uncommon depth and intelligence, side-splitting wry humor, and soft-pedalled wisdom, John has been a rock whose opinions on anything I've listened to and trusted even when I wasn't sure I agreed with them. Throughout the years, he's shown up out of the blue and sat in with our bands, always a much-storied highlight. After taking up guitar during my 1997 sabbatical to sing with students, I was sheepish about playing in front of him. I always drummed in our bands, and he was the real deal on guitar. But I finally shared with him a singer/songwriter recording I made in 2007, which he liked. I'm truly not sure which has meant more to me—when he was such a kind and abiding presence during some serious health scares I've experienced in recent years, or when he announced to the boys that "Rawls can *play* guitar." When I thought about recording the song that accompanies this essay, I was sure he'd want to participate.

Art knows the third friend, **Ed Shockley**, because he's heard me speak about him in a variety of contexts over the years. Don't start me telling stories about him, there's not sufficient space in this essay. A homegrown genius and inveterate newspaper reader, he's the best conversationalist and storyteller I've ever met. He's also one of my favorite drummers and singers, whose playing I admired from across Sussex County before we met when I was a high school junior. We became fast friends during college, "taking tea" after dinner with my future wife and life partner-to-be Sandy and others, swapping yarns and opinions, followed by a nightly ping pong tournament that pitted Ed and another friend Rob against John Render and me. I also recall Sunday afternoon touch football games with all our musician friends after we slept off our hangovers from gigging the night before. Ed is a professional musician, session player, and singer—a living legend in Delaware. Sandy and I have danced to his music and enjoyed his stories and cooking our entire married life. When I stopped playing music professionally for some 25 years in order to help raise our kids and be a professor, Ed always found ways to include me in music making. He also has read and discussed with me almost everything I've written and attended some of my classes and seminars, all while being a talented curator and dealer of antiques and a dedicated stay-at-home father to Buck and husband to Jill.

Drummers are the bedrock of good bands, and we can be somewhat jealous of our proprietary role as keepers of the beat. Laying down a compelling groove is a starkly embodied, usually sweaty undertaking. And while there's no shortage of drummer jokes, there are few people who understand the art and musicality of contemporary drumming—and the importance of Ringo Starr—like Ed and me. When I came back home east in the summers, we would play high-profile gigs with no rehearsal and on two drum sets—one heartbeat in bodies twain. I started playing out on acoustic guitar at Purdue but was reluctant to continue performing when I came to Ohio University in Athens, a well-known music town with so many great players. When I told Ed, he said, "Rawls, you've got a lot to offer as a guitarist, singer, or drummer, and you don't have to shy away from any gig in *any* town. You go for it." Once again, something he said has made all the difference in the unfolding of my life.

I wrote a song called "Turn 'Em Aloose" a couple summers ago when Sandy and I were travelling with our children Brian and Shelley in the Pacific Northwest. I always bring a guitar on trips. "Turn 'Em Aloose" borrows a phrase someone who followed our bands used to quip back in the day. I played the song for Ed soon after we returned home. Encouraged by his response and beginning to feel our mortality due to lingering health concerns and some of our friends recently passing, we decided that it was high time that the four of us—Ed, John, Sherman and me—should finally record an original song together from scratch.

Now I don't know if you have ever composed an original song, but in my experience every single time one shows up in my life, it feels like a miracle, something to be coddled like a child. Despite all our years of friendship and over-lapping musical histories, we four had never done this together. And recording studios don't lie—"every breath you take" and every sound you make get pre-served naked to the world for posterity. After checking everybody's willingness and availability, when I came east two summers ago to play Ed's and my annual gig as a duo on a Friday, he booked another friend Marty's recording studio for the next day, Saturday, June 23, 2018. Although I could tell you a hundred stories about laughing, conversing, crying, getting away with things, and growing older with these treasured souls, our collective essence shone through when I gathered with my lifelong friends John, Sherman, and Ed to record this song.

***

Let's understand that these are busy people, working several jobs along with their family responsibilities—each navigates unpredictable hours and may be called upon and away with little notice. Recognizing these contingencies, we knew we had to operate as nimbly and efficiently as we could. After we scheduled the studio, things were unfolding quickly, and I needed to circulate a "demo" of the song for everyone to hear. We had some luck on this score. Jeff Redefer, a friend of mine and an excellent guitarist, with whom I've played in Athens bands since 2009, designed the studio and teaches recording production at Ohio University. Earlier in the year, he asked me to be "the talent" during one of his culminating class meetings where the students must assume full responsibility for producing a recording of a singer/songwriter. As a result of that session, I had a professional-grade demo of the song "Turn 'Em Aloose."

Even so, I should note two things. First, veteran Emmy Award-winning producer that he is, Jeff couldn't resist suggesting after we had recorded a bluegrass, two-step version of the song ("Humor me, Bill") that I try cutting the tempo of the song in half. Of course, I followed his advice, channeling my best "feel" for Neil Young and Bob Dylan while playing and singing the song again in this funky, slowed-down fashion "while the tape rolled." After having written and performed this song as a two-step for myself and at gigs for several months, this first-time-I-played-and-sang-it, one-take version actually became the one I distributed as a demo. The second thing to note is that because it was a professionally-recorded demo, the file I had to share was too huge to email to my friends.

As Sandy was driving us east, I kibitzed on the phone with Sherman, who resourcefully instructed me in detail about how I could make use of a website designed for sharing large media files on a no-cost trial basis. "That means you can bail on 'em when you're done, Rawls." Taking careful notes while we talked concerning each of the unfamiliar (to me) steps involved, once we finally arrived at my brother and beloved friend Ron's home, I was able to upload and send a demo of the song with a lyrics sheet to Sherman, John, and Ed. As Ed recommended, I also shared the materials with Marty, the recording engineer, so that he could get a feel in advance for the type of song we would be recording in his studio.

All of this was unfolding on the fly. We didn't know who was going to play or sing what, and only Ed had even heard the song. We just "went with it" as we always used to say when we were young(er). As Sandy and I crossed into western Maryland on Interstate 68, I called Ed to confirm the recording arrangements. While we chatted, I could readily tell how much thought and effort he had been devoting to making sure our session would come off just three days hence. For example, Marty's studio was the only one of four Ed had contacted that was available that Saturday, and there were still some questions about whether Marty could have his brand-new primary recording computer fully operational by then. Things were nip and tuck to say the least. Though John had been playing bass in a church praise band recently, he didn't own one, He also couldn't recall when he'd last played electric guitar, something else he didn't own. Ed told me he would bring for John both electric and bass guitars.

I've had significant experience recording on the drums since I did an afternoon session at Columbia Records' 30th Street Studios in New York City when I was 15. I've drummed all the recordings of songs I've written and probably would have anticipated laying down the drum track on this song if I had given it any real consideration. Yet I listened to Ed's wisdom as he described the walkup to our session. Thinking about his many gifts, I knew there was only one person I would want to drum that song. "Edmund, will you play drums on our session?" I asked him as Sandy and I were rolling east.

"Sure," he said, "I'd be happy to." Like so many other times, I felt the grace of our friendship wafting and settling into place as if in a picnic blanket.

On Friday, Ed and I had a great gig at the Milton Farmers Market held outside the Dogfish Head Brewery 17 miles from Seaford, Delaware, where Sandy, John, Sherman and I grew up. It's a very cool affair in which he's included me for the last five years. We both sing and alternate playing drums while he's playing piano or I'm playing guitar. We perform original songs as well as covers that we and our audience members have enjoyed over the past 40 years. Along with other family and friends in attendance, John and Sherman showed up and sat in for a few tunes, and we started getting psyched for Saturday's recording. Returning to their beach house, I played the demo of "Turn 'Em Aloose" for my brother Ron, Barb, my wonderful sister (in-law), and Sandy, and then performed it on guitar for them. They have followed all of our bands over the years and still regularly catch Sherman and Ed performing with a celebrated, ten-piece outfit called The Funsters, which also includes four musicians I played with in Kickback throughout grad school.

FIGURE 16.1 Left to right: Ed Shockley, Bill Rawlins, John Render, Sherman Ward

***

Ron and Barb engaged The Funsters to play at their daughter Niki's wedding to Steve Salata 14 years ago. It was an extraordinary pleasure for me that they hired this band of my friends for this hallmark event in our family. After a gorgeous wedding service, we sat down to a celebratory feast with over 200 people under a large canvas tent festooned with twinkling clear lights. I eagerly anticipated Sherman announcing the new bride and groom for their first dance and then with his fine baritone voice singing Sinatra's "Summer Wind." Meanwhile, Ed walked up, decked out in a black tuxedo (which we've backstage always called "big boy pants" and "monkey suits"). He held in his hand the printed pages of the four sets of songs they would be performing at this high-stakes gala on their packed calendar of gigs. He handed me all four sets, smiled, and said, "Hey Rawls; here's what we're doing. Tell me which songs you want to play."

Realize that this was during my 25-year sabbatical from music when I may not have played the drums for two years or even more. But Ed knew how much this would mean to me, and it also was a gracious display of his confidence in my ability to "cut the gig." At that point our children had hardly ever seen me play music, and it was a distant memory for most of our extended family. I selected a few songs from early in the third set: "Soul Man," by Sam and Dave; "Time Won't Let Me," by The Outsiders; and "Pick up the Pieces," by The Average White Band. Into the second song, I noticed my dad had carefully made his way through the dancing throng and was perched very close to the left side of the stage (where Ed's honey maple Maryland Drums kit is always set up). Dad intently watched me play, something he was too busy to do during the years I was "always in bands." I sensed that something important was clicking for him inside, an overdue recognition, and I could feel it from him to me, too.

Generous and knowing souls that they are, Ed and Sherman called each of my brothers up to sing on the final song I would drum, Wilson Picket's "Midnight Hour." My oldest brother, Rocky, actually was a lead singer for a band when he was a high school senior and still enjoys performing when he gets the chance. His band's equipment and drums were in our basement, and one day after school when I was in fifth grade, I walked downstairs, sat down at the drum set, and just started playing them. With interruptions of varying lengths, I've been playing them ever since. My older brother, Ron, the "father of the bride," has a nice voice, and I swear smiled warmly throughout the entire verse he sang to a highly responsive crowd of his family and friends at his beloved daughter's wedding. Finally, my younger brother, Terry, a true music aficionado, who also plays guitar and drums, delivered his verse with delight and conviction. Yet the true magic happened when Sherman and Ed then cajoled our typically retiring in such settings father Jack Rawlins to take the stage with us. The priceless and for me now eternal moment of Dad–white-haired, becoming frail, slightly hunched, but all-in, and smiling joyfully while surrounded on stage by his four sons–is captured in a black and white photo taken from the dance floor. It graces the top of an oft-visited chest in our home.

***

FIGURE 16.2 Left to right: Ron Rawlins, Terry Rawlins, Jack Rawlins, Bill Rawlins, Rocky Rawlins

The night before the session, Ron, Barb, and Sandy were very encouraging about the song "Turn 'Em Aloose." Preparing to leave the next day, I could tell that Ron was intrigued by the prospect of the session. As I've mentioned, he knows and is friendly with everyone involved and even sang for a spell in John's and my band The Dynasty when we were kids. But that morning, being the good-hearted soul that he is, he was respectful of the mysterious process of recording and of the impending reunion of his brother's tight circle of music-making friends. I couldn't be more grateful that I found the existential clarity in that moment to invite him to join us. I enjoyed having him there, with his upbeat and always-interested-in-others ways and his easy laughter. As someone who has known us all since we were young, he also brought an enriching sense of history. Engineer Marty, Matt, (John's grandson, a talented pianist and composer), and Ron graciously offered the "excess of seeing" (Bakhtin, 1990) that witnesses to creative events embody, which is crucial for the consummation of all aesthetic activity. Moreover, with his usual enthusiasm and resourcefulness, Ron tangibly enacted this role by photographing and video-recording numerous moments of the session. I have shared those materials with the players and have consulted them extensively in writing this account. I thank him again here for such valued contributions.

Greeting and "going on to" each other outside of Marty's converted garage studio, we immediately fell into a rhythm of referencing old stories and experiences in hilarious ways of which Sherman "Woody" Ward is the hands-down virtuoso. Our banter was much like the interactions I highlighted long ago in my first qualitative research report. We continued doing so inside, introducing Ron to Marty, and Matt to everyone, and expressing appreciation to Marty for his mellow, welcoming studio and facilitating our session at such short notice. He'd attended to every detail. From listening to the demo, he'd already selected, tuned, and mic'd a vintage set of Ludwig drums with a deep resonant warm sound that was perfect for the genre of music we were going to play. He'd chosen the perfect snare drum too, punchy and solid, yet also "wet" enough to allow each beat Ed played on it to open out and settle in for an unhurried, fetching groove. Marty achieved this "wet" snare sound by skillfully loosening the snares' grip on the bottom head of the drum just enough to let the sound spread out, relax, and buzz a little. Think a decidedly *un*-military marching band drum sound; think Aretha Franklin's drummers' snare sounds. An accomplished drummer himself, Marty had already put a lot of thought and effort into the session before we arrived, which would make all the difference in the very possibility of us being able to complete what we did in a mere four and a half hours.

We decided that we would first lay down the basic rhythm track of the song. While many people making records these days will start with just a drum track and then layer every other instrument in discrete and fastidiously measured ways, I despise this way of recording. It sounds artificial and soulless to me, "rotten with perfection" as jazz pianist and literary critic Kenneth Burke would say. In contrast, I wanted us to actually play this song together while listening to and feeding off each other. That was the whole point of being there. To this end, Marty had me play my guitar and sing the song a few times in a vocal booth sealed away from the other players so that they could clearly hear me sing through headphones without too much "bleed" from the other instruments. Simultaneously, Marty dialed in Ed's drum sounds and achieved the right amount of presence and punch for John's bass.

Able to hear the others clearly through our headphones and eager to start, I counted in the song. We started playing it to develop together a sense of the arrangement we would be playing, even as we were performing it. Finding myself now finally and suddenly playing this song in the studio with my old friends, it's difficult to capture the feelings of hearing it coming to form and filling out instrumentally from the get-go. Ed's drum part already feels right and knows where the song wants to go. John's bass part lays in and rounds out the song's motion simply, empathically, and musically. Fifty years of making music and growing older together in friendship is coming home to roost. We all know it. Inspired by this moment, I lengthen a musical phrase at the end of the song in a way I didn't on the demo. John and Ed take it in their stride. When we're done, Ed says, "I like what you did there, Bill. But let's play that ending part even twice as long as what you just did." We play it through again with me singing, and Marty says, "Let's record one."

There are different theories about how to make good recordings, but in Ed's, my, and many others' opinion, if you're ready and attuned to each other, your best takes often occur early on. Endlessly striving for "the perfect take," while understandable, is exhausting and takes the joy out of this creative process. So there is a fair amount riding on Marty's suggestion. I count us in again, and we achieve a presentable take, but nobody's life is changed. Even so, we sense something's just around the corner and say some encouraging things to each other about what we're doing. After another good and improving take, one of us says, "Let's nail it this time."

We play the song through one more time, then over our headphones Marty offers one of the happiest sounds you can hear while recording: "I think you should come in here and listen to that one." This means we will emerge from our individual recording spaces and trappings and gather in the control room to listen to Marty play back the take we just performed together. There is deep concentration and silence—except for the track, you can hear a pin drop. Yet gradually people are starting to smile and breathe easier. After the last note, Ed says, "Boys, I think we've got one." This precipitates a round of high fives and collective excitement for what's next. Then lots of laughs and stories are exchanged while Marty works on mixing what we've just done to elicit its most vibrant and warm sonic properties.

Having achieved a strong basic track, it is time to perform a variety of additional vocal and instrumental parts to transform the song from a very presentable group demo into a fully realized record. First, Ed recommends I play another guitar track. Rather than double the kind of funky, intonated style that I used to embellish different moments in the song when singing my "scratch vocal"—like I do performing it solo live—Ed wants me to play a very simple strumming guitar style to provide some additional lateral motion "in the middle of the mix, where you will feel it almost more than you'll hear it." Dating back to the Beatles' *Rubber Soul*, this is an important recording technique used throughout the industry. It is a great idea, which I'm pleased to say I accomplished in one take.

It is then time for John to record the electric lead guitar part. As I've mentioned, it had been a long time since John had played this instrument, and he doesn't even own one. Johnny Guitar Render from the days of old could have smoked this part every way to Sunday in a heartbeat, while uttering quotable one-liners we'd laugh about for years. But now "Poppy" is here four decades down the road, with his grandson watching, and it is clear he is searching and self-consciously reaching with somewhat attenuated "chops" to do everyone proud. With hopefully no pressure, we watch him tune up, settle in, focus, listen, experiment, and try a couple tracks. He has displayed tremendous respect and affection for all of us—even to make the time in his life to be here. Now he is in the unforgiving glare of recording. John being John, and with his friends' encouragement, "stays in the saddle," risks going after what he thinks is right, and gradually crafts a sweet and soulful part that meaningfully shapes and reflects the ethos of the finished song.

Before recording the song's vocals, Ed suggests I dub a tambourine to accent the beats of John's extended guitar lead and continue through the final verse to the song's end. Once I do, he expertly plays a crisp and fluid shaker part that lasts the entire length of the song, holding together its lateral motion and helping it to "swing." I've got news for you; it's no mean feat to accomplish this, especially in one take. It requires experienced rhythm-conscious dexterity and wrist-playing stamina. Try doing it sometime. Either way, you'll feel it throughout this song.

Now three hours into the session, we need to decide who will sing what. The unfolding of this remaining collective effort involves some of my favorite moments because they so embody our characters as persons and friends. All of us are perched at different places in the main room of the studio where the drums, amps, and various instruments are located, and where we performed individually the instrumental over-dubs just described. I distribute a copy of the song's lyrics to everyone, which read:

> Turn 'em aloose, and just watch them walk away.
> They'll be happier there than they ever were here today.
> Turn 'em aloose, and just swallow your pride.
> It's better for them to be gone than growing cold inside.
> Try to be there in the tissue of time.
> Our breath is not our own; it comes to us from everyone.
> You can drink to the wind. You can drink to the sky.
> You can drink to the planet's health before it all runs dry.
> If them clouds burn off—of that mountain in the sky,
> We can sing about it while we sleep and never question why.
> Wake up and dream about the days to come.
> If we pause a little while, we can try to put our thinking caps on.
> Turn 'em aloose, and just watch them walk away.
> They'll be happier there than they ever were here today.
> Turn 'em aloose, and just swallow your pride.
> It's better for them to be gone than growing cold inside.

While we study the lyrics carefully, John finally says, "It's your song, Rawls, and I love the way you sing it. I think you should sing the whole thing."

There are hearty murmurs of support.

"Thanks John; I much appreciate that," I reply. "But there are four verses, and I want each of us to sing one. For me, that's the whole point of doing this."

"So let's each pick one," Sherman suggests. "Rawls, you go first, I'll do the second, and John and Ed can decide which of the last two they'll do." This makes perfect sense to me, so I propose that John sing the third verse and Ed close out the song.

Ed thoughtfully observes, "Bill, you need to start the song, and you should sing the last verse for it to come full circle. I'll split the third verse with John."

John offers, "I think Ed should sing the whole third verse. He's a really fine singer. I'll just lay out."

"But you're a fine singer too," I say to John. "And I want every one of our voices to be heard singing this song."

"Look," Ed says calmly, "Rawls, you start the song. Woody, you sing the second verse. John, you sing the first half of the third one. I'll sing the second half of it. And I'll sing harmony with Bill in the last verse to bring the song home." It's clear that everyone feels good about this inclusive and aesthetic answer to our quandary.

"So let's get to it."

Knowing the page limits for this writing, I can only note in passing the good humor, wisecracking, storytelling, respect, professionalism, and collective encouragement that transpires as we record our vocal parts. As I had deeply hoped, the auditory presence of each of our voices meaningfully embodies and documents the respiration of our moments shared as friends performing this music and growing older together "in the tissue of time." Sherman invokes Sinatra with such swagger and heart. With his depth and sincerity, John reminds me of Johnny Cash. Ed always sings from the depths of a true storyteller, and having Ed so richly enhance the sound of my own voice in the last verse with his ear and gift for harmony is something I always treasure. To round out this collective composition of our voices, we close the session and the song by singing its last phrase in lustrous, enveloping four-part harmony.

Soon after the session, Marty shares an initial mix with Ed and me. Ed offers to add a variety of "sweeteners" to the mix that we didn't have time to accomplish that Saturday. Accordingly, he returns to Marty's studio a few more times and tastefully adds the electric piano, organ, and acoustic piano parts that I believe strongly elevate the final version.

On Thanksgiving of 2018, I share with my friends this recording: www.youtube.com/watch?v=Nvu-WHKwqIM I include selected pictures and videos that Ron took, which then spawn a flurry of emails. In one of them Sherman skillfully emulates while poking fun at our colorful exchanges as friends from younger days. His words recall the rural heritage of our Sussex County musicians' discourse in Delaware where we all grew up and most still live that I once chronicled over 40 years ago in my first qualitative research seminar. As always, Sherman's humorous commentary to me contains more than a few grains of truth:

> Rawls … these emails alone could keep a career like yours alive for another 10 years … holdin' seminars dissectin' the inside communicatin' that's goin' on here that even a fellow traveler like Ed, though swimmin' in his own segregated tribal pool (Lewes) from our sub-culture dish (at Seaford), eventually, with enough spill outta our bowl … embraced these one-liners & story markers as his own. There's a half dozen of these at least, including the one that Ed himself referenced, inside just this small string of emails! There's gotta be a playin', talkin' & singin' Humanities Tour in here somewhere! And I say you're just the Grant-Hound to get us the funding for this Road Show! It's Prairie Home Companion meets Firesign Theater meets Roadhog & his Cadillac Cowboys!
>
> Let me know when to start workin' the logistics for the tour & I'll git a wheel on it right away!
>
> Gimme a Break Mang! SW

Meanwhile, John tells me about his grandchildren repeatedly requesting to play the recording of the song when his large extended family gathered that Christmas. Being an eyewitness to the session, Matt was accorded special storytelling privileges about John's roles playing and singing in the song by his fellow grandkids. And John tells me how much he enjoyed hearing them exclaim several times, "Poppy is a rock star!"

***

For their parts, Carolyn and Art have worked in a dedicated fashion together and with multiple other scholar-teachers for a number of years to create strong argumentative rationales, lucid conceptual considerations, and sterling and affecting exemplars of narrative and autoethnographic inquiry. These labors led directly to the establishment of the Ethnography Division of the National Communication Association, and their collaborative and solo work with personal narrative as scholarly inquiry has not only transformed investigative and writing practices within the Communication discipline but also has influenced scholars across several fields and around the world. I celebrate the author—Arthur—and the caroler—Carolyn—for their songs of life and spirited scholarly works. And I'm grateful for the impetus they have provided over the years for me to realize and relate this unfolding of my own journey as a musical participant and scholar-teacher of communication and friendships.

Forty-five years ago, I left a band to pursue graduate studies in the communication field. Before too long, when I retire from my cherished professional activities, I will return fulltime to making music and continue learning about life with my bandmates, friends, family, and community members.

References

Bakhtin, M. M. (1990). Author and hero in aesthetic activity. In M. Holquist & V. Liapunov (Eds.), *Art and answerability* (pp. 4–256). University of Texas Press.

Bochner, A. P. (2001). Narrative's virtues. *Qualitative Inquiry, 7*, 131–157. https://doi.org/10.1177/107780040100700201.

Bochner, A. P. (2014). *Coming to narrative: A personal history of paradigm change in the human sciences.* Left Coast Press.

Dewey, J. (2005). *Art as experience.* Perigee Trade.

Ellis, C., & Bochner, A. P. (2000). Autoethnography, personal narrative, reflexivity. In N. K. Denzin & Y. S. Lincoln (Eds.), *Handbook of qualitative research* (2nd ed., pp. 733–768). Sage Publications.

Rawlins, W. K. (1992). *Friendship matters: Communication, dialectics, and the life course.* Aldine de Gruyter.

Rawlins, W. K. (2009). *The compass of friendship: Narratives, identities, and dialogues.* Sage Publications.

Rawlins, W. K. (2014). Performance giving life to life. *Text and Performance Quarterly, 34,* 378–381. https://doi.org/10.1080/10462937.2014.904048.

Rawlins, W. K. (2016, May). *Recovering notes on aging: A musical performance autoethnography of surviving wisdom in 60s songs.* Twelfth International Congress of Qualitative Inquiry, University of Illinois, Urbana.

Rawlins, W. K. (2018). Approaching ethnographic research about human interaction as making music together. *Advances in Intelligent Systems and Computing,* 202–209. doi:10.1007/978-3-030-01406-3_17.

17

COMEDIC AUTOETHNOGRAPHY

Nathan Hodges

During the last semester of my Master's program I discovered *The Ethnographic I: A Methodological Novel About Autoethnography* (Ellis, 2004). Before I even finished Chapter 1, still unsure how to pronounce this methodological mouthful, "otto-eth-nog-raf-ee,"[1] I was ready to saddle up with this group of introspective renegades, ride into academic ghost towns and bring them back to life. Carolyn Ellis would lead the charge toting her storytelling six-shooter (known to take out a man's head *and* heart with a single shot) as we kicked open the doors to their social-science saloons and told those Science-is-God Sheriffs and their Generalizability Gangs, "We're operating by our own laws now, boys." We'd leave their egos bruised a darker purple than Carolyn's spurred boots as we rode out of town, pens blazing, and—okay, back to the 21st century.

In this chapter, I consider what it might look like if autoethnographers approach their research comedically. I discuss *why* we need comedy in evocative autoethnography, *what* comedy is (nature/character), *why* comedy matters (functions/aims), and three goals of comedic autoethnography (comedy that embodies the autoethnographic disposition): coping, critiquing, and connecting. I then explain how to do comedic autoethnography, including specific comedic devices you can employ in writing/performing your texts. Throughout, I use examples from my autoethnographies and standup comedy performances, local standup comedy performances I've observed, and excerpts from popular standup comedians.[2]

Evoking evocative autoethnography

I'm still gung-ho about autoethnography, a research method that allows me to most fully communicate my truths, the closest I've come to connecting a USB cable from my squishy noggin' to yours, letting you peruse my browsing history, think what I think, feel what I feel, hopefully evoking from you what's evoked in me. So, what are we evoking through evocative autoethnography?

In a special issue devoted to "Writing Autoethnographic Joy," Myers (2012) observes, "Although there are certainly exceptions, the majority of evocative auto-ethnography relies on experiences of hardship, sadness, and pain. Sometimes the pain is something that is overcome, but sadness and anger are usually at the root of those essays" (p. 158). Hemmingson (2008) writes, "autoethnography has dark tones of seriousness" and is typically about "serious, tragic, and painful personal subject matter." Others tell us if autoethnography doesn't break your heart, then it's not worth doing,[3] and writing autoethnography should make you dig deeper and deeper into the darkness of your own complex sorrows.[4] No wonder Carolyn Ellis brought a box of Kleenex to every "Autoethnography" graduate seminar.

I don't want to change *what* you write about in autoethnography; I want to offer new ways of *perceiving* and *portraying* what you write about. Sadness, anger, tragedy, and painful personal subject matter do not have to be absent or ignored for joy/happiness/humor to exist. Happiness and suffering are not opposites. Bochner (2012) encourages us to think of happiness and suffering as dialectical, not oppositional, that we can "suffer happiness" and "happily suffer."[5] An autoethnography of suffering is not an end in itself but a way of seeking happiness (or joy or meaning). Humor and seriousness are also not opposites. Humor can be a "serious" way of coping with suffering,[6] and comedy and tragedy can be understood dialectically, experiences can be perceived as "comically tragic" and "tragically comedic."[7]

Deadly serious

You're going to die.

Though several people have tried very, very hard not to die, so far everyone has died. Except me and you of course. But history is not on our side in this regard. One of the major problems with death is that the wi-fi never seems to work. Also, you rarely have sex and bugs eat your skin off. No wonder dead people rarely smile. An even bigger problem with death is knowing about it. An even bigger-er problem is what you don't know about it: *when* you're going to die (why do we always find out *after?*) and *how* you're going to die.[8]

If you were my mom's sweet little Shi-tzu, Winston, not only would you not be reading a book about autoethnography (he prefers autoeth*dog*raphy) but instead be playing with/humping my mom's other sweet little Shi-tzu, Daisy, or sitting by your food bowl and making sad noises until someone puts food in it or sleeping, you would also have no idea that play, sex, snacks, and sleep (your existence) will one day not exist. You would have no idea that every time you're let outside to potty and you run over to the woods that a rattlesnake might eat you. You would have no idea that one day you might watch your best friend/sex partner, Daisy, be run over by a car.

Unfortunately, you could never live a dog's life, as great as it might sound, because you're burdened with self-consciousness, a distinctly human quality that exists for as long as you're alive, a quality that, since you learned at some young age that people die (and even worse, that you die), produces a terror so deep that basically everything you do in your life will be motivated by your need to ignore or avoid the inevitably of your death and try to "outlive" it through literal immortality (belief in an afterlife, religion) and symbolic immortality—the sense you are part of something that will outlive you: lineage, nation, work, etc. (Becker, 1973). Other ways you might manage the terror of death: watch videos of bulldogs skateboarding; post a picture of your dinner to social media; covet your neighbor's ox; covet your neighbor's male servant; bear false witness against your neighbor; beat up someone smaller, weaker, and less adept at martial arts than you; paint the Sistine Chapel; purchase sex toys online; obey local, state, and federal laws; participate in a Ponzi scheme; run a marathon; do drugs; be President. Thankfully there are many options, because in what is perhaps the cruelest twist of irony we will experience, it is being alive (as a self-conscious being) that produces our terror of death: "our deepest need is to be free of the anxiety of death ... but it is life which awakens it, and so we must shrink from being fully alive" (Becker, 1973, p. 66). Folks, that's comedy on a cosmic scale.

Though self-consciousness might be a burden, it's also a gift, allowing you to detach yourself from your self. It's also a necessity for humor, an "expression of the freedom of the human spirit, of its capacity to stand outside of life, and itself, and view the whole scene" (Niebuhr, 1946, p. 111–112). Because of your ability to self-detach, you are capable of joking about mistakes and misgivings, and laughing at fears and anxieties, transcending an experience – forgiving yourself and others, and filing away discouragements as valuable life experiences (Burke, 1984; Kimble, 2004).

Now coming to the stage[9]

I'm in a dark, musty basement in Cedar Rapids, Iowa: Penguin's Comedy Club.

"Let's keep the laughs going for your next comedian, Nathan Hodges." A smattering of applause.

I walk towards the stage, my face neutral, perhaps veering toward cynicism. I rarely, if ever, smile on stage, partly as a result of being embarrassed about my crooked, crowded teeth; partly because I do veer towards cynicism. I grab the microphone and scan the room through the near-blinding lights.

"My grandma's dead." Several audience members laugh.

"Parkinson's ... Couldn't shake that one off, Pat." A few audience members groan.

"What, I didn't kill her.... Listen, I love my grandma. I miss her. It's been nearly five years. But I think she's in a better place – not alive with Parkinsons.... One important thing to know about my grandma, she wasn't religious ... at all. But her daughter – my aunt – was.

"Once my grandma was diagnosed, throughout those two years my aunt hounded her to go to church, read the Bible, get saved. And it would make my grandma feel bad. It angered me, preying upon my grandma when she's at her most vulnerable.

"But my grandma resisted until the end…. We're in the hospital room. The whole family is gathered. My grandma has been in a coma for hours. It appears this might be the end. We're all telling stories, crying, reminiscing, my aunt's praying in the corner. All of a sudden grandma wakes out of her coma and looks up at us, entirely lucid, and the first thing my aunt says to her is, 'MAMA, MAMA, did you see Jesus?'

"My grandma looks at her like it's the *dumbest fucking* thing she's ever heard in her life and says 'NO!'… *then immediately dies.*"

"It was beautiful," I say smiling. "I had to leave the room. I couldn't contain myself. I watched my aunt lose her mother and her entire belief system just like that," I say snapping my fingers. "Almost enough to make me believe in God."

Humor⇔comedy

Humor is a frame for experience, a form of perception (Berger, 1997), the difference between what happens and how you understand and express what happens. Asking "*what* is funny?" is a pointless question. The "what" can be anything. There is no given way to frame any experience – death, cancer, drug abuse, racism, school shootings, etc. Even concentration camps can be funny. Even to concentration camp survivors.

Auschwitz survivor Victor Frankl (1959) wrote

> Humor, more than anything else in the human make-up, can afford an aloofness and an ability to rise above any situation, even if only for a few seconds…the attempt to develop a sense of humor and to see things in a humorous light is some kind of a trick learned in the art of living. Yet it is possible to practice the art of living even in a concentration camp, although suffering is omnipresent.
>
> *(p. 54–55)*

Frankl would joke with a fellow prisoner—a surgeon—that if he were to be liberated from the camp and return to his work in the hospital, he would be unable to lose the habits of camp life. He says, "One day you will be back in the operating room, performing a big abdominal operation. Suddenly an orderly will rush in announcing the arrival of the senior surgeon by shouting, *Action! Action!*" (p. 54) which is what the Nazi foreman at his worksite often shouted when supervising the workers. This hope for a future, shared through their funny stories, "was another of the soul's weapons in the fight for self-preservation" (p. 54). In the continual process to make sense of our experiences and represent them in empowering ways, we can try to "squeeze comedy out of life's tragedies" (Bochner, 2000, p. 270).

Humor is the ability to find something funny; comedy is putting humor into action for an audience. There are several genres of comedy with different goals but, in this chapter, I will focus on comedy using "selfhood, subjectivity, and personal experience (auto), to describe, interpret, and represent (graphy), beliefs, practices, and identities of a group or culture (ethno)" (Adams & Herrmann, 2020, p. 2). The only real requirement for something to be comedy is that whatever you communicate makes people laugh. If people aren't laughing, you're not doing comedy. That doesn't mean they need to laugh the entire time or that their laughter needs to be uproarious, or even genuine.[10] Usually making people laugh requires being funny and usually being funny requires recognizing and revealing incongruities.

Incongruity relies on the assumption that within any culture or social experience there is typically congruity (an accepted set of expectations): norms, rules, patterns, values, etc. Comedy requires recognizing norms, rules, patterns, values, etc., establishing them for an audience (building expectations) then subverting/inverting those patterns (violating expectations) and "part of the pleasure of human laughter is it shows how richly attuned our expectations are even if they remain inexplicit" (Boyd, 2004, p. 11).

But not just any expectation violation will do. If I set your house on fire, that would likely violate your expectations, but I doubt you would find that funny. That's because you have no sense of humor. Comedy is grounded in play and thus the incongruity you present to an audience must feel non-threatening (not just physically, but also to their sense of self). There are other ways to violate your expectations: Scaring, attacking, challenging, and making you feel guilty, but these aren't playful and feel threatening so they're unlikely to connect you with someone and produce laughter.

Any incongruence can be perceived as comedic: between the *real world* and what appears real, what we feel and what *is*. As comedian Norm Macdonald (2016) says, "it takes a powerful imagination to see a thing for what it really is" (p. 21); between what we expect to happen and what happens; between what one says and what one does, one's purported beliefs and actual practices (shows like *Last Week Tonight with John Oliver* frequently splice together edited clips of individuals that draw attention to these incongruities); between the expectations of cultural norms and our personal desires; between our unconscious and our conscious, our innate sexual/primal urges and societies that demand we censor them (Freud, 1960); between pretenses of political authority and their underlying fallibility (root of much satire).

Given that surprise is fundamental to producing laughter, comedy acts as an intrusion into the experience of everyday life (Berger, 1997). And what better place to break up the monotony of everyday life than the Bureau of Motor Vehicles:

> The woman behind the desk rattles off questions in a monotone voice without looking up from her form, seemingly annoyed to even be there.
> "Name?" *Nathan Hodges.*
> "Age?" *Thirty-two.*
> "Sex?" *It's been a while.*

A split second of hesitation, then she laughs. My comedic intrusion cut through a façade of bureaucracy, perhaps revealing another reality to her in which her job didn't have to be boring and detached, and words and categories are more malleable than she'd thought. The woman's laughter illustrated to me that "she got it," she identified with what I was saying and doing. Connection is the heart of comedy and autoethnography.

Comedic truth

The truths we seek in autoethnography are "contested, partial, incomplete, and always in motion" (Tullis Owen, McRae, Adams, & Vitale, 2009, p. 185), existing between a storyteller and story listener (Bochner & Ellis, 2016). We expect an audience to engage with a story's tensions, ambiguities, emotional/moral dilemmas, contradictions, and to "live in its reality for a time" (Bochner, 2017, p. 75). The same is true of comedy. Audiences *must* be a *partner* in the performance because *they* decide what's funny by laughing (or not) and thus "audiences turn performers jokes into jokes" (Manwell, 2008, p. 19).

Comedic truth is a truth that exaggerates, distorts, plays with, and draws attention to incongruities, contradictions, failures, and uncertainties of being human and trying to relate to one another. It's neither fictional nor factual, but rather a truth that can be felt through the resonation of laughter. Comedy presents a "world turned upside down, grossly distorted, and precisely for that reason more revealing of some underlying truths than the conventional, right-side-up view" (Berger, 1997, p. 21).

In "The Chemical Life" (Hodges, 2015a), you follow the main character, "you," throughout a day with attention to chemical consumptions and assumptions. The second-person voice and use of footnotes call attention to the ways we ignore or mindlessly read product labels. There are several ways the essay could have been written, particularly given the fear often associated with chemicals. Instead, I look upon life as a "disinterested spectator," one I invite readers to trust and see themselves through. "The Chemical Life" offers an immersive ethnographic adventure that pokes fun at our everyday chemical consumption while inviting readers to question how they understand what is meant by such terms as "healthy," "natural," and "chemical." The opening passage illustrates how the comic frame is employed:

> You are sitting in a McDonald's with a friend drinking a cup of water. Your friend says, "I can't believe they legalized pot in Colorado," while washing down a Big Mac with Diet Coke. When he puts the cup on the table the Diet Coke disintegrates the cardboard and burns a hole through the table. You look around the restaurant. A scraggly-haired woman with droopy sacks under her eyes shoots mayonnaise into her arm with a syringe. Another customer in a business suit snorts artificial sweetener through a straw. Parents season their children's chicken nuggets with hairspray and skin lotion. A woman surrounded by plastic shopping bags puts a French fry into her mouth and lights up the end like she's smoking a cigarette. Your friend pours a bottle labeled *preservatives* onto the rest of his Big Mac … Beep. Beep. BEEP. BEEP. BEEP. A chemical cocktail shoots through your bloodstream as the alarm clock screams at you to wake up.

(p. 627)

This autoethnography seeks to accomplish what Hacking (1999) calls unmasking, "which does not seek to refute ideas but to undermine them by exposing the function they serve" (p. 20). To ask whether the scene described is factually true wouldn't make much sense. We don't know to what extent—if any—it's based on a "real" McDonald's encounter. Instead, readers must reflect upon their own experiences in order to judge the story's validity.

"The Chemical Life" relies on its recognition and employment of various incongruities: between the way some people talk about "health" and their health practices; between the way chemicals are recognized and/or understood as negative in some contexts and taken-for-granted in other contexts; the seeming hypocrisy between the way we understand some people's chemical consumption as repulsive, illegal, or unhealthy and the way we fail to reflect upon our own chemical consumption or see no problem with it.

Comedy as coping mechanism

"*Laughter is the best medicine*"

Lots of unfunny people.

Tragedy and comedy are not necessarily different types of experiences, but different methods for portraying experiences. Kierkegaard even said, "the more one suffers, the more … one has a sense for the comic" (Kimble, 2004). Comedian Tig Notaro (2012) went on stage at Largo Comedy Club in Los Angeles only a few days after discovering she was diagnosed with breast cancer, which was only a few days after her mother unexpectedly died, which was only a few days after she survived a rare, life-threatening bacterial disease, which was only a few days after her partner left her. She scrapped her original set, which consisted of observational jokes about traffic jams, walked to the microphone and started, "Good evening. Hello. I have cancer. How are you? Is everybody having a good time? I have cancer." Notaro spent the next 30 minutes processing her feelings on stage, desperately squeezing comedy out of her tragedies, not just for the audience but for herself: "It's weird because with humor the equation is tragedy plus time equals comedy. I am just at tragedy right now." At times she had to console audience members ("It's okay, it's okay. You're gonna be okay. I don't know what's going on with me"), even as they roared with laughter, at one point telling an audience member, "Sir! This should not tickle you that much. I'm not *that* happy and comfortable."

When I didn't get my way as a child my parents would tell me, "Life isn't fair. Get used to it." I was ashamed: about living in a trailer and my "white trash" family (Hodges, 2016); of how I looked – my crooked, crowded teeth that marked me as poor and unattractive (Hodges, 2015c) and my fat body, a target for derisive comments, physical jabs, and titty-twisters (Hodges, 2015b); of my academic performance – poor grades and being labeled by teachers as a "bad student" (Hodges, 2016); of my seeming inability to make friends and talk with my peers.

My shame cultivated a rage that swelled up inside me, ready to burst at any moment. Comedy offered me a safe way to express this rage and allowed me to stand out, to build solidarity with my peers, a way of coping with my insecurities and perceived deficiencies – of thinking everything's going to be okay, regardless of whether I was poor, fat, stupid, and not "cool." Comedian Judd Apatow (2015) writes, "I always felt the reason I was interested in comedy was that I was on some level hostile and looking for answers" (p. 289).

In order to perceived my experiences comedically I needed some emotional distance. Bergson (1911) tells us comedy requires "a momentary anesthesia of the heart" and encourages us to "look upon life as a disinterested spectator" (p. 5), "curtailing whatever strong emotions one might otherwise have in the situation, be it pity, or love, or hatred" (p. 210).

In "The American Dental Dream" (Hodges, 2015b), I write about being ashamed of my crooked teeth and feeling as if I do not live up to America's cultural standards for straight, white teeth. I show how, using comedy, I therapeutically reframed the narrative I tell about my teeth (Hodges, 2015b). For a while during my undergraduate years, I would treat my snaggletooth as an evil entity, naming it "The Boston Snaggler" (after the infamous Boston Strangler). I would tease friends and sometimes strangers, that The Snaggler had a mind of his own, as I snarled the tooth at them. I externalized the embarrassing tooth, "objectifying and personifying the problem in my life that I experience as painful and oppressive" (Kiesinger, 2002, p. 108), rising above the experience and viewing it with some emotional disengagement. This is a shift from a tragic teeth tale that paints me as a victim to an empowered teeth tale that makes people laugh and projects me as unique and confident (and perhaps a bit strange). However, this reframing is ongoing and, at times—especially when I'm supposed to give a "serious" open-mouthed smile for the camera—feelings of embarrassment sometimes return.

Standup comedian Jesse Reed who describes herself as a "teen mom turned meth addict turned comedian" also uses a comedic frame to discuss her battles with meth addiction. During a set on Comedy Central's popular standup series, "This is Not Happening," she describes how her addiction began: "I get back home to Portland, and quit doing comedy so I could pursue meth full time" and how the addiction progressed to the point where she was drinking her own pee. She was reading a news article about the epidemic of meth addiction in the U.S. and how some addicts had even resorted to drinking their pee to get high because

> meth doesn't metabolize in the body. Goes in meth, goes out meth. Which is why you stay high the whole time.… I don't know what the article was trying to say but what I heard was we're pissing out thousands of dollars of liquid gold.

As someone who grew up in a family ravaged by the drug, I found her depiction of meth addiction hilarious. There are a lot of ways to describe substance abuse, particularly meth addiction. Look no further than the infamous "Faces of Meth" campaign and advertisements produced by the Montana Meth Project to see the fear tactics used to portray the life-robbing tragedy that is meth addiction. In these portrayals, meth addicts beat an old man to death to take his wallet, sell their daughter for sex to get their fix, and lay on dirty mattresses picking imaginary bugs out of their skin until there are open wounds all over their bodies (montanameth. org). What these portrayals leave out is one very important detail about meth: it's fun, an escape from the overwhelming stress and shame of living in poverty. Meth makes you feel you could take on the world. Like there's an invisible angel on your shoulder sweet talking into your ear while holding a gun to your head. Meth gives you a drive that could make you a pro athlete, world renowned artist, or CEO … if you weren't on meth.

Reed was a meth addict. That is a fact. She can't change that. She has to live with the experiences she's been through. Rather than keep her experiences shrouded in silence, where they have the potential to metastasize into shame tumors, and rather than frame her experiences in ways that seek pity from others, she frames herself as a *fool with agency*, and her experiences as learning opportunities that have shaped her into the person she is today—someone who is on stage owning her story in all its *meth*iness. However, she ends her set with a stern warning to the audience: "Here's the thing, don't ever drink meth piss, because it's fantastic, and you won't wanna do any other drugs."

However, comedy can be a way of preventing you from confronting your trauma and despair. Hannah Gadsby's widely-lauded 2018 Netflix special, *Nanette*, starts off fairly typical for a standup comedy show, with jokes about her upbringing in a small town in Tasmania ("Famous for a lot of things. Potatoes … our frighteningly small gene pool."). Later she tells a story in which she was at a bus stop after a night at the pub and was talking with a woman. A guy comes up to Gadbsy and starts shoving her, calling her a "fucking faggot" and "fucking freak" and tells her to stay away from his girlfriend when the girl Gadsby was talking to steps in and stops the guy, telling him, "It's a girl!" I'll let Gadbsy finish the story:

> And he goes, "Oh, I'm so sorry. I don't hit women."
> "What a guy! I don't hit women. How about you don't hit anyone? Good rule of thumb." Then he goes, "Sorry, I got confused. I thought you were a fucking faggot … trying to crack on to my girlfriend."

She continues the set telling funny stories about coming out to her mom and grandma and growing up as a lesbian woman before jabbing the audience:

> Do you understand what self-deprecation means when it comes from somebody who already exists in the margins? It's not humility. It's humiliation. I put myself down in order to seek permission to speak. And I simply will not do that anymore.

The tone of her delivery is serious and the audience applauds. Then just as suddenly as she shifted out of the comedic frame she shifts back in with jokes that poke fun at various times she has been mistaken for being a man ("I love being mistaken for a man, 'cause just for a few moments, life gets a hell of a lot easier.... I'm about to get good service for no fucking effort!"). Her set grows heavier, her words punctuated by applause and sometimes silence, but rarely involuntary laughter, as she knowingly refuses to release the tension she has created, ultimately building to a crescendo:

> Do you remember that story about that young man who almost beat me up? It was a very funny story. I made a lot of people laugh about his ignorance, and the reason I could do that is because I'm very good at this job. I am good at controlling the tension. I know how to balance that to get the laugh at the right place. But in order to balance the tension in the room with that story, I couldn't tell that story as it actually happened. Because I couldn't tell the part of the story where that man realized his mistake. And he came back. And he said, "Oh, no, I get it. You're a lady faggot. I'm allowed to beat the shit out of you," and he did! He beat the shit out of me and nobody stopped him. And I didn't … report that to the police, and I did not take myself to the hospital, and I should have.

Gadsby weaves back and forth between jokes and observations about comedy to "skewer the nature of jokes, arguing that because they inevitably lead to incomplete stories, they evade difficult truths" (Zinoman, 2018). For Gadsby, jokes are not nearly sophisticated enough to deal with the trauma she experienced because they require only two parts—a beginning and a middle (setup and punchline) and required her to "freeze an incredibly formative experience at its trauma point and … seal it off into jokes." She then tells the audience that the answer to coping with our personal and collective traumas is not laughter, but stories:

> Laughter is not our medicine. Stories hold our cure. Laughter is just the honey that sweetens the bitter medicine. I don't want to unite you with laughter … I just needed my story heard, my story felt and understood by individuals with minds of their own. Because, like it or not, your story is my story. And my story is your story.
>
> *(Gadsby, 2018)*

It is likely clear to any viewer watching her speak that traditional jokes are an inadequate medium for her to process her trauma. The pain and anger are evident in her voice. However, her final statements of the night: "laughter is not *our* medicine … my story is *your* story" dismiss how comedy has been used by others—especially marginalized individuals—throughout history to cope with pain and prejudice, and to find meaning in their suffering. And the clear distinctions she makes between "jokes" and "stories" fail to account for the versatility of standup comedy as an art form in ways that go far beyond the traditional setup/punchline format.[11]

Comedy to critique

> "Every joke is a tiny revolution"
>
> *George Orwell (1945)*

Wes—one of my best friends—a 49-year-old white man with moppy gray hair and dark-framed glasses, stands on stage holding a microphone to his mouth. His face looks both grumpy and inviting, a furrowed brow, no smile, but eyes that show curiosity and seek connection.

"I'm a veteran," he says and within seconds the audience is clapping. "No, no, no, no, no," he says gesturing for the crowd to stop.

> I was in the navy for six years, and I don't like this fetishization of veterans. When we obsessively thank vets for their service, we reduce them down to this one aspect of their identity and we ignore other aspects of their identity and their experiences. For example, I was in the Navy with this guy named Sam. And yeah he's a veteran, but he is more than that. He's also a guy who really likes fucking Filipino prostitutes.... Really, I think when people say "thank you for your service" what they're really saying is, thank you ... for growing up poor.

Comedians are able to offer commentary and critique on cultural issues through personal storytelling. Comedic autoethnography creates opportunities for personal and cultural critique, allowing you to complicate everyday life encounters, embrace ambiguous and nonbinary identities, and negotiate socially stigmatized identities through constructing counter-narratives (Boylorn & Orbe, 2014). Comedian Josh Blue regularly makes audiences laugh with stories about his Cerebral Palsy, leveling criticism against our ableist culture while also building identification with the audience (who are part of our ableist culture). During an interview Blue says,

> I take the piss out of myself—pretty much throughout the show, but by doing that it leaves the door wide open for me to take the piss out of you too.... And to point out that you're ignorant about disability.
>
> *(Bingham & Green, 2016)*

He often uses the uncontrollable actions of his right arm in ways that draw attention to the physicality of disability and that challenge audience assumptions that people with disabilities are passive victims in need of pity. In his 2006 special, Blue talks about getting into a fight, and what he calls the "Palsy Punch": "First of all, you don't really know where it's coming from. Second of all, neither do I!"

Self-deprecating humor can allow you to explore your own subjectivity and cultural groups to which you belong, potentially disrupting and subverting the flaws and foolishness of others' thoughts and actions and the ways in which these are culturally learned. Sometimes we self-deprecate as a way of helping us feel we're better than our former selves. Comedy can be a way of claiming dignity, self-worth, and power when it feels we have none.

British comedian Rosie Jones has ataxic cerebral palsy, severely altering her speech patterns, making it slower and erratic. This sometimes leads uninformed individuals to assume she has a cognitive impairment or learning disability. In her set, Rosie draws attention to this incongruity between what other (often able-bodied) expect from her based on her body and speech, and her actual cognitive abilities: "My name's Rosie … and as you can tell … from my voice, I suffer from … being northern."[12] This one line takes her 17 seconds to say. Later in her set she says, "I have a disability called cer-e-bral pa-lsy," she struggles through each syllable of the name, "and I guess the worst thing about having cer-e-bral pal-sy is how long it takes me," the audience already starts laughing as they anticipate the punchline, "to say, cerr-eee-brall" she puts her hand up gesturing for herself to hurry up and say it already, "pall-syyy." The audience laughs. "Blind … deaf … why did they get one syll-a-ble? But the slow talker gets five," she holds up five fingers smiling, "fook-in syll-a-bles?" Her jokes poke fun not only at herself but also at the absurdity of this phrase being applied to this group of people therefore poking fun at the cruel ironies that members of stigmatized groups live with and that those without the disability can take-for-granted.[13]

Comedy to connect

> "Laughter is the closest distance between two people"
>
> *Victor Borge*

Comedians and autoethnographers "call for engagement, identification, and resonance" (Bochner, 2017, p. 75) and a comedian must "establish some or many points of identification with their audience in order to be successful; laughter signals belonging or affirms that they get where you are coming from" (Krefting, 2012, p. 145). The audience/reader has to trust the comedian/autoethnographer is being truthful and authentic, "showing a willingness to be their own worst critic—picking at scabs, exposing warts…striving for an acute self-consciousness and a shameless subjectivity" (Bochner, 2017, p. 71). And according to stand-up comedian, Louie Anderson, no other stand-up understood this better than arguably the greatest comedian of all-time, Richard Pryor:

> Richard was the best at surgically opening himself up on stage … like his whole guts and everything, and laying it out on display. I think he was best at displaying his insides, and that's why you loved him so much because he'd go up there and you'd go, This guy is hiding absolutely nothing from me, and he's being completely honest, but yet he's funny and he's right and he's making me think but he's not making me feel guilty about what I am.
>
> *(Ajaye, 2002, p. 56)*

When Pryor looks within himself and refuses to avert his eyes, pointing out his own flaws and insecurities, he draws attention to the taken-for-granted assumption that he has his shit together—that he has life figured out, that he's in control, that he's always a good person. He *invites* listeners to identify with his experiences, giving them permission to laugh at their own faults and tragedies. Sometimes their laughter is a symbolic "thank you" for making them feel less alone. But it can also help dismantle the shame and despair he may have attached to his experiences. As Wyatt (2016) observed a standup comedian say at the end of his open mic set in Edinburgh, "Doing standup is a very good laxative" (p. 46).

The paradox of comedy is that it both unifies and divides—simultaneously forming a bond and drawing a line—allying you with one group/ideal by differentiating you from you another group/ideal (Meyer, 2000). Comedy can unite you with a group/ideal by allowing you to playfully clarify ideas (i.e. point out incongruities of certain positions, cultural norms) and create mutual identification with an audience (typically marked by laughter). Simultaneously, this clarification contrasts you from other views or social groups (as comedy is built on contradiction), and thus your jokes also allow you to enforce certain norms and/or positions, implicitly or explicitly marking what is acceptable or unacceptable (Meyer, 2000). Thus, comedy can be used to critique unjust social practices and damaging cultural norms and values *and* can be used to justify unjust social practices and perpetuate damaging cultural norms and values.

Doing autoethnographic comedy

Each of these devices are ways comedic autoethnographers can *understand/frame* an experience and also *present* that experience, in order to reveal some new understanding about themselves, others, and culture.

Overall, a comedic voice seems most accessible when writing as a "distanced spectator" (Bergson, 1911), which could include writing in second- or third-person narrative voice, but also simply writing in a way that transforms the emotional and subjective into the literal and objective. In "Weighing Ourselves Down: Scale Stories" (Hodges, 2015c), I describe the emotional connection my mom felt with me when I was born:

> My mom looks up at the blurry ceiling and puts all her weight into one final push. She says she fell in love 'the moment she laid eyes on me.' Her unconditional love taught me one of the most valuable lessons I'll ever need in this life: If you want to make a good first impression, get naked and cry.
>
> *(p. 53)*

I'm not encouraging you to meet someone for the first time naked and crying (because I doubt you'll get the chance for a second impression). I'm poking fun at the sentimental cultural discourse that often accompanies birth stories. Despite the sterile, clinical lights of the hospital room; despite the sweaty, screaming mother who more than likely just shit herself; despite the sleepless agitation of family members; and despite this tiny wriggling, crying, ball of flesh covered in a white, cheese-like substance with a spongy, octopus tentacle attached to it, what do you hear in most birth stories?

Some comedic truths are expressed through *strategic juxtaposition*—purposefully putting together contradictory words, actions, people, ideologies, etc. Other comedic devices used include *exaggeration*—revving up the facts – and *understatement*—downplaying the facts. In order to do this well you must trust the reader. Don't explain the humor or you will kill it (as I've done throughout this chapter). And humor is more enjoyable when it's alive. For example, there is a section in "Weighing Ourselves Down: Scale Stories" (Hodges, 2015c) in which I discuss my time being a vegan. In order to express the contradiction between how veganism is often culturally portrayed as healthy and what I experienced as a vegan and saw from vegans in my community I wrote:

> I discover I can be vegan and eat a steady diet of preservative-filled, chemically-injected junk food, as long as it doesn't have a trace of animal parts in it: Oreo® cookies, Frito® chips, and frozen dinners with dissertation-length ingredient lists. I've met people who call themselves vegan who'd eat deep-fried meatless hotdogs rolled in Chernobyl waste and sprinkled with FD&C #'s 1–100 but wouldn't get within tonguing distance of a boiled egg from a family-owned, free-range, vegetarian-fed chicken.
>
> *(p. 61)*

There are no vegan hotdogs that have nuclear waste in them (at least that's what *they* want you to think). The U.S. Food and Drug Administration has approved a number of food dyes and additives, from Red No. 40 to Yellow No. 6, but there aren't anywhere near 100, and if there were, they wouldn't all be in one food (at least that's what *they* want you to think). I wrote this assuming the reader knows I know that. In order to express the comedic truth that although vegans and vegan living are often portrayed as more natural and healthy, there are plenty of vegans and ways of being vegan that are artificial and unhealthy. In order to do this in a way with which readers could identify and hopefully laugh, I exaggerated the facts about the chemicals and ingredient lists (at least that's what *they* want you to think).

Another common device used to convey comedic truths is *verbal irony*, in which words convey the opposite of their intended meaning and *situational irony* arises through incongruity between what's expected or intended to happen and what happens. For example, in Norm Macdonald's book (2016) he writes: "The plain truth is that Adam Eget is an alcoholic and that's why he doesn't drink. Me, I'm not an alcoholic and that's why I do drink. Life sure is funny that way" (p. 9). An example from my standup: "Took my dog to the dog park this morning … was a lot more fun when she was alive."[14]

In "The American Dental Dream" (Hodges, 2015b), there is a scene in which I'm at the dentist getting my teeth cleaned and notice the irony between what they're using to clean my teeth and what is supposedly giving me cavities:

> Flavored toothpaste is rubbed on a chewy retainer and put on my teeth for cleaning. I choose French vanilla from a menu of delicious flavors: bubble gum, cherry cheesecake, chocolate, banana split, and other flavors that taste like the same sugary stuff supposedly giving me cavities.
>
> *(p. 946)*

Dramatic irony occurs when the audience is aware of something the writer/character seemingly isn't, making the author/performer appear unaware and/or foolish, inviting audience members to laugh at their superiority over the author/performer ("At least I don't do that!") or identify with the author/performer's foolishness and feel less alone ("I'm not the only one!") An example from Norm Macdonald's book (2016) in which he describes his affection for comedian, Sarah Silverman:

> Sarah said she could no longer live in New York, that she was being tormented day and night by some obsessive stalker. This caught me completely by surprise, as I had taken to hanging around Sarah's apartment, hiding in the bushes day and night, watching her come and go, and I had never seen any signs of a stalker.
>
> *(p. 146)*

There's also *postmodern irony* in which you treat something "serious" in a cynical, mocking way, and *post-irony*, in which you treat something that is absurd seriously or un-ironically or you're unclear about whether it's to be taken seriously. Hannibal Buress, during the 2015 Comedy Central Roast of Justin Bieber: "They say that you roast the ones that you love but I don't like you at all, man. I'm just here because this is a real good opportunity for me." Buress delivers these "jokes" deadpan and laughs out loud at his own lines along with the audience who is roaring with laughter. Bieber appears to have a smile on his face. Buress continues in a deadpan delivery, "Actually you should thank me for participating in this extremely transparent attempt to be more likable in the public eye. And I hope it doesn't work."[15]

Are we to take Buress seriously? I get the impression he really is there because it will be a big boost for his comedy career and that he really does believe this roast was a stunt to get Bieber back in the good graces of the public. I also get the impression he doesn't really "like" Bieber, or at least the Bieber he knows but he perhaps recognizes that's not *all* of who Bieber is. For Buress to say this to the audience and to Bieber, as a "joke," as something that was meant to evoke laughter, reveals to me that he recognizes the nuances, that he anticipates Bieber will respond in a way he understands as non-threatening, as "friendly," as a jab from someone who is not an enemy. Buress's statements feel both true and not-true at the same time.

On the page, irony can be difficult to convey as it is rarely revealed through the words themselves. Irony is often *performed* within a specific time and place, to a specific audience, and conveyed through nonverbals (gestures, facial expressions, tone, vocal emphasis, pauses, etc.). Thus context and the interaction between audience and comedian are crucial for interpreting messages as ironic. Goltz (2017) describes this as "ironic performativity ... an embodied perspective by incongruity ... an irony that ... rubs, disrupts, and creates/negates what is said/meant, what is doing/done" (p. 36). This potentially generative tension between *who* is delivering the message, *what* message is being delivered, and *how* the message is delivered: "the relationship between the spoken [/written] text of the joke, the aesthetic delivery, and the performing body ... has the potential to open up a broad interplay and proliferation of meanings—particularly when these elements work in ironic tension/production" (p. 34).

When performed successfully, taken-for-granted rigid belief systems become briefly destabilized, revealing the fragility and arbitrariness of our meanings. One of the reasons irony can be difficult to convey and interpret is it requires more out of an audience than a literal interpretation and a passive consumption of messages. We need critical, self-reflexive audience members/readers. Goltz (2017) suggests

> how we read ironic performativity is as much, if not more, about the audience as it is the speaker/[writer]/performer/comedian...Whether an audience reads offense, subversion, or hope into a joke has as much to do with the specific audience member and the context, as the content of the joke, itself.
>
> *(p. 25)*

Irony doesn't easily pin down truths and doesn't make explicit claims about how the performer or the audience should feel about what is being said. The truths that emerge through ironic performativity are fluid, contextual, and occur *between* a comedian and audience.

Some irony can be difficult to convey through the written word.[16] In many cases, doing autoethnographic comedy might require you to perform live where the context is more obvious, and you're able to interact with an audience, and use your body to convey irony. Even if you're unable, unwilling, or don't desire to perform comedic autoethnography, there are still ways you can *performatively* write irony, such as using "quotes" to show you don't mean "exactly" what you "said." Also, the order and rate in which you reveal details in your stories/jokes is important for creating a pattern/expectations for the audience, building tension, and performing irony. The punchline needs to come as a surprise to work. You can apply this principle to the page by creating a nonlinear reading experience using line breaks, extra spaces, and footnotes.

Stepping off stage

Comedic Autoethnography involves using your lived experiences to describe and/or critique cultural beliefs, practices, and experiences (Adams, Holman Jones &

Ellis, 2015) in ways that: are playful, ironic, absurd; recognize and subvert readers' expectations in terms of word choice, descriptions, pacing, organization; draw attention to and create incongruities; interrogate your vulnerabilities but also step outside your emotions and "look upon life as a disinterested spectator" (Bergson, 1911); suspend disbelief and offer hope that no matter what one has lived through and anticipates living through, everything will be "okay."

Now go write something funny but be serious; this is your life we're talking about. Read the rest of this book first though.

Notes

1 "Evocative Autoethnography." Try saying that 5x fast. You: "that that that that that."
2 I have performed on a weekly basis at comedy clubs and open mics since May 2018.
3 Ellis, 2004, p. 138.
4 Bochner, 2017, p. 71
5 Art did for four years as my advisor. I did for four years as his advisee.
6 "Humor and its attendant joy cannot be deep without the seriousness; and without the 'distance' afforded by the atonement the seriousness is transformed into agonizing anxiety" (Kierkegaard)
7 "The tragic and the comic are both based on contradiction; but the tragic is the suffering contradiction, the comical, the painless contradiction…. The comic apprehension evokes the contradiction or makes it manifest by having in mind the way out, which is why the contradiction is painless. The tragic apprehension sees the contradiction and despairs of a way out" (Roberts, 1987, p. 172).
8 A few possibilities: You laugh so hard reading this chapter that you go into cardiac arrest (Wikipedia "deaths from laughter"). You die peacefully in your sleep decades from now (if the ice caps haven't melted by then … better learn to swim).
9 The following scene is adapted from a bit I've told on stage several times.
10 "An audience member who finds no humor in a joke, by laughing reflexively, still helps generate group laughter which convinces other audience members to laugh reflexively" (Manwell, 2008).
11 Gadsby continues to perform standup comedy. She is currently touring the U.S. performing her new hour special, *Douglas*. She opens her set, "Had I would have known tragedy would be so wildly popular, I might have budgeted my tragedy better" to the laughter of the crowd, dismantling the somewhat arbitrary distinctions between comedy and tragedy implied in *Nanette* (see Krefting, 2019)
12 Referencing the British stereotype that northerners are poor, rough, uncultured.
13 Similar to Carolyn Ellis's (1998) observation about the cruel irony of "lisp" being one of the most difficult words for those with lisps to say.
14 Don't worry. I don't actually *have* a dog. I mean I did, before I left her at the dog park.
15 These lines did not air in Comedy Central's airing of the roast, so Buress tweeted, "This one got cut from the #BieberRoast. I get it," with a meme containing the joke.
16 Which might require talking further about the irony in a footnote. For example, you might simply say (in the text or as a footnote), "Just kidding, folks" or "To be clear, I don't actually believe that racist joke I just wrote, but the fact that I wrote it means I did think it and since I feel the need to explain myself here means I understand that it's racist, and the fact that you read it, understood it, and told your colleague *this guy is a racist* or *that was racist* means the racism was already there before I wrote the joke and what I'm trying to do by ironically performing 'racism' is to make you, me, all of us accountable since we live in a white supremacist culture in which racism exists whether we acknowledge or not, and that when confronted with this 'racist joke' from me, someone who has hopefully earned your trust by now, I draw attention to the

omnipresence and absurdity of such beliefs and open a space for you to interrogate your own racist beliefs and complicity in the perpetuation of whiteness rather than you simply telling others I'm a 'racist,' demonizing me and turning a systemic problem into an individual one, while rhetorically positioning yourself outside this oppressive system, and probably providing you some sliver of self-righteousness, however, I realize irony is built upon ambiguity and requires a number of cues and artistry to do it well so in ironically performing 'racism' I do run the risk of reifying racist logics if I don't perform it well and/or the audience isn't critically self-reflexive and simply interprets the joke without irony [or in a way I didn't intend] that fits into their already racist worldview" (see Goltz, 2017).

References

Adams, T., Holman Jones, S., & Ellis, C. (2015). *Autoethnography*. Oxford University Press.
Adams, T., & Herrmann, A. (2020). Expanding our autoethnographic future. *Journal of Autoethnography*, *1*(1), 1–8.
Ajaye, F. (2002). *Comic insights: The art of stand-up comedy*. Silman-James.
Apatow, J. (2015). *Sick in the head: Conversations about life and comedy*. Random House.
Becker, E. (1973). *The denial of death*. Simon & Schuster.
Berger, P. (1997). *Redeeming laughter: The comic dimension of human experience*. De Gruyter.
Bergson, H. (1911). *Laughter*. Macmillan.
Bingham, S., & Green, S. (2016). Aesthetic as analysis: Synthesizing humor and disability through stand-up comedy. *Humanity & Society*, *40*(3), 278–305.
Bochner, A. (2000). Criteria against ourselves. *Qualitative Inquiry*, *6*(2), 266–272.
Bochner, A. (2012). Suffering happiness: On autoethnography's ethical calling. *Qualitative Communication Research*, *1*(2), 209–229.
Bochner, A. (2017). Heart of the matter: A mini-manifesto for autoethnography. *International Review of Qualitative Research*, *10*(1), 67–80.
Bochner, A., & Ellis, C. (2016). *Evocative autoethnography: Writing lives and telling stories*. Routledge.
Boyd, B. (2004). Laughter and literature: A play theory of humor. *Philosophy and Literature*, *28*(1), 1–22.
Boylorn, R., & Orbe, M. (Eds.). (2014). *Critical autoethnography: Intersecting cultural identities in everyday life*. Left Coast Press.
Burke, K. (1984). *Attitudes toward history* (3rd ed.). University of California Press.
Ellis, C. (1993). There are survivors: Telling a story of sudden death. *The Sociological Quarterly*, *34*, 711–730.
Ellis, C. (2004). *The ethnographic I: A methodological novel about autoethnography*. Altamira Press.
Ellis, C., Adams, T., & Bochner, A. (2011). Autoethnography: An overview. *Forum: Qualitative Social Research*, *12*(1).
Frankl, V. (1959). *Man's search for meaning*. Beacon Press.
Freud, S. (1960). *Jokes and their relation to the unconscious*. W.W. Norton & Co.
Gadsby, H. (2018). *Nanette* [Netflix special]. Netflix.
Goltz, D. (2017). *Comic performativities: Identity, internet outrage, and the aesthetics of communication*. Routledge.
Hacking, I. (1999). *The social construction of what?* Harvard University Press.
Hemmingson, M. (2008). Make them giggle: Auto/ethnography as stand up comedy – A response to Denzin's call to performance, *Creative Approaches to Research*, *1*(2), 9–22.
Hodges, N. (2015a). The chemical life. *Health Communication*, *30*, 627–634.
Hodges, N. (2015b). The American dental dream. *Health Communication*, *30*, 943–950.

Hodges, N. (2015c). Weighing ourselves down: Scale stories. *Departures in Critical Qualitative Research, 4,* 51–69.

Hodges, N. (2016). *Blue-collar scholars: Bridging academic and working-class worlds.* [Doctoral Dissertation]. University of South Florida. Scholar Commons.

Kiesinger, C. (2002). My father's shoes: The therapeutic value of narrative reframing. In A. Bochner and C. Ellis (Eds.), *Ethnographically speaking: Autoethnography, literature, and aesthetics,* (pp. 95–114). Altamira Press.

Kimble, M. (2004). Human despair and comic transcendence. *Journal of Religious Gerontology, 16*(3–4),1–11.

Krefting, R. (2012). Laughter in the final instance: The cultural economy of humor. In J. Batalion (Ed.), *The laughing stalk: Live comedy and its audiences* (pp. 140–156). Parlor Press.

Krefting, R. (2019). Hannah Gadbsy: On the limits of satire. *Studies in American Humor, 5*(1).

Macdonald, N. (2016). *Based on a true story: A memoir.* Spiegel & Grau.

Manwell, C. (2008). *Standup-up comedy as a tool for social change.* Undergraduate thesis, University of Michigan.

Meyer, J. (2000). Humor as a double-edged sword: Four functions of humor in communication. *Communication Theory, 10*(3), 310–331.

Myers, B. (2012). Introduction to writing autoethnographic joy. *Qualitative Communication Research, 1*(2), 157–162.

Niebuhr, R. (1946). *Discerning the signs of the times: Sermons for today and tomorrow.* Scribner.

Notaro, T. (2012). *Live.* [Comedy recording]. Largo.

Orwell, G. (1945). Funny, but not vulgar. *Leader.*

Roberts, R. (1987). Smiling with God: Reflections on Christianity and the psychology of humor. *Faith and Philosophy, 4*(2), 168–175.

Stanhope, D. (2017). *Digging up mother: A love story.* Da Capo Press.

Tullis Owen, J., McRae, C., Adams, T., & Vitale, A. (2009). Truth troubles. *Qualitative Inquiry, 15*(1), 178–200.

Wyatt, J. (2016). Two shits: A connection of some kind. *Departures in Critical Qualitative Research, 5*(4), 43–47.

Zinoman, J. (2018, July 26). If comedy is making you feel bad, you're not paying attention. *The New York Times.*

18

WALKING IN DALLAS WITH DEAD PEOPLE[1]

Deborah C. Breede

Stumbling

On August 21, 2016, my mother died. In the year that followed, my mother's only sister, my Aunt Joan, died. My mother's best friend, my godmother, Aunt Marcia, died, as did two of her three brothers, my uncles, Donald and Henry. In May of 2017, my youngest brother John and I went to three funerals on two coasts in two weeks. Almost one year to the day of my mother's death, our year of loss ended in August 2017 when my adopted brother, Jeff, died unexpectedly in his sleep. He was 54 years old. His wife, Lisa, tried to wake him up, but he was dead. August 2016 through August 2017 was the worst year of my life.

I have written about my mother often. She delighted everyone she met; her unwavering sense of adventure was infectious (Breede, 2016). Her cooking was legendary; her smile, dazzling. She hated wearing glasses, so she always took them off when being photographed (Davis & Breede, 2019). She loved to sing and dance, especially to old Motown (Breede, 2013). I'd often watch her, admiring her sense of style, as she'd move seamlessly through a room, engaging family and strangers alike with grace, warmth, and a laugh that ushered in joy. Three years after her death, I can't remember her, talk about her, or write about her without crying. As I write these words, tears cascade in rivulets down my face. I carry a hole in me where she once lived.

In 2005, doctors diagnosed my mother with Alzheimer's disease. She had shown symptoms years before that. She forgot things. She'd get lost on her way home. She tried to cut tomatoes with scissors. Her diagnosis broke my family's hearts, but those hearts shattered into ever shrinking, ever sharper shards over the next ten years as we watched her decline. By 2010 she couldn't walk or talk, eat without assistance, or bathe herself. She was incontinent and immobile. By 2015 she didn't recognize or interact with anyone. Often, tears would leak from her unblinking eyes as she lay in her room at the Memory Center. Bright cards hanging against the drab beige tile, I would lean over the cold metal rails of the bed and sing her Motown songs that I would play on my phone. Her stiff hand, more claw-like than Mom-like, would rest, unmoving, on the white knit blanket. Sitting next to my mother's hospital bed for the last seven years of her life, I prayed on and off for her to die, despair at her absence intermingled with the joy I felt in hugging her, rubbing her arm, caressing her cheek. She still smelled the same.

Sometimes, I fantasized about kidnapping her. I would take her to the Waldorf Astoria in New York City, her favorite hotel. I would dress her in the red plaid flannel and lace nightgown I bought her. I would crawl into bed with her. I would inject her with morphine while she lay in my arms; the nurses told me they "accidentally" did it for other families who wanted their moms to stop suffering. She would drift off peacefully, back to knowing who she was. Back to knowing how much she was loved.

I thought when she died I would feel relief because of the toll her Alzheimer's took on our family. All I felt was emptiness and loss. We all miss her desperately. Every night my father still sits in his Lazy Boy, across from the TV, which is next to her picture, sipping his martini, and talks to her, aloud. Her absence is cavernous in our lives.

During the year of loss, I taught my classes, I worked on a book, I served my institution, I went through the motions. I have few memories of that year. In January 2017, I decided to submit to the National Communication Association annual conference in Dallas. Since I'd never been to Dallas, and had been absent from the conference circuit that previous year, it seemed a good time to begin again.

It was a busy conference. While in Dallas, I felt oddly compelled to go to Dealey Plaza, the site of the JFK assassination. I wanted to see the book depository, visit the memorial, buy some souvenirs. I wanted to pay respects for my mom. She adored John F. Kennedy. Like her, he was a Catholic. Like her, he was a champion of social justice. Like her, he believed that we could do so much better. Like her, he was a hero. The first time I remember hearing my mother scream, watching her sob, or comforting her in a loss was on the day he was assassinated.

I played hooky for the morning conference sessions and walked to the convergence of highways that frame the memorial. I took pictures, read the historical markers, wandered around the park. On the walk back, I stopped in a McDonald's to use the bathroom. The bathrooms were locked, which was unusual to me. When I obtained the key from the security guard, he told me that a woman died of a heroin overdose in one of the locked stalls earlier that morning. He stated this matter-of-factly, handed me the key, and walked away.

When I returned to my hotel room to prepare for an afternoon of conference sessions, I checked my cell phone. I had several missed calls with messages, and scrolled through my log deciding whom to call back. My hand froze. I had missed a call from my Aunt Joan, who had left a voice message. She had been dead for six months. I stared at the phone for a long time. I decided to hit play. I still have the voice message:

Hi Debbie Doots, it's Aunt Joan. I just wanted to wish you a happy new year. We're going to Panda Palace like we do every year. We went to Canada today to get our prescriptions, and we got you that bourbon you like. Hopefully when you come, we'll be able to do the same. OK. Have a wonderful new year honey. I'm going to turn my phone off so you don't need to call me back. All right. I love you. Bye bye.

My Aunt Joan had called me on December 30, 2016, as we were preparing for my scheduled visit to see her in Bellingham, Washington the following month. Our January 2017 visit is a golden memory. I remember watching her in her warm brick kitchen as she, my uncle, and my cousin sang and tossed pasta together. We had cocktails every evening at 4:00, bundled up, and sat on her back deck, watching the deer emerge from the woods to graze in her yard. We drank countless bottles of wine watching her crime dramas; she was crazy for NCIS and other "detective" shows. She insisted on taking me sightseeing, where we broke down on the side of Interstate 5, and had to spend the next four hours in a car dealership as they repaired the car. We ate popcorn, watched soap operas, and picked out the cars we would buy if we had the money. My uncle took pictures of us as we posed around our Corvettes and Camaros, wrapping our scarves around our heads and necks, and sashaying across the salesroom floor in front of our "new cars." We talked a lot about my mom.

My Aunt Joan died the following May. I received the voice mail message in November. As I listened to my Aunt Joan's message, I sobbed uncontrollably for several minutes. After a while, I began to take deep breaths, slowly getting control of my emotions. I assumed the call had originally gotten lost in cyberspace, appearing on my phone almost eleven months later. I remember sitting on the side of my hotel room bed, both feet planted flat on the floor, staring out the window. My breath, in long intervals, went in, and out. In and out. I don't remember what I thought about. After what seemed like a long time, I started writing. Writing became a "method of inquiry" (Richardson, 2002; Richardson & St. Pierre, 2005) for the next several hours. At around 6:30 that evening, my roommate, Jenn, came in to change out of conference attire and get ready to go out. She asked me if I wanted to join her. I said no, I was on a writing binge. She left, I ordered room service, and continued writing. When she returned around midnight, I asked her to read a very early version of "Walking in Dallas with Dead People."

Rambling: theoretical and methodological positionalities

Theory and method will merge here. Autoethnography does that. It blurs then blends boundaries, divisions, and standpoints. It individualizes human experience through its collective commonality. It is unique yet shared. It is "mermaid song" (Gergen & Gergen, 2011). It tells by showing. It is oxymoronic. Bochner (2008, 2012, 2014), Ellis (1993, 1995, 1996, 1999, 2012; Ellis & Rawicki, 2013, 2014, 2019; Ellis & Patti, 2014) and Bochner and Ellis (1996) often represent the dialectical nature of both autoethnography and the experience of death, loss, and grief.

In much of this extensive body of work, now spanning almost a half a century, one question remains implicit, "What should ethnography be in the 21st century, especially in light of the past 100 years?" (Ellis, 2000; Bochner, 2000). Ellis suggests it is "an interrogation of the inner self ... a process of identity, self-knowledge and empowerment" (10/12/2000). Yet autoethnography is a systemic experience; she warns us of

> the ethnographic fallacy; we must "always assume that there are larger forces at play ... be detailed in your research, verify stories, interview family members, look at geography, analyze artifacts—do as detailed and thorough a research job as possible. Approach your research from a systems theory perspective".
> *(Ellis, 9/21/2000)*

Each of us is an individual set of systems, and we are all part of larger systems. The events of our daily lives often seem random, but they are not.

Frequently depicting the seemingly inconsequential moments of caregiving and the subsequent loss of loved ones, Ellis (1996, 2010) uses such moments to illustrate the dualities of joy and pain within our shared human experience. She asserts that we must "voice-the representation of participants ... voices differ from writer to writer. Voices differ within the writer; write your soul. Sharing stories is a way out of the dilemma" (9/21/2000).

As Ellis further explains, "Autoethnography opens up spaces between yourself and another person. If you're not exploring those openings, you're really only doing a very partial job with your autoethnography" (9/28/2000). As an auto-ethnographer, I open up and walk these spaces between myself and my loved ones. Exposing individual and shared vulnerabilities, I am able to break down barriers, relying on emotion and body as opposed to logic and mind. According to Ellis (2000) and Bochner (2000), these methods help assuage the pain of loss and grief and honor "our ethical obligation to love." Ellis calls this "academic philanthropy" (10/12/2000).

Applying these epistemologies in this piece, I represent the universality of loss and grief within the everydayness of the ordinary experience of walking. Using performative autoethnography, I hum poetry and rhythm together within the context of Dallas, a city grown famous through death. Walking, then, becomes a metaphor. De Certeau (1984) characterizes the "ordinary practitioners of the city" as " ... walkers, Wandersmanner, whose bodies follow the thicks and thins of an urban text they write without being able to read it. These practitioners make use of spaces that cannot be seen" (p. 93). They are inactive; they are acted upon. De Certeau suggests they "elude legibility," resulting in a "manifold story that has neither author nor spectator, shaped out of fragments of trajectories and alterations of spaces: in relation to representations, it remains daily and indefinitely other" (p. 93). I borrow from and apply Bourdieu (1998) to extend de Certeau and allow the Wandersmanner a bit of agency in their walk. Still "shaped out of fragments and trajectories of alterations of space," I "plunge into the particularity of a temporal reality, historically located and dated" (Bourdieu, 1998, p. 2) by framing the act of walking as "a generative principle of distinct and distinctive practices … a habitus" inclusive of "classification schemes that make judgments" (p. 8). As I walk through Dallas, I simultaneously become auteur and performer of grief, and like grief, walking becomes both repetition and ritual, "predictive" (p. 10) in its distance, and that distance is physical, emotional and social.

Lefebvre (1991) within his theoretical introductions of rhythm analysis, observes that "rhythms in all their multiplicity interpenetrate one another … rhythms are forever crossing and re-crossing, superimposing themselves upon each other, always bound to space" (p. 205). He poses a theoretical question:

> Is it possible to envision a sort of rhythm analysis which would address itself to the concrete reality of rhythms, and perhaps even to their use (or appropriation)? Such an approach would seek to discover those rhythms whose existence is signaled only through mediations, through indirect effects or manifestations.
>
> *(p. 205)*

He suggests that such rhythm analysis could one day supersede psychoanalysis in validity, as rhythm analysis is "more concrete, more effective" and better suited to not only applications within the field of anatomy, but also within interpersonal and social relationships. He goes on to theorize that such fields of inquiry would employ the performing arts "in ways that cannot be reduced to the discrete and fixed determinants of analytic thought" (pp. 205–206).

It is in this spirit that I present "Walking in Dallas with Dead People." Its geographic space is a city, but that space is not bound by distance alone, but by time and rhythm. The rhythm of walking is the rhythm of the city is the rhythm of grief. It is part poem, part memoir, part ballad. It is a dirge and a dream. It is an ode to my mother; it is a swan song for all who struggle toward death. It is a tribute to the women who have shaped me. It is an indictment of our country's mental health and larger health care crises. The piece is a collection of these remnants—memories of my loved ones and our times together, articles of their clothing, the smells and tastes of them, the horrors of inadequate and overloaded social service structures. Like these remnants, like these rhythms, like grief, like the humans within it—it is fragmented. I wanted to represent people and places forsaken by an overwhelmed system as they live and confront death and near death, the wanderings and wonderings within and outside of a place. The geographic place fugues into other places, other spaces. The place frames the piece, motivates the piece, and mourns multiple losses.

Presented as a poem, "Walking in Dallas with Dead People" emulates Waka Poetry. Waka poems are traditional, "yet far more performative" than some Japanese poetic forms; they are especially useful when "the poem maker and/or the poem itself mimes the act of 'expressing' that which might be felt in certain emotional, social, or sensory circumstances" (Kamens, 2002, p. 380). Thus, Waka poetry is representational. It relies on inference and metaphor, often fragmented, seemingly foreign. Rejecting narrative temporarily, this performative autoethnography is abstract in nature, relying on seemingly disconnected images to convey loss, death, and grief. Its setting is in Dallas, but it reminds us how the body travels even after death through the bodies of the living people it has impacted. As a result, both the living and the dead are eulogized in this piece, set in a place whose history is death.

Dallas has trafficked and prospered in death. Its downtown historical markers commemorate Indian massacres of white settlers and white settlers' massacres of Indians. They commemorate Mexican massacres of white settlers and white settlers' massacres of Mexicans. They commemorate one of the most famous presidential assassinations of the 20th century, and the absence of markers silently commemorates the stories of a million undocumented deaths. While I was in Dallas, a woman was stabbed repeatedly with an ice pick, a schoolboy was knifed to death by other children who wanted his backpack, and a homeless person was murdered in a homeless encampment. A woman died of a heroin overdose in a McDonald's bathroom. Countless automobile collisions, drug overdoses, and accidents claimed lives. Like many large cities, at night the sidewalks, back alleys, and doorways become bedrooms for homeless people, many of whom are ill. And as is typical in large cities with large homeless populations, the morning papers are full of stories of the deaths of these people and many others. Dallas becomes a metaphor for death.

And so, I present:

Walking in Dallas with Dead People

At night, in big cities,
I wander the streets like a homeless person
Patchwork clothes
I wear the remnants of people
Who I've loved in my life
All dead.
A mosaic
A sign of something yet to come.
No one bothers me if I look like nothing
A woman
Shattered
Shredded
No one notices me.
I'm free.
Picking through the alleyways
Smoking an occasional joint
As I walk
Invisible.
I carry them with me
Every person
Every story
Every clinging memory
So fresh
So close
So shadowy.

Their voices still call to me as I walk
They still fill my day
With conversation and
Cunning.
Their voices are real on the phones
That I collect
Like lunchboxes
Light and airy.
"We went to Canada today."
The hollowness of that empty place in me is cavernous.
"We bought you bourbon."
Walking
The red eyeball in the locked Dallas garden stares at me
Unforgiving.
Walking
I can look up
Gaze skyward
Secure in my distance
In my loneliness.
Walking is not death.
In the plaza by the McDonalds
Crooked torn men sit in wheelchairs.
In the plaza by the McDonalds
You never find money as you're walking by.
Only agonizing acorns
Screeching
Shouting
Broken
Angry.
Like me
But they can't leave.
Walking
Balconies call
Cajun in their smells
Their fleur de lis.
Walking
Rich gumbo life engulfs me
Wrought iron protects me
Fences and gates secure.
Upstairs porches whisper,
"Is that girl smoking a joint?"
Soon, it will be different.
New Orleans knows Jenn
Grinning, lilting, dancing.
Dogs sniff discarded sandwiches in Congo Park.
Walking.
In Boston, walking with my mom,
Winding winding through wending ways
Wishing she were really here
Walking.

We wandered through graves in countless Southern cemeteries
Brick streets
Old old
Divided like the neighborhoods
Walking.
When I ate pizza in the window
Pizza Margherita
Her name, walking
Grated pecorino, pizza, pinot noir
Walking.
Life
Warm whiffs of dough and garlic
Wafting, walking, walking.
Walking through Texas
Walking without her, without them
The chiseled rocks and faces
The nebulous ghosts
The sense of all that was that is gone
Walking
Through Austin
Crazy acorn people banging their heads against brick walls
Walking.
My frayed and worn Converse cry out
"Enough!" But I keep walking
Walking, walking
White and black
Pink and red
Stars and stripes
And even more silly
Shoes
Walking, walking.
When we walk
We listen.
We smile.
We look left and right as we cross the streets.
We're careful
We hold hands as we cross.
We say please and thank you.
My canvas pullover is old.
My jeans are threadbare.
They're tired.
They've seen a lot.
They've been washed hard and hung out to dry.
My jeans are Texas.
They don't fit in.
Walking.
When I walk, sometimes I cry.
I can't help it
I'm walking, and everything is too beautiful and too sad
All at the same time.

Simultaneous
Like everything.
That's how it is.
Beauty and loneliness
Surround me.
Sometimes butterflies flit by
Walking.
When I eat pizza Margherita in Dallas,
It's OK
But not like the pizza in Boston
Not like the pizza in Norfolk
In New York
In Naples
The pizza that is us
All these people who travel with me
All the time
All the ins and outs
Not like the pizza that is our blood
That pulses through us
Rich with the smell of earth and cheese and bread.
Rich with them.
Rich with you.
Sicilians are strong, they say.
Him and her.
Her and him.
They can walk.
Walking through Venice
Mothers and daughters stroll arm in arm.
I wake her up and tell her we have to walk.
When I walk in Washington
Very early in the morning
Kisses still wet as I walk
Wet wet dog kisses everywhere
She's waiting when I'm done walking.
She tells me they don't eat breakfast.
None of them do.
They're walking.
Jenn tells me her mom is happy I'm here in Dallas with her.
We've walked a lot together.
We've walked down dark highways where there are never any cabs.
We've walked through Flatirons and Foggy Days.
We've walked when it rained and when it shined.
We've walked through Tampa, and Texas, and Trauma
We've walked
Brown skin
We've walked.
She doesn't walk as fast as me
She's not as furious
But we walk.
When I want to walk with Jenn, I call her.

For the others, I must walk.
Walking through the jungle, sometimes I hitchhiked.
I was always a little afraid.
I walked through swamps and cities,
Miami and Maryland
Baltimore
Brownstones
Brown skin.
In Memphis,
I walked fast.
She wasn't there.
I was always a little afraid.
Sometimes,
I don't know where I'm walking.
I just walk.
Sometimes
Mimosa trees with pink flowers are with me.
Their wispy feather flowers make me smile
But I still walk.
Walking makes me very hungry.
I have to watch my pennies because I am homeless.
I eat bread and cheese
The creamy crunchy sharpness of it all
Goes good with red wine.
I eat in Balboa Park in San Diego where she lives.
They play softball there
And fly jet airplanes.
They walk the ball field.
I walk the bus stations.
I sit in bus stations in London and Paris.
I walk through train stations in Australia and Spain.
I sit in front of the bus station in Dallas
Eating a sandwich.
The acorns are angry.
They chatter.
They can't walk.
My feet become fatigued when I walk.
They blister.
They moan.
They worry.
I forget.
They complain constantly.
Not like them.
They generally don't complain.
They rarely did.
There are a lot of dead people in Dallas.
They've been shot driving by in convertibles
Blood stain
Pink dress.
They've been stabbed with knives and with ice picks.

They've been mourned
Morning screams echoing echoing
Coming home to her screams that morning.
I was only six.
They are not sad.
They are also homeless now.
Their stories are like ours
Like all stories
They lived
And then they died.
They might walk somewhere else one day.
But today they walk with us.
I like things that are tattered.
I don't like things that are tethered.
They gnash their teeth.
They can't walk.
When things are tattered
Topsy turvy
Tumultuous
They are easy to walk through.
In Florida and on freeways
They walk with me.
They are persistent.
They neither give up
Nor do they go away.
They can't be stopped.
They are walking.
We've always liked to walk through graveyards
She and I
Graveyards, junkyards, navy yards
Places where you can't forget.
You can only remember
The madnesses
In the minutes
As they tick tick tick
Keeping step
Keeping time
Faithful and precise
Never forgetting.
It's easy to hear.
It's easy to feel
And not to feel
To think about the dry yellow leaves
The rusted automotive parts
The grays and the oranges
The oranges
Glistening in the marmalade on a Sunday morning
The oranges packed carefully in boxes
Nestled in sawdust
Nestled in waxed paper

Nestled in plastic bubbles
The years marking the packings
The passings.
Oranges then strawberries
Peaches then watermelons
Cantaloupe, honeydew,
Her favorites
Wet with tears
Always wet with tears
The corrugated box now empty.
I don't sleep outside anymore.
It's too hard.
Too cold.
Too concrete.
I like wispy things
Whispering all the time.
I stay with friends,
In hotels
In farmhouses and beach houses
In mansions and cottages.
Never outside.
Outside is for walking.
When I walk,
I wear their clothes,
Hem-less
Homeless
With missing buttons
Their clothes smell like them still.
I can smell them still
All around me
Whispering
Whispering
"Walk with us."
Aunt Joan's gold and black velvet coat
Torn shreds flapping around my ankles
Wispy in the wind.
Aunt Marcia's butterfly scarves,
Silky,
Wispy,
Flowers jumping, dancing, flapping.
Carol's linen
Nanny's embroidered sweater
Too big
Too small
Walking
Wearing
Where-ing
Wonder-ing
Where they are.
They're walking.

Their clothes are homeless too now
Like me.
I wash my hands in a locked bathroom.
It's how we keep clean
How we keep warm
Walking
Whining
Whimpering.
They whisper …
"It will get better.
You'll keep walking."
Walking in Dallas with dead people.

"The clamorous traffic of tropes ends here – for now" (Kamens, 2002, p. 403).

Note

1 The author wishes to thank Andrea Bergstrom, Jennifer Erdely, Margaret Fain, Cassandra Hill, and Ronald Pelias for their feedback on early drafts of this work.

References

Bochner, A. P. (2000). *Class lectures*. Summer workshop in writing. University of South Florida, Tampa, FL.

Bochner, A. P. (2008). Fathers and sons. *Qualitative Inquiry, 14*(7), 1321–1328. doi:10.1177/1077800408322682.

Bochner, A. P. (2012). Bird on the wire: Freeing the father within me. *Qualitative Inquiry, 18*(2), 168–173. doi:10.1177/1077800411429094.

Bochner, A. P. (2014). *Coming to narrative: A personal history of paradigm change in the human sciences*. Left Coast Press.

Bochner, A. P., & Ellis, C. (Eds.) (2002). *Ethnographically speaking: Autoethnography, literature, and aesthetics*. AltaMira Press.

Bourdieu, P. (1998). *Practical reason*. Stanford University Press.

Breede, D. C. (2013). ReMembering mother: Reconstituting voice and identity through narrative with Alzheimer's patients. *The Journal of Loss and Trauma, 18*(5), 461–471. doi:10.1080/15325024.2012.714225.

Breede, D. C. (2016). *Searching for George Clooney: Aging, Alzheimer's, and the costs of care at end of life. Death, Dying, and Beyond: Understanding Ourselves at the End*. University of North Carolina's End of Life Symposium, Charlotte, NC.

Breede, D. C. (2019). *Walking in Dallas with dead people*. Doing Autoethnography Conference, St. Petersburg, FL.

Davis, C. S., & Breede, D. C. (2019). *Talking through death: Communicating about death in interpersonal, mediated, and cultural contexts*. London: Routledge.

de Certeau, M. (1984). *The practice of everyday life*. University of California Press.

Ellis, C. (1993). "There are survivors": Telling a story of sudden death. *The Sociological Quarterly, 34*(4), 711–730.

Ellis, C. (1995). Speaking of dying: An ethnographic short story. *Symbolic Interaction, 18*(1), 73–81. doi:10.1525/si.1995.18.1.73.

Ellis, C. (1996). Maternal connections. In C. Ellis & A. P. Bochner, (Eds.), *Composing Ethnography: Alternative forms of qualitative writing* (pp. 240–243). AltaMira Press.

Ellis, C. (1999). Heartful autoethnography. *Qualitative Health Research*, 9(5), 669–689.

Ellis, C. (2000). *Class Lectures*. Advanced Qualitative Methods. University of South Florida, Tampa, FL.

Ellis, C. (2009). Autoethnography as method. *Biography: An Interdisciplinary Quarterly*, 32(2), 360–363. doi:10.1353/bio.0.0097.

Ellis, C. (2010). *Final negotiations: A story of love and chronic illness*. Temple University Press.

Ellis, C. (2012). *Revisioning an ethnographic life: Integrating a communicative heart with a sociological eye*. Blue ribbon papers: Behind the professional mask: The autobiographies of leading symbolic interactionists. Howard House/Emerald Group Publishing, Ltd.

Ellis, C., & Bochner, A. P. (Eds.) (1996). *Composing ethnography: Alternative forms of qualitative writing*. AltaMira Press.

Ellis, C., & Patti, C. (2014). With heart: Compassionate interviewing and storytelling with Holocaust survivors. *Storytelling, Self, Society*, 10(1), 93–118. doi:10/13110/storselfsoci,.10.1.0093.

Ellis, C., & Rawicki, J. (2013). Collaborative witnessing of survival during the Holocaust: An exemplar of relational autoethnography. *Qualitative Inquiry*, 19(5), 366–380. doi:10.1177/1077800413479562.

Ellis, C., & Rawicki, J. (2014). More than mazel? Luck and agency in surviving the Holocaust. *Journal of Loss & Trauma*, 19(2), 99–120. doi:10.1080/15325024.2012.738574.

Ellis, C., & Rawicki, J. (2019). The clean shirt: A flicker of hope in despair. *Journal of Contemporary Ethnography*, 48(1), 3–15. doi:10.1177/0891241617696809.

Gergen, M. M., & Gergen, K. J. (2011). Performative social science and psychology. *Historical Social Research*, 36(4), 291–299. www.jstor.org/stable/23032295.

Kamens, E. (2002). Waking the dead: Fujiwara no Teika's Sotoba kuyo poems. *The Journal of Japanese Studies*, 28(2), 379–406. doi:10.2307/4126814.

Lefebvre, H. [Translated by Donald Nicholson-Smith] (1991). *The production of space*. Blackwell Publishing.

Richardson, L. (2002). Writing sociology. *Cultural Studies–Critical Methodologies*, 2(4), 414–422.

Richardson, L., & St. Pierre, E. A. (2005). *Writing: A method of inquiry*. In N. K. Denzin & Y. S. Lincoln (Eds.), *The Sage handbook of qualitative research* (pp. 959–978). Sage.

19

FORGET MY PERFECT OFFERING

A mother daughter

Silvia M. Bénard Calva

Wondering

Mexico City, Mexico. December 30, 2018.

I've come to Mexico City to visit and tend to you, mother. It is 2:13 am and this is the fifth time you ask me to walk you to the bathroom. The day before, I had mentioned I was going to a conference in a few days, and I still had to get my paper finished.

"Ay, *mi hijita*," you said, "and I'm not letting you sleep."

"Don't worry mom," I replied, "I came to Mexico City to spend time with you."

I realize I probably won't be getting much sleep and plunge into my memories of Aguasacalientes, Mexico, in 2005, when I wrote two short articles, "¡Ay, Aguascalientes!, ¿yo qué hago aquí? [Ay, Aguascalientes, what am I doing here?]" (Lachevre, 2005) and "¿Tengo vocación docente? [Do I have a teaching vocation?]" (Lachevre, 2005), both from the bottom of my heart and with an unbearable need to speak up. At that time, I used a pen name—Renata (for Renato Rosaldo, the anthropologist) and Lachevre (my great grandfather's mother's name). There was no sociological aspiration in those texts, because at that point I viewed sociology as something completely alien to my daily life, and, what's most important, there wasn't an intention to let readers know who I was.

A few years later, in Long Island, NY, 2009, I was still trying to understand what I was doing living in that middle-sized city in Mexico and doing research using grounded theory to make sense out of long interviews with others in a similar situation, that is, being settled there but originally being born and raised in Mexico City when I came across some information for a seminar called ResearchTalk, which had a number of workshops, two of which drew my attention. One was *Autoethnography*, to be taught by Carolyn Ellis, and another one was called *Narrative Ethnography*, to be taught by Harold Lloyd Goodall. At that time, I had no idea who they were, but when I read the titles and the short descriptions of the workshops, it seemed to me that they suggested to do research following their personal life experiences, something that sounded similar to what I had published under a pen name.

When I first enrolled in the workshops, I had a two-day introductory session to autoethnography. Hallelujah! Carolyn taught me that it was legitimate to write about my own story to make sense out of lived experiences with a sociological perspective and it was a turning point in my long journey of inquiry. By writing about my migration from a large metropolitan area and my settlement in Aguascalientes, I could reach a deeper understanding of the conundrums posed by that painful process of accommodation which I lived through as I moved from one of the largest cities in the world to a middle-sized city in Mexico. However, in the following two days I spent in Long Island, I learned how Bud Goodall gave meaning to his own life history by doing research on his father's life (Goodall, 2006). Furthermore, Carolyn and Bud also taught me about the importance of good writing. That was the beginning of all the years I have spent trying to master the art of narrative inquiry.

Still, it wasn't until a few years passed and I was in Blacksburg, VA, in 2012, with my daughter, with whom I travelled to spend four months of my sabbatical year there, that I stumbled into something that turned into another cornerstone for my train of thought. It was after Kris Tilley-Lubbs invited me to Virginia Tech as a visiting scholar. During my visit, one of my major tasks was to find and review articles and books on autoethnography that were not available in Mexico. It was then that I came across Art Bochner's "It's about Time: Narrative and the Divided Self" (1997), in which he engaged the division we academics draw between life and work and, just as Carolyn had driven me to view sociology from another perspective and—alongside Bud—had taught me the importance of good writing. Art's article opened my eyes to understanding why in academia, as we are expected to set the personal aside and focus on rational thought, we experience depression.

Listening

Meeting Carolyn and coming across Art's article, reminds me of that beautiful Anthem written by Leonard Cohen (1992) in which he refers to how light filters through cracks, implying that there is some good in that which can appear to be negative at first sight. Those dark big university buildings, both in Mexico and the United States, began to show their cracks and, as years passed by, those became even more evident. During my years as a professor at a public university in Mexico (2003–present), light came through the cracks as I read about autoethnography and began to practice it in research, teaching, and everyday life.

When I wrote my abstract for the Symposium on Autoethnography and Narrative Inquiry (St. Petersburg, FL, 2019), quoting Leonard Cohen's legendary *Anthem,* I still had not read Art's article "Bird on the Wire: Freeing the Father within Me" (Bochner, 2012), which also mentions a song written by Cohen. Now that I have read that article too, I understand better why I have such a personal connection with Art and his writings: His father is to him what my mother is to me.

At present, I see a mother who is different from the one who raised me; that same person who had a thousand things to do before turning her attention to me, her seventh child; beating me constantly, and shaming me for being overweight. Nowadays, she is an 89-year-old woman who asks me to walk her to the bathroom, because she cannot stand by herself. She says that everything I do is well done and tells me how gorgeous I look. However, I've already lost the opportunity to have a "real talk" with her, for now she has trouble hearing and cannot sustain long conversations, because she gets easily tired. I side with Carolyn as she states:

> Taking care of her feels natural, as though she is my child. The love and concern flowing between us feels like my mom and I are falling in love. The emotionality continues during the four days and nights I stay with her in the hospital. My life is devoted temporarily to her well-being. She knows it and is grateful. I am grateful for the experience.
>
> *(Ellis, 2004, p. 134)*

Carolyn's description of her interactions with her mother when she was in a similar condition to mine have accompanied me during these four and some years whenever I visit my mother in Mexico City. Carolyn's narrative makes my time with my mother more bearable, as I bear witness to how fast she has aged. More importantly, it makes me feel that I can be that good daughter who, in many ways and regarding many things, she had pointed out I was not.

Having a loving, caring, and down-to-the-basics interaction with my mother has, to a certain extent, allowed me to heal. We don't talk much. In that sense, I'm closer to how I was when I flew away to go to graduate school in Austin. But being there for her now, and not treating her the way she treated me when I was dependent on her, gives me peace and a sense of forgiveness that go beyond words. When I realize I myself am being kind, I trust there must've been significant happenings in the way she raised me that make me appreciate it, even though my most present memories circle around how she could not stop battering me once she started, her constant "you are so self-centered," and her disapproval and shaming regarding my fat body. One unforgettable moment regarding my looks revolves around her taking me to see the doctor who was monitoring my weight. She and I were sitting in the car as we saw a brimful bus stop next to us in a red light. Just like that, she dropped a comment: "Can you believe that, being as many poor people as there are and in so much need, having to take the bus, we are sitting in a car alone and paying a doctor so that you stop eating?!"

Numbing

I had given up on my mother many, many years before 2018. It happened when I moved out of the house in my last undergraduate year and moved to Austin, TX, a couple of years later. Once living in the USA, I immersed myself in an everyday routine, which involved putting up with the high standards of the academic program, combined with a part-time job as a research assistant. It was then that I experienced, without noticing it, a subtle socialization process: the overload of academic work allowed me to put my feelings aside. That was functional to me. As Art so beautifully wrote, I was "working hour after hour, day after day securing a safe dwelling in the sacred spaces of introspective solitude" (Bochner, 2012, p. 169).

I also thank Art for saying: "When you beat me, I learned to hate you. I didn't realize until much later how much rage and resentment I felt. When I was a kid, I was not allowed to feel" (Bochner, 2012, p. 170). I had never met anybody who said it so boldly and clearly. My mother used the same words as his father, "Don't cry," and she would continue beating me until I stopped crying. I very well know what he means when he talks about rage and resentment.

My father, contrary to my mother, regulated all manifestations of happiness: we kids were not allowed to laugh too much or too loudly.

It has taken decades for me to start recognizing my emotions. The other day I talked with a group of dear friends from Al-Anon—the world-wide organization of friends and family of alcoholics—about how we learn to block our feelings. We agreed that numbing is a slow, profound and hardly noticeable process we go through to deal with pain. The problem is that numbing drags good emotions together with the bad ones, both of which make life worth living.

***

Thus, for many, many years, I thought the same as Art: "I was sufficiently aware of my anger and pain not to take a chance of passing them on to children" (Bochner, 2012, p. 170). I told myself that someone with my upbringing should not raise kids. But years went by, years in which I cultivated the art of numbing— as I had learned to do through primary socialization and later mastering the art in graduate school. However, this allowed me to rethink the decision I had made of not becoming a mother. In fact, a condition I negotiated with my partner was that if he wanted to marry me, he had to promise me he wouldn't want to have kids.

Two years after we got married, I got pregnant without consciously intending to. I didn't know whether or not to go on with the pregnancy, but I thought it over for weeks, talked to my partner about options, negotiated ways to raise our baby so that I could have a professional career, and after we agreed on raising the child together so that both of us could have a professional life, I finally decided to go ahead and carry on with the pregnancy. At that point, my major concern was how I would be able to finish my dissertation and take care of a newborn at the same time. So, I let very important, year-old issues that dealt with me never being entitled to become a good candidate for raising children, pass me by.

Six years later, after three unsuccessful attempts and a miscarriage, I got pregnant again. This time I was stubbornly convinced that I wanted to have a girl. I didn't take into consideration if I would be psychologically and physically capable, or if my unstable marriage could bear raising another child. At age 39, I had a newborn girl and a seven-year-old boy (for an utter description of these years, see, Bénard, 2014).

Mothering

I knew what I was deprived of as I grew up. Therefore, I tried as hard as I could to be aware of my children's needs—for food, water, sleep, warmth, attention, help—and I made my best efforts to listen to them, talk to them, let them make decisions, have fun, learn joyfully, just anything I could think of.

On the one hand, all that heavy load I had put on my shoulders kept me from realizing that I was often responding to my deprived childhood, not to my kids' needs. Since I felt so many things had been lacking while I was dependent on my mother, I overdid my everyday efforts to fulfil their needs: don't eat until they are not hungry, don't rest if they need anything, don't sleep if they are awake, suffer when they are in pain, worry when they do, contribute with their obligations when they need you to. As years went by, such attention resulted in my own disadvantage: I was permanently tired, quite depressed, resented my partner and unsatisfied with my professional career.

On the other hand, I got the trace of my parents' lifestyle deeply ingrained inside me (see deAnda & Geist-Martin, 2017; De Linos Escario, 2018). This was something I was unaware of. That strong sense of duty and a permanent state of work overload that I recreated within my own family—the same as my parents did with us—which followed the path of being always working, trying to make sure everything was under control, never taking the time to stop and enjoy life, or just do nothing and take pleasure on spending time with my children. It was all about work. I even saw the time I spent playing with my kids as duty and obligation.

Besides those learned traits of life I inherited and carried on my back, there was another one that wasn't directly related to my upbringing: having an academic career. That was something I had worked very hard on, and I thought it to be the most fulfilling feature of my life. When my son was born, I had been in the field of sociology for more than ten years and in graduate school for seven. My career was the one thing I never wanted to give up no matter what. My life, particularly during the years I had been a graduate student, was focused on sociology seminars, master's thesis, comprehensive exams, proposal, dissertation, and working as a research assistant and teaching assistant. The four years before my partner moved to Austin to live with me, I virtually did nothing but devote myself to study and work. I was certain that sociology was my calling.

***

When I look back at the load I put on my shoulders during the years I raised my kids, I wonder why I would put myself in such a destructive situation. Why was I willing to raise children under such high expectations of what I could do better than my parents and have an academic career on top of that. To make things more intricate, I moved to my partner's hometown when my son was two and a half, and I was still working on my dissertation. That move translated into almost forgetting about his support as a partner for he became a high government official and put most of his energy into doing a good job. Therefore, he could not find the time and energy for household chores and, even worse, he constantly lobbied for mental, emotional, and moral support, all of which I dutifully forced myself to provide (Bénard, 2014).

> Playing Lego with my son, sitting on the rug in his room.
> How many afternoons have we played Lego?
> How many hours have I spent playing while my husband is working?
> His work is so important.
> He works for the governor!
> I play Lego.
> His time is spent on important decision making.
> Mine is spent playing Lego.

Today, as I read this to revive my memories, I wish I could play Lego again. I wish I could also plant the avocado seed after supper, as my daughter, my son and I did so many times. I wish I could laugh with them and get wet from the garden hose as we filled our plastic pool. Play, play, play with them. Give myself a break and take the opportunity to offset my troubled childhood. But, instead of doing so, I turned my attention to others and not to myself.

***

I had a lot of support from domestic workers during some of those years. After arguing with my partner about him not being around, we hired a domestic worker under the agreement that she would do some chores at home in exchange for having a place to live. She and another woman who worked full time took care of all the chores except taking care of the kids, unless they got sick and had to miss school, or had to be left alone if my partner and I had to attend social events or, sometimes, go to the movies or supper by ourselves. I wish they could read these lines as I express my gratitude to them both. One of them, Martha, is an icon of our wellbeing. She worked with us for about 14 years, keeping the house perfectly clean, cooking dinner, washing and ironing clothes. She was always there for us. I sometimes even had to tell her to go home, to quit working, to stop ironing certain things—she even ironed men's underwear! I don't know how I would have survived without her. My thanks to Martha, she is part of our family history, and we remember her with love and gratitude. My daughter yearns for her often. Thanks to Mary too for making our lives easier. She took care of the kids during the nights we went out, kept the garden watered and clean, and dealt with the people who went home to provide gas, water, etc. while I was at work. I remember how we teased her about being the public relations person in the family.

***

All things considered, I realize now that my mothering had many flaws no matter how far I wanted to avoid my parents' parenting, particularly my mother's. I did not follow her violent ways, and I tried to be there for my kids, even though I worked as a researcher for six hours a day until I got divorced and then started working full-time as a professor in a public university that same year. At that time (2003), my daughter was six, my son 13.

The problem was not only how I overloaded myself with duties but also the fact that I hindered my children's capability of becoming self-sufficient. Their needs were covered either by me or by Martha and Mary, so I overprotected them and thus blocked their way to further independence. They felt they were the center of my universe, and they were! But when my partner and I got divorced, Mary emigrated to the USA to work as a temporary worker, the kids spent four days a week with me and three with their father. That gave me a break from motherhood hours, which, of course, I filled with working at the university to cover the 40 hours a week I had to be there.

Naively, again, as in many of the decisions I had taken regarding marriage and family, I thought my son and daughter were going to be fine with their father while I had time on my own. I never thought how hard it was going to be for the three of them to be together. My ex-husband was working fewer hours than when he was a high government official, but still, he left the kids alone for many hours while he was at work. The children were not being taken care of as they had been before the divorce.

Many years had to pass before I realized my children needed a more stable environment. But by the time that became clear to me, the only way I would've got them back all week long would've been by making a legal claim. The result of that would've hurt my children even deeper and would very probably have turned them against me. So, we all had to adapt to an arrangement that put a lot of burden on their shoulders and a lot of guilt on mine.

As I write this, and whenever I think about it, my stomach gets upset. I wish I could jump out from the chair and return to the past to fix things for my kids. I reprehend myself: How could you be so stupid?! How could you think they were going to be fine after they got used to you, with the help of Mary and Martha sorting so many things out for them and for their father when we all lived together?! I screwed it. You did your best, Silvia, I then try to convince myself. And he did as he knew. That was all we could do.

I fell far short from the high standards I had set myself as a mother. I wish I had the nerve to let my mom know. However, I don't, because whenever I complained about something she did wrong, she always replied, "With my best intentions, *mi hijita*." she said it often before she had the stroke, and I hated it. No, no, no, mother, I silently told myself whenever I heard her saying that. I will be much better than that, for "the road to hell is paved of good intentions," as my father often said. I will work hard, day and night, not to be like her. Still, she would sure be proud to know my daughter uses what she knows about our relationship to complain: "Exactly mom, just like grandma, with your best intentions!"

Then, I try turning to a higher being—a god, a goddess, the universe, something. Nowadays, becoming more spiritual has helped me surrender and accept that things just were the way they were. Thanks to Leonard Cohen's Anthem, I tell myself not to expect to be perfect.

Discerning

July 14, 2019. Mexico City.

I'm back to taking care of mom. Back to basic everyday chores. Going to the bathroom many, many times at night, convincing her to eat as much as possible, being aware of her medicine intake schedule and trying to keep her awake during the day. Short talks, loud and clear, and no more big decisions.

Night one. I can't sleep. Again, I feel the urge to ask her for something that is very important to me. Should I do it? Should I forget about it? Should I tell my sisters? What if my mom says no? And if she puts conditions in exchange?

Forget about it, Silvia, I tell myself, it is not worth it. Rest, you need to get some sleep before she starts calling you to take her to the bathroom. Why is that one thing so important? It should not be. I don't want to ask her. She may be hurt and think you want to take advantage of her condition. No, no, no. You are not going to do it!

Day two. It is Saturday. My sisters and their families come to my mother's house for dinner. This event has taken place for more than forty years. Every Saturday, my sisters, their sons and daughters, and now their kids too, come to my mother's. I want to believe she enjoys those gatherings. Mom always makes sure that there is food for around ten people. She asks the two domestic workers who live at her home now to start cooking and clean the house. On Saturday, one of my sisters comes to bathe Mom, help her brush and dry her hair, and put her make-up on. Then, someone must help my mom walk downstairs from her bedroom to the dining room. She sits with her guests for about three hours, trying to listen to what they talk about, interacting with them, and eating very little food.

As years have passed, fewer members of the family go to those Saturday gatherings. Many of us have moved out of Mexico City. My brother and his family, who live in Mexico City, gave up on the gatherings many years ago. My son, who lives with my mother now, eats with her sometimes. When I share those meals, I must gather the courage to sit there to witness the way they talk about politics, poverty, race, gender, and family. Some comments I have heard coming from my sisters, their partners and some of my nieces and nephews are difficult for me to hear and almost impossible to cope with, as they come one after another, receiving the support of many of those present and who have now taken over that dining room.

In one of my last visits, my daughter and I were on vacation. I wanted to see my mother and my son. Before our arrival, the three of us had agreed on doing things together. We wanted to go to a museum on Saturday morning. My son and daughter said that, if we couldn't make it back at 3 pm, we could go to a restaurant and skip grandma's supper. However, my mother and I did not get much sleep on Friday night, and I was exhausted Saturday morning. I did not go the museum and instead stayed around for supper. It was my opportunity to see my family.

Saturday, 1 pm. I go to the bathroom to get ready, not only physically, but mentally and emotionally. I do my best to look as nice as I can, knowing how important image is in my family. I am not thin. In this family, that very much is held against me but, well, it's too late—nothing to be done about it before supper,

I tell myself in front of the mirror. Right after, I read the daily page in the book *Valor Para Cambiar*:

> Today, I will live in the present, where I will try to find something that I can appreciate. If there is pain, I will accept it as well. But pain must not completely overshadow the agreeable things that are present in my reality. I will participate in benefiting from my happiness; I can begin a dialog during supper or laugh with a friend. Just for today, I can even allow myself to sing.
>
> *(Al-Anon, 2018, p. 195; translation is mine)*

I take a few deep breaths and walk to my mother's bedroom to escort her and, with the help of my sister, walk her downstairs to the dining room. Some of the guests are already there; others are coming soon. We start sitting down at the table. It will be nine adults and four kids.

The dining room has a large glass table and ten chairs—originally for eight children, my father and my mother. Now we include more chairs and table places almost every time we use it. Each of us has an assigned space. However, today my commonly used place at the table ends up too close to that of a man, the partner of one of my sisters, with whom I have had trouble at the dining table due to his comments around politics, women, gays, and ethnic minorities.

Today, he came to sit at the dining table once I had taken a seat—strategically far from my customary place and closer to my mother. He sat next to me and started asking me about Aguascalientes. Without saying a word, for there was lots of noise and everybody wasn't seated yet, I just stood up and moved to another free chair as far from him as possible.

Then, we are having green sauce enchiladas (with chicken for some, with cheese for the vegetarians), beans, rice, and salad; the kids are having pasta. Some of us are drinking table wine, others are drinking soda, juice, or water. We are all finally seated and enjoying the food, when my niece and her husband start talking about their vacation. The day before, they had come back from Whistler, Canada, where they had spent a week with their three kids. The man I had sat away from cannot wait to tell us that he has been there before and that he knows it is beautiful—he even names a local river. He then asks my niece's husband if he knows which river he is talking about, and the guy answers he doesn't know. Then, the man goes on and on and on, telling everyone his opinions about the place and interrupting the other guests as they want to talk. Meanwhile, keeping in mind the passage I read from *Valor Para Cambiar* to prepare myself before dinner, I decide to start talking to my niece and her husband, who were sitting close to me, and to see the pictures they were showing us on their cell phone. I had succeeded this time.

Dessert time. We are having a great variety of pastries and chocolate cake from my mother's Austrian cuisine bakery: Yes! We are enjoying the best part of the meal. Suddenly, Canada comes back to the table. So far, it had all seemed fine to me. I had been able to stay safe. I even felt appreciated as, when talking about Canada earlier on, I had said the countryside was so beautiful, and my mother mentioned I had lived in Saskatchewan for some time when I was a teenager. This time, the man comments: "Canadians are very nice people." Yes—many around the table agree, but then he pops off, "Yes, white Canadians are very nice." And nobody says a word. They just go on talking about other things, as if the comment was normal and acceptable. I can feel a heat rising inside my body. I look at him furiously while he pretends everything is fine. Two minutes after that, I decide I've had enough. That's it! I stand up and leave the table.

Healing

I have seen how my two sisters who live in Mexico City have not only taken over my mother's dining room, but many other spaces as well. One of them administers her health, her house, and the few assets she has left; the other oversees what is left of my mother's business, the bakery. As my mother has lost control over many decisions regarding her person, her house, her assets and her business, my two sisters want to take over and keep my mother, my three other sisters, my brother, and I, at the margins.

Lately, I have been struggling with that reality. After going to visit and coming back so many times with irritable bowel syndrome (which started on a visit a couple of years ago), I decided that my health was more important than their decisions. Besides, I left home more than 35 years ago—moved out before I went to graduate school, lived in Texas for six years and went back to Mexico City for three before I settled in Aguascalientes 28 years ago. In contrast, my two sisters stayed in Mexico City—geographically, physically and symbolically. We used to have those Saturday meals even before their sons and daughters were born. They have been by my mother's side since, and, whether I like it or not, the three of them have developed their own dynamics and decision-making mechanisms. So, at present, I try to accept the way they have settled their interactions and decision-making. It was not only the two of them, but also my mother who, along their side, constructed—day after day, year after year—the way things are now.

On my third day there, I decide I will do it. I wake up with the strength to ask my mother and get a *no* as a possible answer. Today, my mother and I will spend most of the day alone. I will make sure to find the right time to ask her. I prepare breakfast for both of us and take it to her bedroom. We sit down and start to eat.

Then, I ask, "Mom, my desk at home is too high for me. Do you think I could use my father's desk? Nobody uses it now, and I would feel very fortunate if I were able to enjoy it. You know, I spend a lot of time writing and reading, and I need a comfortable place to do it. And you have witnessed how much I've always liked it."

"Yes, you can," she responds.

"Really?! Thanks mom! I think I deserve it. The twins [one of my sisters and my brother] have gotten many things from the old house and, well, from all my siblings, I'm the one who uses a desk the most. Well … I will not say anything about the others. Thanks, mom, thanks!"

"Yes. You are the most learned, you deserve it. Just tell your brother. He will notice the empty space in the office as soon as that desk is gone. You tell him that I gave it to you."

"Of course, I will give him a call. And my sisters? I don't want to tell my sisters."

"I will tell your sisters."

She goes on eating with little interest, as she always has, though this has worsened after her stroke four years ago. I continue drinking my second or third cup of coffee and eating a slice of sachertorte. That is my favorite breakfast when I go to her house: coffee and the taste of a variety of cakes and pastries left from Saturday's supper.

***

FIGURE 19.1 This is the rolltop desk my mother gave me. According to the source I consulted, it is an Original WM. Schwarzwaelder & Co. Rolltop desk (*Collector's Weekly*). This type of desk was built in Chichester, NY, where William Schwarzwaelder and his descendants ran the factory during the 1800s and 1900s, until it ran out of business in 1939.

***

Years ago, I asked my mother to give me that desk when she did not need it anymore. My father was the original owner of the rolltop desk. He died almost 30 years ago, exactly one month after my son was born. He knew how much I liked it, and I had asked him to give it to me whenever he decided he did not need it anymore.

"Fredy," I humorously refer to him as such, "when you decide you don't need that desk anymore, would you give it to me?"

"Uy, *mi hijita*, that will probably be after I die."

About 20 years after he died, there was an occasion in which one of my sisters told me my mother said I had offered to buy the desk from her. *Buy it?* I told myself. Hmm, I will probably have to do that if I ever want it to see it in my house. My mother, my mother, she is so concerned about money. I don't care. I refuse to give money the weight it has in my family of origin. So, if she wants money, I will buy it from her whenever I can.

However, on Saturday night, I decided I would not buy it from her. With that resolution in mind, a difficult part of asking for it was to get "no" as an answer. "Why you and not any of your sisters or your brother?" I imagined her asking. The other part was to get her to offer me a chance to buy it. The latter possibility was rather easy to deal with, because my perspective on money has not changed. So, the first difficulty was grounded in the fact that I wanted it to be a present, a token of her recognition of me, a constant of me getting something that was especially meant for me, for she knew how much I liked it and she also knew, for me in particular, how much it meant to have my father's antique desk.

Therefore, when she said yes, it was not only a desk I got. I got her acknowledgement that there was something unique of me that she valued. In her eyes, I am the most learned, and that matters. I am not like my sisters who stayed, who are there, close to her and, in many ways, are like her. She approves their ways of life as mothers, grandmothers and sentimental partners, and affirms their self-sacrificing attitude. I have been, according to her, inadequate, self-centered, rebellious, and fat.

Inheritance, I can feel it now, is a recognition of who you are and why you deserve what you get from your ancestor. It is not about the money. It is an assessment of who you are to that person.

Finally, mother! I got your recognition that I am someone, that you see me, despite my not being what you expected me to be as a woman for so many years. Thank you, mom. My gratitude goes to you. We are at peace.

Acknowledgements

I want to thank my son and my daughter for reading this piece and letting me know they were fine with what I mention about them. I also want to thank my niece Aline Bénard, for reading this, not only to copy-edit my English, but also giving me comments about the content of this article. Elena, one of my sisters who lives in Baja California Sur, also read a final draft and made comments and suggestions. It was good to listen to her opinion as she has had a much more friendly relationship to my mother than I have.

Estefanía Díaz helped me review the literature on mother-daughter relations and she, María de la Luz Luévano, and Magdalena Aranda made comments to drafts of this article. I extend my gratitude to Javier González, my psychoanalyst, for helping me realize the deep meaning of my mother's present. I am also in debt to Tony Adams and Carolyn Ellis, for their careful and loving suggestions on how to make this a better piece.

References

Al-Anon (Central Mexicana de Servicios Generales de los grupos de familiars) (2018). *Grupos de familia Al-Anon, Valor para cambiar. Un día a la vez en Al-Anon*. Mexico.

Bénard, S. (2014). *Atrapada en provincia. Un ejercicio autoetnográfico de imaginación sociológica*. Universidad Autónoma de Aguascalientes.

Bochner, A. P. (1997). It's about time. Narrative and the divided self. *Qualitative Inquiry 3*(4), 418–438. https://doi.org/10.1177/107780049700300404.

Bochner, A. P. (2012). Bird on the wire. Freeing the father within me. *Qualitative Inquiry 18*(2), 168–173. doi:10.1177/1077800411429094.

Cohen, L. (1992). *Anthem*. Columbia Records.

Collector's Weekly (n.d.). Original Wm Schwarzwaelder & Co. Rolltop Desk (early 1900s). www.collectorsweekly.com/stories/60869-original-wm-schwarzwaelder-and-co-rolltop?in=474-activity.

deAnda, C. D., & Geist-Martin, P. (2017). Memory as insight: Navigating the complexities of generational mother-daughter relationships. *Qualitative Inquiry 24*(6), 406–412. https://doi.org/10.1177/1077800417743526.

Ellis, C. (2004). *The ethnographic I: A methodological novel about autoethnography*. Altamira.

De Linos Escario, A. (2018). Madres e hijas: ¿se hereda el modelo de maternidad? *EMPIRIA, Revista de metodología en Ciencias Sociales 39*, 175–199.

Goodall, H. L. (2006). *A need to know. The clandestine history of a CIA agent*. Left Coast Press.

Lachevre, R. (2005). ¡Ay Aguascalientes!, ¿yo qué hago aquí? In Salvador Camacho Sandoval (Ed.), *La vuelta a la ciudad de Aguascalientes en 80 textos* (pp. 219–223). Universidad Autónoma de Aguascalientes.

Lachevre, R. (2005). ¿Tengo vocación docente? *Revista Parteaguas, 1*(1), 40–44.

20

EPILOGUE

Autoethnography as a warm idea

Arthur P. Bochner and Carolyn Ellis

We express our deepest appreciation to the editors and authors of the chapters in this book who have honored us by continuing, cultivating, widening, and elevating the ideals and promise of an autoethnographic way of living and writing. We receive your book as a heartwarming and compassionate gift, an act of extraordinary generosity that we will always treasure. Over the course of our academic lives, we have joined with and come to think of you as our extended family—as close friends, former students, collaborators, co-researchers, and confidants. Your connection to us is not fleeting or momentary but rather stretches over years and, in some cases, decades. Together, we share a prolonged history, joyful memories, and precious moments. We cherish these ties and find it impossible to convey fully how profoundly your presence has enriched our lives.

The beginning

In January 1990, Art attended a campus presentation in which Carolyn spoke passionately about her image of a fresh, innovative kind of sociology. She imagined research that would center on emotions and represent lived experiences in ways that would make social life accessible and readable. "In the form of stories," she said. This mode of sociology would challenge the widely held belief that introspection and subjectivity had no meaningful role to play in the work of social scientists. In her talk, Carolyn was not content merely to theorize something new. She also read narrative excerpts of episodes from a book she was working on that showed what this sociology felt and looked like (Ellis, 1995/2018).

Sitting in the back of the audience, Art listened with a sympathetic ear. Carolyn's project appeared harmonious with his own theorizing about communication studies. In his work, he had proposed that communication should not only be *what* we study but *how* we study, the goal being to move closer to the phenomena we want to understand (Bochner, 1978, 1981). In "Forming Warm Ideas," Art endorsed the ideal of catalytic thinking that produces warm ideas rather than cold facts: "By warm ideas I mean ideas that compel us to move closer to our subject matter, open up new lines of thought, extend our territory into new avenues of inquiry, and amplify our understanding beyond what we knew before" (Bochner, 1981, p. 77). The stories Carolyn told that day had this catalytic effect on Art. They kept him close to the events and feelings surrounding them. Carolyn's ethnographic compositions made it difficult, if not impossible, for Art to distance himself from the grief and loss she described.

Thickening the plot

In the months that followed that first chance meeting, the two of us shared an exciting optimism about what we might be able to create together. We conversed endlessly about fashioning a kind of social science that would be not so much *about* people as *on behalf* of them, showing what it might mean to live well while afflicted by the losses and tragedies of ordinary life. Refusing to hide behind academic jargon, we invited readers to become witnesses to our experiences and encouraged them to feel in their guts the truth of our stories. We believed that there were others out there like us, who had a taste for daring, intimate, embodied, and evocative tales that could make a difference in the world—stories of relational living together, decision making, and coming apart; illness, disability, and loss; family trauma, domestic abuse, and incest; obsession, addiction, and depression; privilege, inequality, and oppression.

Our initial test of this premise occurred in 1992, when we co-constructed our first joint publication (Ellis & Bochner, 1992). In that relationship story, we underscored the importance of creating an "experience of the experience" that can provide an opportunity to ride the active currents of lived experience without fixing meanings once and for all (p. 98). The story we told acted back on us emotionally and cognitively, evoking new feelings, ideas, and understandings of our experience. By attending to how other people heard and reacted to our jointly constructed tale, we learned that though many felt the ambivalence, pain, and confusion in the relationship dilemma we faced, others did not necessarily empathize or directly identify with us. These diverse responses made us aware of similarities and differences between their worlds and ours. Through the reflexive process of writing and performing our experience, we gained a perspective on our story we did not have before. Our understanding of the range of meanings our story had conveyed deepened and widened. We could see that the process of writing a lived experience for others to witness offered extensive possibilities for healing.

Optimism for an artful science featuring autoethnography

Eventually, we conceived of what we were doing as a moral and existential practice. We were using personal narratives as a means of channeling readers' own moral experiences as they engaged with other people's suffering, pain, trauma, and inequality. Gradually, we lost interest in social science as a "creature science" (Becker, 1968, p. 389) demanding an array of technical (computational) skills. Instead, we opted for inspiration over obligation, going all in on the existential calling of the human sciences (Bochner, 2012). We were seeking a humane, qualitative field of inquiry that required us to develop caring relationships with others instead of standing apart from them in the name of objectivity and rigor.

Was such a project possible? Could qualitative inquiry evolve into an artful science? Could it become a poetic blending and bending of science, literature, poetics, and politics through which self-conscious and reflexive writers and/or performance artists express the beauty and tragedy of lived life? Could the human sciences become more human by encouraging and sanctioning forms of representing lived experiences that enable readers and audiences to bring their own mindful attention to other people's experiences of love, hate, joy, injustice, and deep pain? In other words, could our autoethnographic project become a warm idea?

Enter autoethnography

Soon after this publication, we began using *autoethnography* as an inclusive term that could cover and sanction various kinds of first-person composition within its fluid and expansive boundaries. Autoethnography touched people where they lived, inviting and encouraging a wider community of qualitative researchers to see themselves as one of us and attach themselves to the ideals of an autoethnographic way of living and working (Ellis & Bochner, 2000; Bochner & Ellis, 2016).

At this point, both of us were senior professors. We felt secure, respected, and protected in our department. Still, neither of us had forgotten where we had started and how difficult it had been to feel at home doing existential qualitative research and first-person writing in the mainstreamed social sciences. For too long, seasoned scholars eager to do something different, as well as new students of qualitative inquiry, had felt stifled and constrained—if not crushed—by discredited methodological directives and inhibiting writing conventions. Now, we were in a position in the university to advance the project of autoethnography and, as Stacy Holman Jones (2018) observed, "use our insider knowledge and privilege to identify and get resources to others who might have otherwise been excluded or left to fend for themselves in the academy."

Of course, we had considerable help along the way. For more than 20 years, at three different academic presses, Mitch Allen supported and promoted our project through the *Ethnographic Alternatives* and *Writing Lives* book series that offered publication opportunities for writers experimenting with novel forms of expressing lived experience and blurring boundaries between humanities and social sciences. Meanwhile, starting in 2005, Norman Denzin offered a home base through the International Congress of Qualitative Inquiry, an association and annual meeting that from the beginning featured autoethnographic work. Each year, this Congress attracted scholars, teachers, writers, and performers from around the globe who eagerly broke from the conventions of third-person, silent authorship and experimented with the genre-bending and messy-text forms of autoethnographic representation. We welcomed the many scholars who walked similar paths to ours, including students who came through our graduate program in narrative and autoethnography at the University of South Florida (for example, the three editors of this volume and other contributors), as well as scholars from countries outside the U.S. and in disciplines beyond communication and sociology.

Who we are, what we want

As the stories and essays in this volume show, autoethnographers seek the good and focus on the fullness of living. Thus, we obsess over the question, how can we make life better? We ask what kind of moral world we can possibly construct. We seek a deeper engagement with human subjectivity, especially our own. Desiring to make our societies—and ourselves—better than we are, we confront the pain, suffering, injustice and inequality we find in the world. We pursue evocative depictions of real people, refusing to hide our insecurities beneath layers of technical language and jargon. We realize that we are engaged in a moral practice when we attend to decisive existential experiences of real people engaging in the art of living, seizing on love and joy, and struggling to cope with what life throws at them—ambivalence, desire, melancholy, illness, disappointment, dread, discrimination, loneliness, disability, despair, entrapment, injustice, and mortality. We are a community of storytellers who perpetually muster the courage to face contingency by engaging in the principled, political, and practical work of autoethnography with the goal of giving meaning to our lives and to the lives of other people touched by our work.

To be alive is to be uncertain. Sometimes this fact is hard to accept. But this is the place from which we all start. Autoethnography offers an avenue into connecting with the vulnerability and suffering uncertainty brings into our lives, because autoethnography itself is a genre of doubt, a vehicle for exercising, embodying, and enacting ambiguity. The shape of autoethnography is not the exclamation point (!) but the question mark (?). We autoethnographers are in the habit of picking at our scabs, exposing our warts, vacillating between angst and anger—all in order to strive for an acute self-consciousness and a shameless subjectivity that can enable us to show how a person might endure life's injustices, pain, and suffering, escape them, or remedy them. We do this not to present ourselves or others as victims trapped in their plights, but as survivors writing and rewriting ourselves to become better societal and family members who might live nobler lives, comfort others in the process, and contribute affirmatively to the world in which we live.

So, has our autoethnographic project become a successful warm idea that brings us close to others, focusing on lived experience, caring relationships, and a better world? We think it has. We hold up as evidence the more than 40,000 entries on autoethnography in Google Scholar, the numerous disciplines and international venues in which autoethnography is practiced, and the many book series, textbooks, collections, journals, and international conferences that include and focus on autoethnography. Autoethnography as we conceived it began as a humble, experimental attempt to break away from numbing and alienating writing practices by broadening and blurring boundaries between humanities and social sciences. It has grown rapidly—even exponentially—into a vast array of polymorphous auto-ethnographic forms such as evocative autoethnography, critical autoethnography, analytic autoethnography, performance autoethnography, queer autoethnography, poetic autoethnography, arts-based autoethnography, and others.

Our hearts are warmed by the passion and care performed in the chapters and editors' introduction to this volume. These stories give us hope that future qualitative work will continue to honor compassion and kindness. We are hopeful that personal narrative as a practice might assist us to appreciate and cope with the deep-rooted problems of poverty, inequality, climate change, and racism demanding our attention today in the wake of COVID-19 and the murders of George Floyd and many others.

This is a brief rendering of what we imagine we have been doing all these years. Of course, like everyone else, we lived in the middle, hoping that one day the work itself would justify an attempt to look back and understand it retrospectively. Actually, we never anticipated autoethnography would occupy the significant position and legitimacy it now holds in the human sciences. Because we live in the middle, we always risk making a muddle of our memories. Perhaps it is best to recognize that the story of autoethnography has no beginning, and where it will go is a story that you, the reader, will contribute to authoring in your time.

References

Becker, E. (1968). *The structure of evil: An essay on the unification of the sciences of man*. The Free Press.

Bochner, A. P. (1978). On taking ourselves seriously: An analysis of some persistent problems and promising directions in interpersonal research. *Human Communication Research, 4*, 179–191. https://doi.org/10.1111/j.1468-2958.1978.tb00607.x.

Bochner, A. P. (1981). Forming warm ideas. In C. Wilder-Mott & J. Weakland (Eds.), *Rigor and imagination: Essays from the legacy of Gregory Bateson* (pp. 65–81). Praeger.

Bochner, A. (2012). Between obligation and inspiration: Choosing qualitative inquiry. *Qualitative Inquiry, 18*(7), 535–543. https://doi.org/10.1177/1077800412450152.

Bochner, A. P., & Ellis (2016). *Evocative autoethnography: Writing lives, telling stories*. Routledge.

Ellis, C. (1995/2018). *Final negotiations: A story of love, loss, and chronic illness*. Temple University Press.

Ellis, C., & Bochner, A. P. (1992). Telling and performing personal stories: The constraints of choice in abortion. In C. Ellis & M. Flaherty (Eds.), *Investigating subjectivity: Research on lived experience* (pp. 79–101). Sage.

Ellis, C., & Bochner, A. (2000). Autoethnography, personal narrative, reflexivity: Researcher as subject. In N. K. Denzin & Y. S. Lincoln (Eds.), *The handbook of qualitative research* (2nd ed., pp. 733–768). Sage.

Holman Jones, S. (2018). *Becoming wild*. Paper presented at International Congress of Qualitative Inquiry. Urbana, Illinois.

INDEX

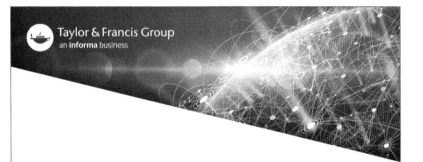

9 780367 476694